HSIAO CHIN AND **PUNTO**

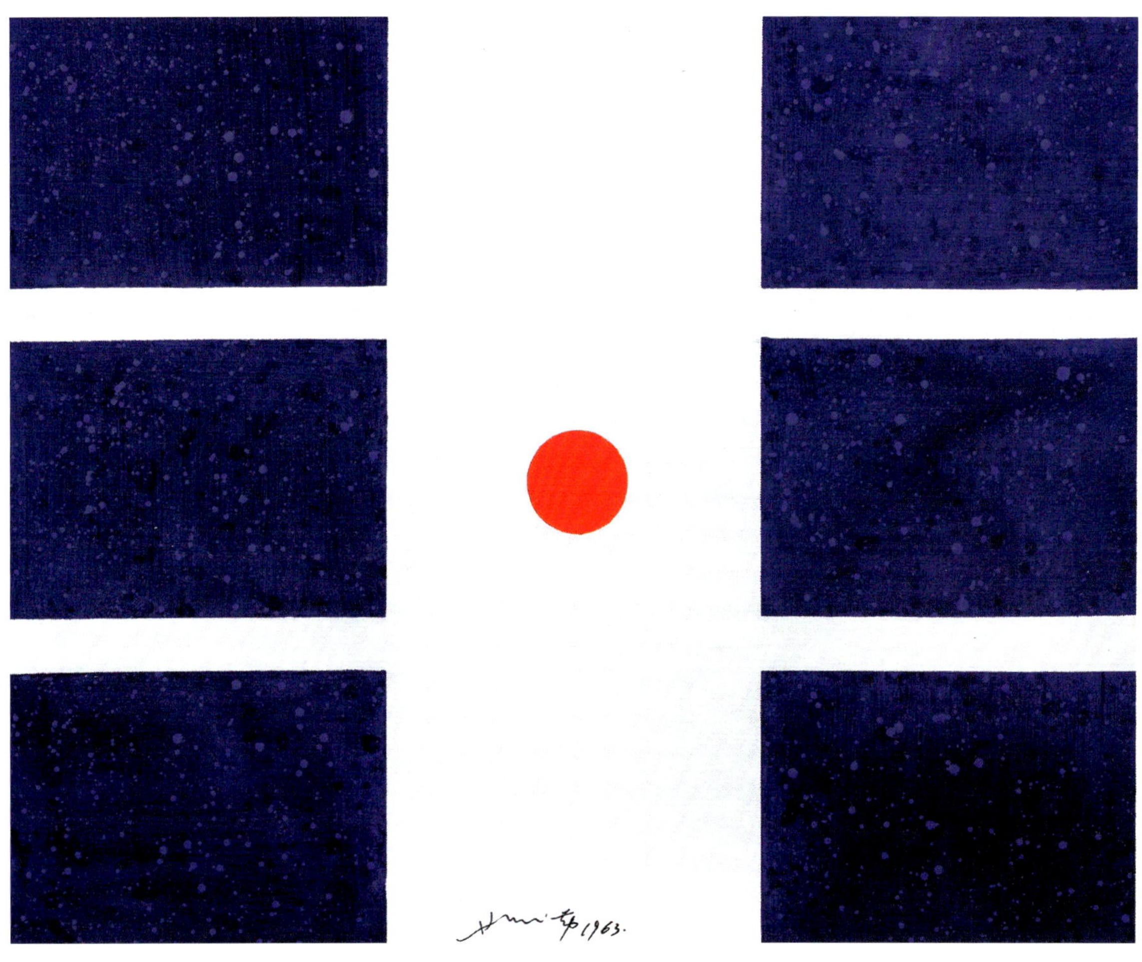

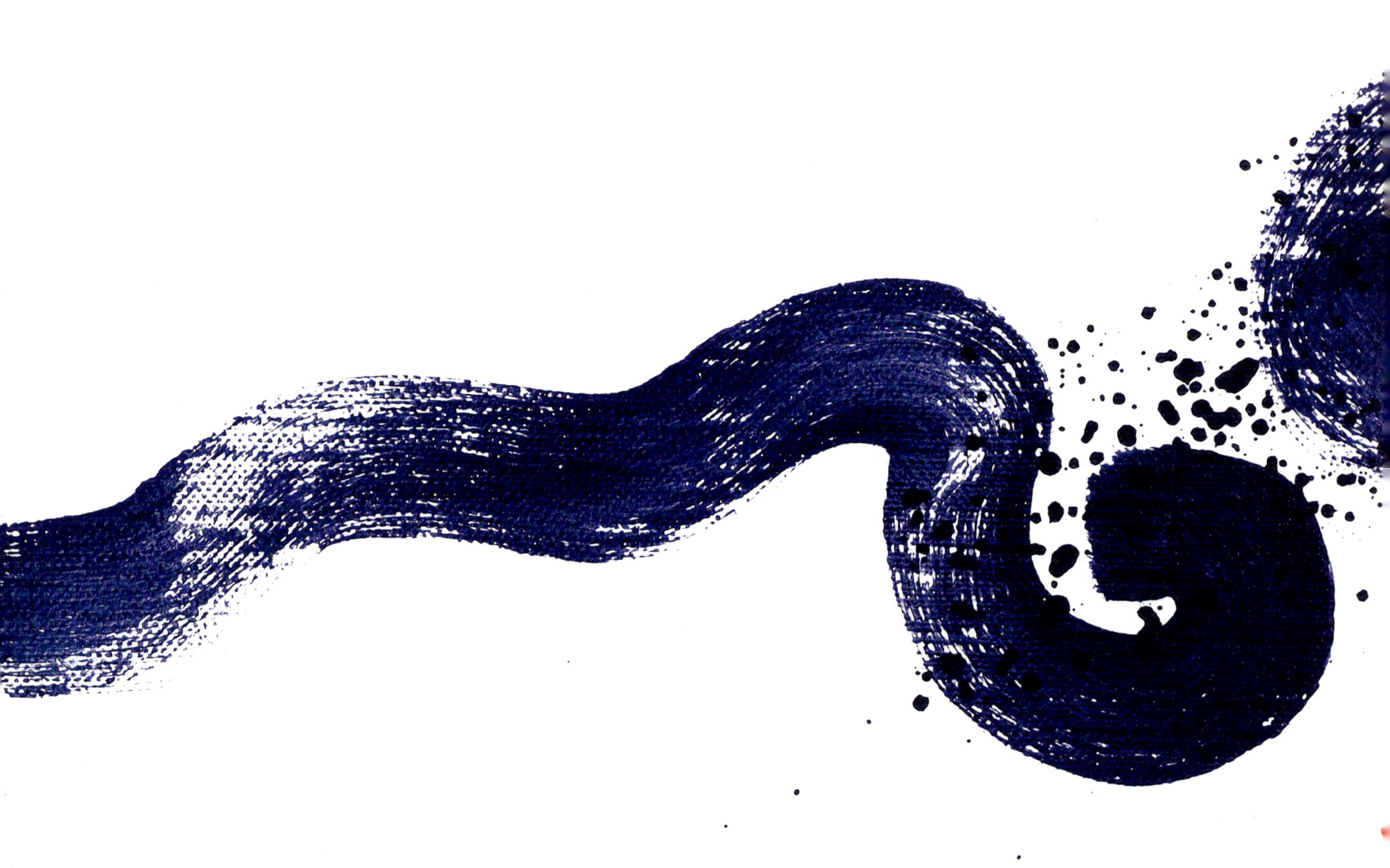

HSIAO CHIN AND **PUNTO**

Mapping Post-War Avant-Garde

JOSHUA GONG

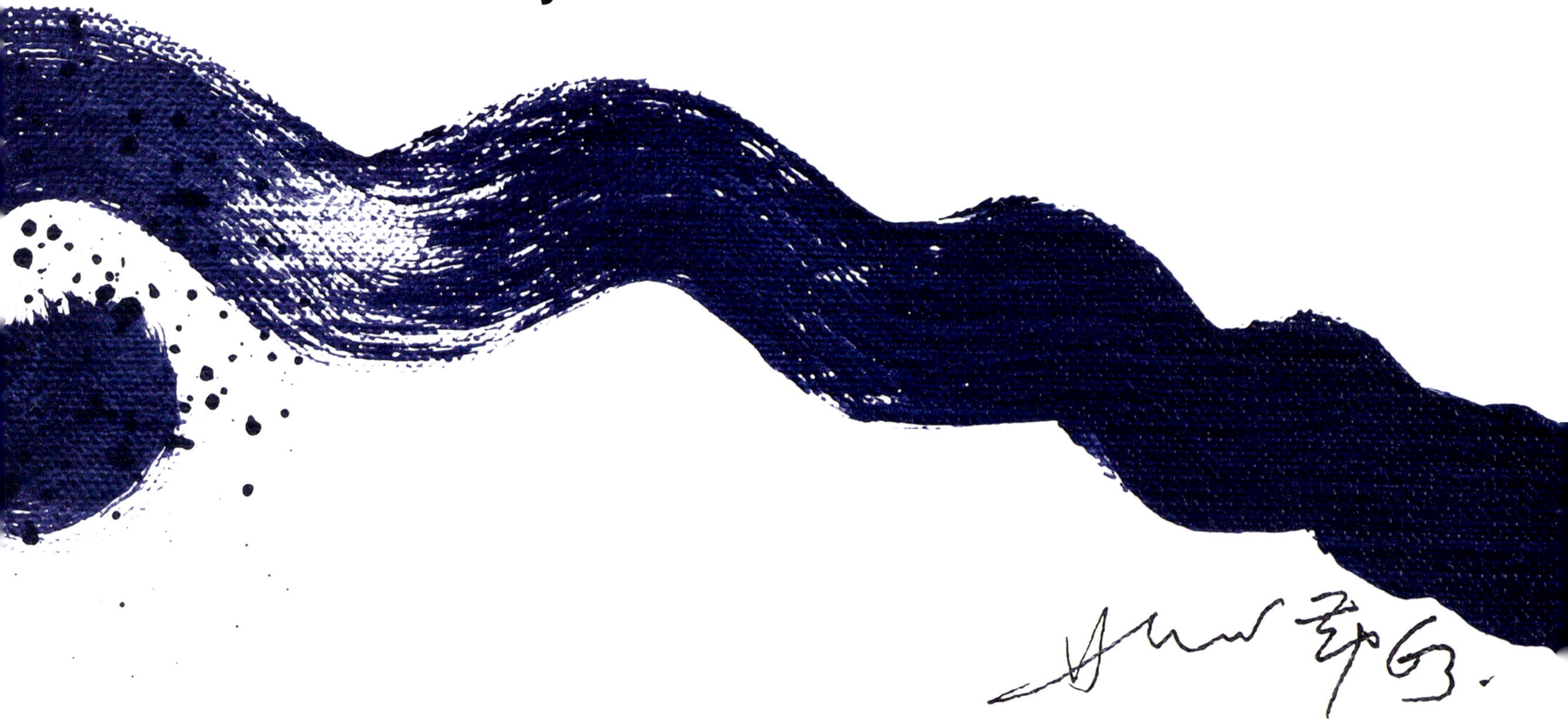

UNICORN

Hsiao Chin selected museum and public collections

A. Calderara Foundation (Fondazione A. Calderara), Vacciago
Antonio Mazzotta Foundation (Fondazione Antonio Mazzotta), Milan
Art Gallery of Ontario, Toronto
Art Society of Dusseldorf (Kunstverein Düsseldorf), Dusseldorf
Cantonal Museum of Fine Arts (Musée Cantonal des Beaux-Arts), Lausanne
China Art Museum, Shanghai
Detroit Institute of Arts, Detroit
Dimension Endowment of Art Foundation, Taipei
Fogg Art Museum, Cambridge, Massachusetts
Gallery of Modern Art of San Marino (Galleria d'Arte Moderna di San Marino), City of San Marino
Guangdong Museum of Art, Guangzhou
Guimet National Museum of Asian Art (Musée national des arts asiatiques Guimet), Paris
Haus Lange Museum (Museum Haus Lange), Krefeld
Historic Center of Visual Art of the University of Parma (Centro Storico d'Arte Visiva dell' Università di Parma), Parma
Hong Kong Museum of Art, Hong Kong
Kaohsiung Museum of Fine Arts, Kaohsiung
Metropolitan Museum of Art, New York
MGM Cotai Chairman's Collection, Macau
M+ Museum, Hong Kong
Municipal Museum and University of Macerata (Galleria Civica e Università di Macerata), Macerata
Municipal Museum of Cagliari (Galleria Civica di Cagliari), Cagliari
Municipal Museum of Gibellina (Galleria Civica di Gibellina), Gibellina
Municipal Museum of Marsala (Galleria Civica di Marsala), Marsala
Municipal Museum of Modern Art (Museo Civico d'Arte Moderna), Modena
Municipal Museum (Städtisches Museum), Bochum
Municipal Museum (Städtisches Museum), Leverkusen
Municipal Museum (Städtisches Museum), Monchengladbach
Museum of Brindisi (Museo Brindisi), Brindisi
Museum of Contemporary Art (Museo de Arte Contemporáneo), Vilafames
Museum of Contemporary Art of Barcelona (Museu d'Art Contemporani de Barcelona), Barcelona
Museum of Contemporary Art, Skopje
Museum of Modern and Contemporary Art (Museo d'Arte Moderna e Contemporanea), San Gimignano
Museum of Modern Art, New York
National Art Museum of China, Beijing
National Gallery of Modern and Contemporary Art (Galleria Nazionale d'Arte Moderna e Contemporanea), Rome
National Library of Wales, Aberystwyth
National Museum of History, Taipei
National Museum of Wales, Cardiff
National Taiwan Museum of Fine Arts, Taichung
New York Public Library, New York
Palace of Diamond (Palazzo dei Diamanti), Ferrara
Philadelphia Museum of Art, Philadelphia
Randers Museum of Art (Randers Kunstmuseum), Jutland
Rose Art Museum, Waltham, Massachusetts
State Gallery of Stuttgart (Staatsgalerie Stuttgart), Stuttgart
Taipei Fine Arts Museum, Taipei
Zhongshan Museum of Art, Zhongshan

Published in 2020 by
Unicorn, an imprint of Unicorn Publishing Group
5 Newburgh Street
London
W1F 7RG
www.unicornpublishing.org

ISBN 978-1-912690-83-1

10 9 8 7 6 5 4 3 2 1

Designer: Isobel Gillan
Editor: Elisabeth Ingles

Printed by Gomer Press

The use of artworks, photos and archival materials in this book is authorised by Hsiao Chin Foundation.

Photographer / Jian-Hui Chung

Courtesy of Hsiao Chin Foundation and 3812 Gallery

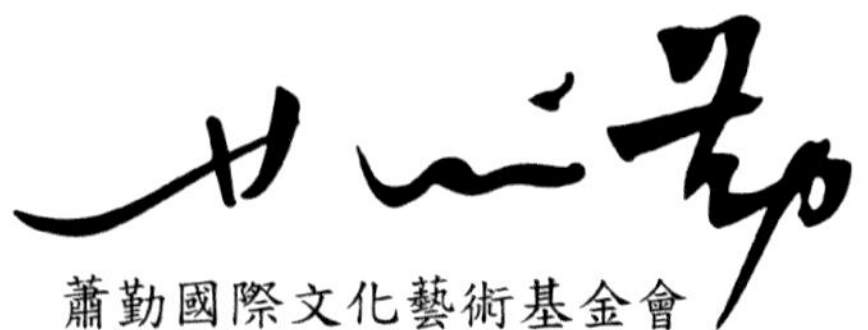

3812 gallery
London | Hong Kong

www.hsiaochin.com
www.3812gallery.com

CONTENTS

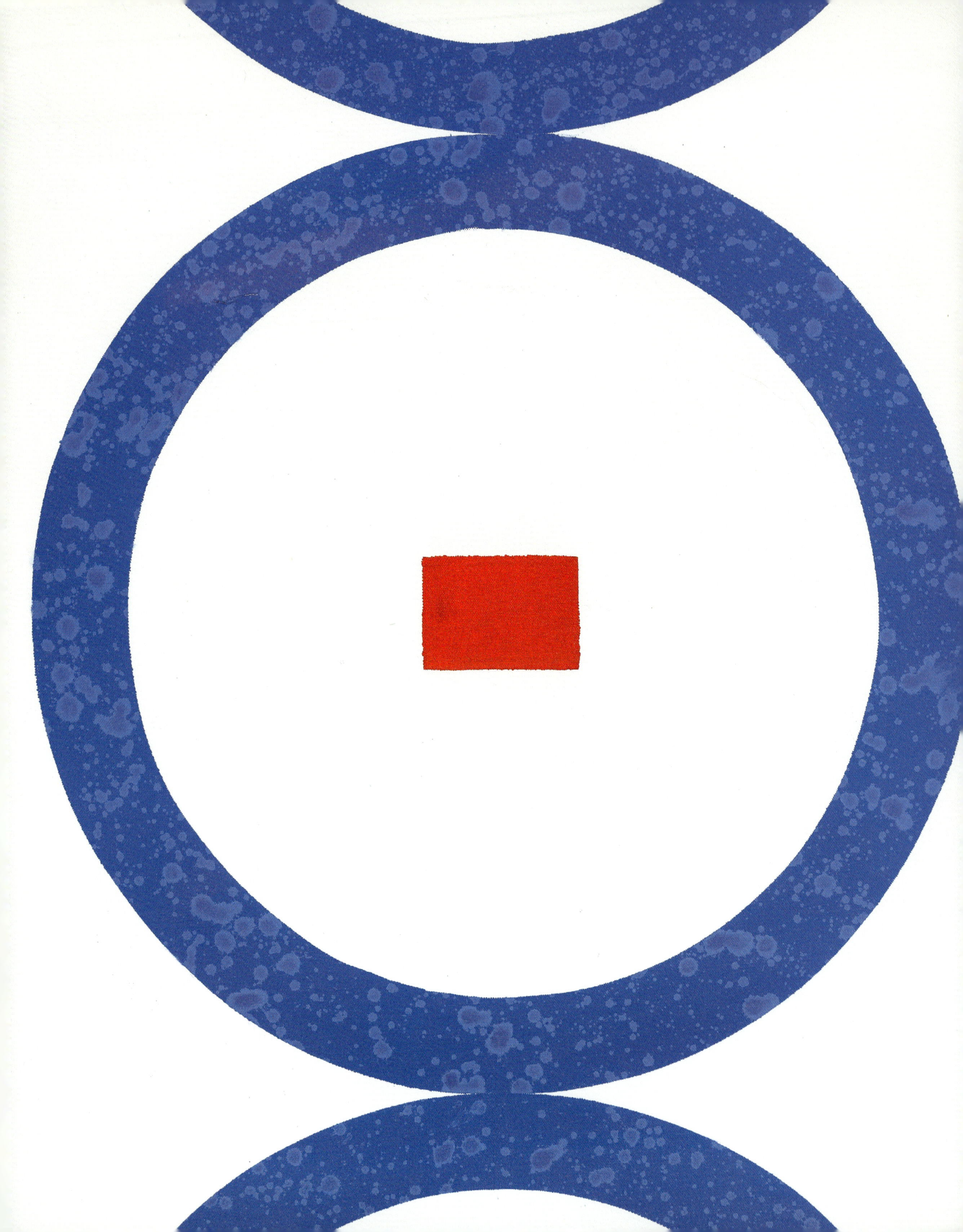

THE OMNIPRESENT VITALITY IN THE UNIVERSE

Hsiao Chin
Kaohsiung City, February 2020

I have always viewed the future and everything in its development calmly and with deep tranquillity and honest immanence. Meanwhile, I name the profound, intangible and omnipresent vitality in the universe, Chi (炁).

In my paintings Chi has numerous and vivid appearances. Chi represents the ubiquitous life force; meanwhile the law of nature is the source and spring of Chi. I tried to interpret and master many themes based on my personal understanding of dialectic, such as void and substance, action and stillness, Yin and Yang, the strong and the weak, the limited and the infinite, and thus create my work.

With close scrutiny and sensible observation, my attention has returned to the origin of the universe, guiding the flow of Chi to reflect the appearance of everything. With meta–physical phenomenology, it is attempted that through the phenomenon the ontology is revealed and through the revelation the concept interaction between the external and the internal can be realised. I observe how nature operates through a macroscopic view, while understanding changes microscopically, through which the strong fluctuation of Chi at the verge of the infinite and beyond can be felt. The natural force initiating the chaotic state can be seen and the vastness of the universe can be experienced. The forever-expanding force reflects the concrete living experience, natural phenomena and cosmic inventory. All are inspiring for my creation and immediately at my disposal.

Since the end of the 1950s I have personally detested and resisted the superfluity of *Art Informel* and pursued more profound spirituality. Because we shared the same goal, Antonio Calderara, Kenjiro Azuma and I worked together for the sincerity and purity of art-making. It requires artists to have a depth of spirituality and strong determination in order to overcome struggles. We decided to form an art movement in Milan, aiming at presenting spirituality … therefore the Punto International Art Movement was realised.

The manifesto states:

> Purity of concepts and reasons for creation are conditioned on the understanding of the 'finite' within the 'infinite', and on the grasp of the reality of thought and the true meaning of life.
>
> 'Man' is the finite condition within the infinite universe. The art practitioner should be an oracle of the human spirit and the spokesperson for its ideas. Thus, his explorations of ideas, spiritual pursuits and contemplations of life should come before others. Only in this way can they be transmitted to others and contribute to the evolution of the human spirit.

In June 1965, Galleria L'Elefante in Mestre, near Venice, held the twelfth Punto exhibition. Such an international movement was officially recognised by the liberal arts circle and our significance in art history was acknowledged.

In May 1966, the last Punto exhibition was held at Galleria Fanesi in Ancona, Italy, and the Italian art critic G. Binni wrote:

> Could it be that only the recipients of secret teachings can understand the philosophical roots of Punto? That is not the case. In this world, some people truly live, while others only exist like plants. Some people use their brains to think, while others only act on the teachings they hear from others. Some people adapt to other people, while others cannot. Some people are free, while others are not. The people in Punto belong to the first category, while others belong to the second.

Indeed, I used to declare openly: 'Dear friends, I hope that we can all join in the first category.'

This year I am eighty-five, and the Hsiao Chin Foundation has recently hosted a retrospective exhibition at our Hsiao Chin Foundation Art Centre. I coined *New Energy* as its title, reiterating my idea in making paintings: 'Regardless of distance or alienation, there will be a meaningful connection as long as there is clarity on the consensus.'

(opposite, detail see page 71) Hsiao Chin, *The Cycles (Il cicli)*, 1963

HSIAO CHIN

Edward Lucie-Smith

Non-Western artists very often do not receive full credit for their participation in Western or even in fully international art movements. To some extent this seems to have been the case with Hsiao Chin. He has worked in a wide variety of different environments, and was, in the 1960s, one of the leading members of the Punto group, which featured both Western and Chinese artists. For avoiding the white horror in Taiwan during the 1950s and 1960s, Hsiao Chin chose to go abroad to release himself from political turbulence and ideological constraints in Taiwan; meanwhile he was also not subject to the ideological restrictions that governed artistic activity in mainland China, in the decade from 1966 until 1976. He has nevertheless, as this book amply demonstrates, been very much a prophet for what the West regards as characteristically Chinese ways of thinking. He was, for example, deeply interested in both Daoism and Buddhism, moving gradually from one to the other.

As the text of this book notes:

> 'Daoism focused on simplicity and its nihilistic thinking is more for hermits. Hisao Chin was interested in helping and communicating with the rest of the world, which corresponded with Buddhism.'

In the more than sixty years since the 1960s there has been a gradually shift of focus within the Western art world itself. Perhaps the most important aspect of this change has been the appearance of a genuine pluralism. That is to say, the Western art world no longer sees itself as the dominant force in artistic creativity - the unchallenged centre for experimentation and for what used to be called Modernism. As we have moved into the Post-Modern epoch, art has become ever more visibly plural. What we have now is a conversation between different aspects of innovation, based in turn upon different sources, many of them non-European. Artists who belong to different traditions both accept things from cultures that are not their own, but also reject or simply ignore others, which seem to them to conflict with what they have inherited from their own deep-rooted past.

Hsiao Chin is a striking example of this complex process of combined assimilation and rejection. Western taste is inclined to classify him as an abstract artist, pushing abstraction to its furthest boundary in its rejection of anything that hints at figurative references. For Hsiao Chin, this embrace of doctrinaire non-figuration seems to be something that is essentially irrelevant to what he wants to achieve. The roots of this attitude are to be found in the fact that in traditional Chinese ink-painting the boundaries between the figurative and the non-figurative have never been firmly fixed, because painting and writing (forming Chinese characters) are basically the same activity. Hsiao Chin's paintings are basically mysterious signs.

In that sense he is not a Modern or even a Post-Modern artist in any accepted interpretation of those terms. He is in fact someone who offers signposts towards an artistic future that has not as yet fully revealed itself. He indicates paths that painting may perhaps be ready to take. It can be no surprise, looking at China's age-old fluency in using symbols in art, that a Chinese artist should be in the vanguard today.

(opposite, detail see page 90) Hsiao Chin, *Dancing Light-15*, 1963

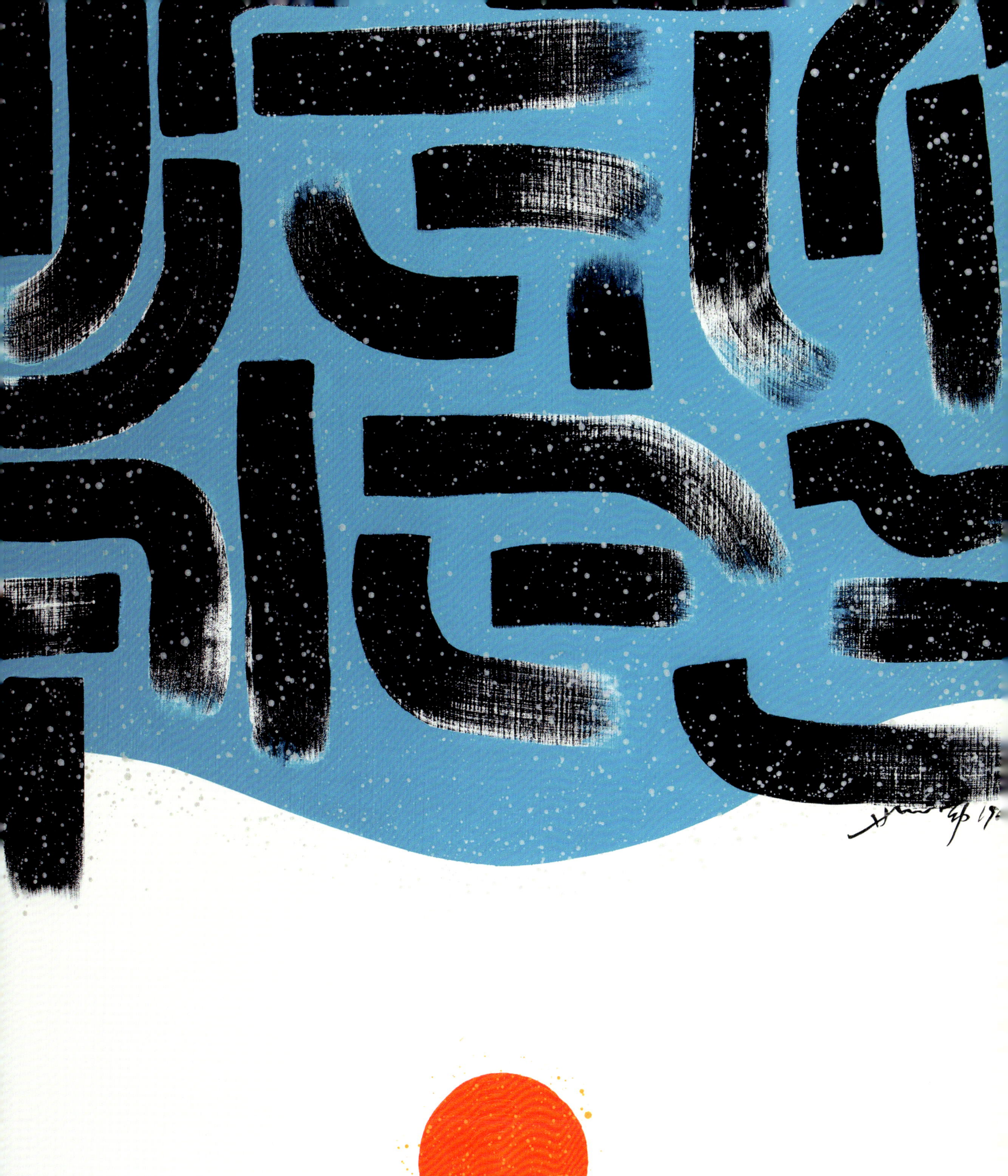

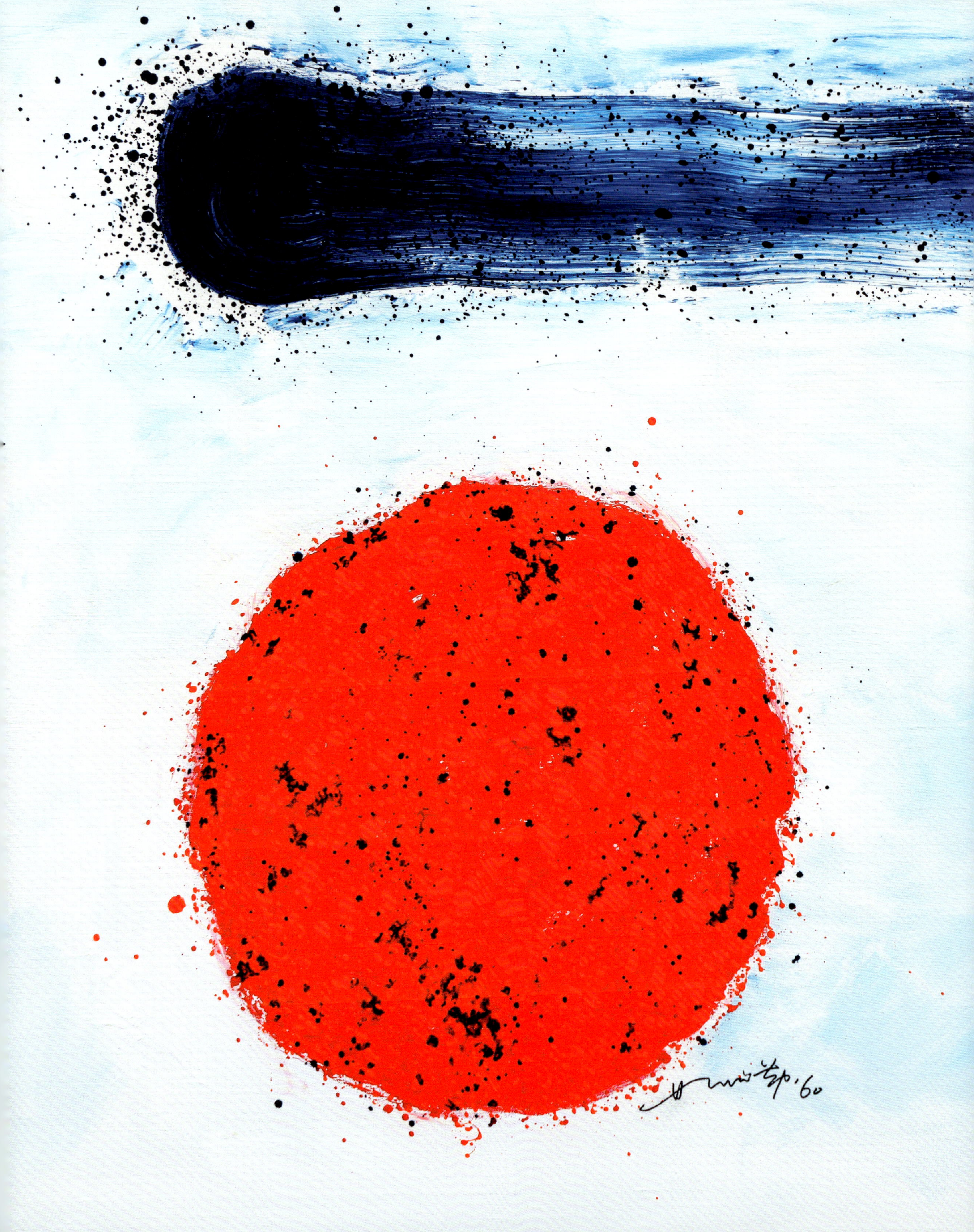

PUNTO AND ITS HISTORICAL SIGNIFICANCE

From 1961 to 1967, within only six years, thirteen Punto exhibitions were held across the world, showing as many as twenty-six artists participating in the movement. Hsiao Chin initiated the project with his fellow artist friends and they were able to exhibit their art to the public, which was historically remarkable considering its Cold War background. Organising a series of international art movements, with artists from Asia, Europe and South America, was itself a symbol of internationalism, disregarding the tension between the Eastern and Western blocs.

Not only has Punto tackled how art could progress, present itself and represent its practitioners, but its anti-*Art Informel* nature directly distinguished it from the other trends of the 1960s. Punto has insisted on its 'conceptual purity',[1] defending the autonomy of art from both the formal and the social approaches to art.

The post-war European avant-garde world

In summer 1956, on being offered a scholarship by the 'Chinese and Spanish Cultural and Economic Association', Hsiao Chin embarked a journey of art in Europe. He realised his path to abstraction as early as 1958, while his Eastern origin enabled him to interpret spiritual movements with Chinese concepts. Hsiao Chin fully understood the essential philosophy behind abstract art. He put it thus:

> The so-called informal [*sic*] often makes people feel 'I don't understand', but we have to understand that the performance of painting was in abstract form from the beginning of history, the so-called 'understanding' is just an explanation of the surface image, painting is not as literature, it does not need any narrative object to explain it, although previously painting had the existence of image, but it was only expressing abstract composition through images. Expressing inner feelings of an artist (such as philosophical, religious, loving, poetic, etc.), these elements are the nature of painting, that is, it can be expressed without images (with colour, rhythm, organisation of material, imagination, composition, etc.).[2]

His comment on abstract art demonstrates that not only did he understand the difference between representationalist images and Expressionist pictures, but also that his idea about abstract art was in accord with those invented by Kandinsky, Malevich and Mondrian: abstract images project a new realm based on internal movement. Therefore Hsiao Chin was able to break the shackles of the ready-made and pursue the full extent of creativity.

The history of European art in the post-war era witnessed the end of European cultural predominance in the West.[3] Artists and thinkers had begun to reflect upon the very question of progress (via evolution and revolution). There are several sceptical views on the nature of the human condition, the value of modernity, as well as the gravity of culture; art should be developed by extension of these paths.

Hsiao Chin confronted the European cultural crises that were unprecedented, as so many aspects of the occidental model of civilisation were annulled. Politically, the British Empire could no longer maintain its hegemony, and the power vacuum had immediately and spontaneously been filled through capitalist American and Communist Soviet influences. Germany and the whole of Europe were divided

(*opposite, detail* *see page 38*) Hsiao Chin, *TY-89*, 1960

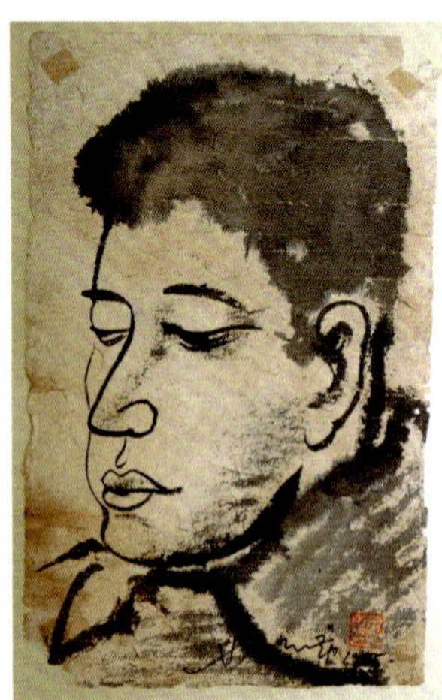

Hsiao Chin, *Self-portrait*, 1955, Ink on paper, 32 x 20.5cm

(*right*) Members of the Ton-Fan Art Group with Li Chun-shan (From the left: Ouyang Wen-yuan, Li Chun-shan, Chen Tao-ming, Li Yuan-chia, Hsia Yan, Ho Kan, Wu Hao, Hsiao Chin, and Hsiao Ming-hsien)

(*far right*) The first 'Ton-Fan Art Group Inaugural Painting Exhibition-Chinese & Spanish Modern Artists Joint Exhibition' took place at Taipei News Building, Taiwan & the Galleria Jardin in Barcelona, November, 1957

by the Eastern and Western blocs, and so entered into the Cold War. Paris – the modern cultural and art capital – had declined, or, rather, its internationalism started to spread all over the world. As early as 1940, Harold Rosenberg had already pointed out that Paris presents the 'modern' culture, and it is the 'international culture', and it is 'falling'.[4]

At one point, New York was thought to be taking the former position of Paris (as an international pioneer) in the field of contemporary art, as John-Franklin Koenig experienced at first hand during his time in Paris.[5] However, the American art circle offered a national style – American Abstract Expressionism – the cultural value behind which is, in a way, using a national value system to standardise an international one. It is quite the opposite of the French avant-garde stance.[6] Therefore, the pre-war art order had waned, and many nations and regions were trying to establish new ones, or an 'absolute' order was questioned. It is believed that after the war, not a single European school or centre received the attention that New York did, but also the true nature of modernism turned out to be questionable.[7] On the other hand, as Europe had become the buffer between two superpowers during the Cold War, the political, economic and cultural environment was further complicated, sometimes very intensely, sometimes less so; in between, a sense of freedom and the reversing of colonisation could be felt. Modern art, the concept of which was generated in France, and which the United States had admired and followed, in the 1950s was ambiguously conveyed through action paintings and colour fields.

Hsiao Chin was from the Western system, as he was formally educated in Taiwan (the Republic of China). It is assumed that during his college training, the proper standard was still the European one, namely, from the essential Classical art to Post-Impressionist style or the Cubist approach.

Hsiao Chin's mentor Mr Li Chun-shan (李仲生) was one of the earliest Chinese artists dedicated to promoting modern art. Li Chun-shan did his art training in Japan and was the first Chinese artist to blend surrealist ideas into painting.[8] Even though Li Chun-shan took up the modern style and insight from the West, nevertheless he had not limited his fellow students to any pre-established doctrines. Traditionally, Chinese pedagogic methods were 'inoculative' and dogmatic; luckily for Hsiao Chin, Li Chun-shan was inspirational. He encouraged Hsiao Chin in searching for new possibilities in art rather than copying examples by old masters. During the art course, Li Chun-shan had observed and realised that Hsiao Chin was talented at bold and vibrant colouring; therefore the teacher spent some time studying Fauvism to help the young student realise his potential.

Meanwhile, he also taught Hsiao Chin the iconography of Chinese art, especially the Beijing Opera, so that his pupil was not confined by any particular regional visual cultures. But he would not revise students' sketches or allow them to copy his drawings, so that all of his students could explore their distinct pictorial languages.[9] Later on, some Chinese art historians or critics would even go so far as to comment that Hsiao Chin was too Western[10] and his work reveals no sign of a Chinese context, which is a misunderstanding. Hsiao Chin's entire art career was deeply rooted in Chinese culture.

The reason why he presented such an impression to the public is that he inherited Chinese ideas and his work reflected Eastern philosophy at a much more profound level. Unlike some artists, especially many who experienced the '85 New Wave, Hsiao Chin did not borrow or collage Chinese symbols superficially.

In Taiwan, Hsiao Chin was the co-founder of the first modern artists' organisation, Ton-Fan Art Group (東方畫會).

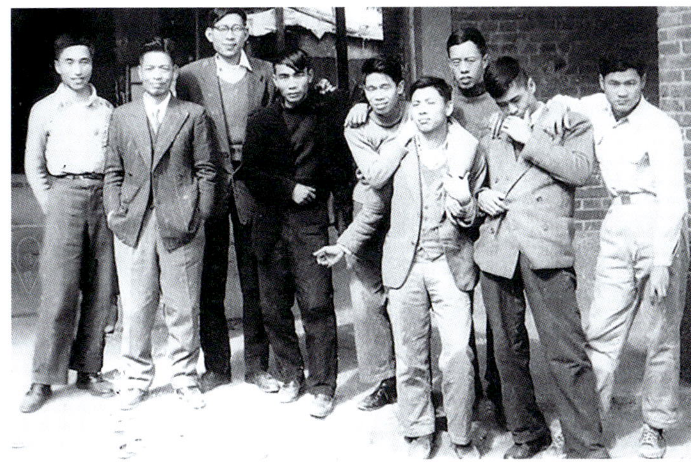

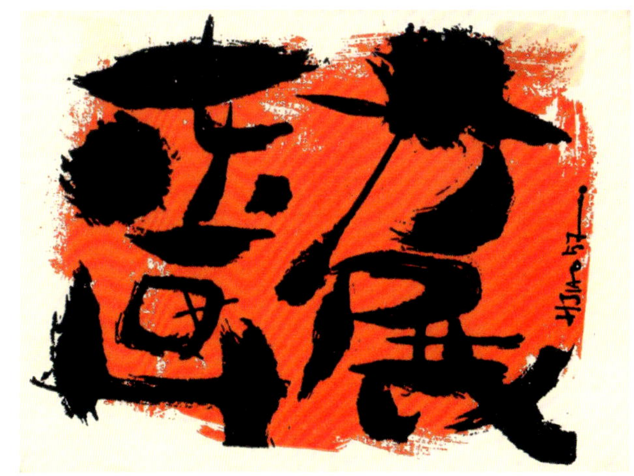

It was a non-official association, and there were eight like-minded young artists in the group. It was initiated on 31 December 1955, just before Hsiao Chin was offered a scholarship to study in Spain.[11] In May 1956, the influential Fifth Moon Art Group (五月畫會) was established by Liu Kuosung (劉國松) and his fellows. With artists of Ton-Fan, they were the most pioneering avant-garde artists in post-war China. It could be said that Ton-Fan is the first modern group; however, because of restrictive censorship under the Nationalist Party regime, they were not officially registered by the government until 1956, by which time Hsiao Chin had already gone to Spain.[12] Nevertheless, Hsiao Chin carried Ton-Fan's collective mission to Europe: to promote Chinese avant-garde art.

Before Punto, Hsiao Chin devoted himself to organising exhibitions for Ton-Fan. The name in Chinese literally means the East – the name of the group succinctly manifested their ideal.

Thanks to Li Chun-shan's unique way of educating the Ton-Fan artists, Hsiao Chin developed his independent and critical judgement on art. In summer 1956, he arrived in Madrid. But he was not satisfied by the conservative style taught at the Royal Academy of Fine Arts of San Fernando (Real Academia de Bellas Artes de San Fernando). Therefore he decided to forfeit his scholarship and go to the more flamboyant Barcelona, where Picasso, Dalí and Miro remained active, and it was one of the centres of *Art Informel*.[13]

Hsiao Chin's art education in Europe remained *informel* as well. Traditional Salon art (representationalist) had been overturned by the Impressionists nearly a hundred years before. Paris during the Third Republic (1870–1940) witnessed the decline of 'classic art' and the rise of multiple non-official art tendencies: Impressionism, Post-Impressionism, Fauvism, Cubism, Surrealism and to some extent Dadaism (despite its origin in Switzerland). Artists, especially the avant-garde ones, were people of modern society. American art historian Meyer Schapiro has pointed out that early Impressionism had a moral aspect: the artists 'reflect in the very choice of subjects and in the new aesthetic devices the concept of art as solely a field of individual enjoyment, without reference to ideas, and motives, and they presuppose the cultivation of these pleasures as the highest field of freedom for an unenlightened bourgeois detached from the official beliefs of his class.'[14]

Hsiao Chin recognised how significant individual criticism was, embraced contemporary society and decided to learn from different fields in society rather than the institutionalised art academies. He organised Ton-Fan and the subsequent Punto to expand the Eastern-rooted art ideals into a much broader horizon.

It can be said that Hsiao Chin is the first Chinese artist after World War II who successfully made an international showcase of contemporary Chinese art.

In Barcelona, Hsiao Chin joined two art associations (Real Circulo Artistico de Barcelona and Cercle Maillol Français).[15] The former was an influential local organisation with members from all over Europe and South America. Hsiao Chin was one of only two Chinese artists in the institution, which was located in the city centre and had two floors. The ground floor was spacious enough for all kinds of exhibitions, and the first floor had a library, a space for indoor drawing, and a bar, where artists were able to study and exchange their ideas. The Cercle Maillol was a famous French art institute; the Barcelona branch was established in 1947, and every year it selected talented artists and offered them a scholarship to study in France (for one year or half a year). In the society, Hsiao Chin participated in lectures and seminars, and watched films. It was also in

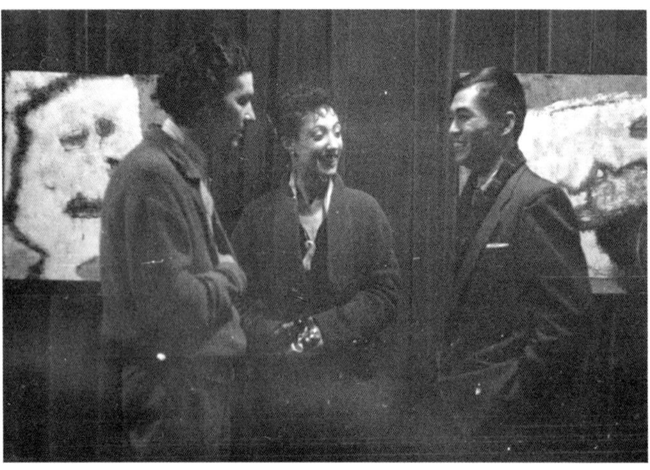

Hsiao Chin's first solo exhibition was held in Museo Municipal de Mataró in Barcelona, 1957

(*right*) Hsiao Chin with Chao Chung-hsiang (first person on the left) at the China House in Barcelona, 1957

(*far right*) Hsiao Chin in his studio in Barcelona, 1959

this circle that Hsiao Chin befriended a great many Spanish art informalists, such as Antoni Tàpies, Joan-Josep Tharrats and Modest Cruixart, who in September 1948 established *Daul al Set*. The group was heavily influenced by Dadaism and Surrealism, and through its magazines, Hsiao Chin became familiar with the art of Paul Klee, Joan Miró, Antoni Gaudí and Francis Picabia.[16] As with his direct contact with European avant-garde culture, Hsiao Chin started writing reports and articles and introduced the developing *Art Informel* to the Chinese audience in Taiwan. Through writing, he was able to map the trajectory of modern art and realise the significance of Eastern philosophy to the Western avant-garde.

Hsiao Chin saw how challenging it was for Western art to evolve by the end of the nineteenth century.[17] Impressionism focused on the study of optical science; nevertheless it had already stepped away from the imitating tradition current since the Renaissance. Subsequently, the Expressionist and abstract artists rapidly shifted from depiction of the external to the search for inner feelings. World War I led artists to explore the irrational, non-sense, automatism, hence Dadaism and Surrealism. Hsiao Chin realised that the solution to the crisis of European civilisation was not just Eastern exoticism but globalisation, with regional equilibrium, when national autonomy could affirm vibrant originality.[18]

Hsiao Chin was immersed in the various trends of Western art, but he kept a critical mind and acutely pointed out the flaw in *l'art pour l'art* ('art for art's sake') as well as the less convincing slogans of the *-isms*:

> Although many of those Western modern, contemporary, avant-garde and Post-Modern schools of art do not necessarily have profound import (which is the most important part of its eternal value), their courage, rebellion, challenge and innovation are commendable. This is the momentum that keeps art always on the cutting-edge of the era. The artist should not only be a creator of foresight, but also be a voice of social conscience and insight.[19]

It can be said that the post-war era for European art was a most kaleidoscopic time: Parisian dominance in art started to wane; many European countries started to explore different trends, as European reconstruction culture was to be defined in the field of art by artists such as Lucio Fontana, Piero Manzoni and Yves Klein,[20] who departed from the previous European avant-garde legacy (from Cubism and Dadaism to Surrealism); abstract-form and conceptualist-oriented art in the 1950s and 1960s proliferated in Europe. Those art trends can be loosely labelled as *Art Informel*.

Art Informel was primarily theorised in 1952 by Michel Tapié, a French critic, in his book *Un art autre* ('Art of Another Kind'), referring to an approach that is neither abstraction nor figuration. Instead, it endeavours to seek a much more authentic way of reconstructing the Western cultural foundation after the crisis created by World War II.[21] Tapié realised that the mirage of many art groups, as well as their cultural stances, did not offer a real possibility for the future and Dada represented the latest effective revolution in changing the concept of art.[22] Similarly, Jean-Paul Sartre confronted the same issue and tackled the problem with existentialist ideas, which resonate in the art of Alberto Giacometti. Sartre discovered the absoluteness of being and emphasised the inevitability of decision-making required of human beings, regardless of their social and physiological circumstances.[23] In Britain, Francis Bacon's terrifying figures expanded the ideas of German

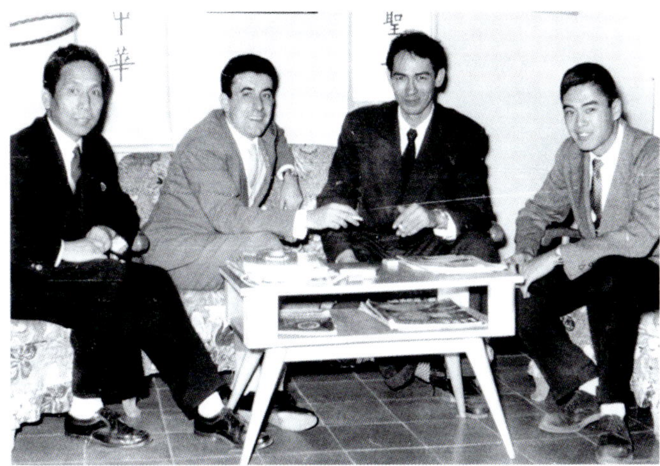

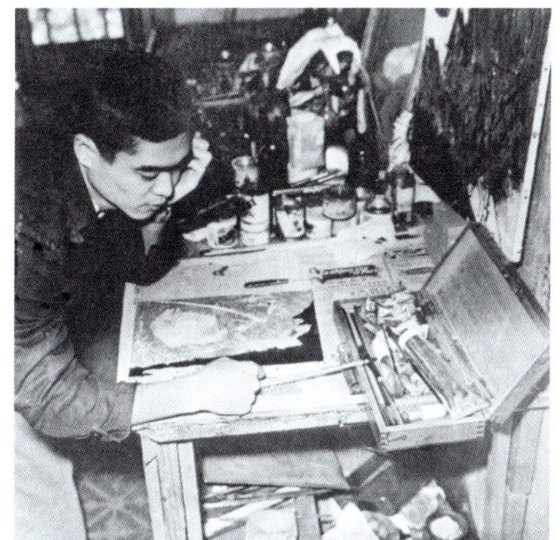

Expressionism, with his personal experience reflecting individual identity and sexuality. With the advancement of sciences, Cybernetic rationality appeared in art, mandating the purity of aesthetics.[24]

Post-war Europe unfolded infinite possibilities for Hsiao Chin, and he later recollected the impact:

> Another important matter when I first arrived in Europe was 'seeing'. I looked around everywhere, tried to see as much as possible, anything related to art. Visual art is expressed in visual language, and for visual language. First, you have to study with the 'eyes' before feeling with the 'heart' and analysing with the 'brain'.[25]

As has been illustrated, Hsiao Chin was in the crucible of a visual explosion, and he was about to contribute to this tapestry of art history.

From Ton-Fan to Punto

1957 was a very significant year in Hsiao Chin's career: he had his first solo exhibition at the Museu de Mataro, and from 1957 he officially signed his name as 'Hsiao 勤', indicating his attempt to combine Eastern and Western cultures.[26]

During this period, Hsiao Chin's painting remained figurative, but the abstract tendency gradually emerged on canvas. His solo exhibition was well received, and the Barcelona art circle started to pay more attention to this young artist from the 'mysterious' Far East. Of course, it was not the Oriental myth that made Hsiao Chin recognisable; rather, it was because of his capacity to absorb current trends with his unique pictorial rendering. Hsiao Chin began to utilise painterly strokes in forming images, which was derived from Chinese calligraphy;[27] meanwhile Fauvist colouring and emotions were more accessible for a Western audience. The Eastern–Western fusion style marked a new beginning: a stylistic change.

It was also in 1957 that Hsiao Chin had been selected by Salon del Jazz (Barcelona) as one of the ten outstanding young artists. It was a great honour, considering that he was a foreigner, and it simply kick-started his career. One of the most positive responses from the media was that Juan Eduardo Cirlot included his work in the art history book *Arte Contemporáneo*, which suggested that not only was Hsiao Chin qualified as a good artist, but also that he was acknowledged as the representative of the *Zeitgeist*.[28]

With a good reputation being built, Hsiao Chin secured individual success when he was signed up by Sala Gasper in 1958, a prestigious gallery in Barcelona. It helped him significantly, so that he could spend more energy on thinking about art rather than the cost of food and rent.

Because Hsiao Chin was in direct contact with contemporary movements in the West, he sent many letters to the other members of Ton-Fan, which inspired their art-making with fresh images and concepts. They felt that an exhibition to present their art and ideas was becoming necessary. Because of intense political restrictions, the first Ton-Fan exhibition was held in collaboration with a few artists from Spain to indicate that it was not 'Communist', so that the Taiwanese government would give permission for them to exhibit in Taipei. Hsiao Chin invited Juan José Tharrats, Will Faber and many Spanish artists, although the exhibition mainly showed the work of the Ton-Fan members.

The exhibition space was located in a newsagents' premises (台北市衡陽街新生報新聞大樓). When it opened on 9 November 1957, the audience was excited to see the new art, as the exhibition served as the first showcase of the avant-garde in Taiwan after the war. The show was

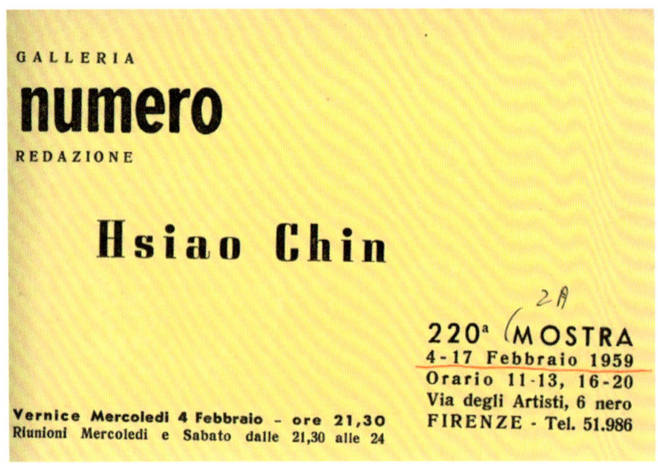

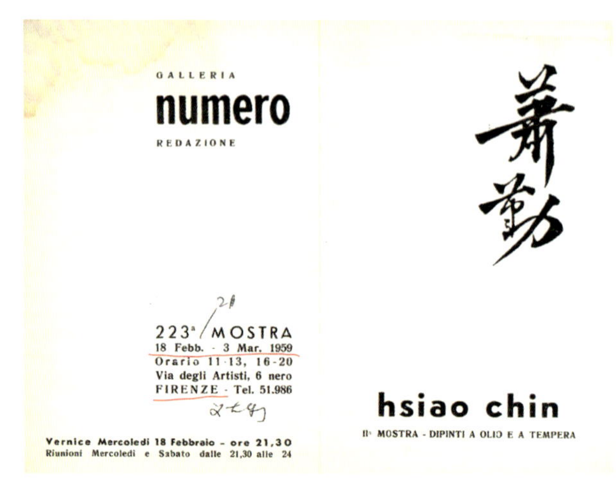

(*above left*) Hsiao Chin's first solo exhibition in Italy at Galleria Numero in Florence, February 4-17, 1959

(*above right*) Hsiao Chin's second solo exhibition in Italy at Galleria Numero in Florence, February 18-March 3, 1959

(*left*) Ton-Fan Art Group Painting Exhibition at Mi Chou Gallery in New York, January 5-30, 1960

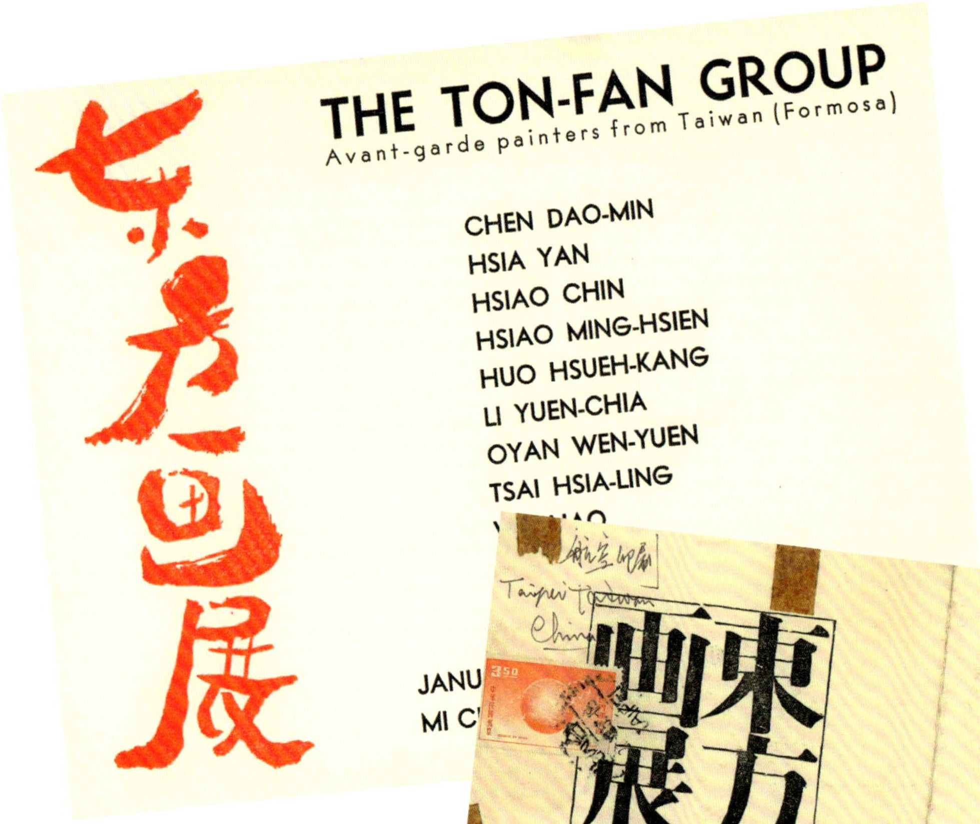

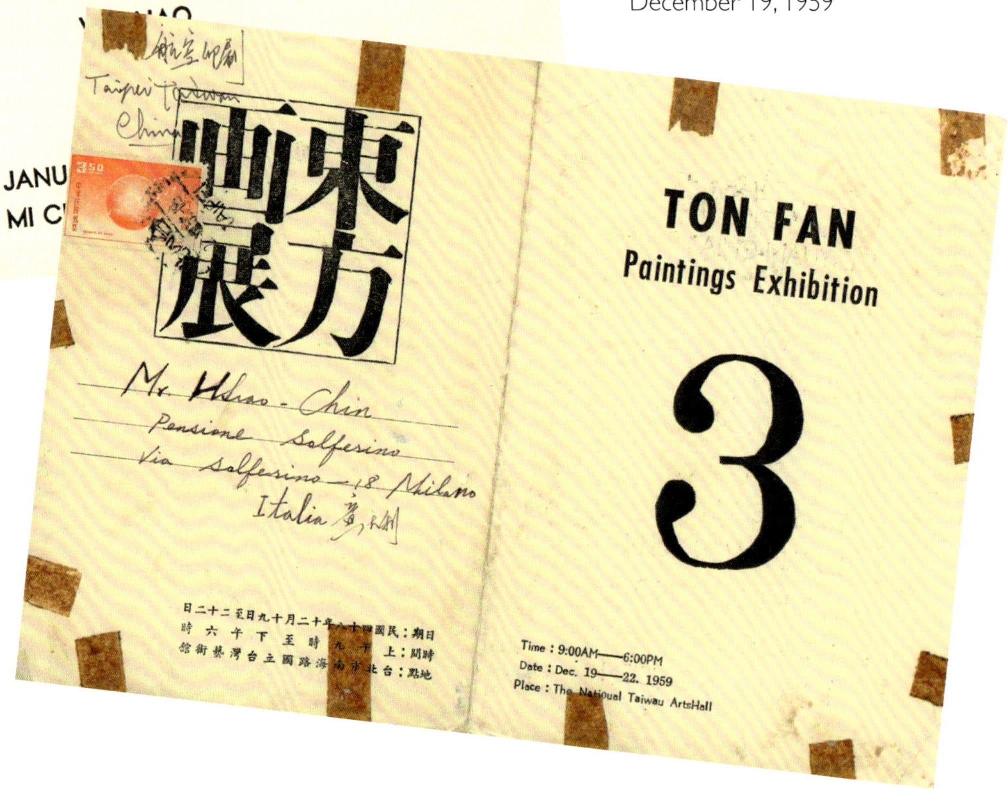

(*below*) Ton-Fan Art Group Painting Exhibition at The National Taiwan Arts Hall in Taipei, December 19, 1959

(below) Taiwan Provincial Museum, Taipei. Catalogue of the 25th Anniversary Joint Exhibition of Ton-Fan and Fifth Moon Art Group, June 16-22, 1981

(right) Ton-Fan Art Group Painting Exhibition in Macerata, November 21-29, 1959

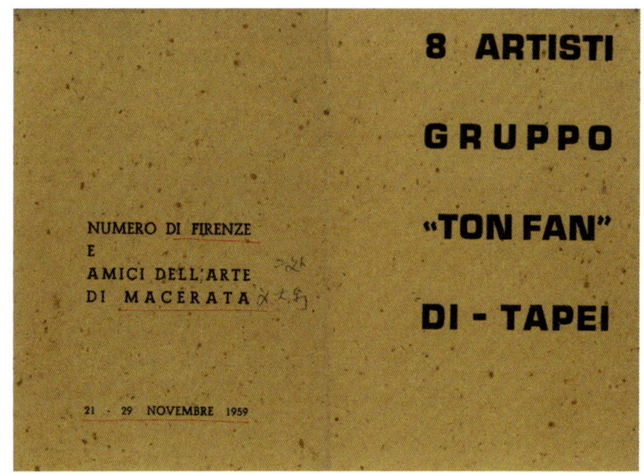

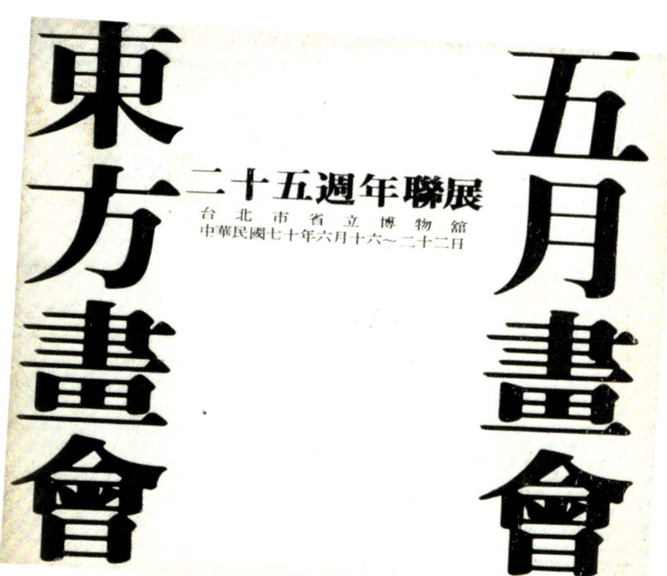

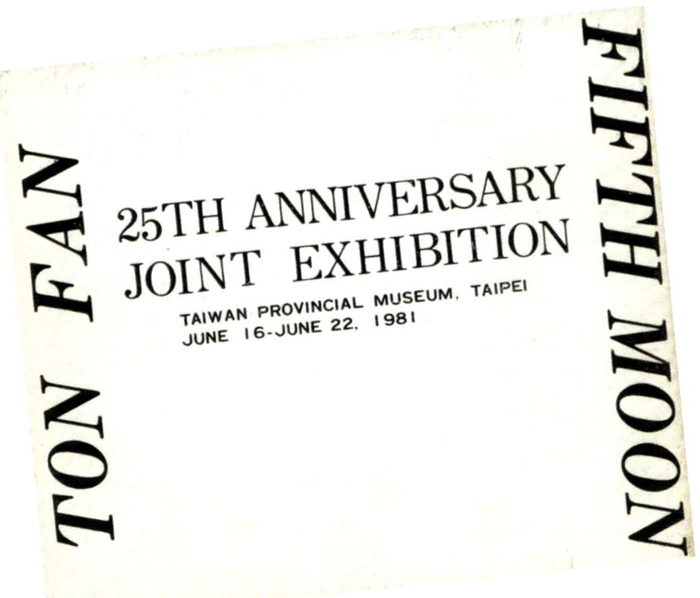

self-funded, without public sponsorship. It was held for only three days; nevertheless, it electrified the public.[29] The reaction was bipolar: many adored the works, while other visitors thought the paintings were merely imitating the Impressionists, and they started to question about how Ton-Fan (Eastern) it was.[30]

At that time, the modernisation of Chinese art had not been entirely accepted by many people in either mainland China or Taiwan, for various reasons. First of all, many traditional Chinese painters were taught to follow the examples set by the old masters. Furthermore, since the end of the Imperial regime, China had always been engaged in civil wars and wars against the colonialist invasions. Therefore there was not a stable tradition of growth for art. In addition, after the war, Taiwan was ruled by the Nationalist government, which saw itself as the legitimate Chinese cultural inheritor and tried to maintain Chinese traditions, in comparison with the mainland Communist regime, who wanted to break and reshape the 'old art'. Modernisation of art was a collective goal for Chinese artists from both sides of the Taiwan channel. Members of Ton-Fan endeavoured to utilise this exhibition to explain to the public what modern art was.

Hsiao Chin organised the first exhibition for Ton-Fan in Galleria Jardin, Barcelona, and through this the artist gained experience in setting up group exhibitions – it certainly helped him to arrange Punto.

In this exhibition, Hsiao Chin put his new paintings on display. Those paintings already showed some stylistic changes, which became more apparent in Punto.

Ton-Fan is seen to be the benchmark in Chinese art history, because it inherited the legacy of the short-lived Juelan (決瀾社, 1932–35), the first modernist art group in China, which was disrupted by the war. Ton-Fan supported Hsiao Chin's moral responsibility to redirect Chinese art

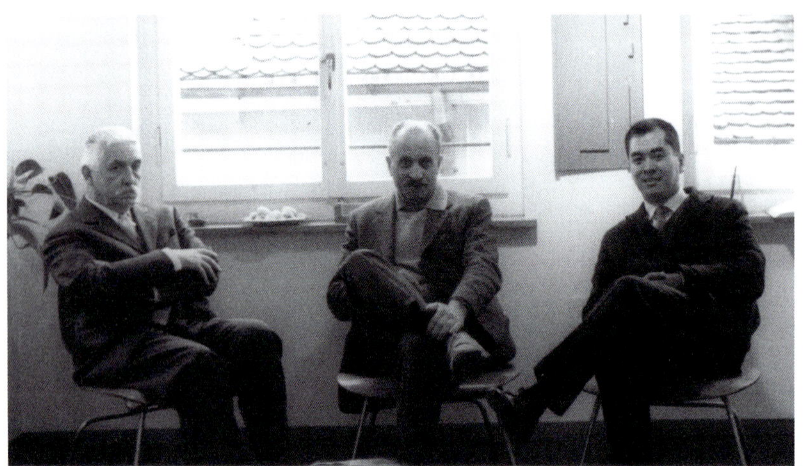

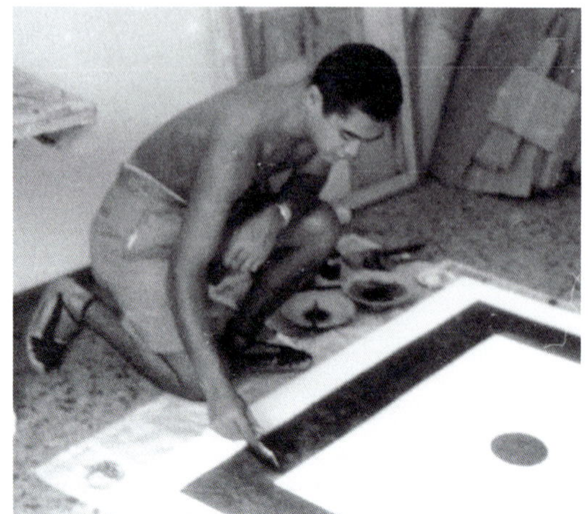

to modernisation, more than twenty years earlier than the mainland Chinese artists, who were able to resume studying Western avant-garde art in the 1980s.[31]

Nevertheless, situated as he was in an international environment, Hsiao Chin was ready to embrace the next avant-garde wave.

Again in 1957, his Ton-Fan fellows participated in the São Paulo Art Biennial. This international event was established in 1951 by the Italian entrepreneur Francisco Ciccillo Matarazzo Sobrinho, following the pattern of the Venice Biennale. Hsiao Ming-hsien (蕭明賢) was the recipient of an honorary award at the Fourth Biennial, and Alfred Barr was on the award jury.[32] Possibly through the success of his friend Hsiao Ming-hsien, Hsiao Chin started to pay attention to art biennials. In summer 1958 he visited the Venice Biennale for the first time, and it offered an excellent opportunity for him to absorb the new trends. At the biennials, he saw works by Mark Tobey and Mark Rothko regularly displayed. Hsiao Chin had already encountered paintings by the two masters in art journals and magazines, but to experience the originals was still spectacular. Tobey visited China in the 1930s and was influenced by Chinese calligraphy. This helped Hsiao Chin recognise the power and depth of Chinese art. Rothko's painting presented a lyrical contemplation and meditation, and its powerful spirituality had a significant impact on Hsiao Chin.

Apart from Venice, Hsiao Chin made a grand tour in Italy that year: he visited Florence and Milan, which led him eventually to leave Spain and migrate to Italy. In Florence, he met Fiamma Vigo, the owner of Galleria Numero. Vigo was passionate about abstract art. She was also a painter and used her money and gallery space to support young artists. Hsiao Chin left a few of his paintings at the gallery.

Unexpectedly, he received an invitation from Vigo in February 1959 to put on a solo exhibition there. During that year, Hsiao Chin was travelling back and forth between Spain and Italy, and by the end of that year he had decided to settle in Milan.

It was in Milan that Hsiao Chin started a much more ambitious project: Punto. Punto not only transcended Ton-Fan but also carried the aims of many European art groups when more international artists joined it.

Punto as a truly international movement

Hsiao Chin sensed an urge to shift his art stylistically and spiritually. This was because, by the end of the 1950s, *Art Informel*, like many art movements in history, had become less self-evident; art forms with similar pictorial languages were prevalent in the art market, which diluted its authenticity and its initial revolutionary intentions. Hsiao Chin observed the situation and felt that *art informel* had already become aberrant, turning out to be a parody of emotional catharsis. The fountain of creativity seemed to have dried up.

Hsiao Chin later recalled how he felt about *Art Informel* in the late 1950s:

> The 1950s was a time when non-representational art was in fashion in Europe, and action painting was in fashion in America. These once vibrant Western art movements, by the end of the 1950s, were trending towards uncontrolled releases of emotion or games of skill, losing their original spiritual depth and vitality. This of course also reflects the crisis of the consumerist attitudes that were then sweeping Chinese and Western society.
>
> At the time, I was opposed to the flood of non-representational, emotional art, and pursued a deeper level of spirituality. I was not alone.[33]

I pittori della galleria

D'ARENA
CALDERARA
MAMPASO
MELONI
MIGNONI

opere di:

BALLA	BUSSE	CARRÀ
CASSINARI	CONTE. M	DE CHIRICO
DE PISIS	DOVA	FARRERAS
FONTANA	GUTTUSO	LATTANZI
LÉGER	LUCIO	MANZÙ
MORANDI	MARINO	PASOTTI
SERRANO	SIRONI	PICASSO
SUAREZ	THARRAS	SOLDATI
VELA	VIOLA	UTRILLO

punto|1

azuma
bologonesi
calderara
cosentino
de luigi
fontana
hsiao chin
li yuan-chia
maino

7 maggio ore 21

Galleria Cadario s.p.a. Milano
via della Spiga 7 telefono 79.41.04

(*opposite far left*) Photo taken during the exhibition at Galerie Suzanne Bollag in Zurich, 1967. From left to right: Calderara, Peschi and Hsiao Chin

(*opposite left*) Hsiao Chin in his studio, 1962

(*above left and right*) The invitation of the first Punto Exhibition at Galleria Cadario, May 7, 1962

(*right*) The statement of Punto International Art Movement, 1962

punto | 1

capire la condizione di finito nell'infinito è intuire nella realtà del pensiero la verità di essere: nella purezza dell'idea la ragione di operare

comprendre la condition de fini dans l'infini est concevoir dans la réalité de la pensée la verité d'être: dans la pureté de l'idée la raison de opérer

in ihrer wahren bedeutung die beschaffenheit und besondere eigenschaft der vollendung in der unendlichkeit zu erfassen, heisst, in der verwirklichung des gedankens die wahrheit des daseins zur erkenntnis heranreifen zu lassen: in der reinheit der idee, den anlass zum wirken

to understand the condition of the finite in the infinite is to perceive the true essence of beeing in the reality of thought: in the purity of the idea the impulse to operate

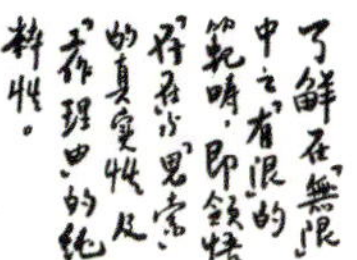

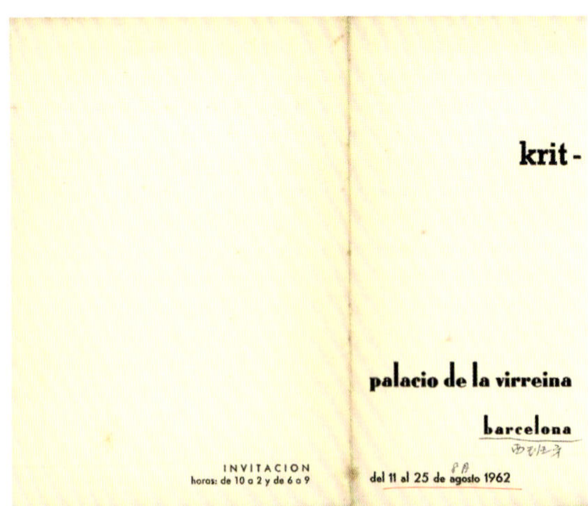

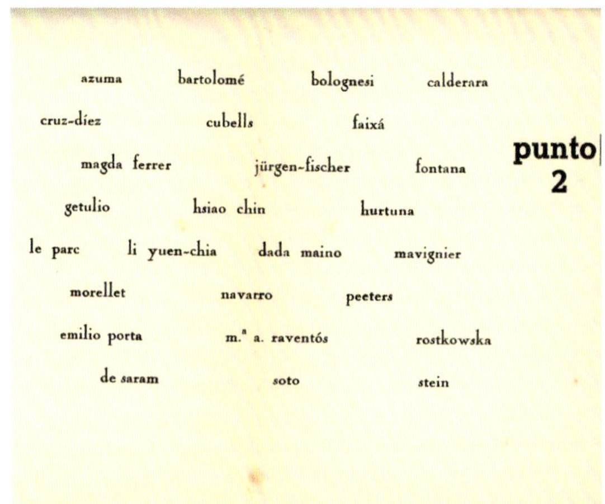

(*left*) The second Punto Exhibition at the Palacio de la Virreina in Barcelona, August 11, 1962

(*opposite, detail see page 57*) Hsiao Chin, *The Origin of Chi-3*, 1962

If Ton-Fan represented Hsiao Chin's mission to present 'Chinese-ness' to the world avant-garde, Punto then can be seen as a new departure, pushing European art forward through its enlightenment. Punto could be said to be a phenomenological way to solve the crises caused by Modernity. Phenomenology aims to recover the lost origin of knowledge by recognising that 'meaning' is a relationship of human consciousness, which must be traced back to a pre-objective intuition of 'things themselves' in their 'flesh and blood presence'.[34]

Punto (an Italian word, meaning 'dot') represents the origin of image: all lines, surfaces and spaces are initiated by a dot. Hsiao Chin and the Punto artists believed in the infinite possibilities of art, which has to be retraced to the beginning of image-making: the dot. Even though Punto was thought to be an abstract art movement, nevertheless its intention was not to create a new world on canvas ('non-objective'), as Kazimir Malevich and Wassily Kandinsky had in mind.[35] Instead, Punto aims at purity in the intention to make art, appreciating the conditions of creating, and realising what life is.

Punto was translated into Chinese later by the Taiwanese curator Huang Chao-hu (黃朝湖) as 龐圖 (páng tú), and despite its phonetic interpretation, the Chinese word, meaning *Grand Image*, expressed Hsiao Chin's vision appropriately. Punto is an organic expression, in search of the lost joy of being and making.

Looking for the truth had been a cliché in the avant-garde: nearly all movements and groups claimed that they were valid and right. The Dadaists expressed this by believing that nonsense is the human condition, while the Surrealists tried to reveal the truth through automatism and the subconscious. Punto's approach was not associated with the irrational. Reason is a relative term. The rational and the irrational are a duality that resides in human nature. One can endeavour to explain the human condition by distinguishing them, but one will never succeed in separating them entirely. The same can be said of abstract and representational art.

Punto in form may seem to be abstract, but its concept was closer to Buddhism and Phenomenology. In Punto, Eastern and Western philosophy found their collective quest to know about our existence by tracing the pre-objective intuition, the origin of being.

In Milan Hsiao Chin befriended Lucio Fontana, Antonio Calderara and Kenjiro Azuma (吾妻兼治郎), and they often discussed and found similarities in their art pursuits, discovering that they were comparable with each other. They were thus able to share and exchange ideas. Hsiao Chin, Calderara and Azuma are the three founders of Punto.

Following an introduction by Hsiao Chin, one of the Ton-Fan artists, Li Yuan-chia (李元佳), was able to join the conversations by post, because at that time he was in Taipei.[36]

Milan in the 1960s was an international, cosmopolitan city. With the support of the Marshall Plan, the economy and artistic life flourished, and it was summarised as the *miracolo italiano*.[37] Major European abstract artists were regularly shown here: Yves Klein, Cy Twombly, Lucio Fontana, Alberto Burri, Piero Manzoni. In a way, they were all working with abstract images for a conceptual breakthrough. Fontana at that time was already well established in Milan; he founded Spatialism in 1947 and remained internationally influential during the post-war era. He was fascinated by the artists from the East and decided to join them on an equal footing.

Hsiao Chin at that time was interested in Daoism as well as the naturalist and minimalist way of image-making it inspired.[38] He changed his palette from oil pigments to watercolour. The flow of life is like the stream of water,

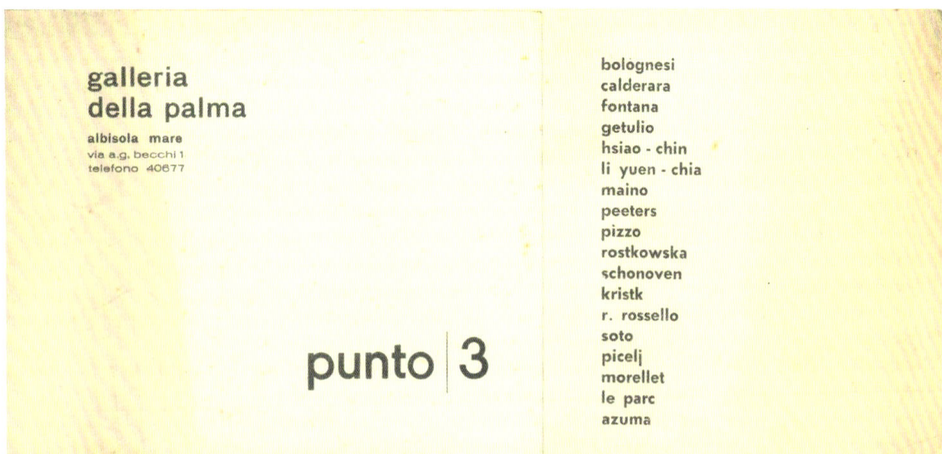

(*left and opposite*) The third Punto Exhibition at the Galleria Della Palma in Albissola, August 20, 1962

Daoism suggests, so Hsiao Chin wanted to make his images asymmetrical and lively. Water also consists of a dot, a drop or an atom. Atoms flow through the universe and the human body, forming the world and every life.

The idea of Punto attracted many artists in Europe, and two more artists joined them: Mario de Luigi, an abstract artist from Venice, and Eduarda Emilia Maino, a female artist who later joined the famous Zero Group. The first Punto exhibition was held at Galleria Cadario in Milan on 7 May 1962. The artists' manifesto was succinct:

> Purity of concepts and reasons for creation are conditioned on the understanding of the 'finite' within the 'infinite', and on the grasp of the reality of thought and the true meaning of life.[39]

The Punto exhibition enabled the artists to present their ideas through actions; nevertheless, the first Punto show was a beginning, a process in which artists strove to deal with the fundamental crisis of European civilisation. The logical way of thinking derived from the Ancient Greeks, the rationality based on empirical observation encouraged by the Enlightenment, and the irrational aspects of the human mind represented by the Dadaists and Surrealists, formed a chain, the trajectory of the *Zeitgeistgeschichte* (the history of the spirit of the time), belonging to a Euro-centric mode, and it did not fully accept an alternative thinking system. Van Gogh, Gauguin, Matisse and Picasso were interested in non-European art, and the art historian Norbert Lynton categorised the artists as 'New Barbarians';[40] nonetheless, it can be said that the renegades of modern European society were looking for salvation, a second chance, via a kind of *chinoiserie*.

Chinoiserie, the vision of Cathay, according to the art historian Hugh Honour, was the imaginary world of the Europeans; even though the fantasy shed light on a new world, it was still fundamentally a European world.[41] The East is a source of *chinoiserie*, but no less and no more.

Punto differentiated from false internationalism by including artists from both hemispheres of the world. It achieved direct communication, in which Eastern and Western artists collaborated equally and successfully. Furthermore, its historical significance was recognised by both the market and the academic world, by both Western and Eastern official sponsors.

As early as in 1935, the philosopher Edmund Husserl had already pointed out the cause of the crisis of European Man and offered the solution:

> In our continually streaming perception of the world we are not isolated but rather stand within it in contact with other men.… In *living with one another* each can participate in the life of the other. Thus, in general, the world does not exist for isolated individuals but for the community of men; and this is due to the communalisation of the straightforwardly perceptual.… It is only by making oneself understood that we have the possibility of *recognising* that the things which one sees are the *same* as those which the other sees.[42]

Punto can be seen as the first attempt in the modern era by the participating artists to bridge geographic differences in dealing with the validity of painting. Before joining Punto, Lucio Fontana had already questioned the 'purity' of painting as discussed by Clement Greenberg. Greenberg claimed that because modern art is progressive, therefore it should identify and differentiate the essential elements from the inessential.[43] In this way, not only pure art and the quintessential property of media can be distinguished,

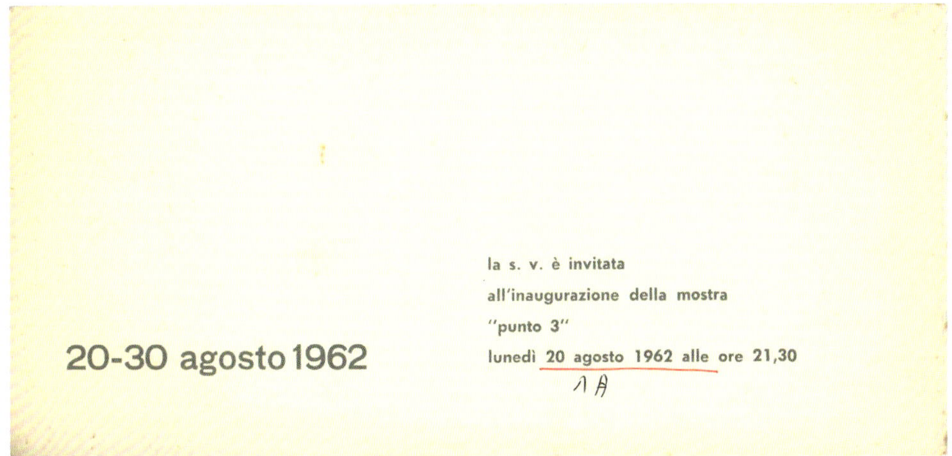

namely flatness and the delimitation of flatness, but also art can move forward. Fontana was a ceramicist and sculptor, which enabled him to see paintings from a three-dimensional angle. He slashed canvas, damaging the 'flatness', and so through this deconstructionist method a new epoch in painting was created. Jaleh Mansoor commented: 'Fontana's act exposes the way any gesture is determined rather than being a projection on to a surface.'[44]

As early as 1946, Fontana declared that 'man has exhausted pictorial and sculptural forms of art', and he wished art could be intrinsically valid and unsullied by 'our ideas'. By 'our', he included himself.[45] Hsiao Chin offered Fontana a new opportunity to pursue his path. In Spatialism, Fontana believed change is the perpetuity of the universe, which is the essential idea of Buddhism, while Buddhism did not only recognise this but further extended it to the idea of *Sūnyatā* (空 Kong): all things are empty of intrinsic existence and nature. *Sūnyatā* corresponds with *lakṣana* (相 Xiang), appearance. The visual is the representation of the abstract essence (*Sūnyatā*). In order to project or determine the essential nature of time and space, it is necessary to go back to the primal stage of painting: Punto.

This action is not aggressive, violent or destructive, as Fontana or Western avant-garde had hitherto progressed. Punto does not deny the validity of history, nor does it claim to advance it. Punto is organic and is interested in the relationship between the nature of the universe and its representation as well as its movement, namely the interaction between *Sūnyatā* and *laksana*.

Punto, in this sense, goes beyond existentialism (focus on humans); instead it seeks the universal (human existence and circumstance). Punto explores the substance and the spiritual. Dots, lines, colours, and the forms generated by them, all have their lives, movements and correspondence with their surroundings.

On the surface, Punto seemed to be another *Art Informel* movement – however, its philosophy is conceptualist.

The Punto artists believed:

> 'Man' is the finite condition within the infinite universe. The art practitioner should be an oracle of the human spirit and the spokesperson for its ideas. Thus, his explorations of ideas, spiritual pursuits and contemplations of life should come before others. Only in this way can they be transmitted to others and contribute to the evolution of the human spirit.[46]

It is clear that Punto is not playing around with form, but has a moral mission.

Thirteen Punto exhibitions

The first Punto exhibition was successful, and the group was immediately recognised internationally. The municipal government of Barcelona sponsored the second exhibition. It was held at the Palacio de la Virreina, and was by far the largest Punto exhibition. Twenty-six artists from eleven countries participated. The show featured the Chinese artists Hsiao Chin and Li Yuan-chia, the Japanese Azuma, the Italians Calderara, Lucio Fontana, Dada Maino, Mario De Luigi, Getulio Alviani, Ettore Sottsass, Enrico Castellani, Zoren, Sergio Dangelo, Mario Nigro and Umberto Peschi, the Spaniards Cubells, Faixa, Magda Ferrer and Maria Asuncio Raventos, the French François Morellet and Joël Stein, the German Klaus Jürgen-Fischer, the Dutch Henk Peeters, the Argentinian Julio Le Parc (a winner of the Grand Prize at the Venice Biennale), the Brazilian Almir Mavignier, the Venezuelans Jesús Rafael Soto and Carlos Cruz Diez, and the Polish Rostkowska de Saram.

文星雜誌社－國立臺灣藝術館－現代文學社

五十二年七月二十八日至八月六日

上午九－十二時
下午二－五時

謹訂於
七月二十八日（星期日）起
在國立臺灣藝術館畫廊
舉行「龐圖國際藝術運動」運台展
PUNTO INTERNATIONAL ART MOVEMENT EXHIBITION
JULY 28–AUGUST 6, 1963 NATIONAL TAIWAN ARTS HALL

敬請蒞臨參觀

臺北市南海路47號藝術館畫廊

蕭 勤	封答那 (FONTANA)	杰都里奧 (GETULIO)	卡爾代拉拉 (CALDERARA)
	比 卓 (PIZZO)	彼德爾司 (PEETERS)	吾妻兼治郎 (AZUMA)
李元佳	索扎司 (SOTTSASS)	阿爾芒多 (ARMANDO)	卡司代拉尼 (CASTELLANI)

(*left*) The invitation of the fifth Punto Exhibition held at The National Taiwan Arts Hall in Taipei, July 28, 1963

(*below*) Some of the artists of Punto International Art Movement

(*opposite, detail see page 84*) Hsiao Chin, *Light Energy*, 1964

All of them played significant roles in the history of art in the 1960s, and some of them even became leaders of their region. The scale of the second Punto illustrated how attractive and significant Hsiao Chin's idea was to the post-war art world.

Nine days after the second exhibition, the third Punto was shown at Albissola, a ceramic art centre in Italy. There were eighteen artists in total participating. Because of the tight schedule the Spanish artists did not take part, but some new artists contributed. They included the leading Zero Group member Jan Schoonhoven from the Netherlands, R. Russell and Pia Pizzo from Italy and Piceli from Yugoslavia.

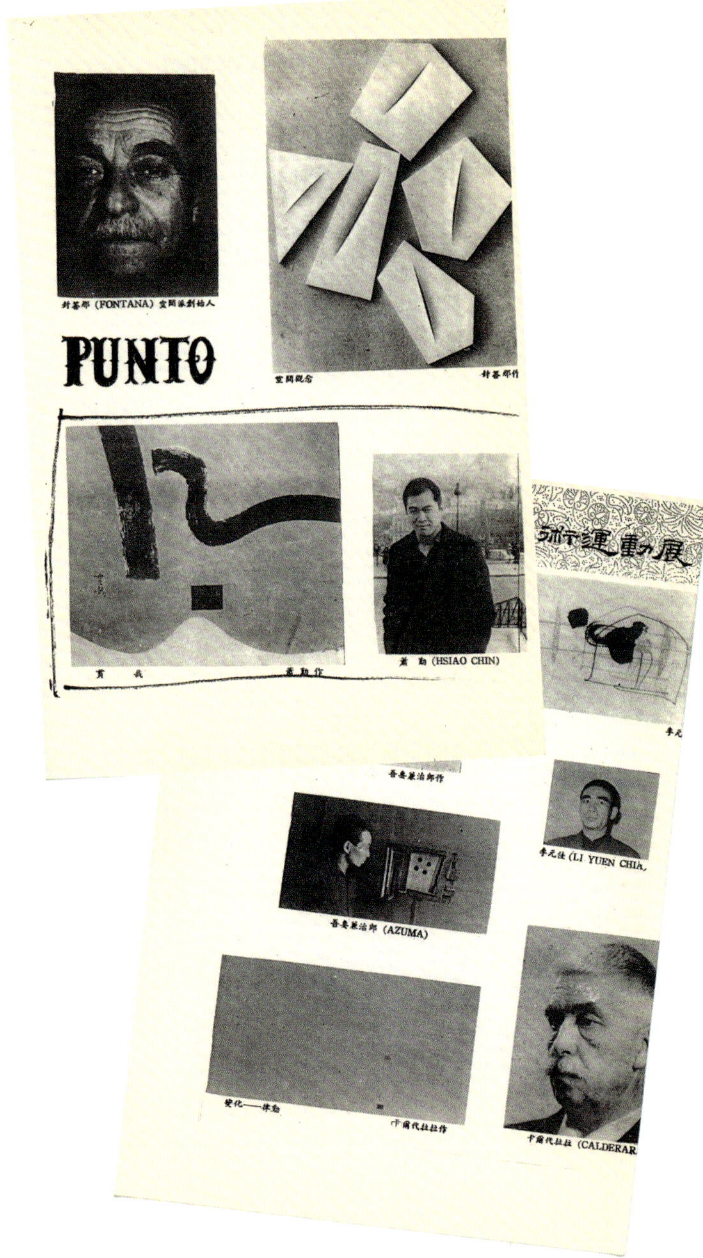

The three Punto exhibitions electrified the landscape of world art at that time. The Punto movement formed a camp against non-representationalism, and indirectly inspired Zero Group and Op Art to crystallise their direction.

The movement not only called artists from two blocs on board, but also attracted artists from the countries of the Non-Aligned Movement. All the same, Hsiao Chin sensed a problem in organising the exhibitions with too many artists, and to some extent, its spiritual purity was hard to maintain.

Hsiao Chin and the original members reflected upon what went wrong and clarified their initial intention. They decided to simplify the operation. Four founding members remained: Hsiao Chin, Lucio Fontana, Antonio Calderara and Kenjiro Azuma. An additional four artists were included: Eduarda Emilia Maino, P. Pizzo, Bolognese and Wout V. Even though Punto was not specifically a feminist movement and Hsiao Chin as a male artist was responsible for operating it, the female artists were treated as equals.

In comparison, the Surrealists and American Abstract Expressionists emphasised their masculinity, power and

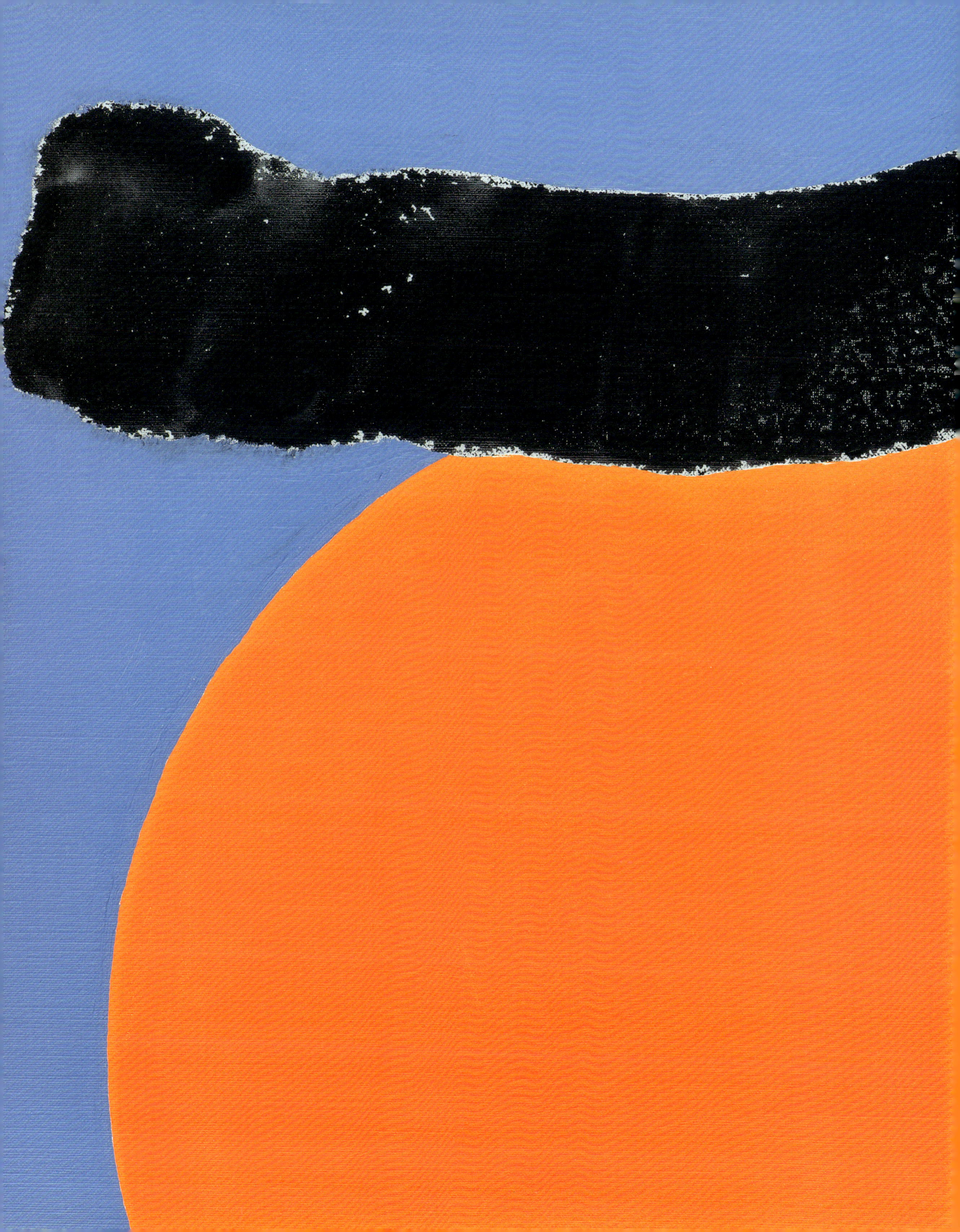

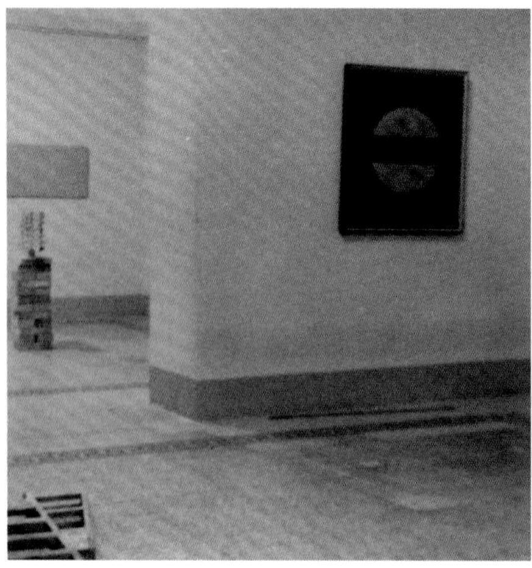
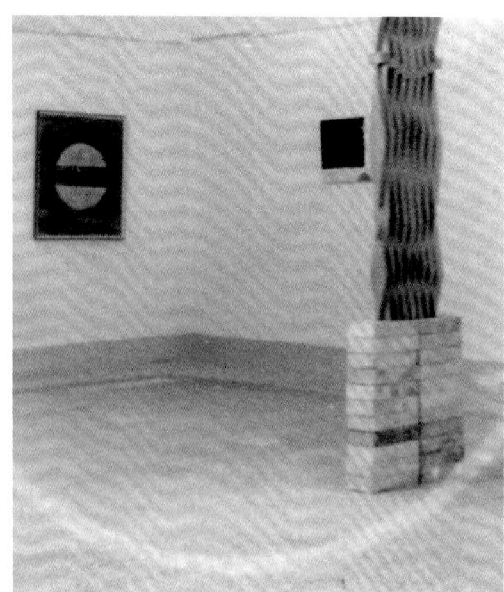
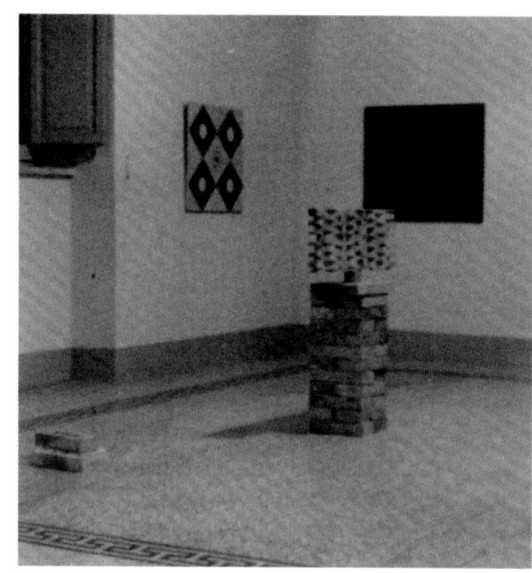

cultural dominance. Allegedly, the Surrealists praised feminist merits, but women, to some extent, were still treated as muses in the traditional sense.

Punto did not aim for cultural dominance, as it did not believe in societal hierarchy. Its spirituality did not exclude the secular; rather, it chose to transcend. Transcendence is not the same as negligence.

The feminist elements in the fourth Punto also can be discerned by its patronage. It was the female gallery owner Fiamma Vigo who provided Galleria Numero in Florence to support the movement.

The importance of the fifth Punto is embodied by its exhibition locale: the National Gallery, Taipei. It was in summer 1963, six months after the fourth exhibition, that Punto travelled to the East. For Hsiao Chin this exhibition gained the confidence of Eastern culture, before consumerism subconsciously contaminated society in Taiwan.[47] Three founders out of four were artists born in the East, and most of Punto's ideas were derived from Eastern philosophy. A state-sponsored exhibition in the East therefore completed one of its goals. Through the international exhibition spaces Punto traced art back to the root of cultural globalisation. For Taiwan and Chinese art, it brought back a new taste and style, different from the traditional Expressionist paintings (寫意). Punto was shocking because the audience in Taiwan was not familiar with such kinds of abstract art.[48]

The sixth exhibition, in May 1964, continued this journey. This time the show was located in the municipal modern art museum of Macerata. The famous Jesuit missionary Matteo Ricci was born in this central Italian town. Father Ricci was an intelligent scholar, whose fluent scholarly Chinese (a kind of Chinese Latin, used by cultured people in China) enabled him to establish an intimate friendship with many Chinese intellectuals in the late Ming dynasty. Ricci brought paintings and optics, among other sciences, to China, and some extent, enlightened Chinese visual culture. The sixth Punto in return reciprocated Ricci's contribution to the cultural exchange between East and West.

In summer 1964, Punto had its seventh exhibition in Venice, at Galleria Gritti. There were seven artists showing their work. Pia Pizzo, Umberto Peschi (a Futurist sculptor) and Zoren collaborated with Hsiao Chin, Calderara, Azuma and Li Yuan-chia. The art critic Toni Toniato, after viewing the artworks, believed that Punto marked a new beginning for the purification of ideas and forms in contemporary art. The seven artists became the core players in Punto.

On 12 December 1964, the seven artists put on the eighth Punto exhibition in Galleria 2000 in Bologna. Bologna was a cultural centre in the early Renaissance and its university is the oldest in the world. The show could be seen as a homage to intellectuals. The Italian philosopher Francesco Saba Sardi found that Punto showed remarkable originality, not following fashions and trends. Furthermore, he believed the unique signs that the artists employed were temporally and geographically boundless. The artists were thought to be constructive, and in spite of their stylistic differences and various cultural roots, they shared a compelling vision.

After the eighth exhibition, another major player in *Art Informel* joined them: Sergio Dangelo. He is one of the founders of *Movimento Nucleare*, an important group in the 1950s, who contributed to the Cybernetic movement. They believed that the truth lies in atoms. Dangelo's contribution to Punto indicated his acknowledgement of his artistic stance: from *Art Informel* to intuitive, spiritual art. The ninth exhibition took place at the Galerie S. Bollag in Zurich, Switzerland, on 7 May 1965.

The eight artists continued their journey by holding the tenth and eleventh exhibitions with the support of Galleria

(*left*) The sixth Punto Exhibition at The Municipal Modern Art Museum of Macerata in Italy, May 3, 1964

(*right*) The seventh Punto Exhibition at Galleria Gritti in Venice, Summer 1964

(*below*) Hsiao Chin, *In the Deep of Darkness (Nel profondo delle Tenebre)*, 1965
Acrylic on canvas
130 x 161cm

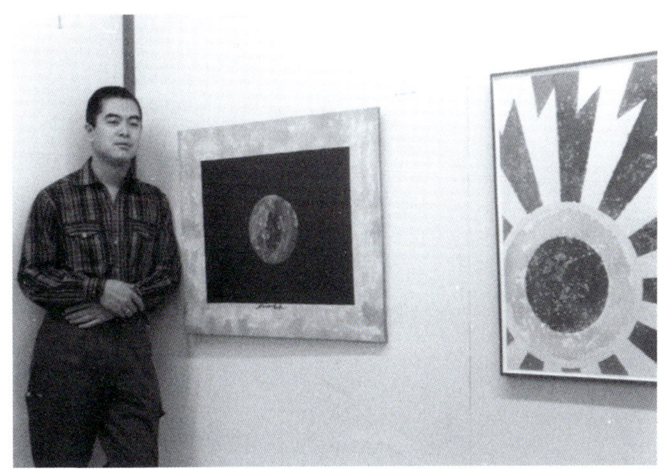

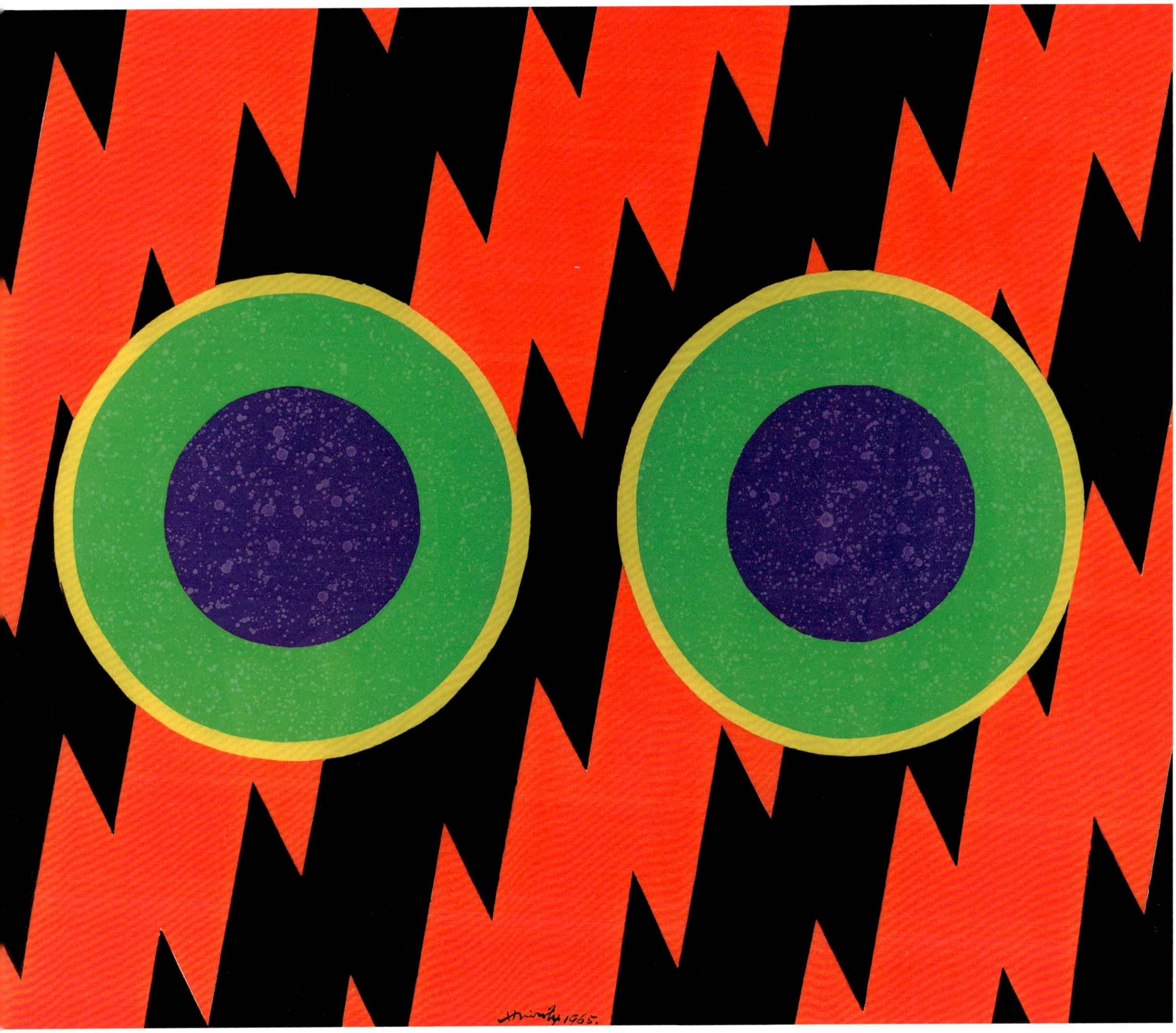

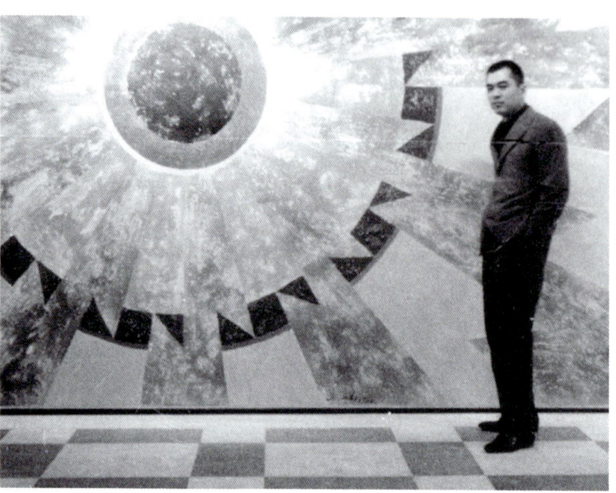

(*far left*) The eighth Punto Exhibition at Galleria 2000 in Bologna, December 12, 1964

(*left*) Hsiao Chin participated in a group exhibition of Chinese modern painters in Rome, January, 1965

(*below*) Hsiao Chin
Con Tour, 1965
Acrylic on canvas
130 x 160cm

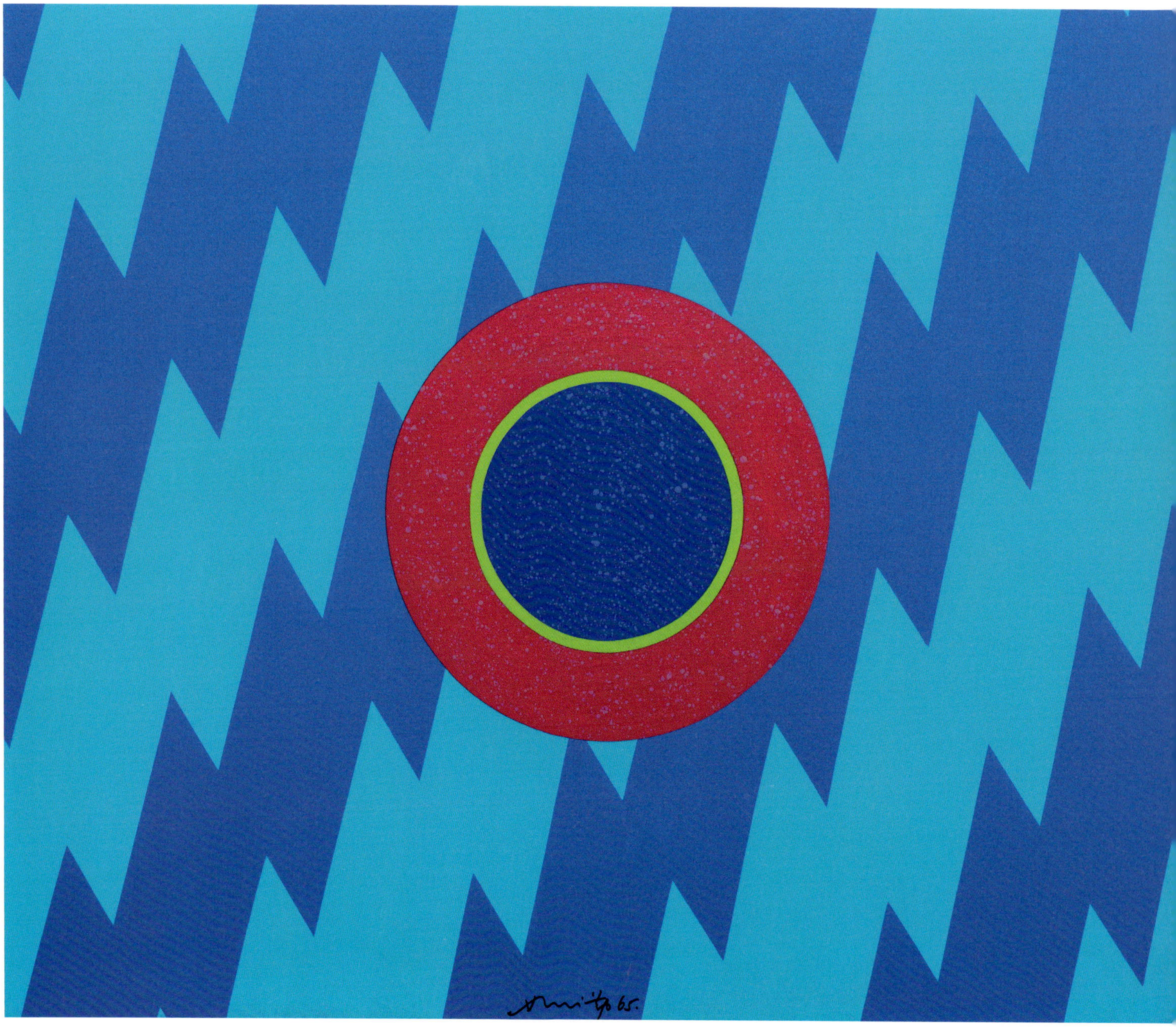

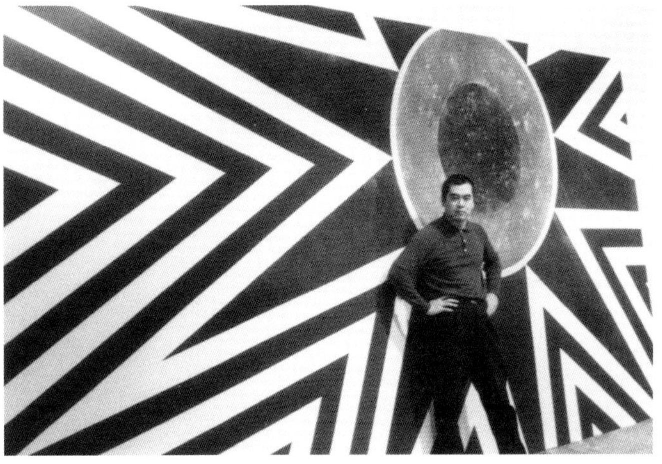

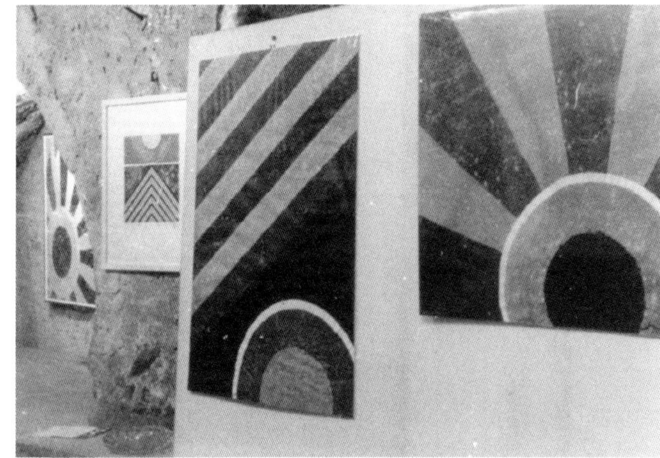

(*above left and right*) Hsiao Chin's exhibition at Signals Gallery in London, 1966

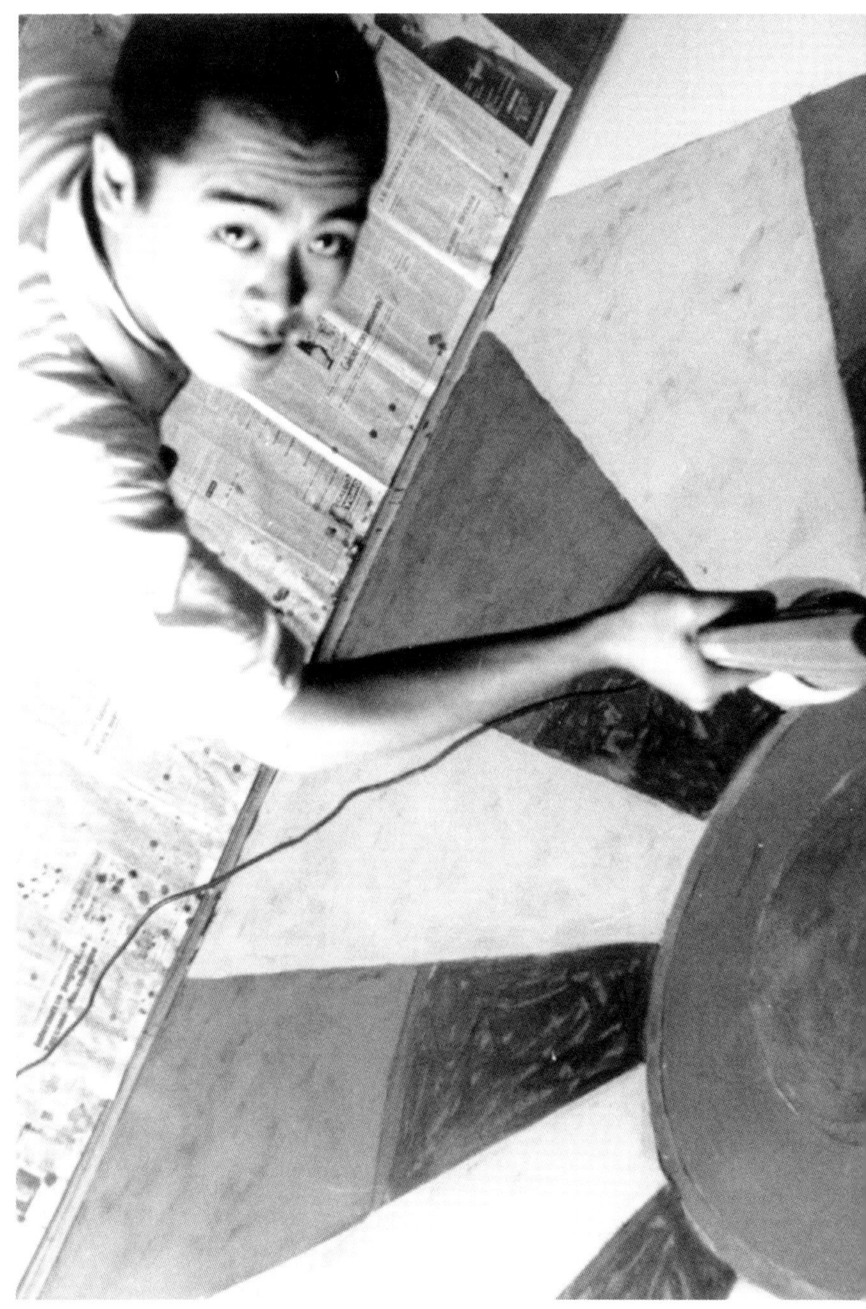

(*right*) Hsiao Chin painting in Milan, 1964

Numero in its branches in Florence and Rome respectively. It was the peak time of Op art and Pop art. Nevertheless, Punto was not affected by the turbulence caused by these two. Even so, it is arguable that if Pop art is superficial, critics and thinkers had noticed that the society of the spectacle had become self-evident.[49]

The twelfth exhibition received great support from publishing houses. A monograph was published for the Punto group. V. Scheiwiller generously printed separate brochures for each artist and then edited them into a new monograph. The exhibition took place at Galleria L'Elefante in Mestre near Venice on 26 June 1965.

In 1965 Punto held four exhibitions, touring to different places in Italy, and with wider support from various cultural contributors, such as critics, artists, galleries and publishers: the idea of Punto was taking root in multiple cultural fields. However, Hsiao Chin acknowledged that Punto seemed to be making its place in art history and the artists were rigorous and pure; but their 'elitist' visual projection turned out to be less accessible.

The artist later commented:

> Only a few artists with deep spirituality and determination can carry on the struggle for ideas such as these, and only a small number of people will be able to accept them. They are difficult to 'adapt for the masses'. This also made it very difficult to gain support from art dealers, and some were even manufactured by them in collusion with art critics.[50]

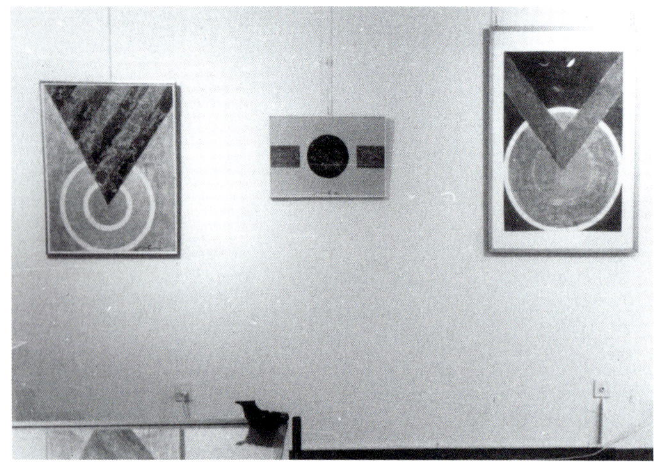

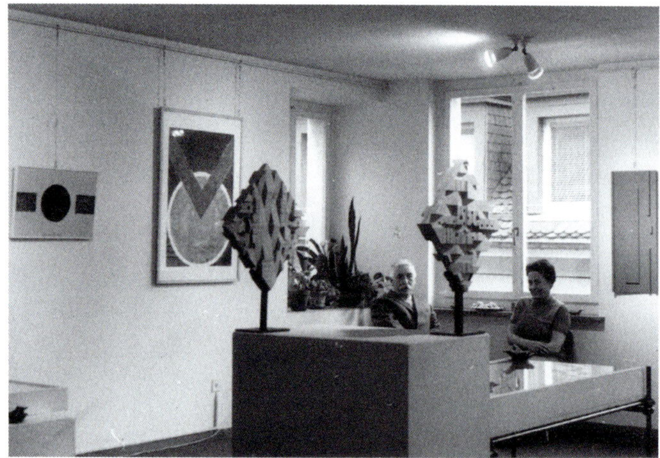

On 14 May 1966, Punto had its final exhibition at Galleria Fanesi in Ancona, in central Italy. Kenjiro Azuma was not able to participate this time. Two artists joined the show: Mario Negro (a Minimalist Italian painter) and Ho Kan (霍剛, a Ton-Fan member). The Italian critic G. Binni reflected upon the meaning of Punto after viewing the exhibition:

> Could it be that only the recipients of secret teachings can understand the philosophical roots of Punto? That is not the case. In this world, some people truly live, while others only exist like plants. Some people use their brains to think, while others only act on the teachings they hear from others. Some people adapt to other people, while others cannot. Some people are free, while others are not. The people in Punto belong to the first category, while others belong to the second. [51]

Such a comment exaggerated the 'others', but Punto's creativity is undeniable. Hsiao Chin wished that every individual could enjoy their existence in the first category, and it is also what Punto international is about. Punto would not exclude the people who are looking for intellectual independence and visual liberty.

During an interview, Hsiao Chin explained and identified the role of an artist:

> It's very difficult to live in this age although it's also our task to attempt to reciprocally bring such different cultures closer together, to choose the best part because positive, to unite them in order to create a 'true culture' of tomorrow.[52]

The Punto movement may have terminated after 1966 in a historical sense; however, its positive attitude and the passion for a brighter future have always resided in all civilisations, whether in the past, the present or the future. Reviewing Punto in the second decade of the twenty-first century, its art remains fresh, vibrant, and the *flâneur* (dilettante) would be surprised to discover this shiny pebble on the shore of art history.

Punto and its legacy

Hsiao Chin admitted that he was the main cause of the end of Punto, as in 1966 he moved to London for six months, then to New York for more than three years.

In the second half of the 1960s, the economy of Milan, as well as the whole of Italy, started to reach stalemate, and the development of contemporary art was eclipsed by New York with movements such as Neo-Dada, Pop and Minimalism. Hsiao Chin's sale did not go well with his agent Giorgio Marconi. Fortunately, at the time Signals Gallery in London invited him to prepare an experimental exhibition. Hsiao Chin found the London art scene was not as active as the Continental ones he was used to. When he returned to Milan after six months, he sensed that many local artists were venturing to New York. So he was excited to visit the city to explore new possibilities. He befriended a famous art director, Gordon B. Washburn, who at that time was the director of Asia House Gallery there.[53] Through Washburn's recommendation, Hsiao Chin was signed by the Rose Fried Gallery, the leading abstract art agent at that time, who represented masters such as Mondrian and Kandinsky. Hsiao Chin was recognised as the leading Chinese abstract artist, and the gallery was happy to organise a solo exhibition for him.

(*far left*) The ninth Punto Exhibition at Galerie Suzanne Bollag in Zurich, May 7, 1965

(*left*) The ninth Punto Exhibition at Galerie Suzanne Bollag in Zurich, May 7, 1965. Calderara at the exhibition site.

(*right*) Exhibition at Galleria Civica d'Arte Moderna in Modena, February 1, 1975

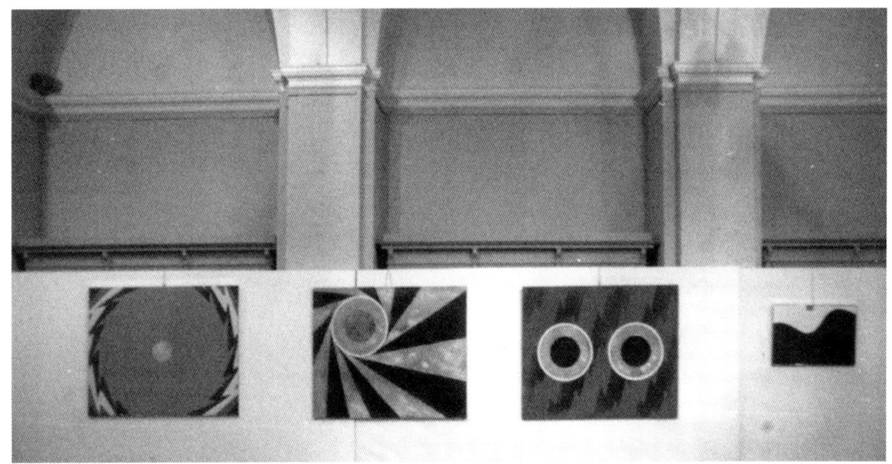

In New York, Hsiao Chin was challenged by the cultural shift, especially between the Minimalist and the Pop, and he contributed to the hard-edge style.

Meanwhile, he was more interested in Buddhism. During the Punto period, his pictorial language derived from the mixture of Daoism and Buddhism, but it became clearer that he was gradually more inclined to Buddhism.

Daoism focused on simplicity and its nihilistic thinking is more for hermits. Hsiao Chin was interested in helping and communicating with the rest of the world, which corresponded with Buddhism.

In 1977, Hsiao Chin started the Surya international movement, which can be seen as the result of his further meditation. Nevertheless, the spirit of Punto has never been extinguished.

How to maintain the maverick vibe as an artist is very challenging, after the waves of Pop, minimalist and conceptualist art, and most important of all, Post-Modernist concepts became prevalent in recent consumerist society. Hsiao Chin witnessed the paradigm shifts and his artistic integrity has not been contaminated. His work evolves, deepens, grows, while his reflections and meditations on human conditions have become more profound day by day and year by year.

Punto was a unique international art movement. It was philosophised by artists from the East and the West, and was recognised globally. It inherited both the European avant-garde inclination to creativity as well as the Eastern way of negating the advancement of violence, seeking peace in tracing the original intent of making art. Because of its unique characteristics, Punto stepped out from many abstract art groups and its universalism was well celebrated. Punto did not seek to be ahead of time or any avant-garde group; rather it circled back to speculate on the origin of art (the issue of painting as a medium, to be specific in Hsiao Chin's case). Time appears not to be linear in Punto, and space shifts and transforms. In a way, Punto transcended modernism and can be categorised as a Post-Modernist movement.

In Chapter Two, a detailed analysis of the form will justify the Post-Modern-ness of Punto.

---

1 Maggie Wu, 2018, *Legend of the Rambling King: Side View of Hsiao Chin*, Kaohsiung City: Punto Press, p. 106. [吳素琴:《逍遙王外傳:側寫蕭勤》, 龐圖出版社2018年].

2 *Ibid.*, pp.83–85.

3 Hugh Honour & John Fleming, 2002, *A World History of Art*, 6th edition, London: Laurence King Publishing, p. 842.

4 Harold Rosenberg, 1962, 'The Fall of Paris', *Tradition of the New*, pp. 209–20. Quote from *Art in Theory, 1900-2000: An Anthology of Changing Ideas*, 2003, ed. Charles Harrison & Paul Wood, new edition, Blackwell Publishing, pp. 550–53.

5 John-Franklin Koenig, '*Abstraction chaude* in Paris in the 1950s', *Reconstructing Modernism: Art in New York, Paris and Montreal 1945–1964*, ed. Serge Guilbaut, The MIT Press, p. 13.

6 Rosenberg, 1962, 'The Fall of Paris', *op. cit.*, pp. 550–53.

7 Norbert Lynton, 1992, *The Story of Modern Art*, 2nd edition, London: Phaidon, p. 257.

8 Hsiao Chin, 2017, *A Historical Dialogue with Art*, Vol. 1, Kaohsiung: Punto Press, p. 37. [蕭勤:《與藝術的歷史對話》(上), 龐圖出版社2017年].

9 Hsiao Chiimg-jui, 1995, 'The Manifestation of Tao-Hsiao Chin's Continuing Progression of Life', *Hsiao Chin: the odyssey, 1953–1994*, Taipei: Taipei City Museum of Fine Arts [蕭瓊瑞:《流動的生命——以象成道的蕭勤》,《蕭勤的歷程:1953–1994》,台北市立美術館1995年].

10 Lu Peng, 2007, *A History of Art in Twentieth-century China*, Peking University Press, p. 617. [呂澎:《20世紀中國藝術史》,北京大學出版社2007年].

11 Maggie Wu, *Legend of the Rambling King: Side View of Hsiao Chin*, p. 54.

12 *Ibid.*

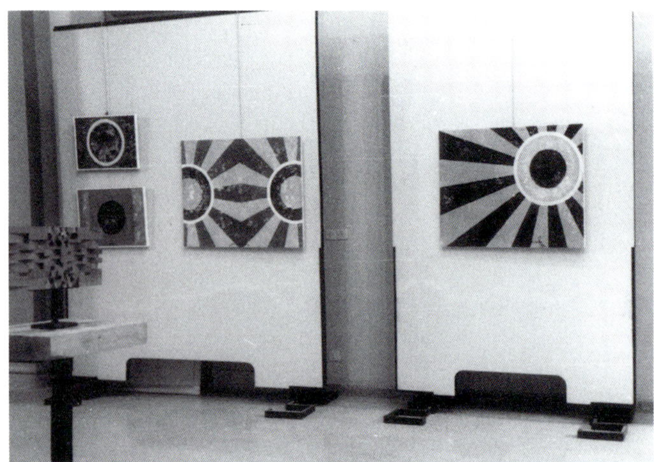

(*left*) The tenth Punto Exhibition at Galleria Numero in Florence, 1965

(*right*) The eleventh Punto Exhibition at Galleria Numero in Rome, 1965

(*right, middle*) The catalogue of the twelfth Punto Exhibition at Galleria L'Elefante in Mestre near Venice, June 26, 1965

(*far right*) The *Universe Projection* series by Hsiao Chin was exhibited at Signals Gallery in London, 1966

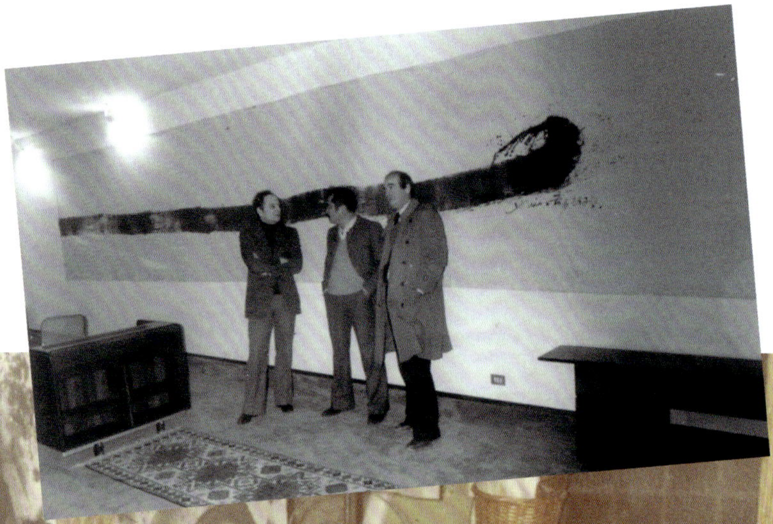

(*left*) The Surya group exhibition at the City Museum of Macerata in Italy, 1978. Hsiao Chin with the Deputy Governor of Macerata (first person on the left), who is also an art critic, and the Macerata transportation officer who is an art collector.

(*below*) Hsiao Chin with Mr. & Mrs. Liu Kuo-sung, Hou Tieh-hua, Huang Bo-yung and Hsiao Ming-hsien in New York, 1967

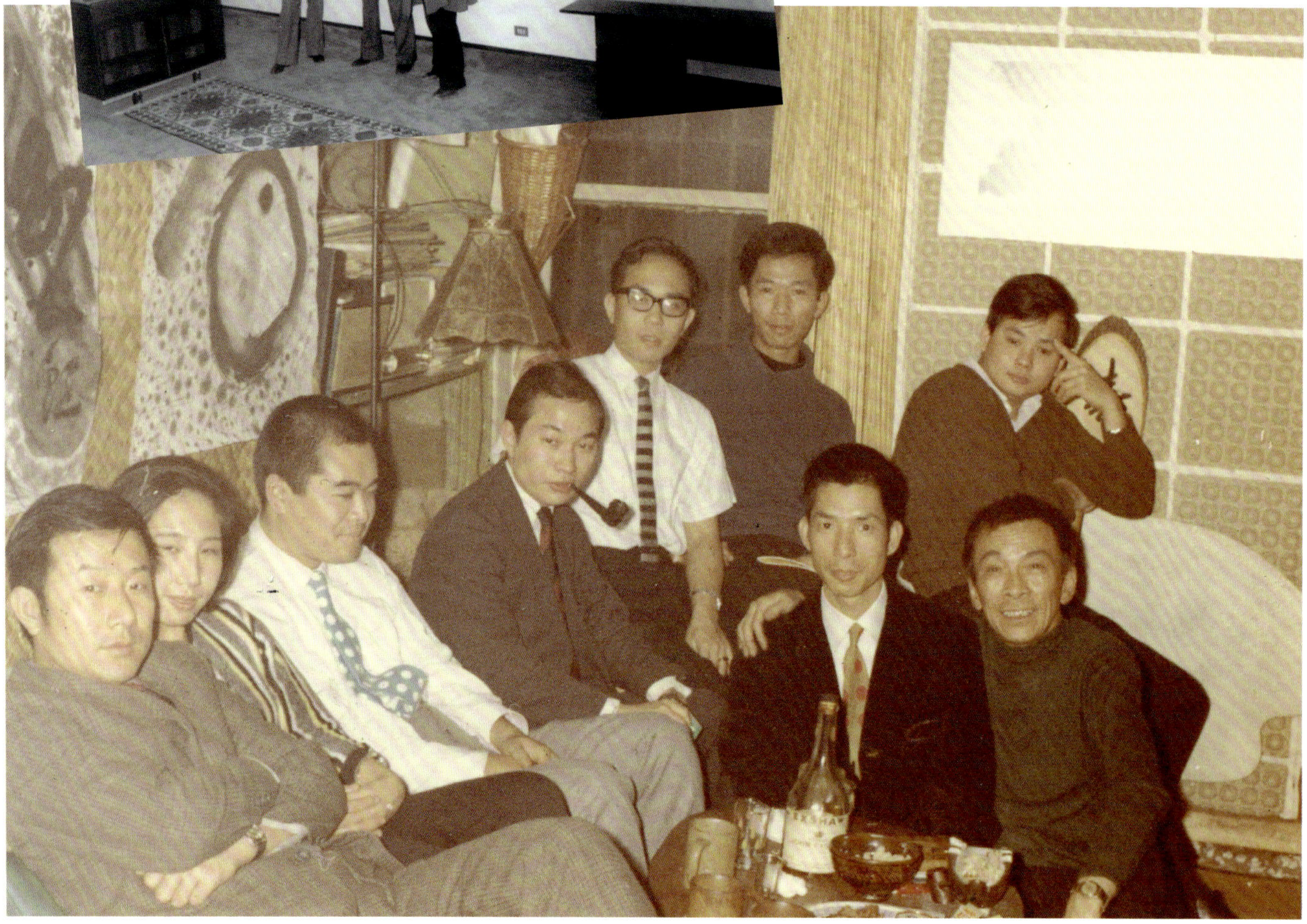

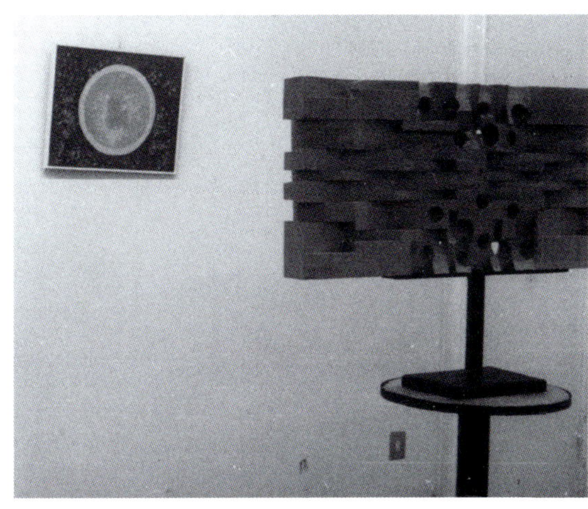

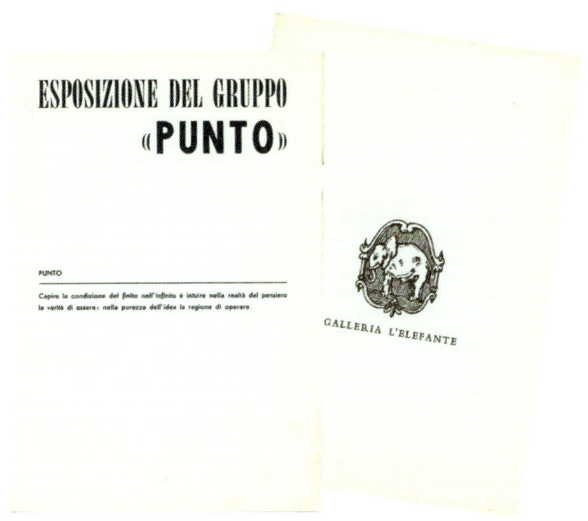

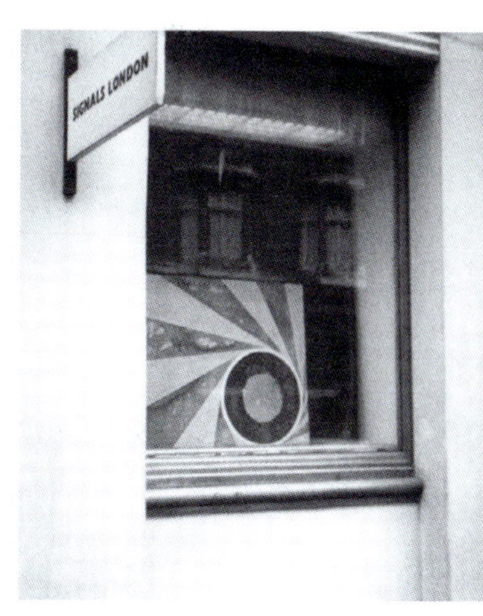

13 *Ibid.*, p. 72.

14 Meyer Schapiro, 1979, 'The Nature of Abstract Art', *Modern Art, 19th and 20th Centuries: Selected Papers*, reprinted in 2011, New York: George Braziller, pp.192–93.

15 Maggie Wu, *Legend of the Rambling King: Side View of Hsiao Chin*, p.72.

16 *Ibid.*

17 Hsiao Chin, *A Historical Dialogue with Art*, p. 49.

18 *Ibid.*

19 *Ibid*, p. 51. [originally 'Ton-Fan Art Group - our Words', *Artist Magazine*, vol. 199, 1991, 《藝術家》].

20 Benjamin Buchloh, 2007, *Art since 1900*, London: Thames & Hudson, p. 322.

21 John J. Curley, 2018, *Global Art and the Cold War*, London: Laurence King Publishing, p. 70.

22 Michel Tapié, 'An Other Art', *Art since 1900*, p. 629.

23 Jean-Paul Sartre, 1948, 'The Search for the Absolute', *Alberto Giacometti: Sculptures, Paintings, Drawings*, New York: Pierre Matisse Gallery.

24 John J. Curley, *Global Art and the Cold War*, pp. 72–80.

25 Hsiao Chin, 1983, '1957, My First Solo Exhibition in Mataro Barcelona', *Artist Magazine*, Vol. 96, pp.69–71.

26 Maggie Wu, *Legend of the Rambling King: Side View of Hsiao Chin*, p.84.

27 Hsiao Chin, '1957, My First Solo Exhibition in Mataro Barcelona', pp.69–71.

28 Juan Eduardo Cirlot, 1958, *Arte contemporaneo: origen universal de sus tendencia*, Barcelona: Edhasa.

29 Hsiao Chin, *A Historical Dialogue with Art*, p. 229.

30 Hsiao Chiimg-jui, 1991, *The Fifth Moon and Ton-fan: The Development of Chinese Modernisation of Art in Taiwan*, Taipei: Dongda Press, p. 120. [蕭瓊瑞:《五月與東方:中國美術現代化運動在戰後臺灣之發展(1945～1970)》,台北:東大圖書1991年].

31 Lu Peng, *A History of Art in Twentieth-century China*, p. 617.

32 http://www.bienal.org.br/exposicoes/4304#posts.

33 Hsiao Chin, 1983, 'Punto Art Movement', *Artist Magazine*, Vol. 103, p. 66-69. [蕭勤:《藝術家》, 1983年12月第103期].

34 Richard Kearney, 1986, *Modern Movements in European Philosophy*, Manchester: Manchester University Press, p. 18.

35 James Bartos, 2019, *The Geometry of Beauty*, London: Unicorn Publishing Group, pp. 27–58.

36 Hsiao Chin, 1983, 'Punto Art Movement', *Artist Magazine*, Vol. 103, p. 66–69.

37 Jaleh Mansoor, 2016, *Marshall Plan Modernism: Italian Postwar Abstraction and the Beginning of Autonomia*, London: Duke University Press, p. 55.

38 Hsiao Chin, 'Punto Art Movement', *Artist Magazine*, pp. 66–69.

39 *Ibid.*

40 Norbert Lynton, *The Story of Modern Art*, p. 13.

41 Hugh Honour, 1973, *Chinoiserie: The Vision of Cathay*, reprinted paperback edition, London: John Murray, p. 5.

42 Richard Kearney, 1986, *Modern Movements in European Philosophy*, Manchester: Manchester University Press, p. 23.

43 Norbert Lynton, *The Story of Modern Art*, p. 244.

44 Jaleh Mansoor, *Marshall Plan Modernism: Italian Postwar Abstraction and the Beginning of Autonomia*, p. 72.

45 Lucio Fontana, 1946, 'The White Manifesto', Quote from *Art in Theory, 1900–2000: An Anthology of Changing Ideas*, 2003, ed. Charles Harrison & Paul Wood, New Edition, Blackwell Publishing, pp. 652–55.

46 Hsiao Chin, 'Punto Art Movement', *Artist Magazine*, pp. 66–69.

47 Hsiao Chin, 'Punto Art Movement', *Artist Magazine*, p. 247.

48 Hsiao Chin, *A Historical Dialogue with Art*, p. 229.

49 Guy Debord, 1983, *Society of The Spectacle*, Detroit: Black & Red.

50 Hsiao Chin, *A Historical Dialogue with Art*, p. 249.

51 Maggie Wu, *Legend of the Rambling King: Side View of Hsiao Chin*, p. 113.

52 Luca Zaffarano & Hsiao Chin, 1987, 'Ten questions asked to Hsiao Chin', in Pola, Francesca edited. *Un Viaggio Attraverso L'universo.* Milan: Robilant+Voena Gallery, 2015, pp.59–60.

53 *Ibid.*, p.164.

Hsiao Chin
Pintura-DK, 1959
Oil on canvas
61 x 37cm

Hsiao Chin
Pittura-CB, 1959
Oil on canvas
70 x 50cm

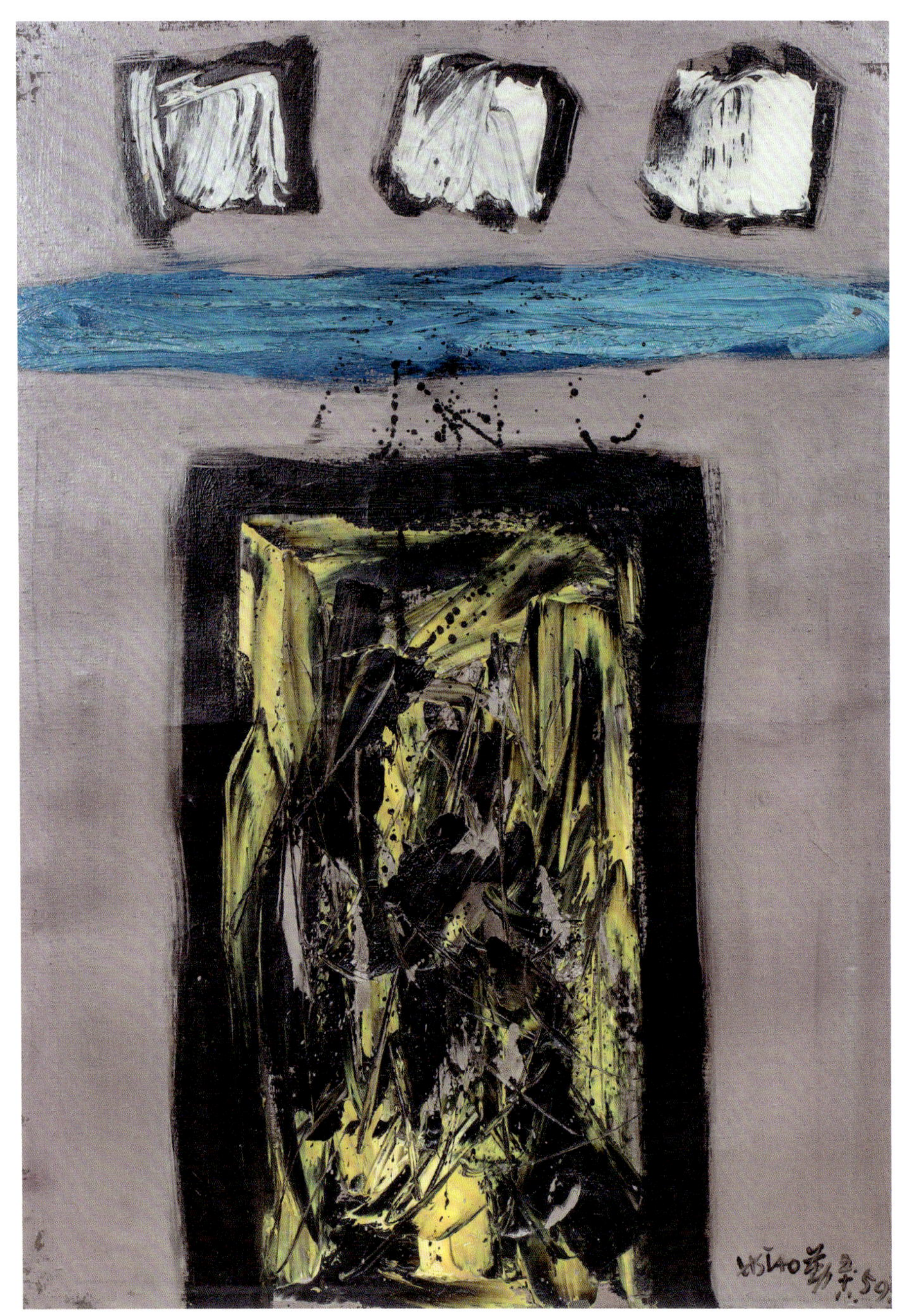

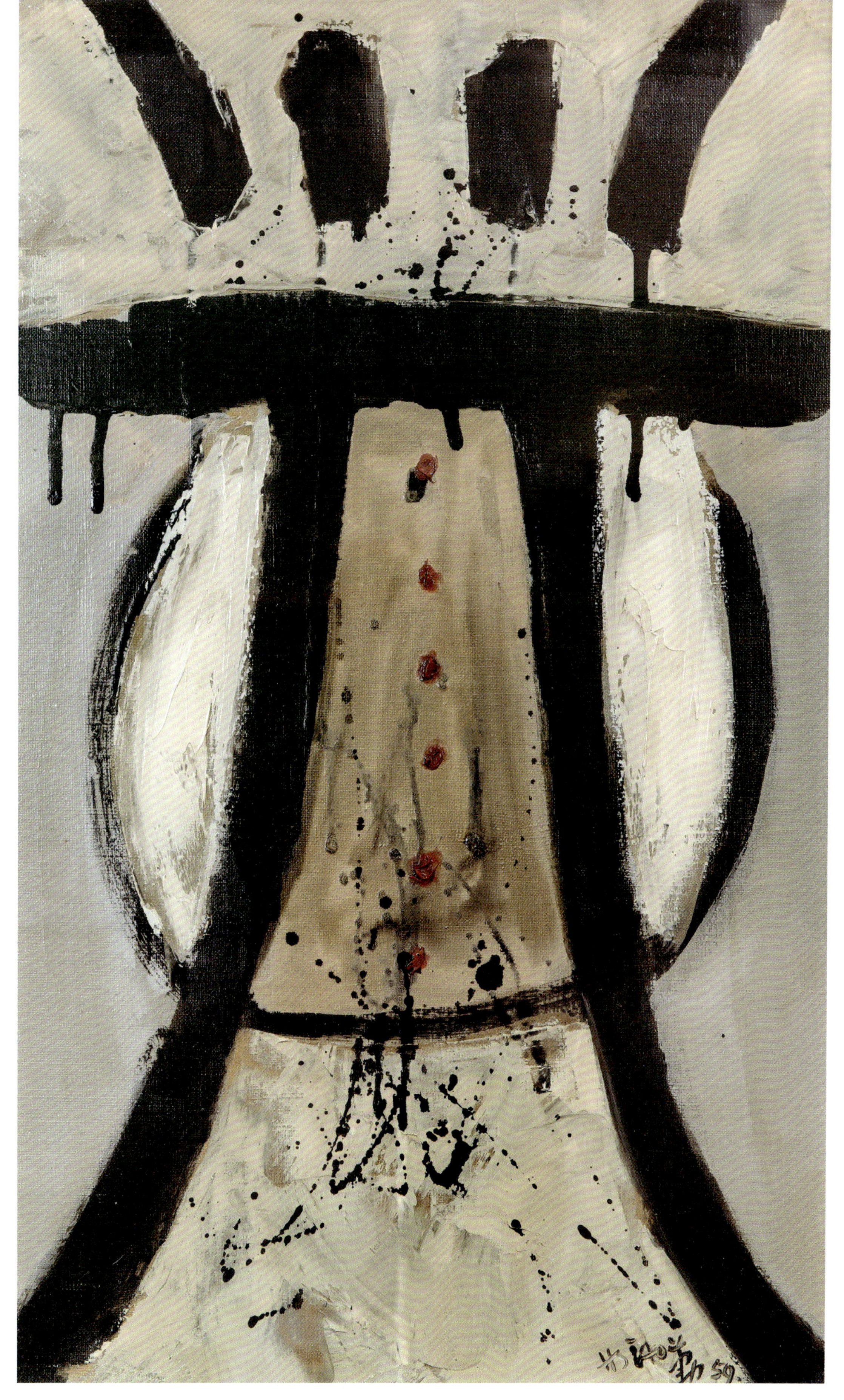

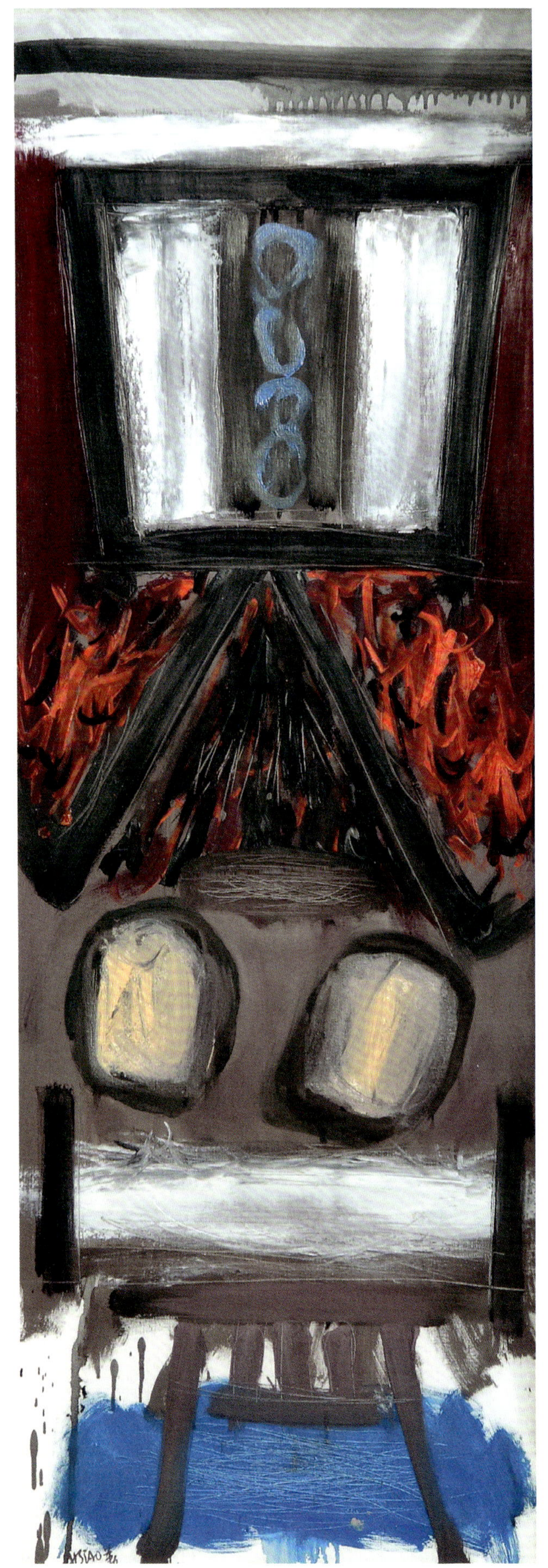

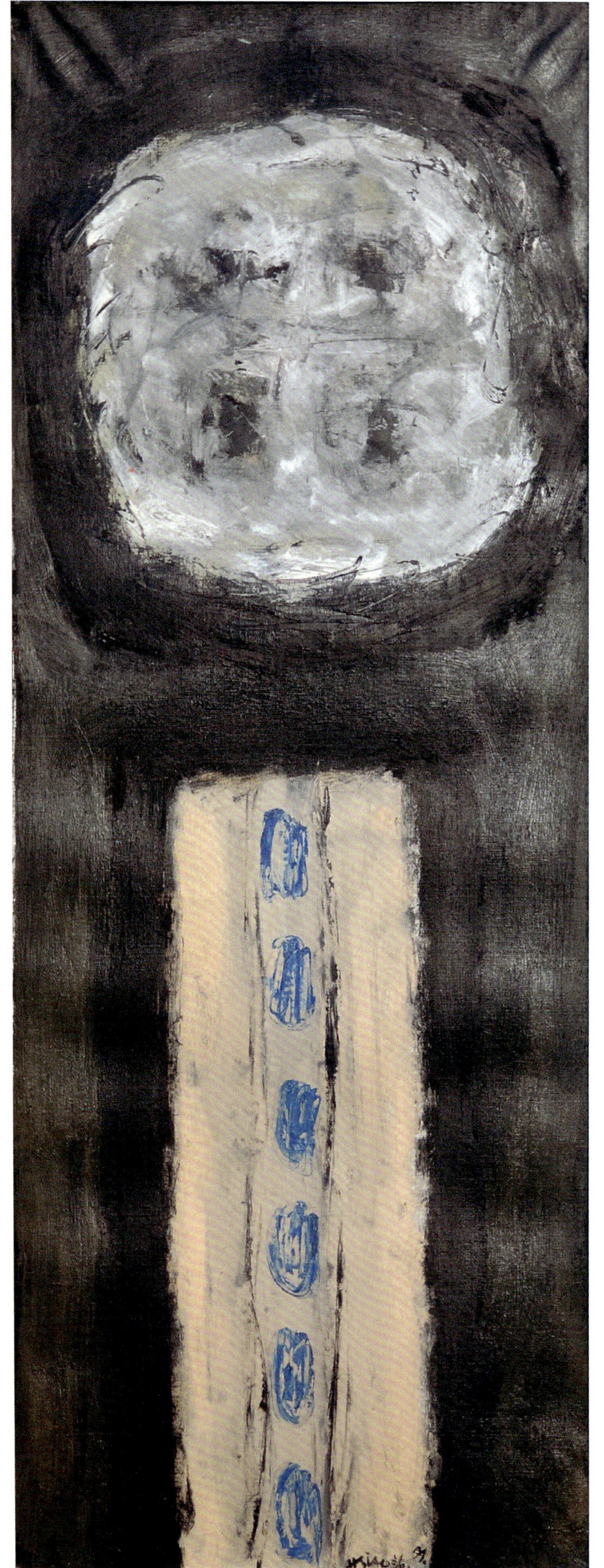

(*far left*) Hsiao Chin
Pintura-AS, 1959
Oil on canvas
138 x 48.5cm

(*left*) Hsiao Chin
Pittura-BM, 1959
Oil on canvas
119 x 45cm

Hsiao Chin
MC 201-60, 1960
Oil on canvas
70 x 100cm

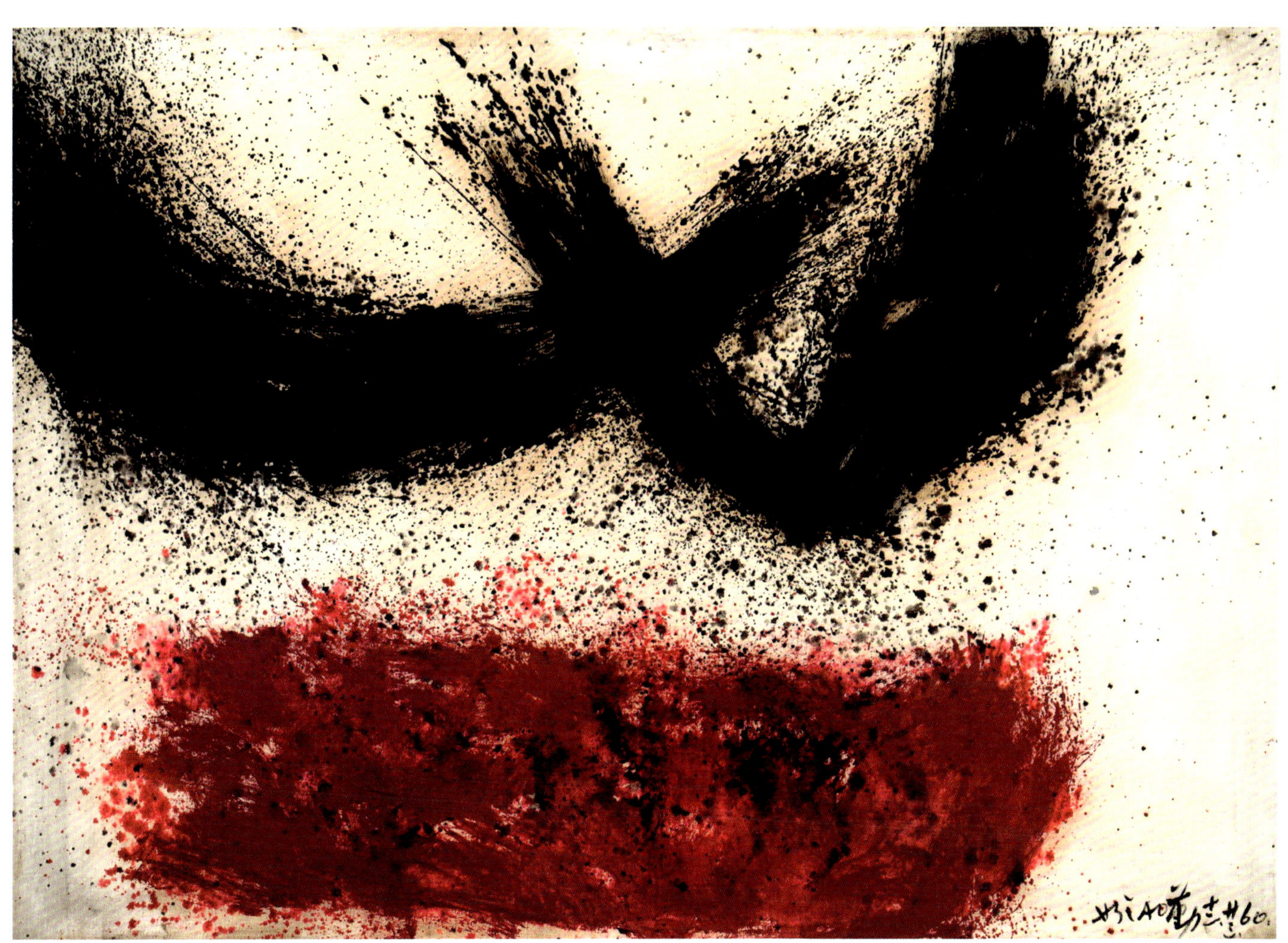

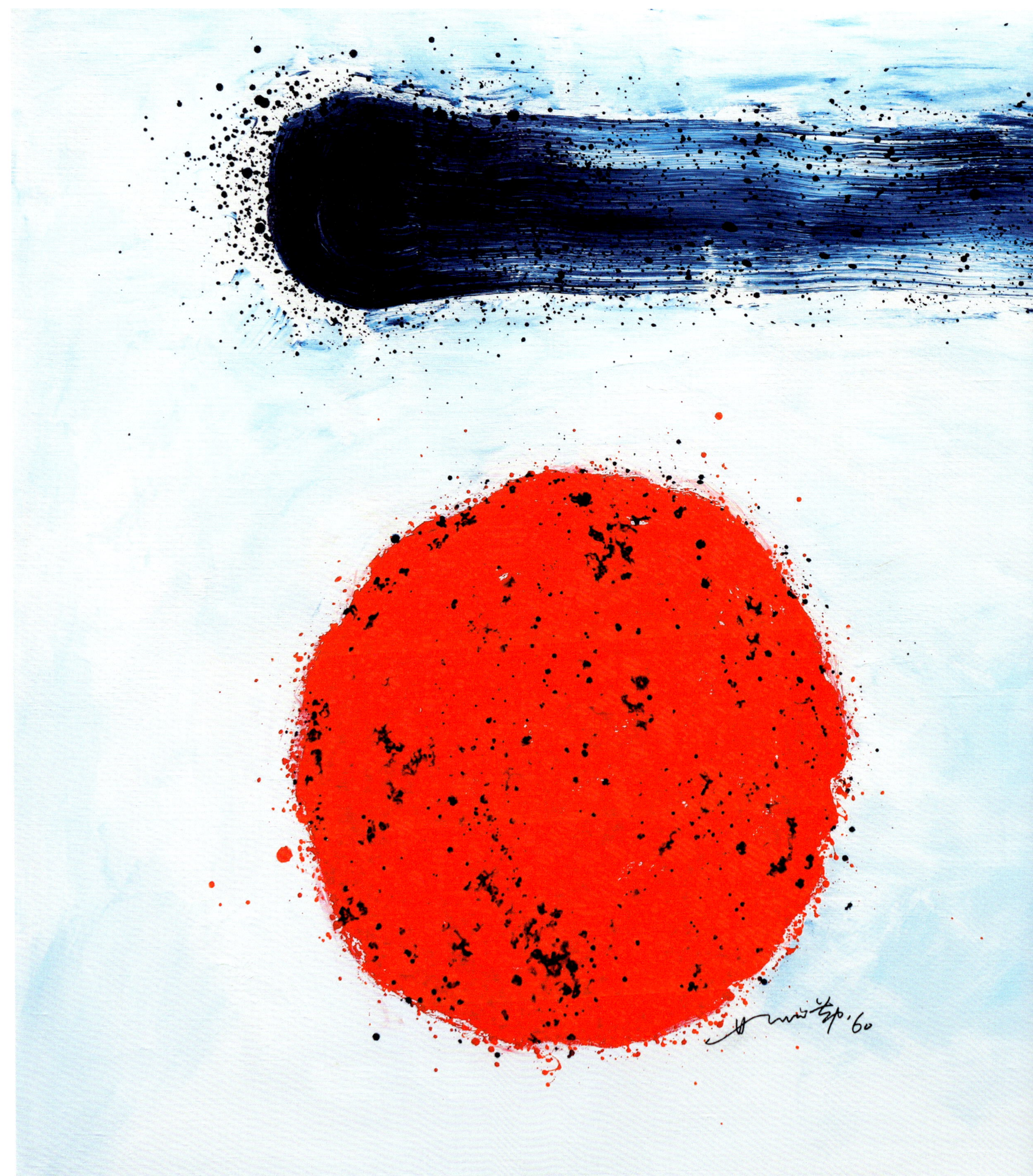

Hsiao Chin
TY-89, 1960
Acrylic on canvas
110 x 140cm

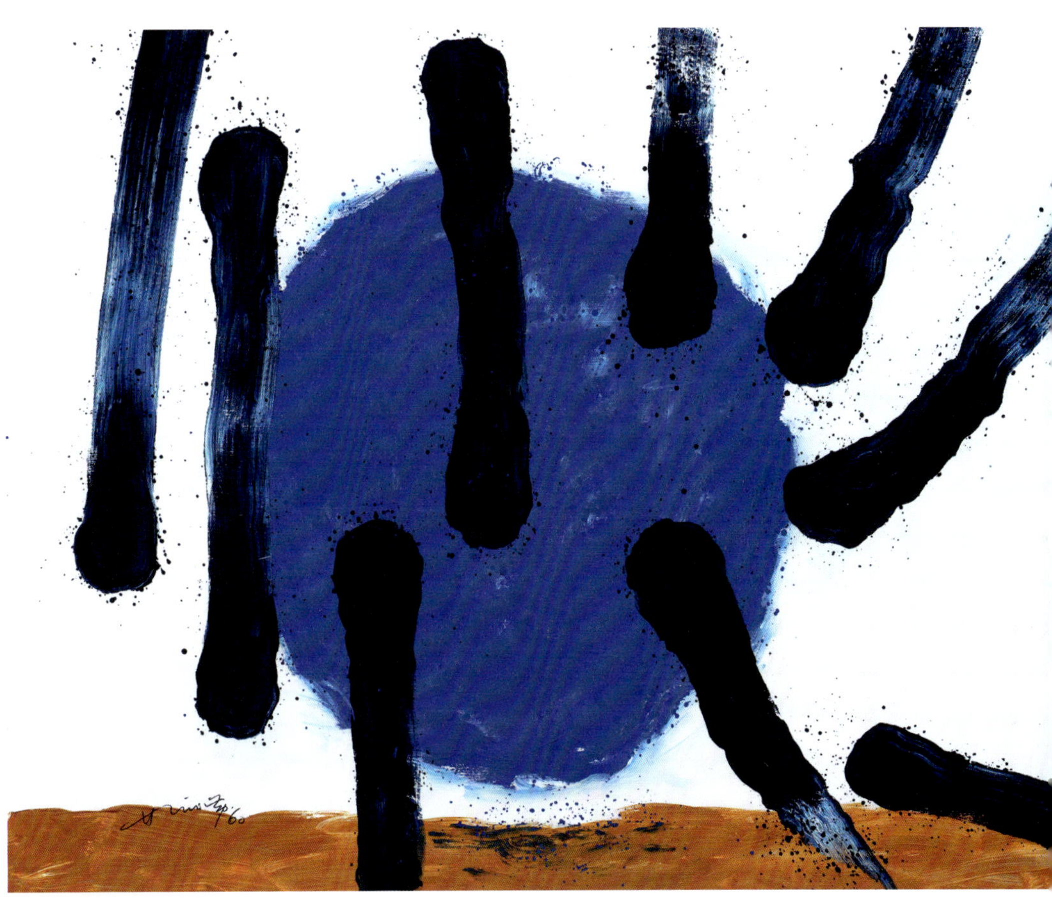

Hsiao Chin
UA-91, 1960
Acrylic on canvas
110 x 140cm

Hsiao Chin
Crouch, 1961
Acrylic and ink on canvas
140 x 110cm

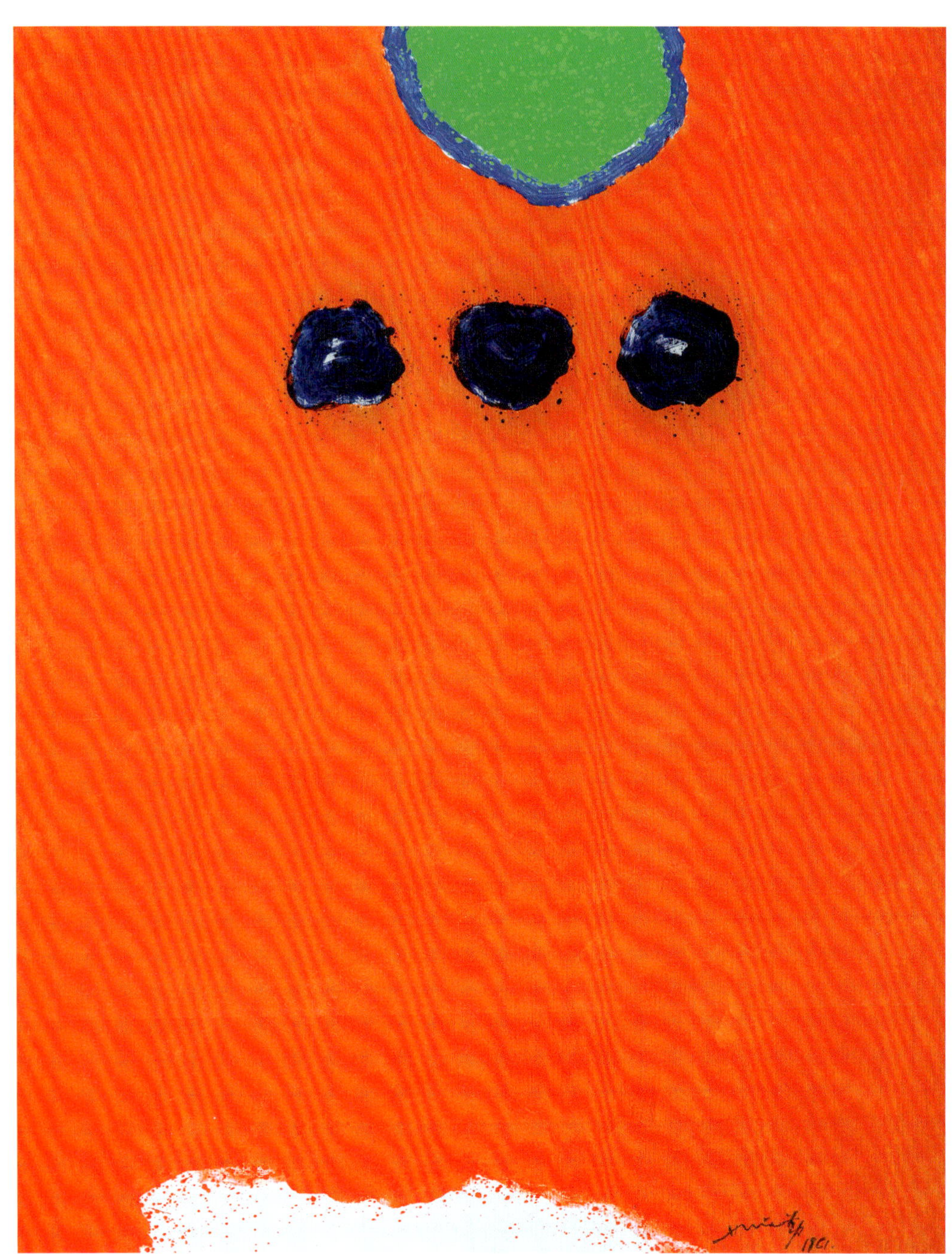

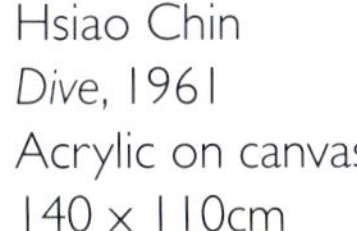

Hsiao Chin
Dive, 1961
Acrylic on canvas
140 x 110cm

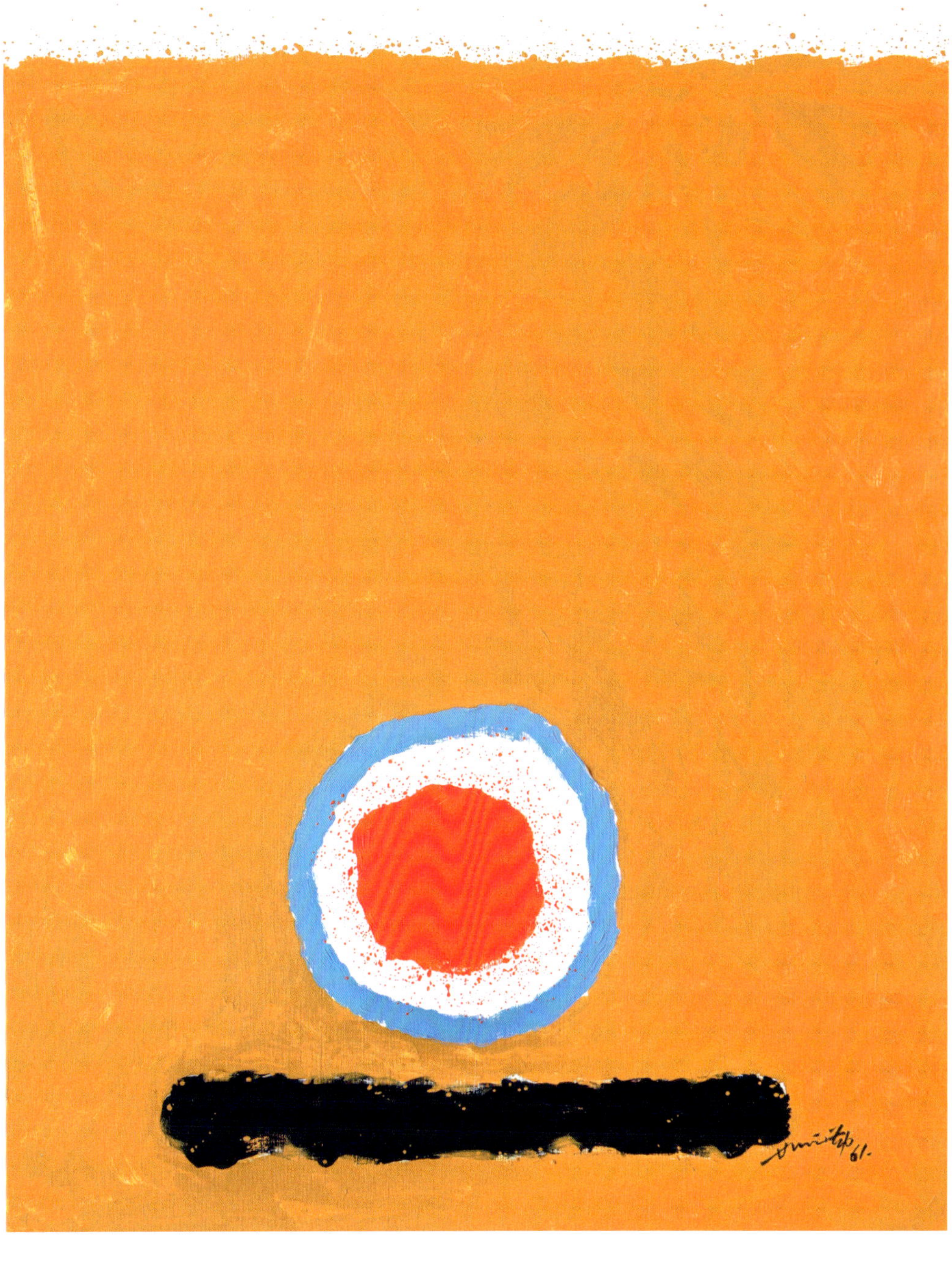

Hsiao Chin
L'ombra della Luna, 1961
Acrylic on canvas
140 x 110cm

Hsiao Chin
Discover, 1961
Acrylic on canvas
140 x 110cm

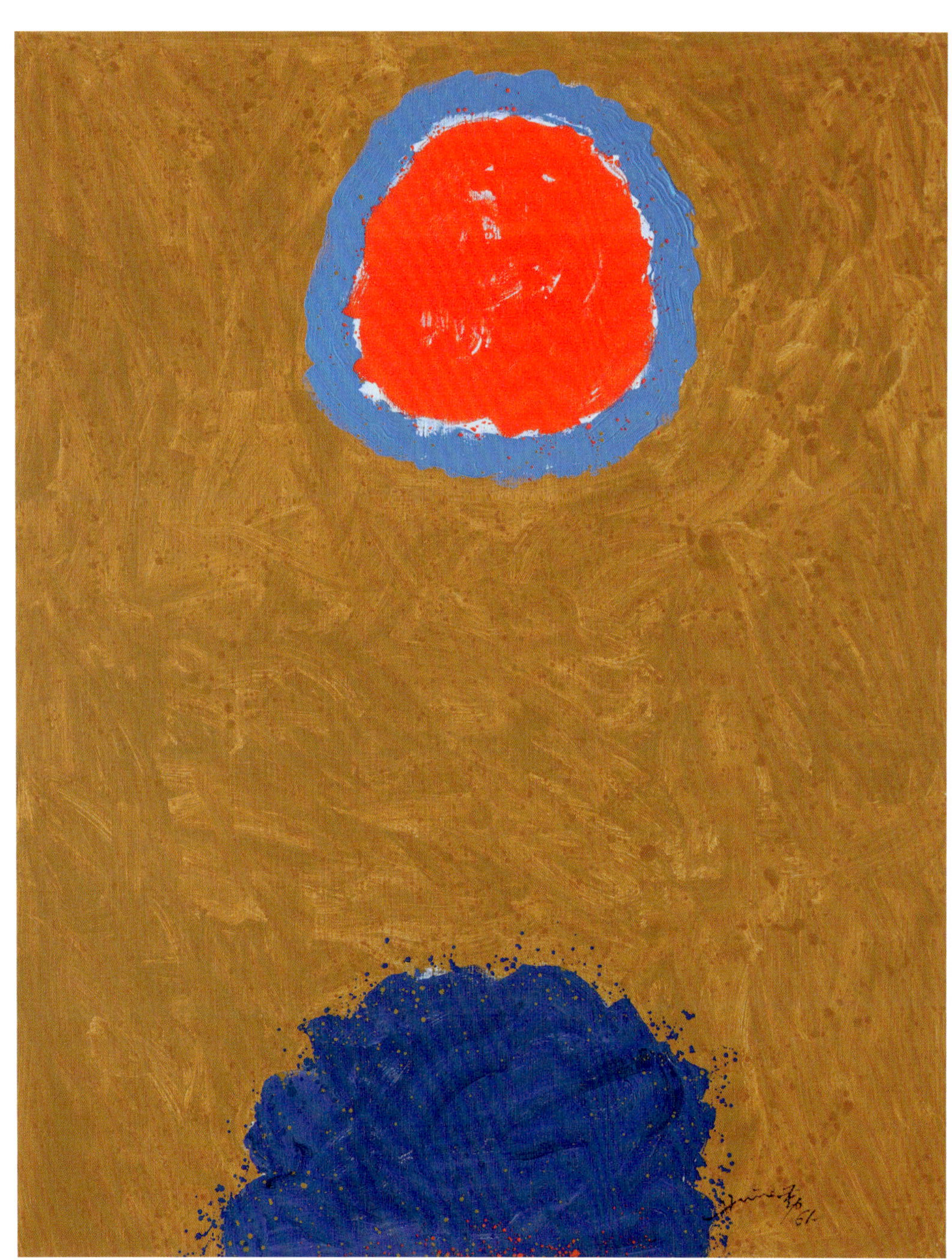

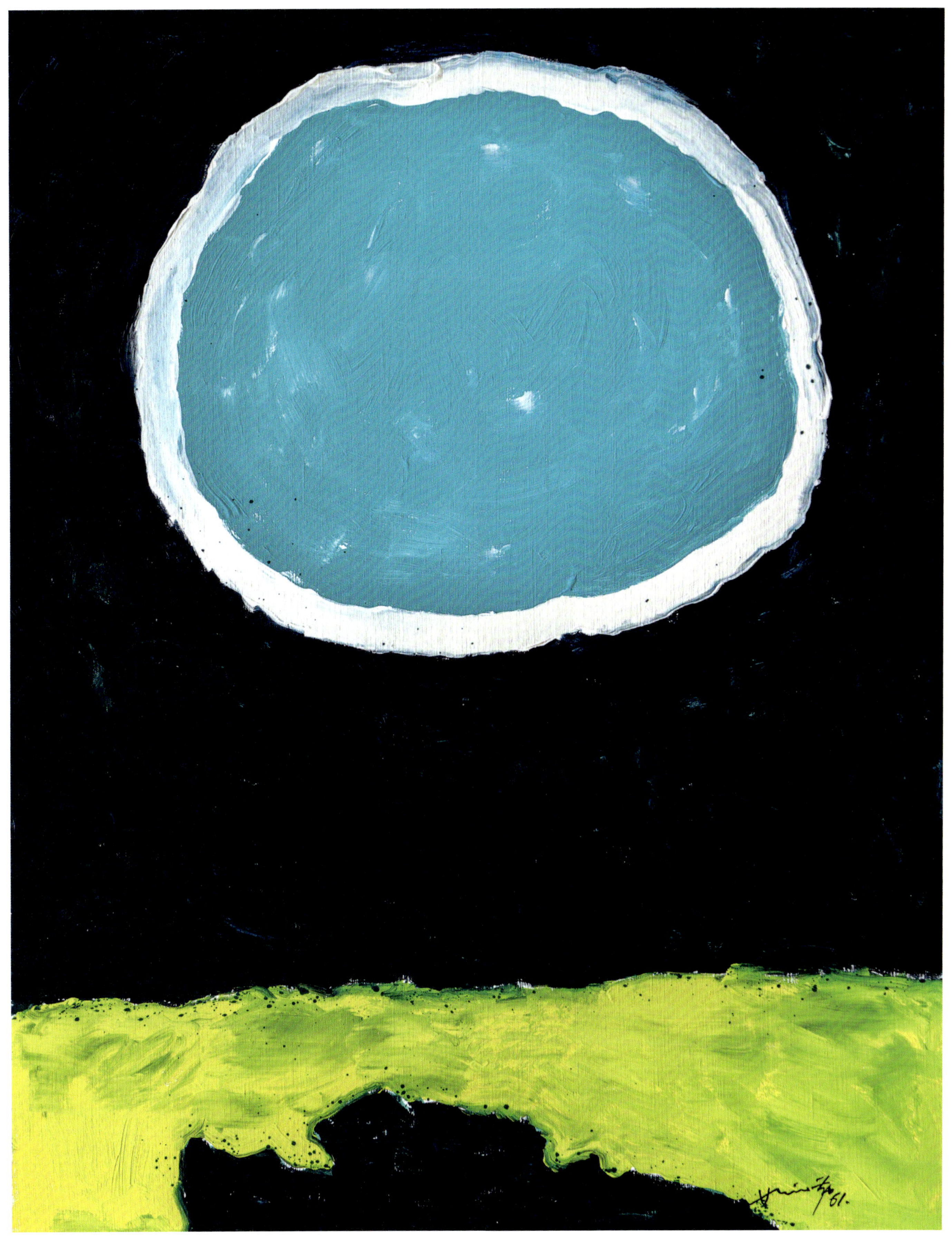

Hsiao Chin
All Ways Energy
(Le forze di Quattro Parte)
1961
Acrylic on canvas
79 x 101cm

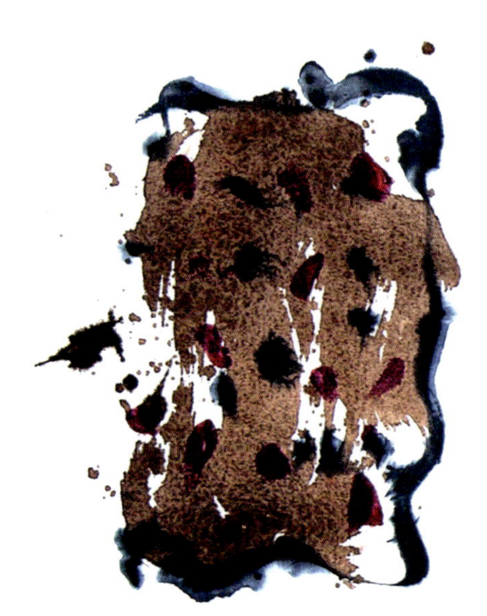

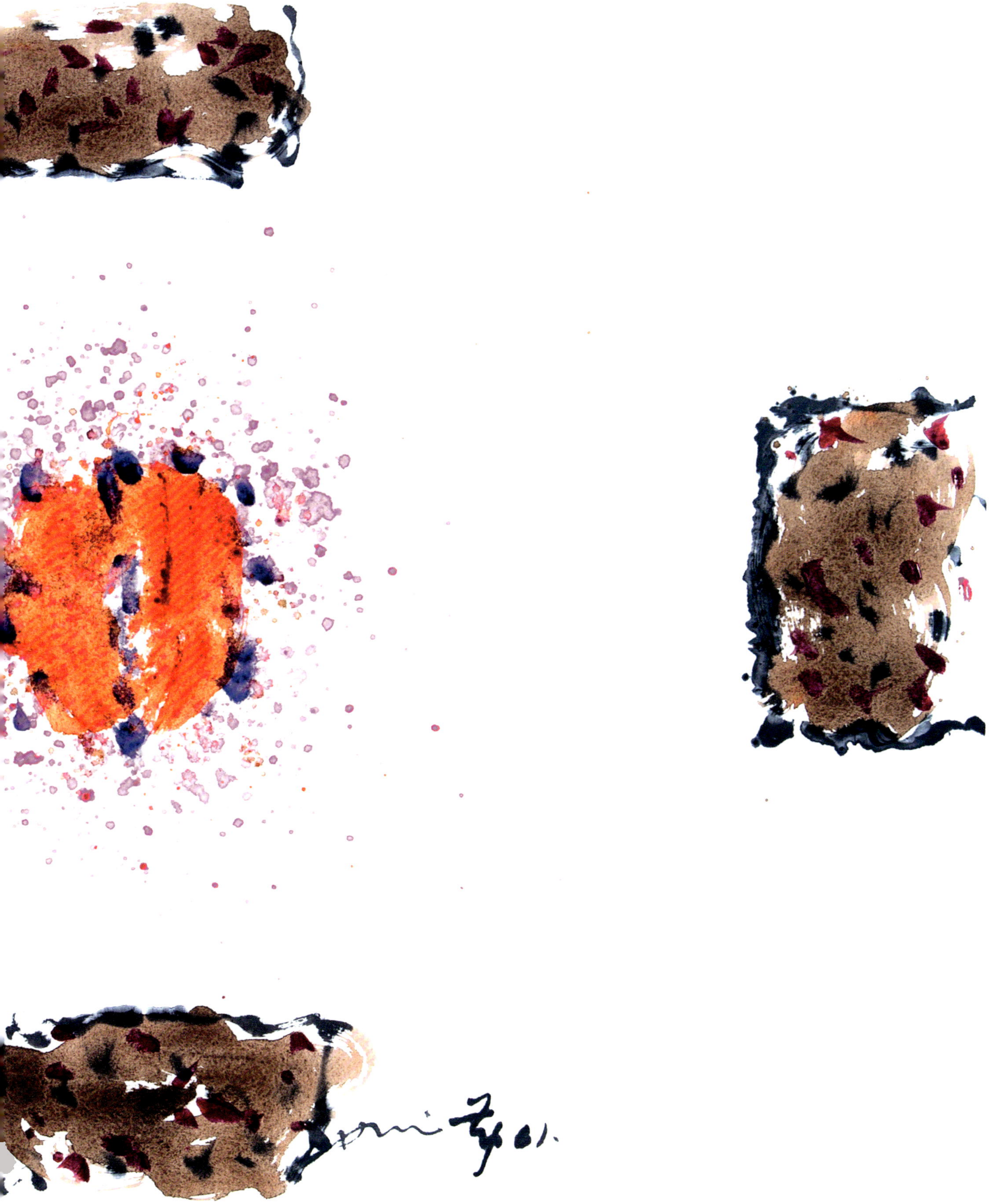

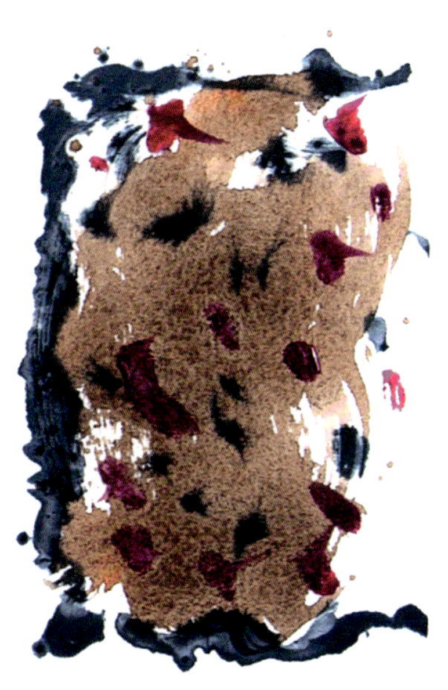

Hsiao Chin
Il silenzio, 1962
Ink on canvas
80 x 70cm

Hsiao Chin
Tao, 1962
Acrylic on canvas
69 x 64cm

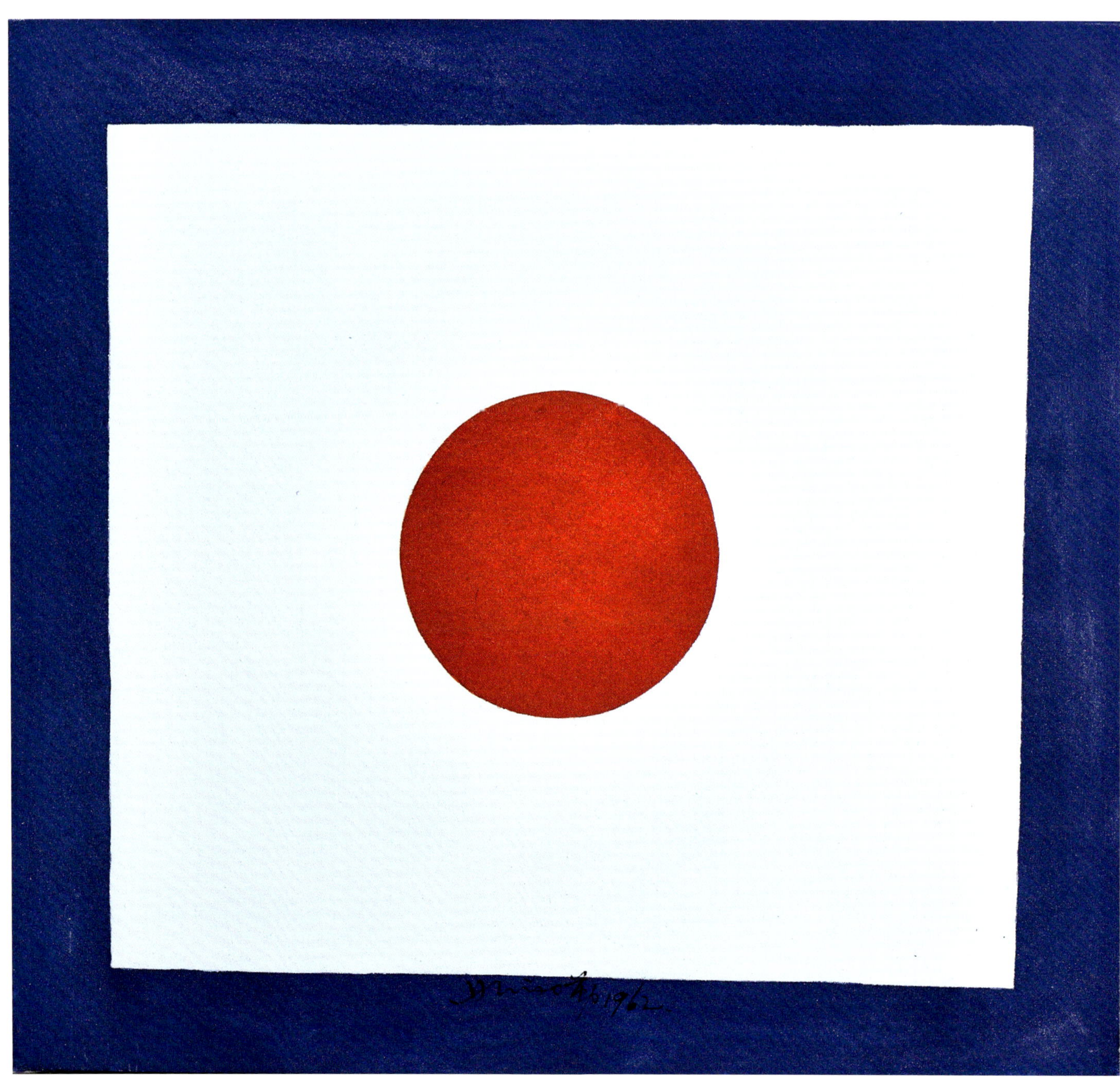

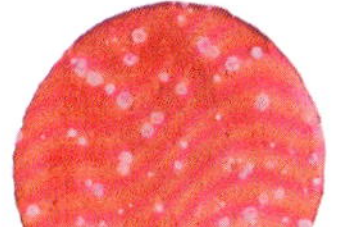

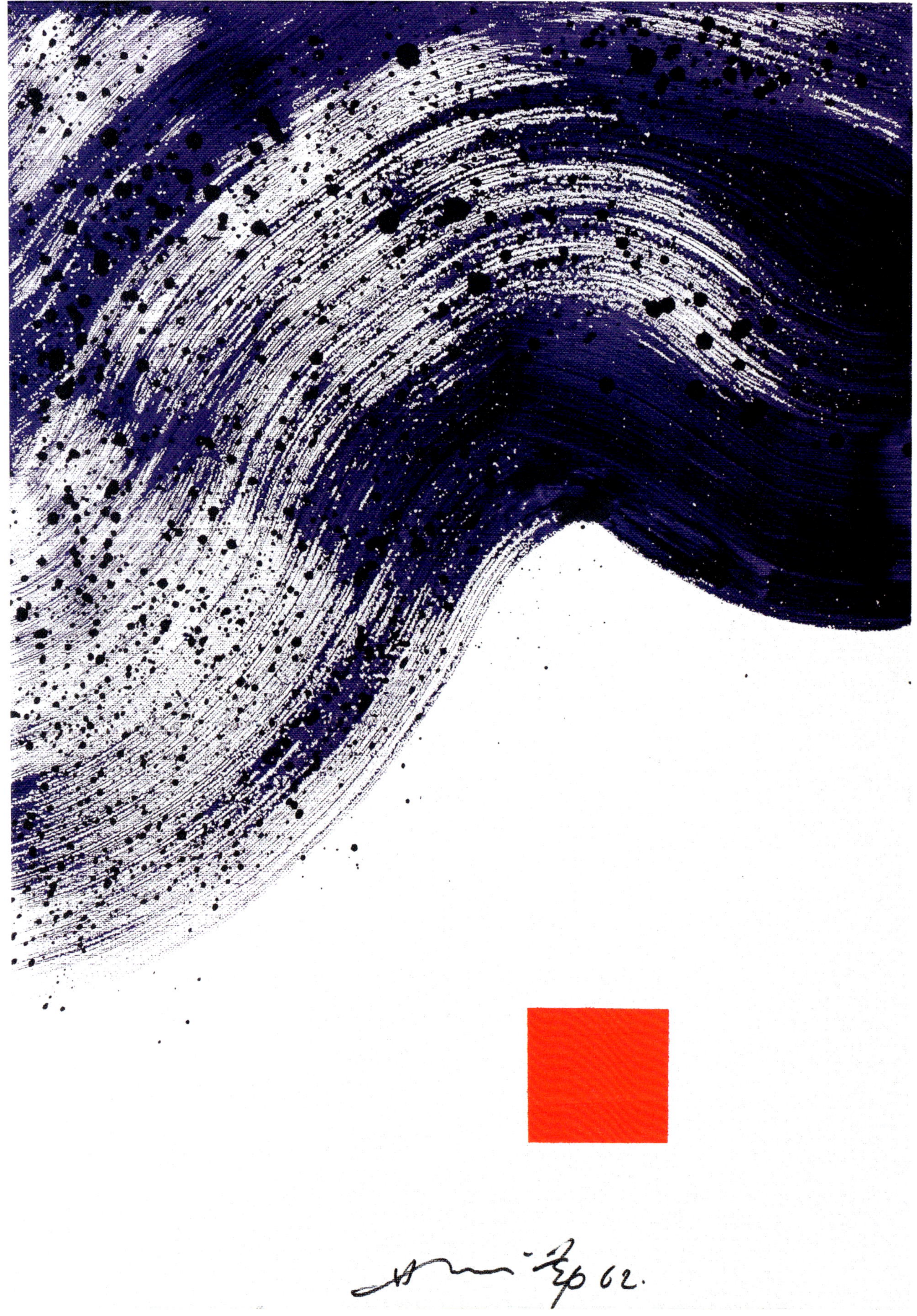

Hsiao Chin
The Beginning of Tao-2, 1962
Acrylic and ink on canvas
70 x 50cm

Hsiao Chin
The Beginning of Tao-3, 1962
Acrylic and ink on canvas
70 x 80cm

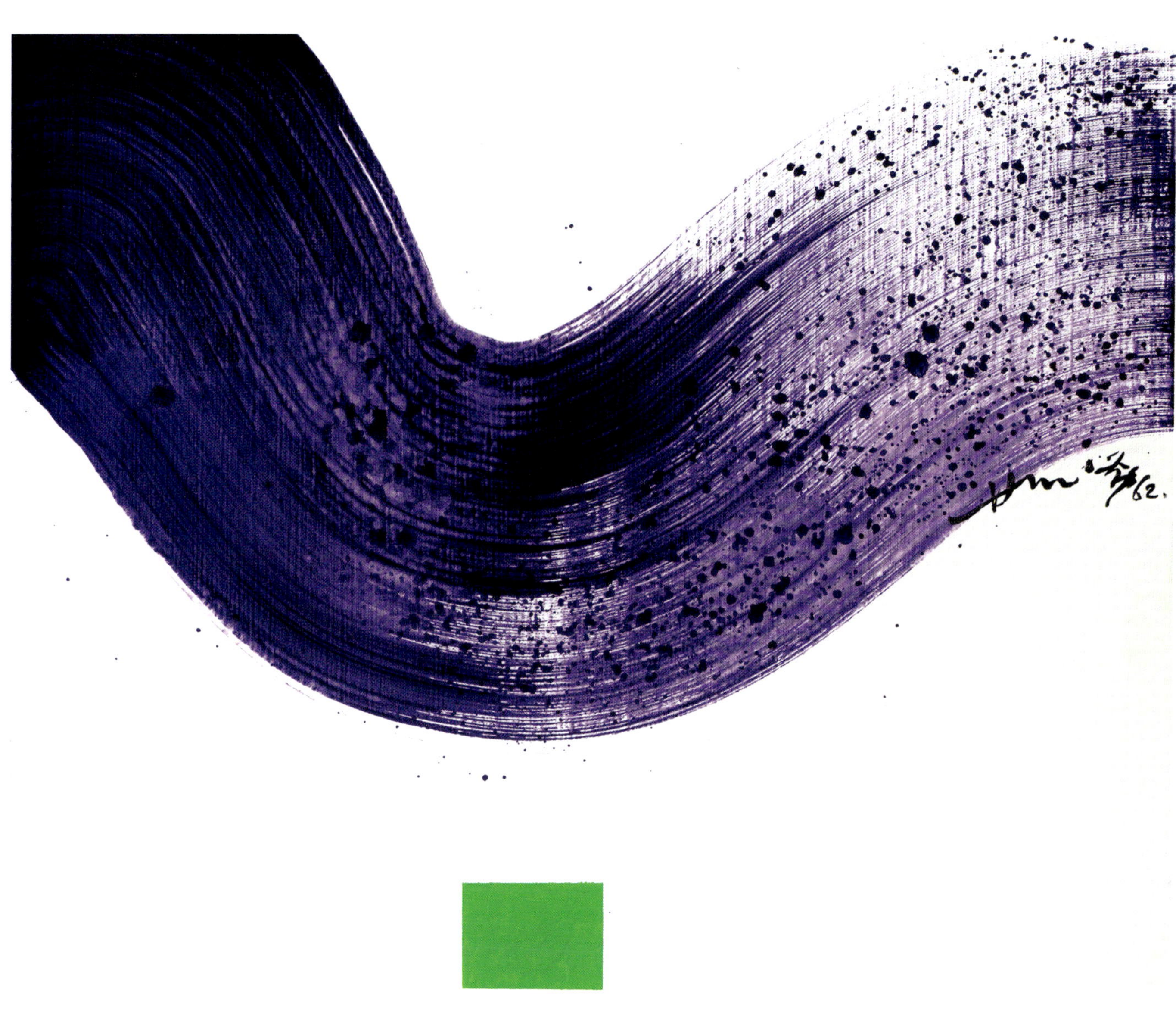

Hsiao Chin
Protection for Kindness
(Conservare la debolezza)
1962
Acrylic on canvas
60 x 80cm

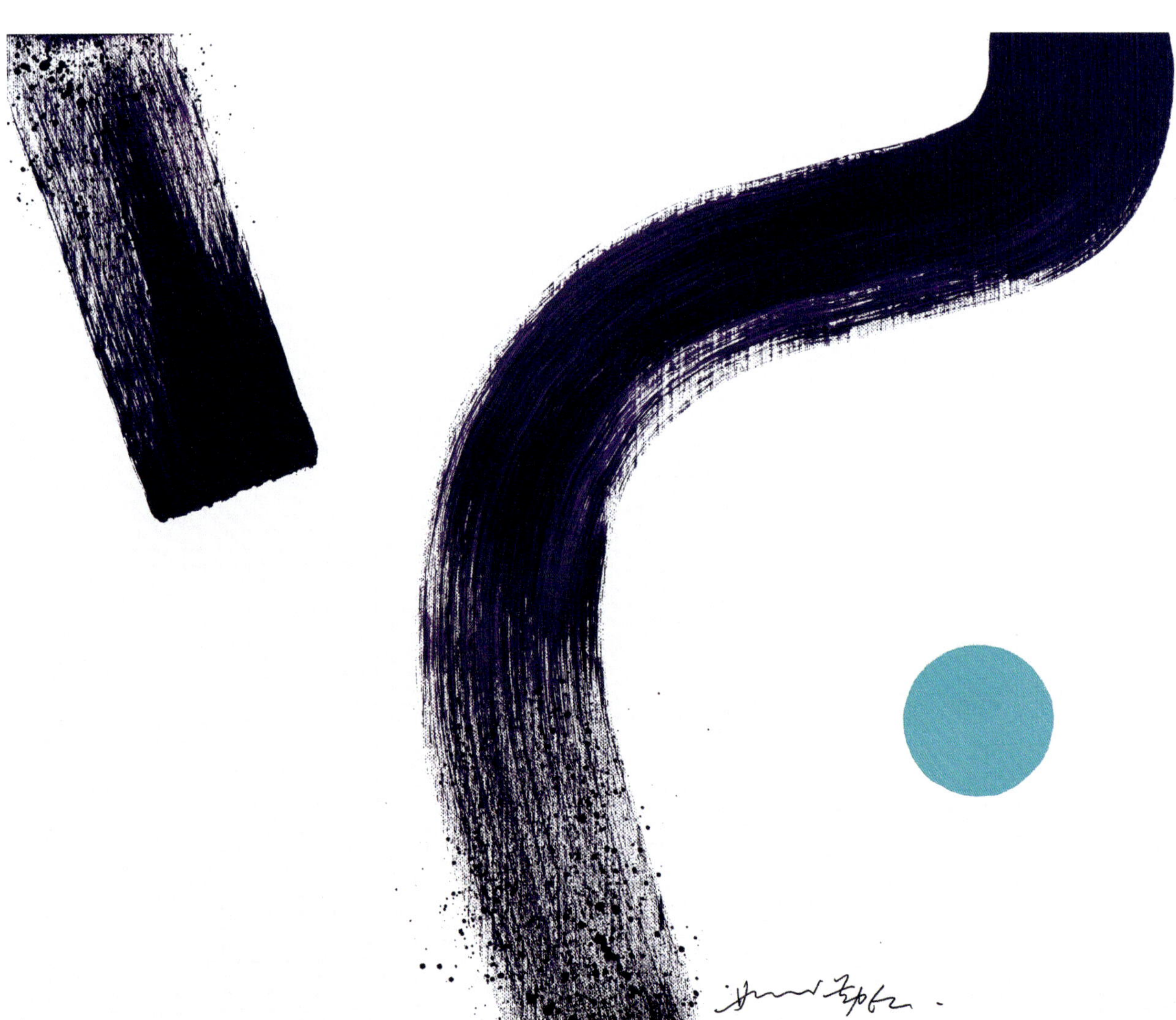

Hsiao Chin
The Awakening, 1962
Acrylic on canvas
50 × 60cm

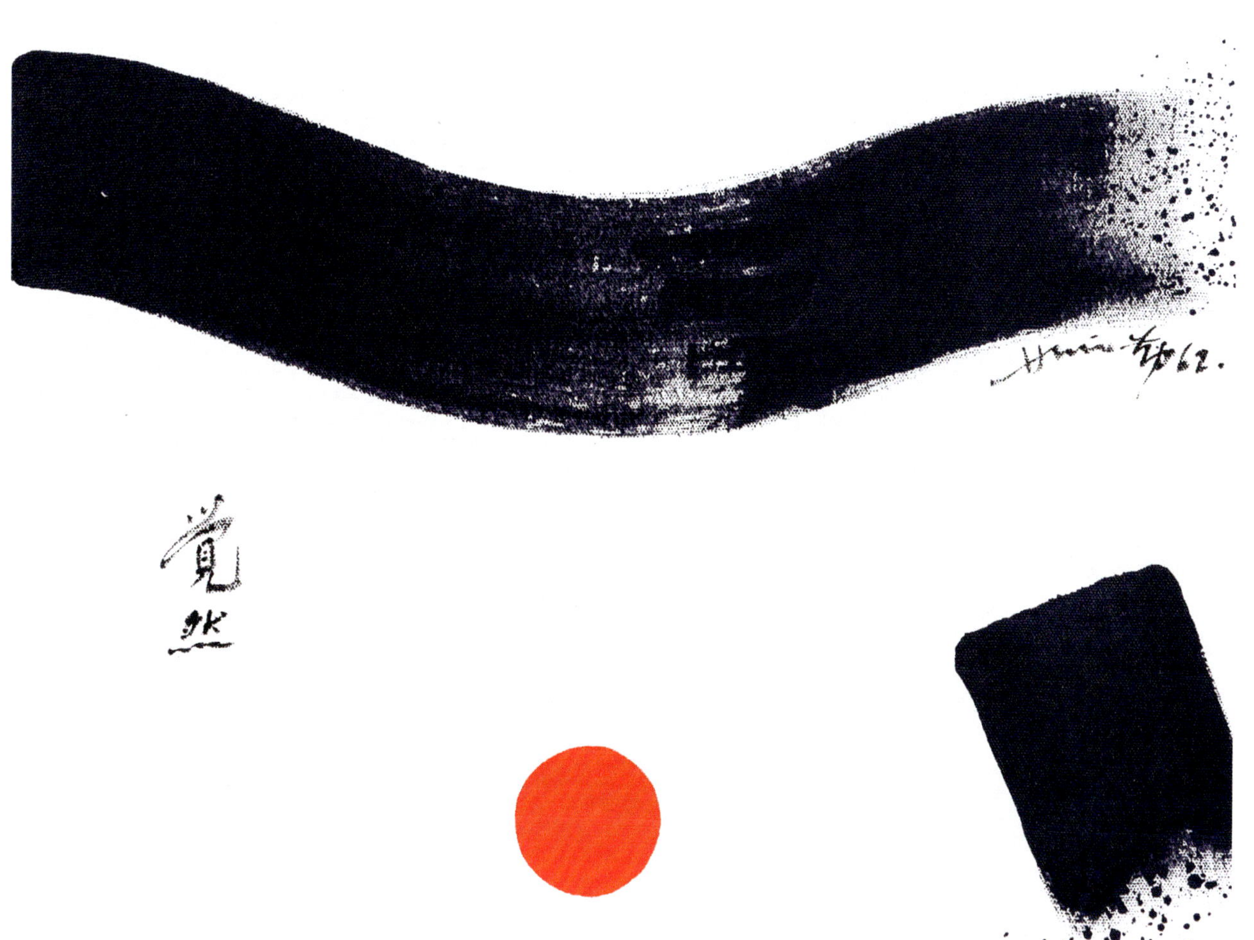

Hsiao Chin
Contemplation, 1962
Acrylic on canvas
70 x 90cm

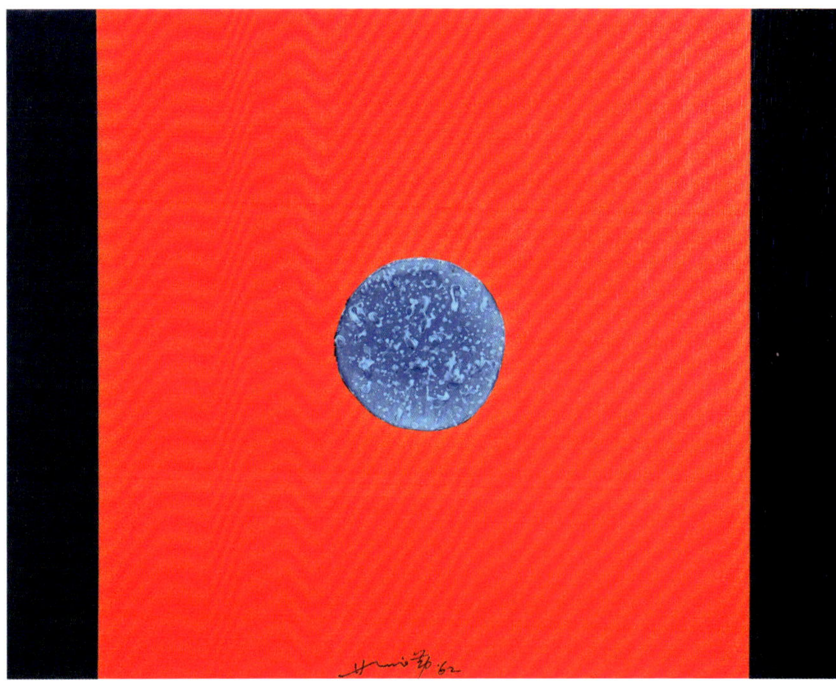

Hsiao Chin
Heat, 1962
Acrylic and ink on canvas
70 x 90cm

Hsiao Chin
Il Tornare, 1962
Acrylic on canvas
90 x 110cm

Hsiao Chin
The Origin of Chi-1, 1962
Ink on canvas
50 x 70cm

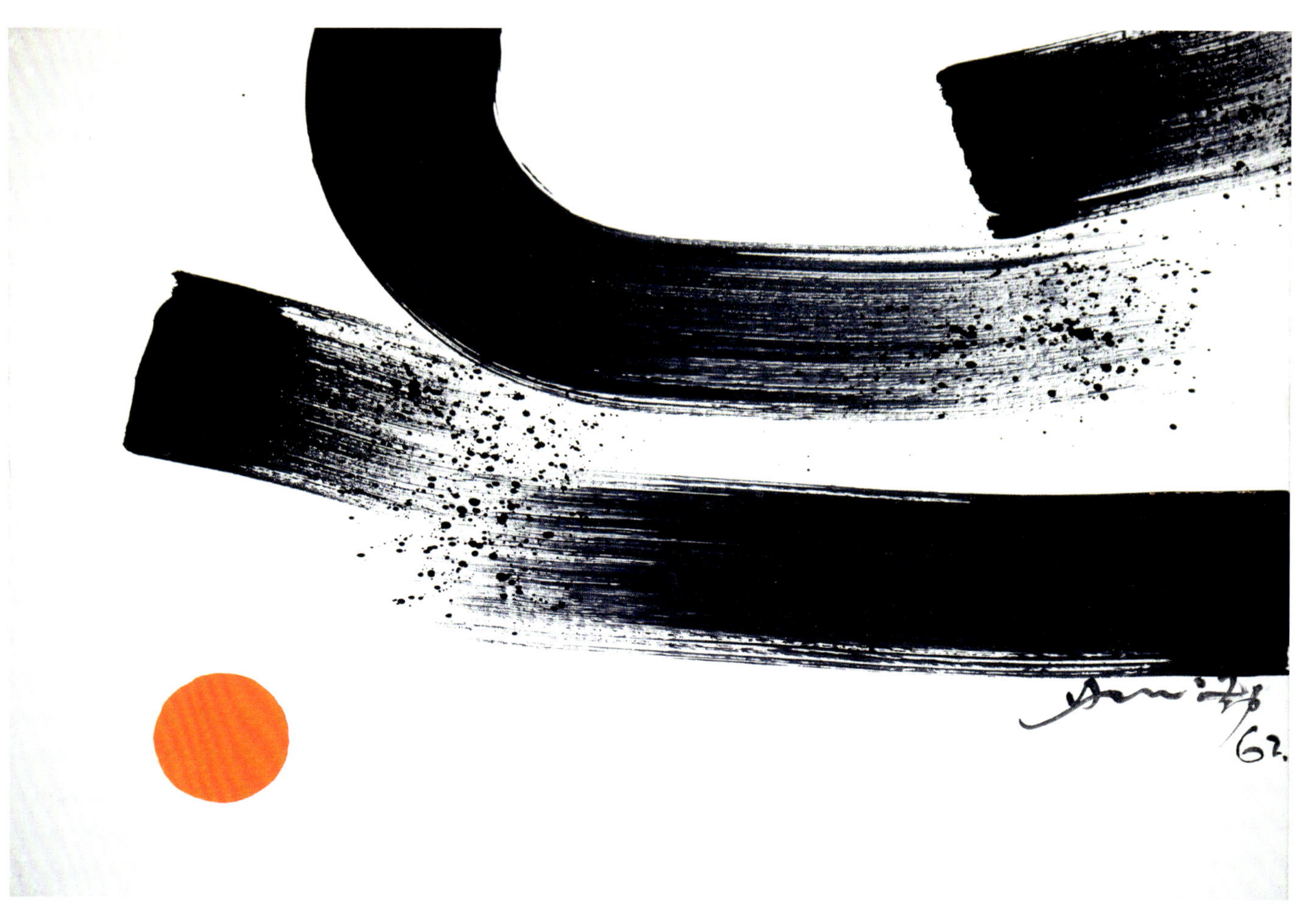

Hsiao Chin
The Origin of Chi-3, 1962
Ink on canvas
40 × 60cm

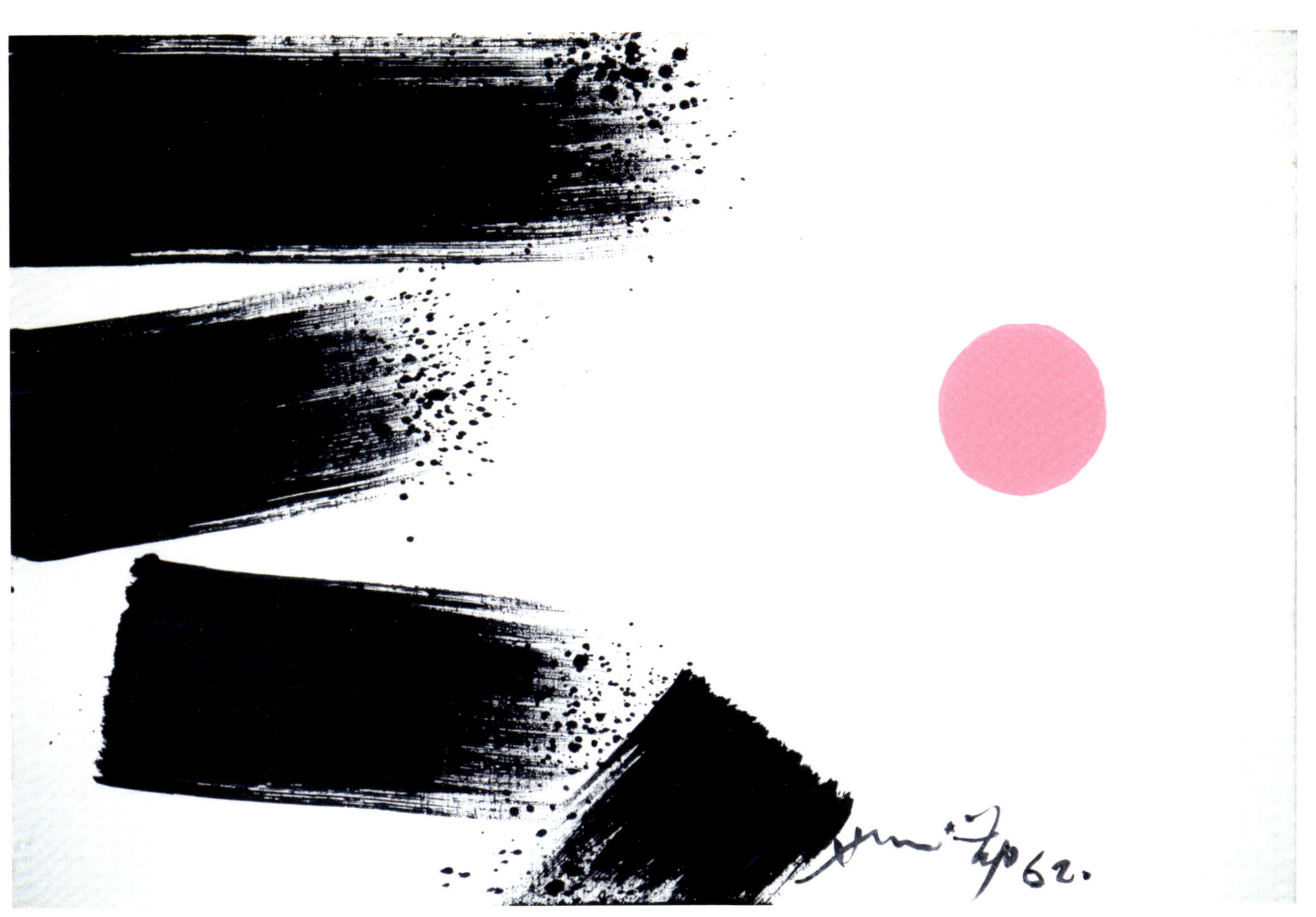

Hsiao Chin
Forward Looking, 1962
Ink on canvas
70 x 90cm

Hsiao Chin
Il silenzio, 1962
Acrylic and ink on canvas
100 x 80cm

Hsiao Chin
The Origin of Chi-4, 1962
Ink on canvas
40 x 60cm

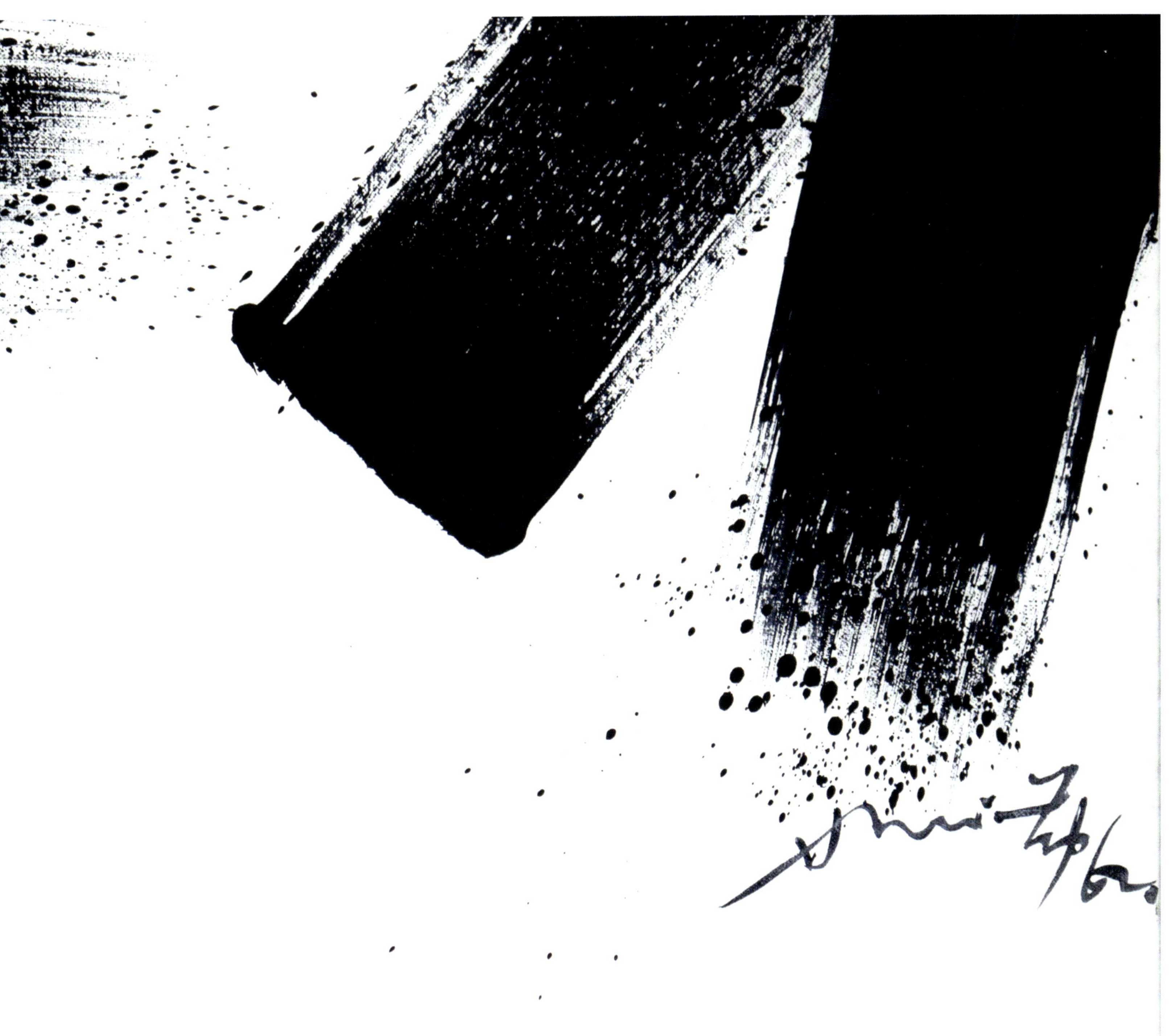

Hsiao Chin
Untitled, 1962
Acrylic and ink on paper
70.5 × 80cm

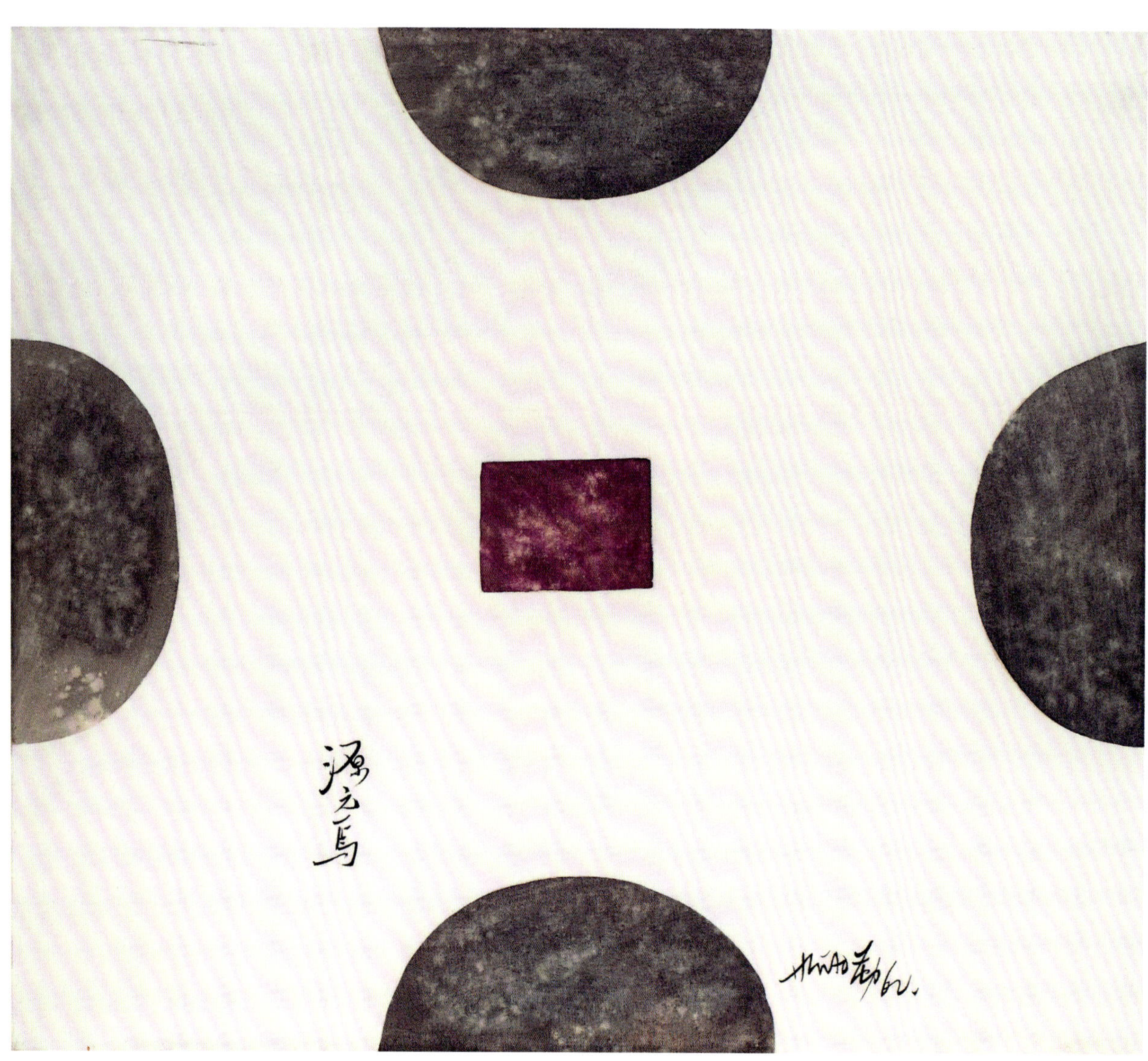

Hsiao Chin
Untitled, 1962
Acrylic on canvas
100 × 130cm

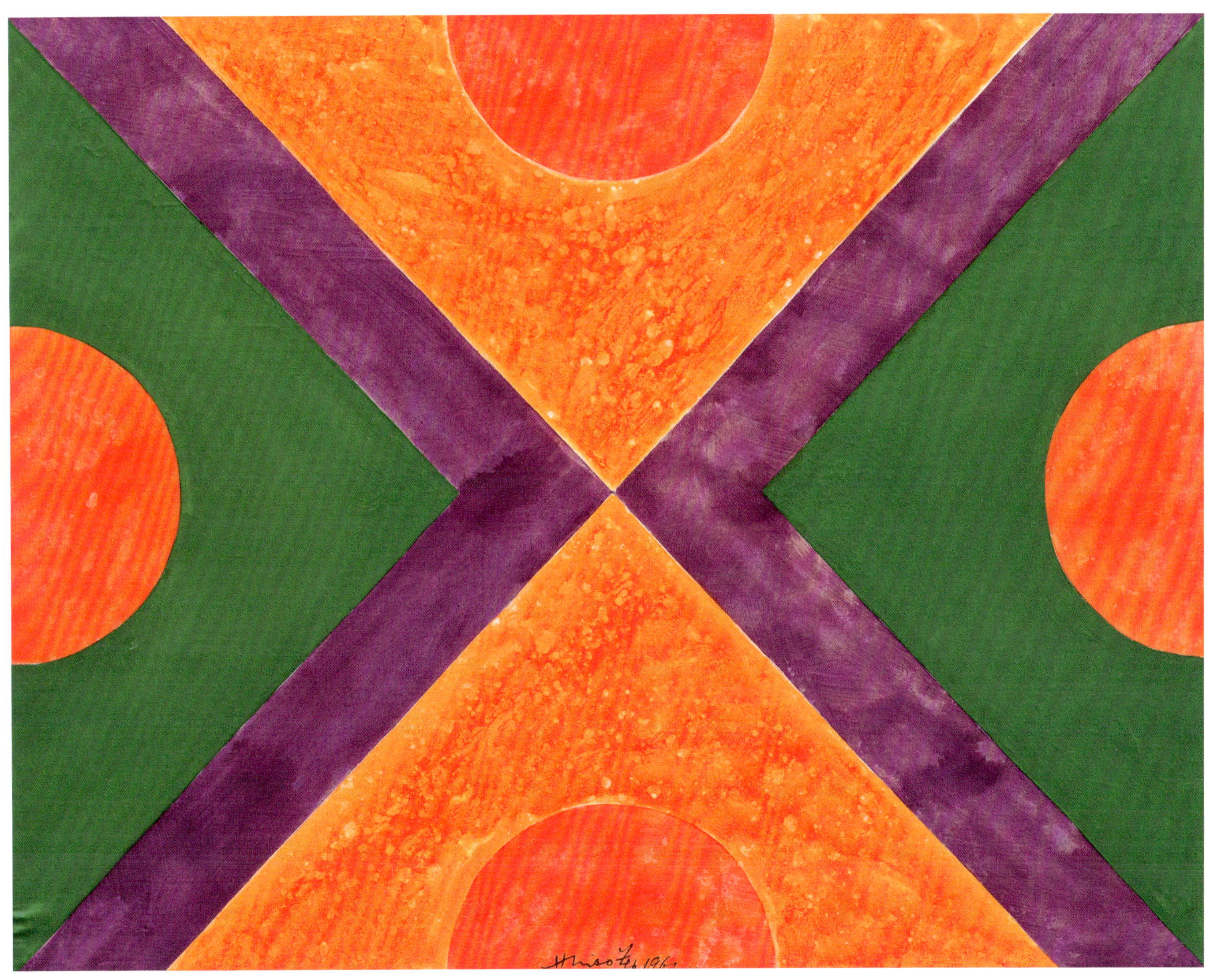

Hsiao Chin
Parallelism of Tao, 1963
Acrylic on canvas
60 x 50cm

Hsiao Chin
The Travel of Tao-1, 1963
Acrylic on canvas
60 x 80cm

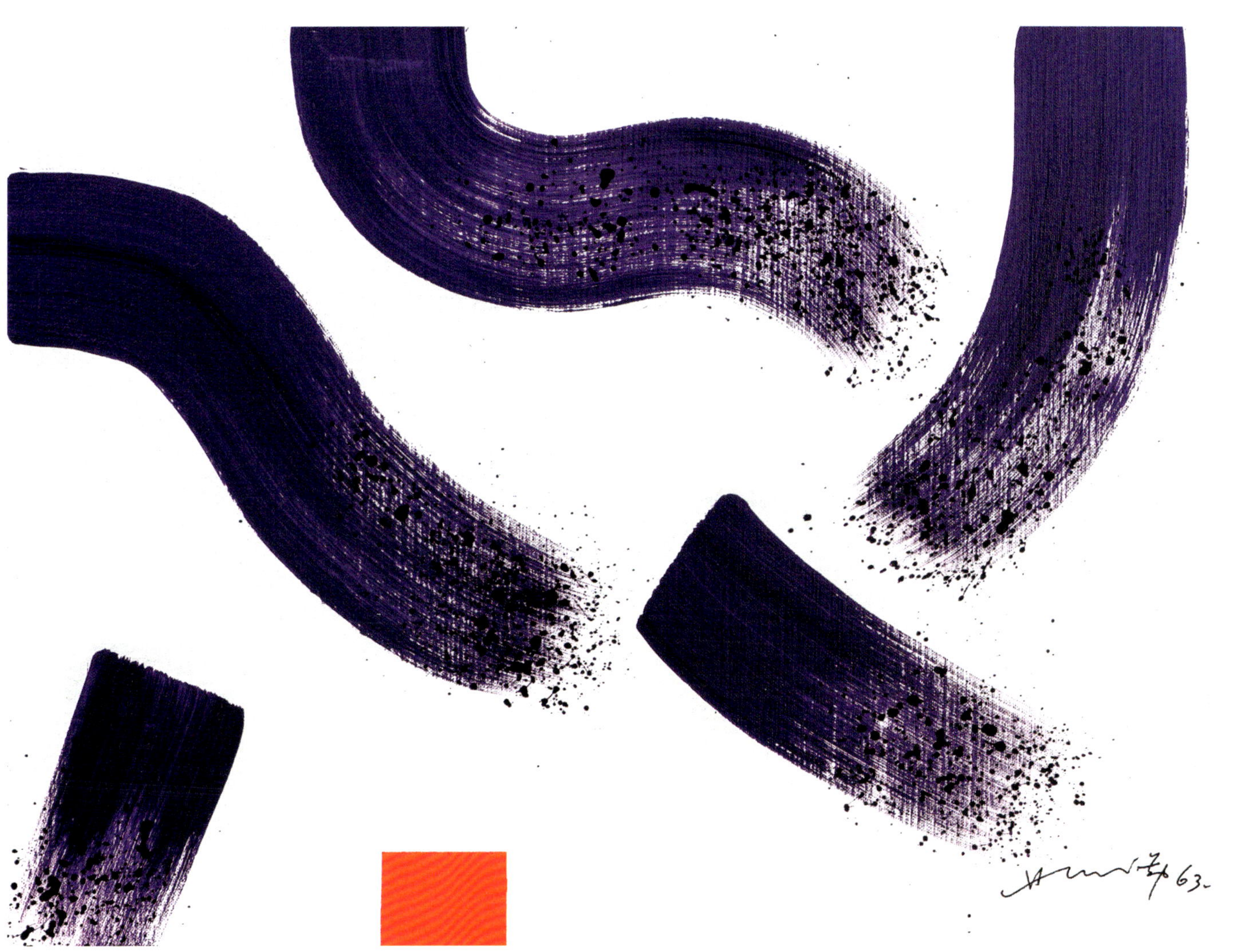

Hsiao Chin
Incroci di Tao, 1963
Acrylic on canvas
90 x 70cm

Hsiao Chin
The Travel of Tao-2, 1963
Acrylic on canvas
50 x 70cm

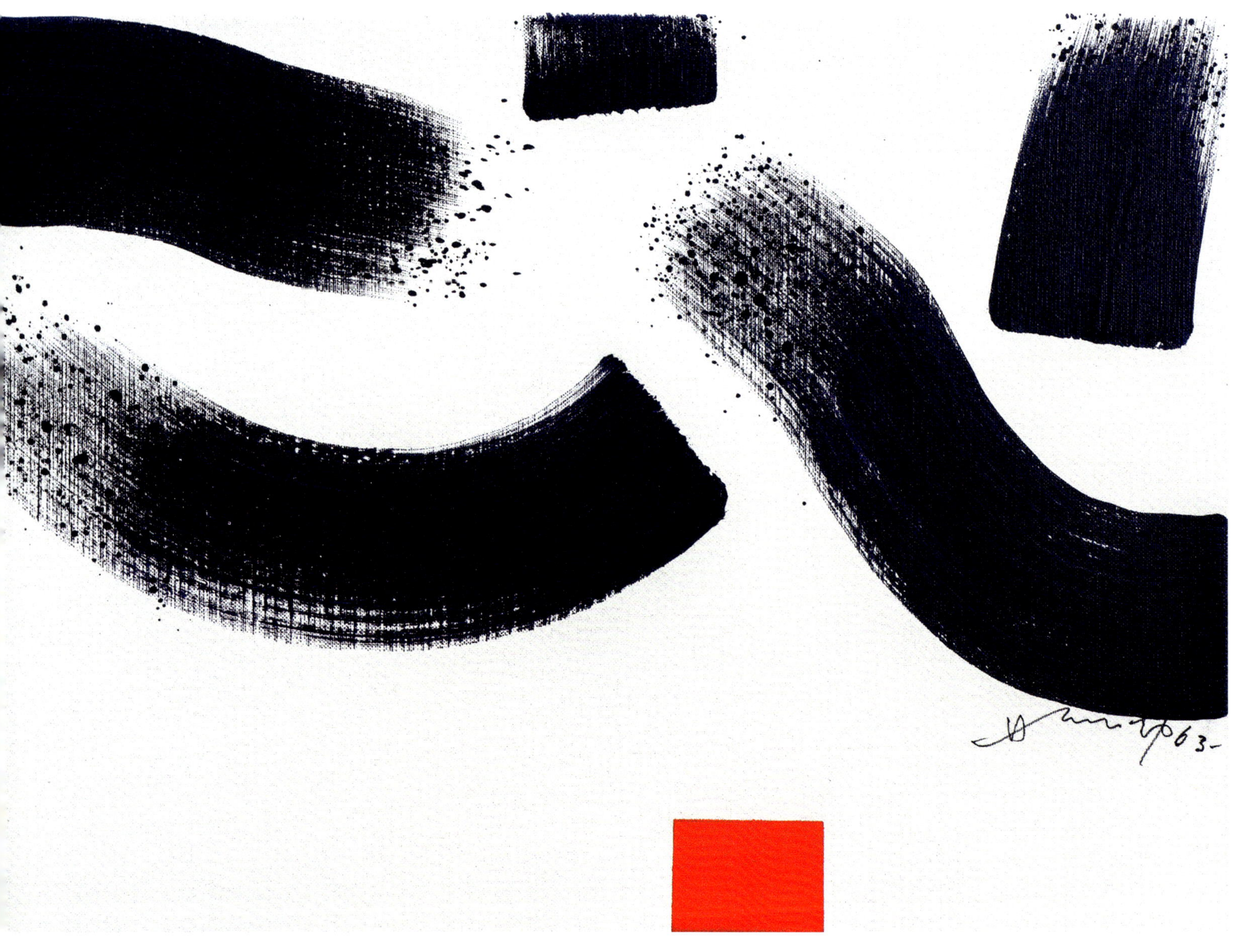

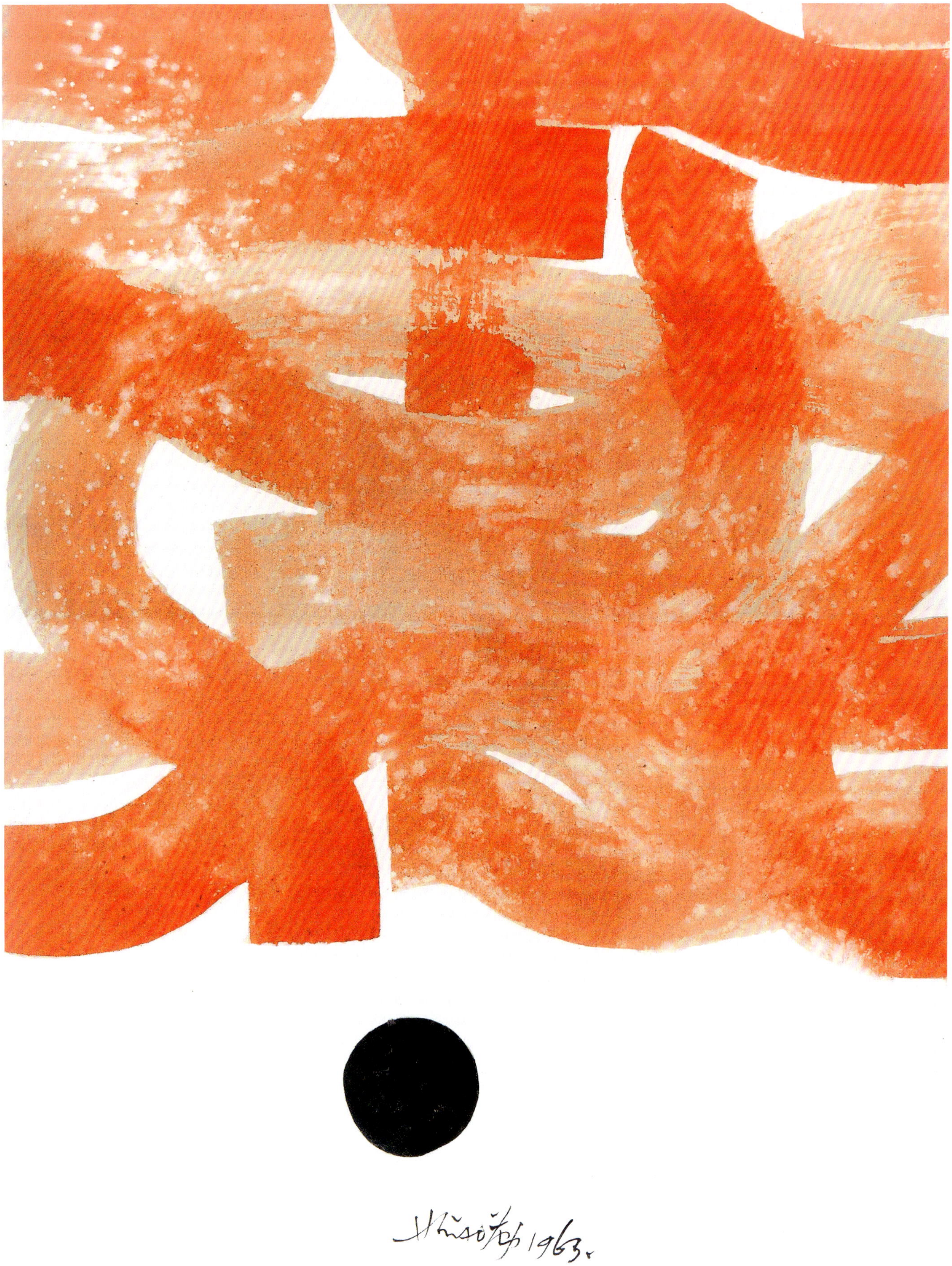

Hsiao Chin
Untitled, 1963
Mixed media on paper
63 x 86cm

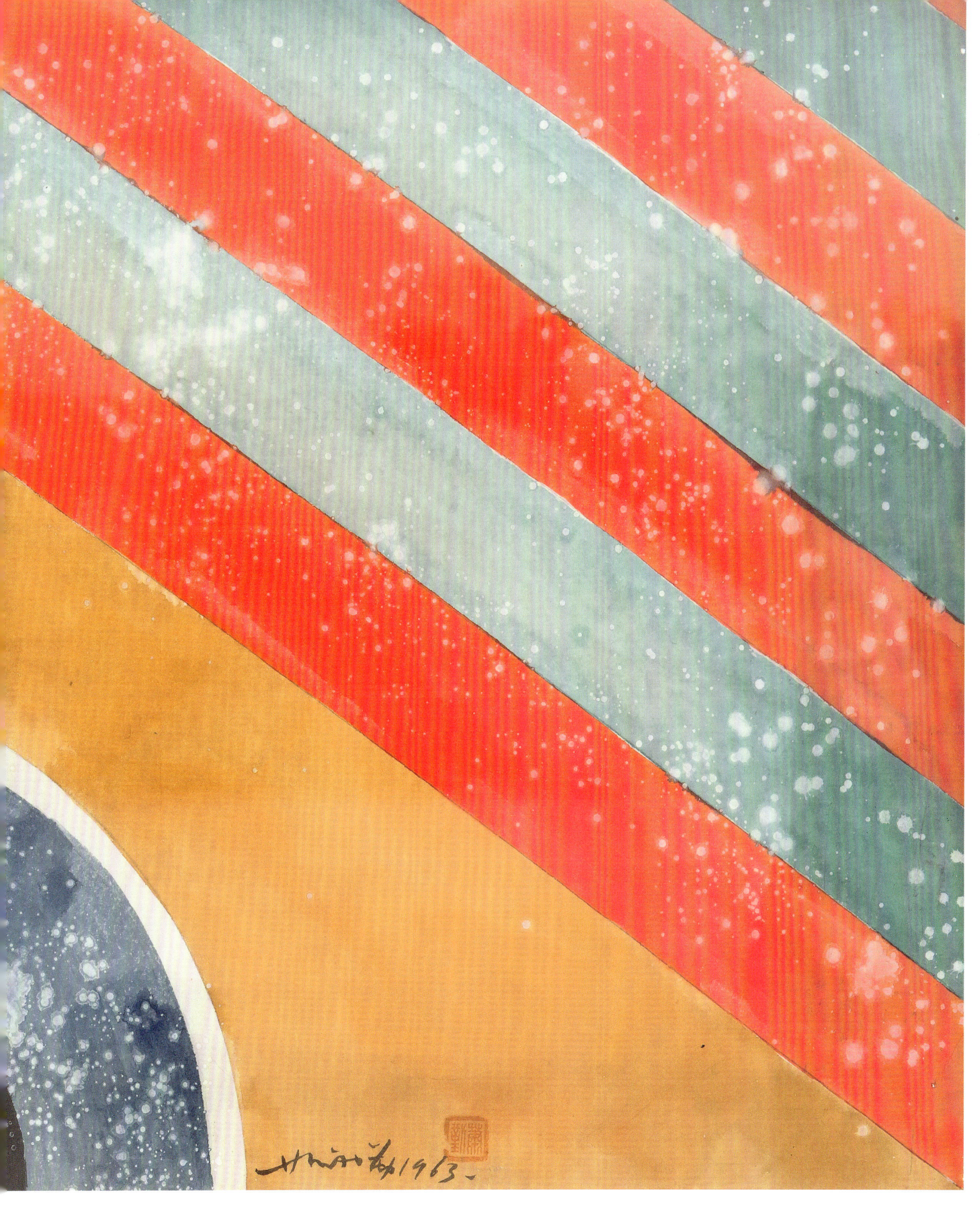

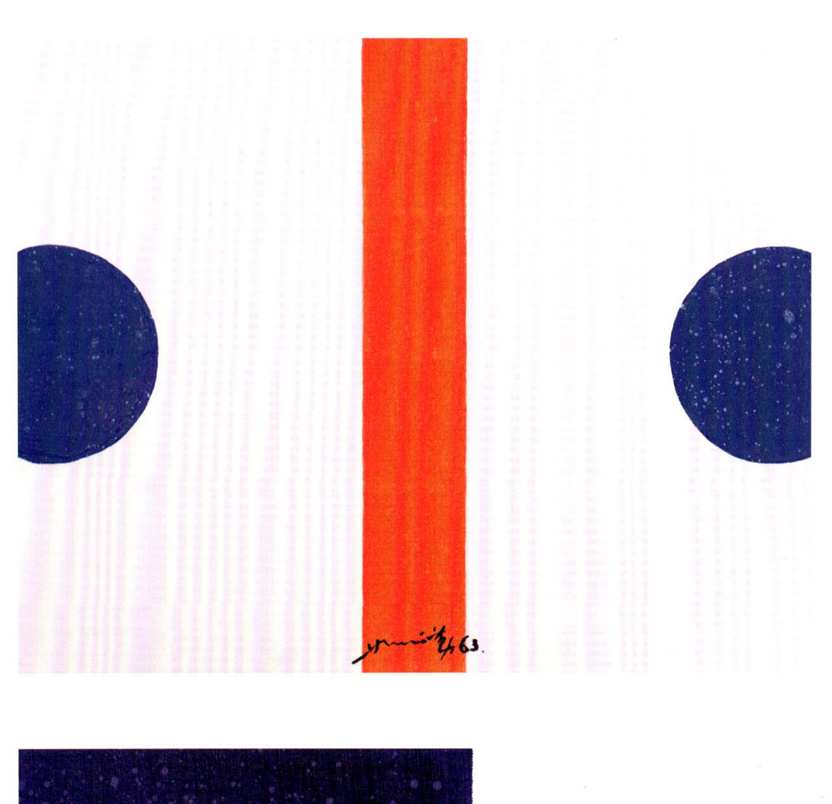

(*left*) Hsiao Chin
Il predestino, 1963
Acrylic on canvas
70 x 90cm

(*below*) Hsiao Chin
Great Earth, 1963
Acrylic on canvas
80 x 100cm

(*opposite*) Hsiao Chin
The Cycles (Il cicli), 1963
Acrylic on canvas
120 x 76cm

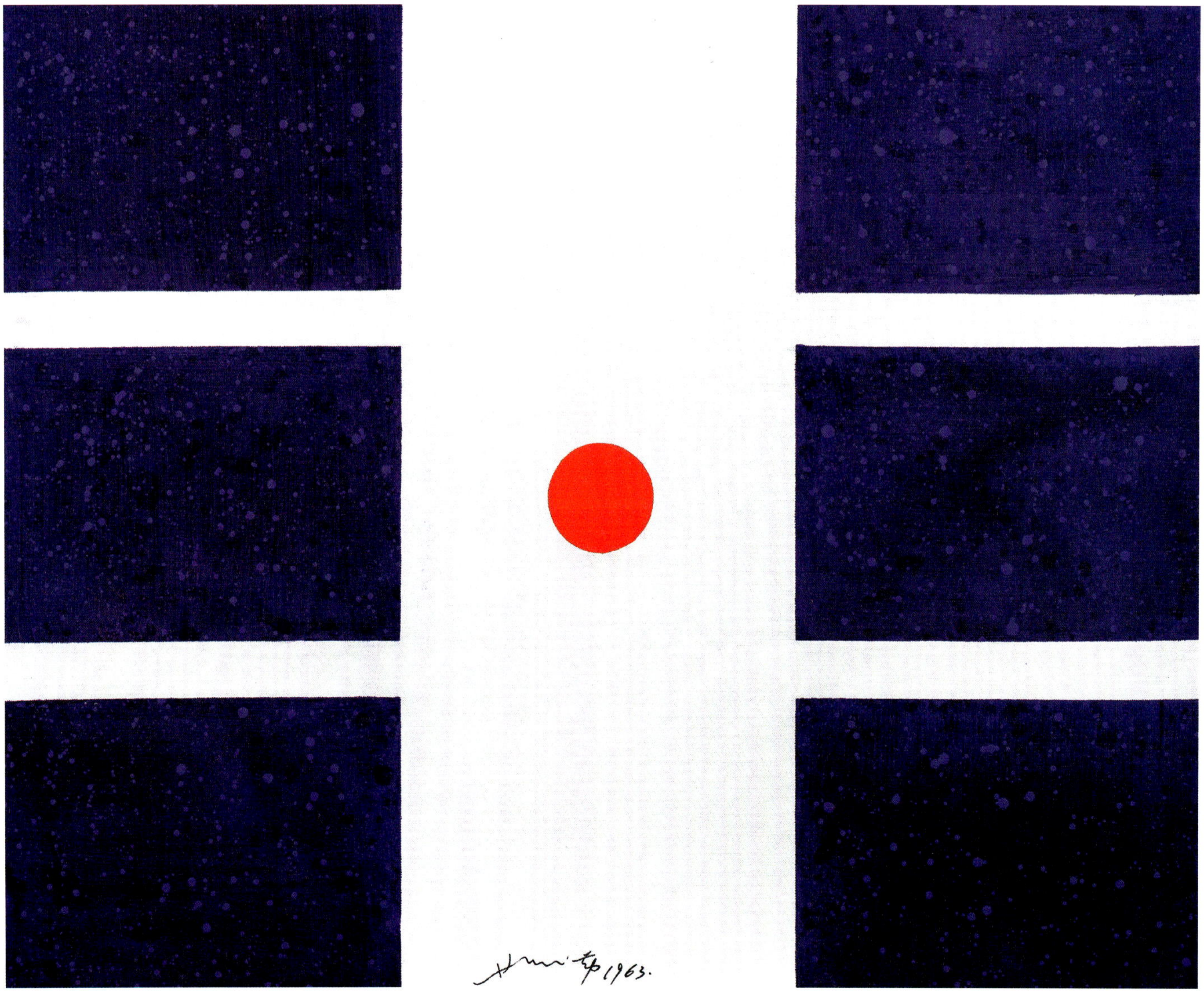

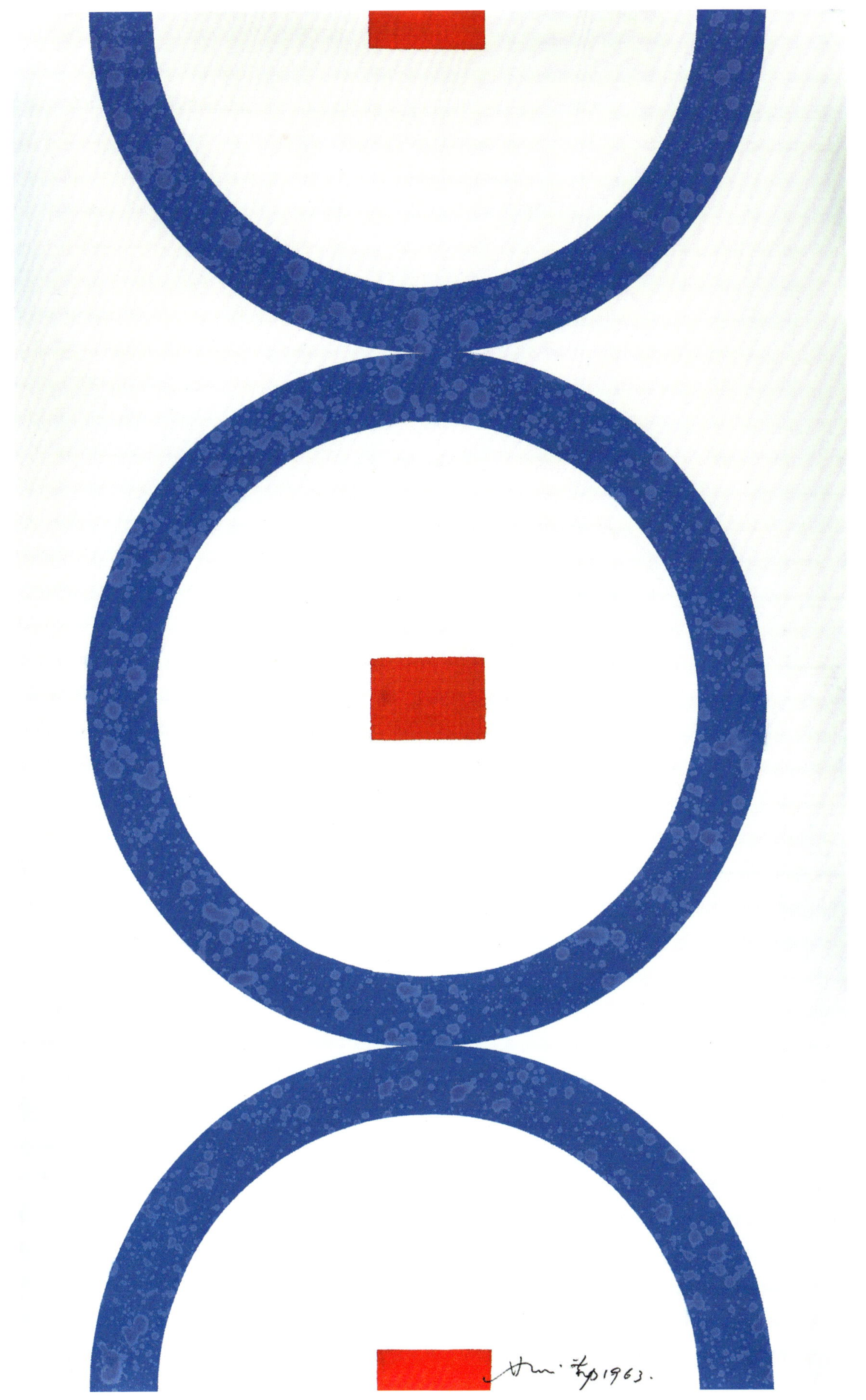

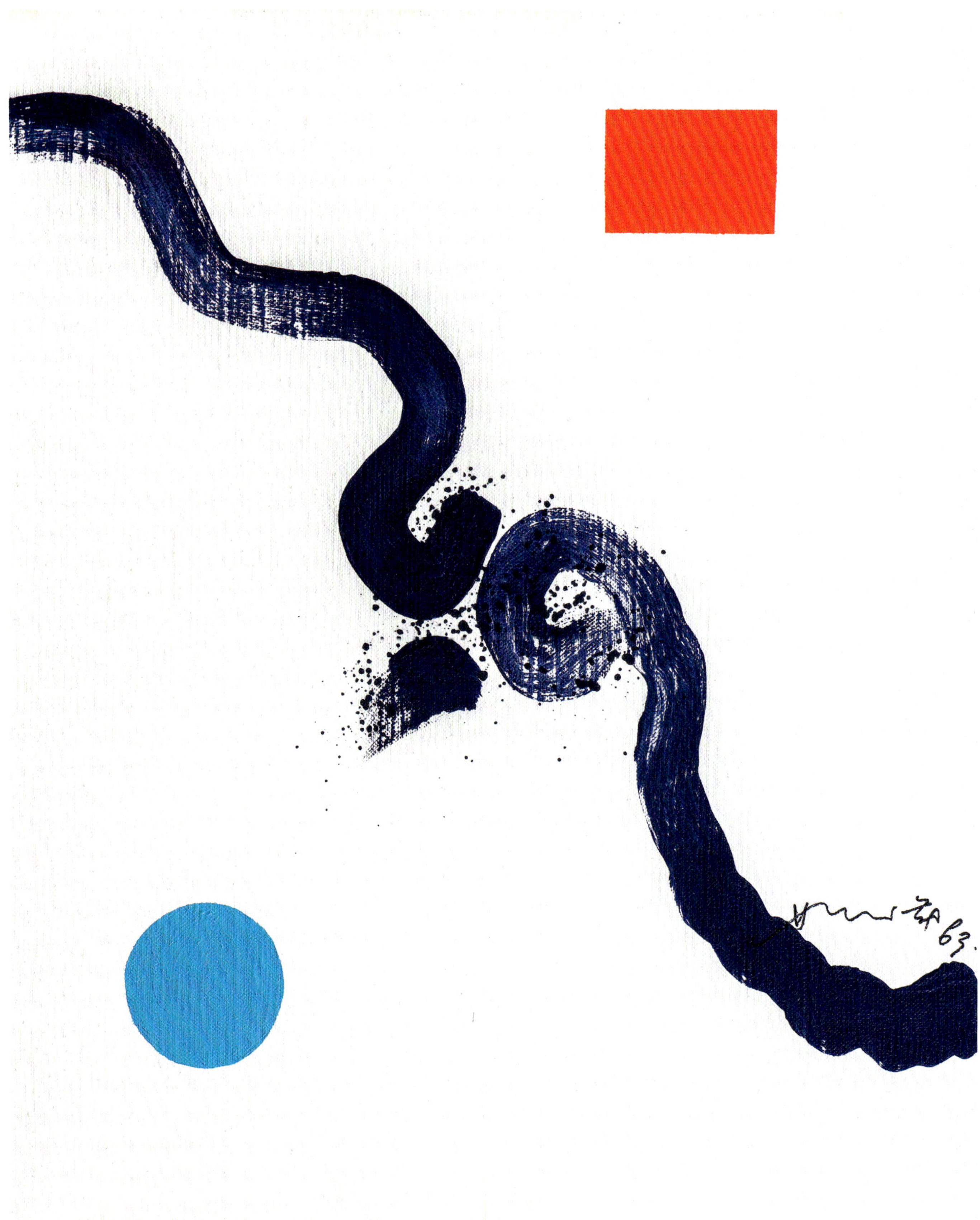

Hsiao Chin
Illuminated Heart-1, 1963
Acrylic on canvas
60 x 50cm

Hsiao Chin
Illuminated Heart-2, 1963
Acrylic on canvas
50 x 60cm

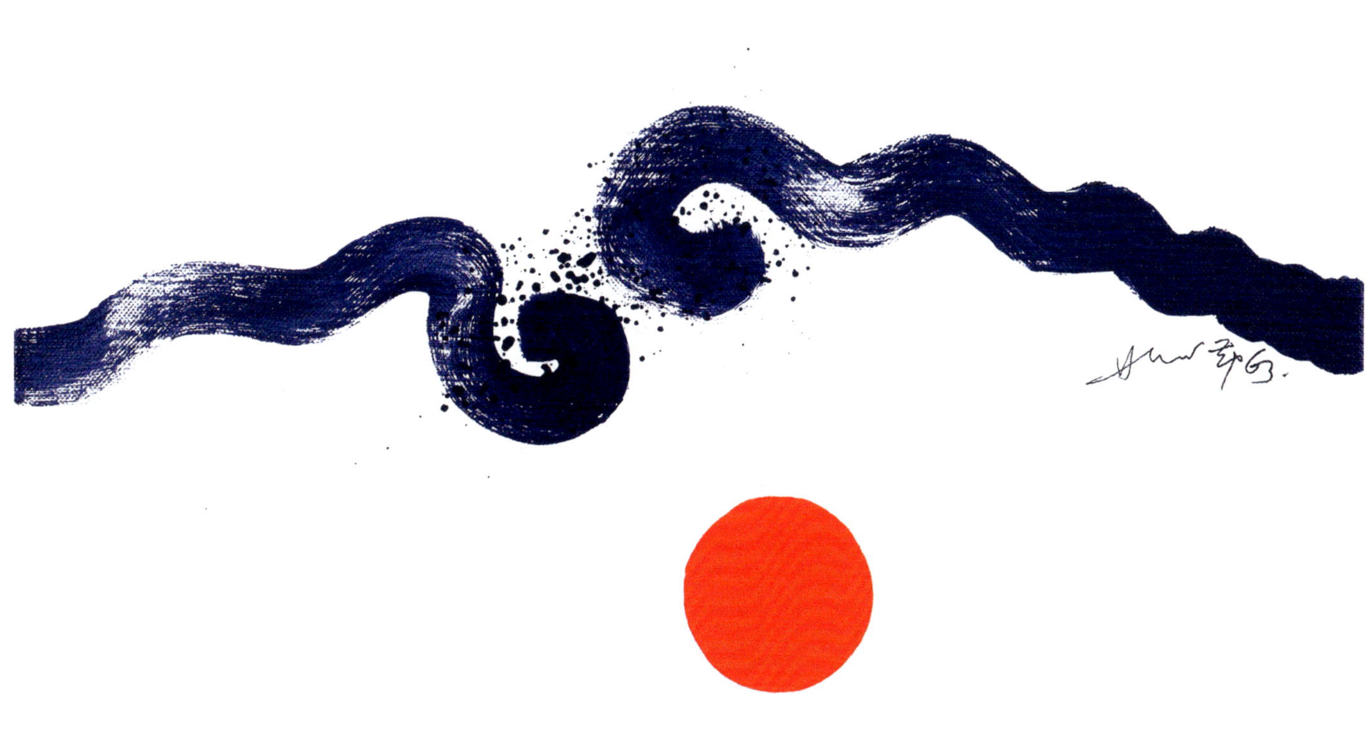

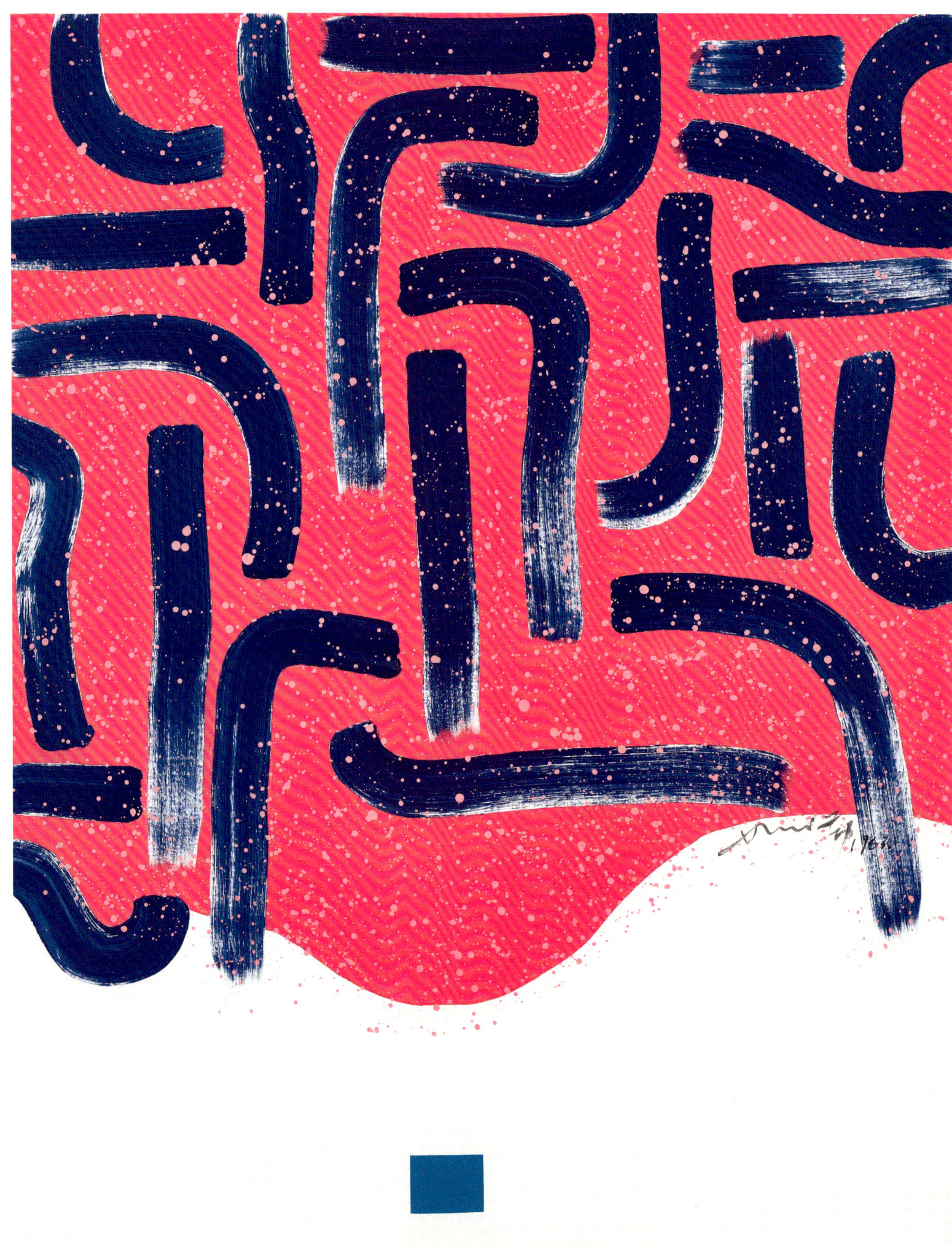

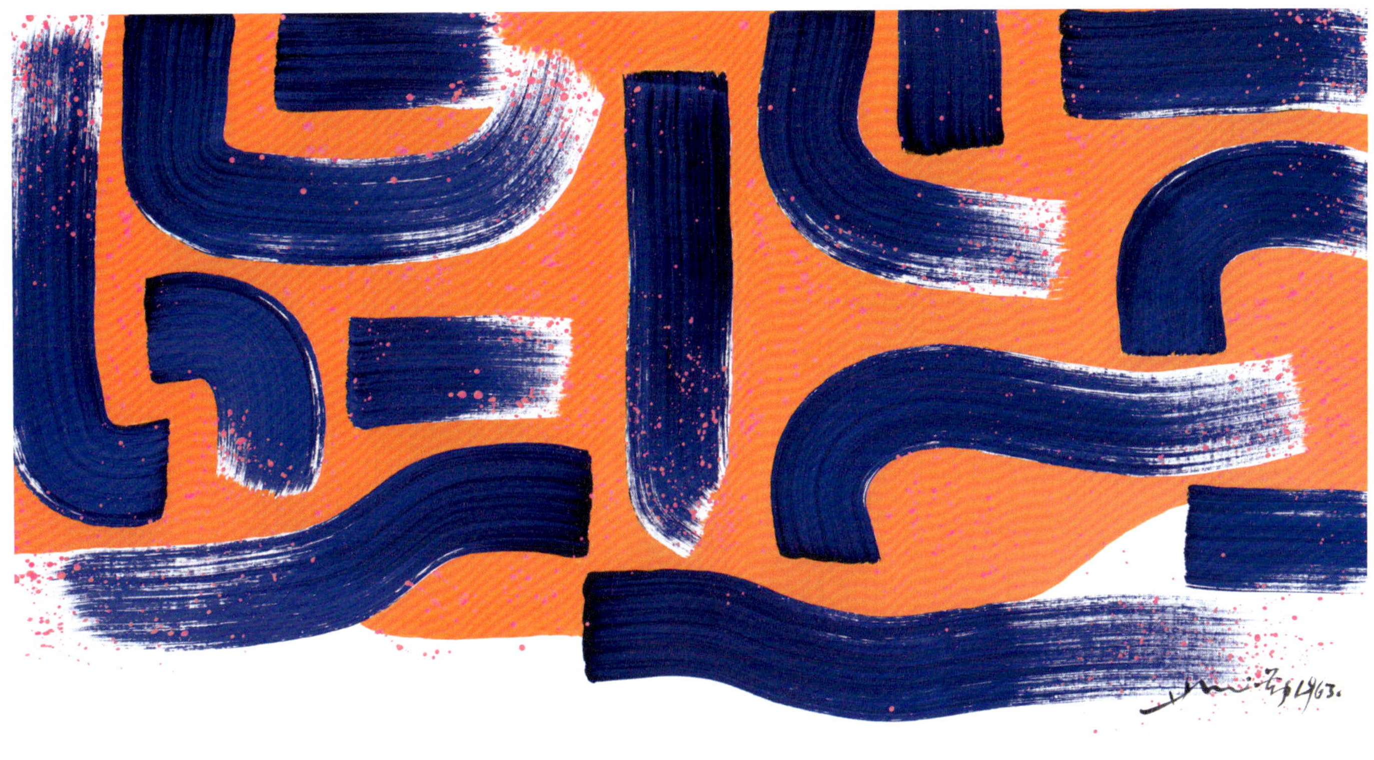

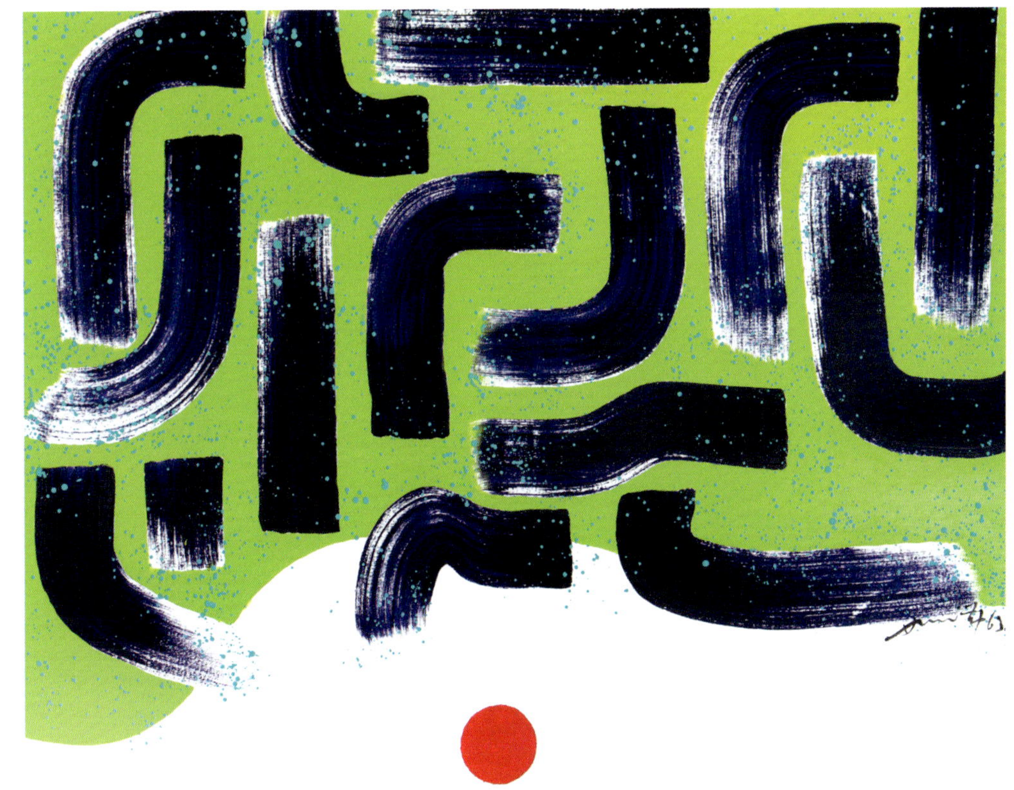

(*opposite*) Hsiao Chin
Dancing Light-5, 1963
Acrylic on canvas
140 x 110cm

(*above*) Hsiao Chin
Dancing Light-6, 1963
Acrylic on canvas
90 x 140cm

(*right*) Hsiao Chin
Dancing Light-7, 1963
Acrylic on canvas
110 x 140cm

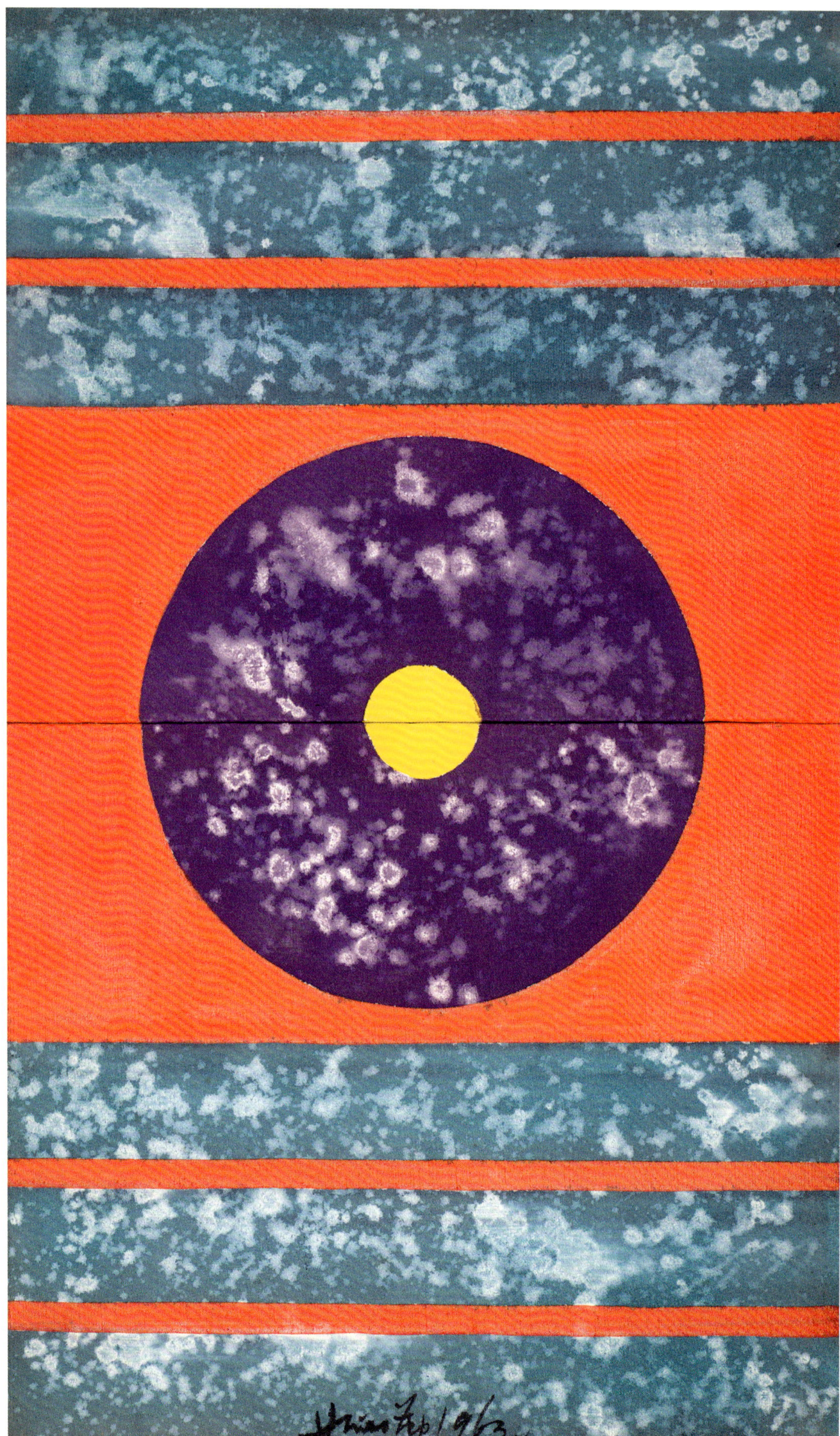

(*opposite*) Hsiao Chin
Elevation, 1963
Ink on canvas
100 x 60cm

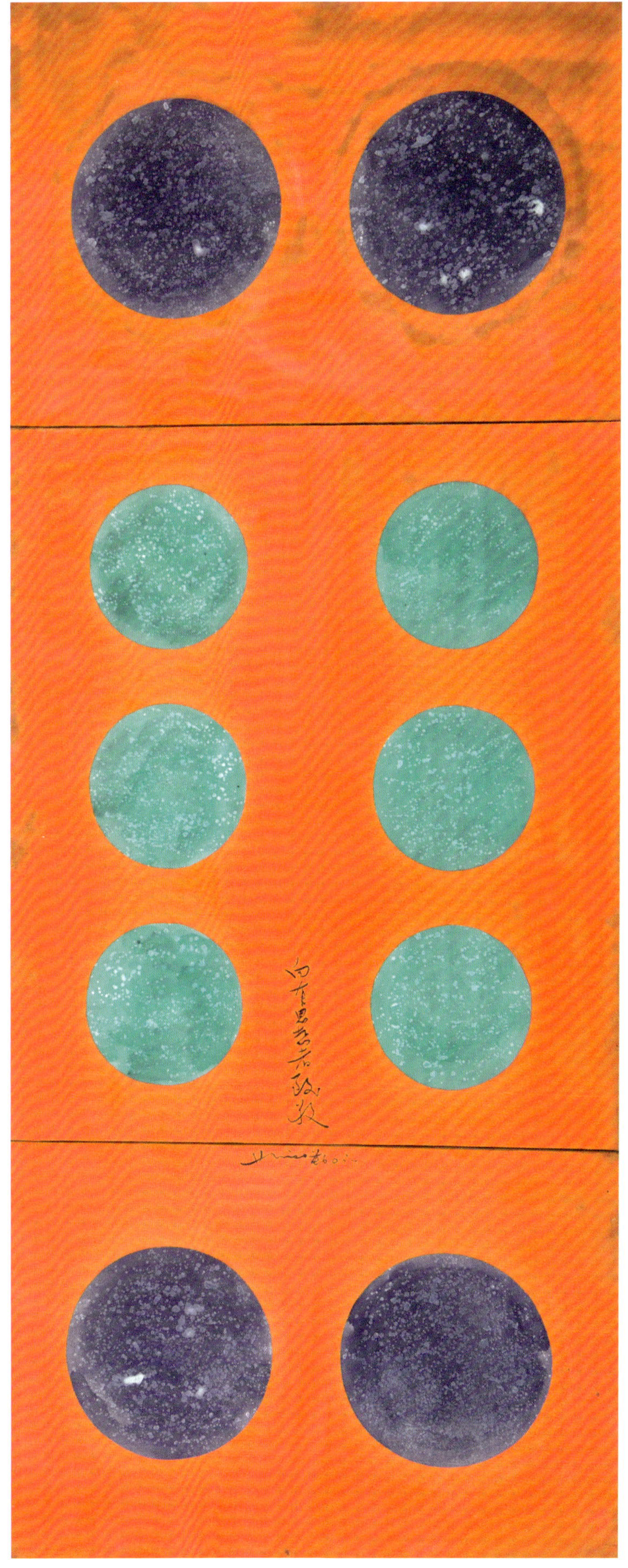

Hsiao Chin
Homage to Thinkers
(Omaggio ai pensatori)
1963
Acrylic on canvas
220 x 90cm

Hsiao Chin
The Link, 1963
Acrylic on canvas
110 x 90cm

Hsiao Chin
Tao, 1963
Ink on canvas
60 x 70cm

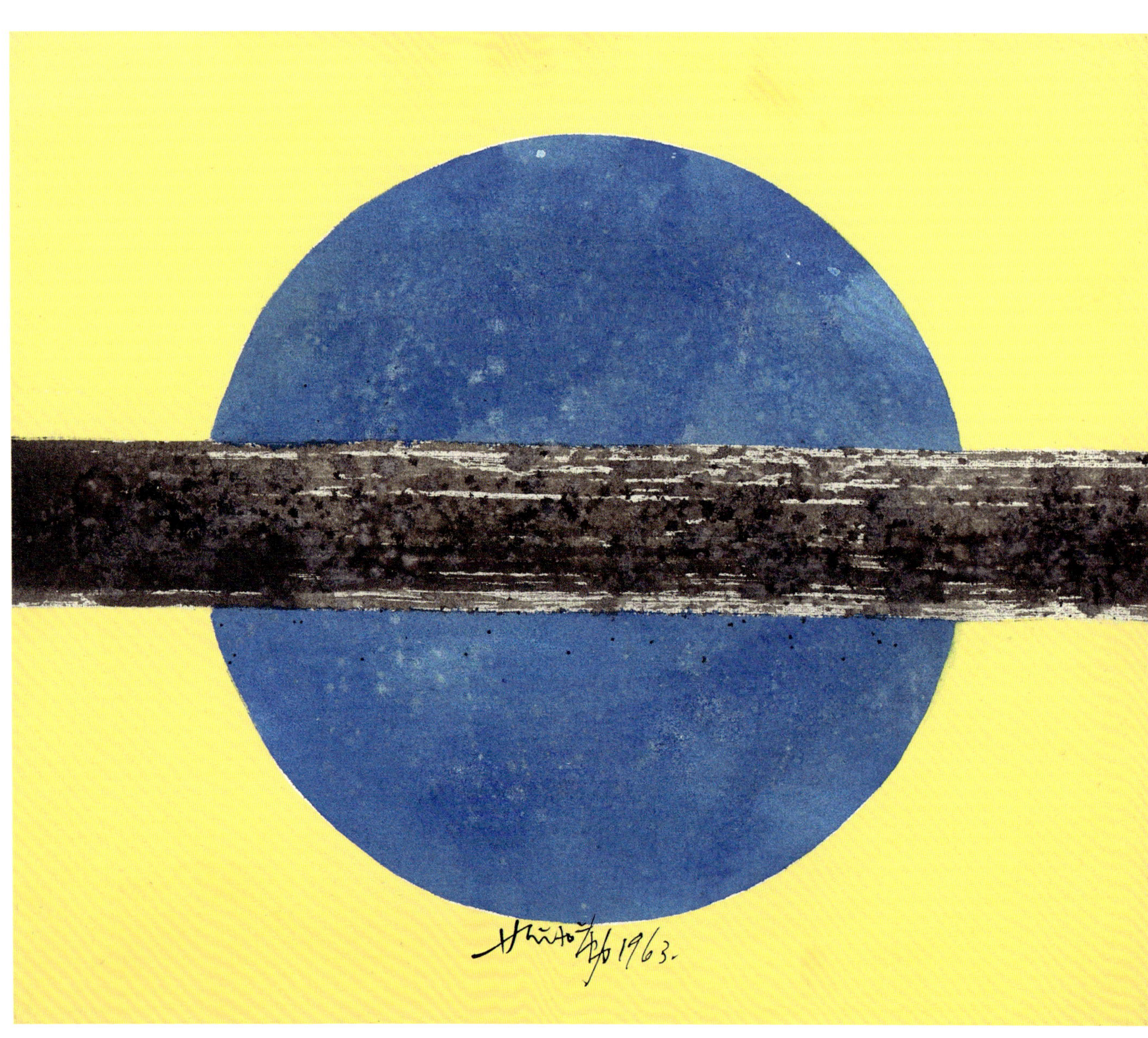

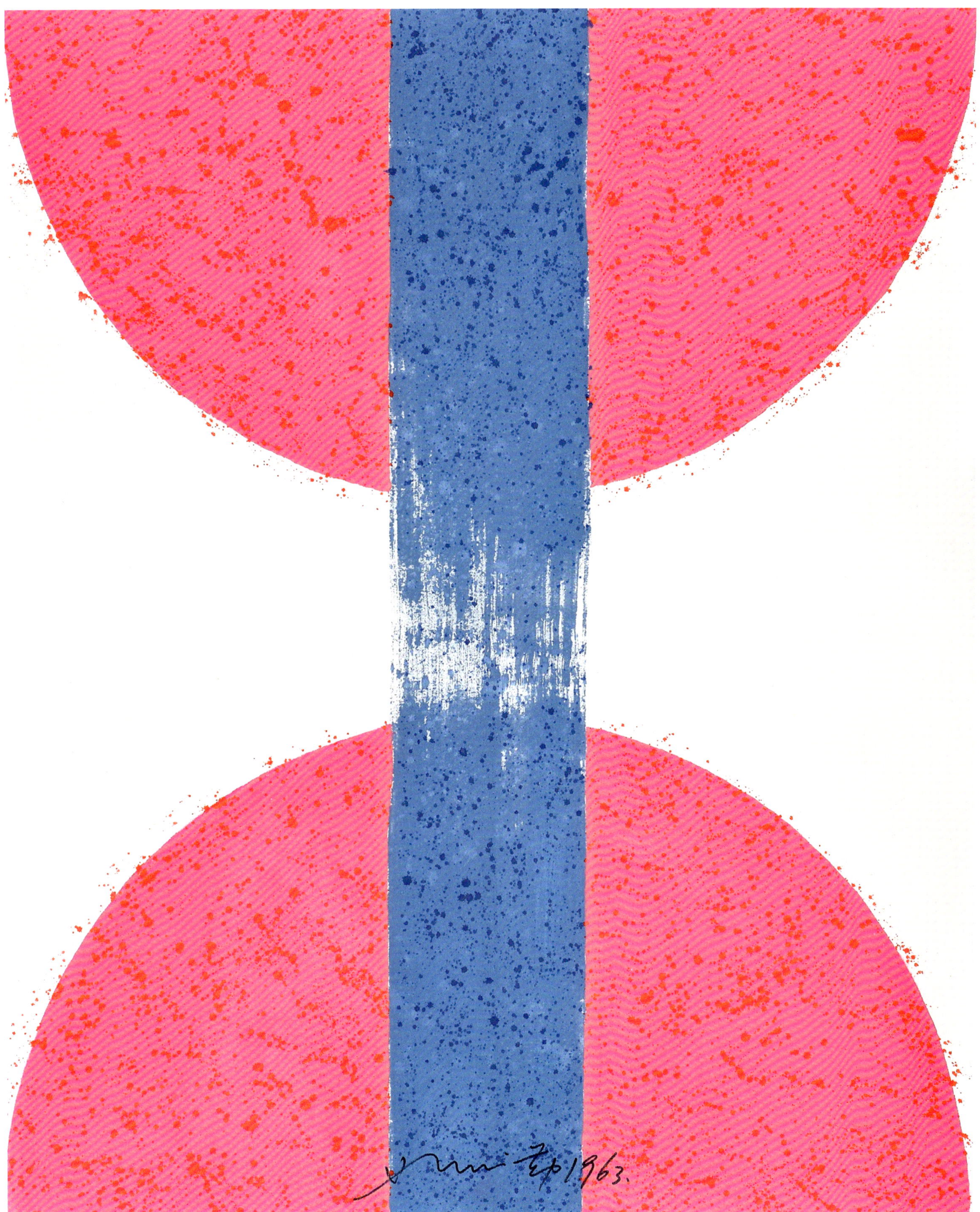

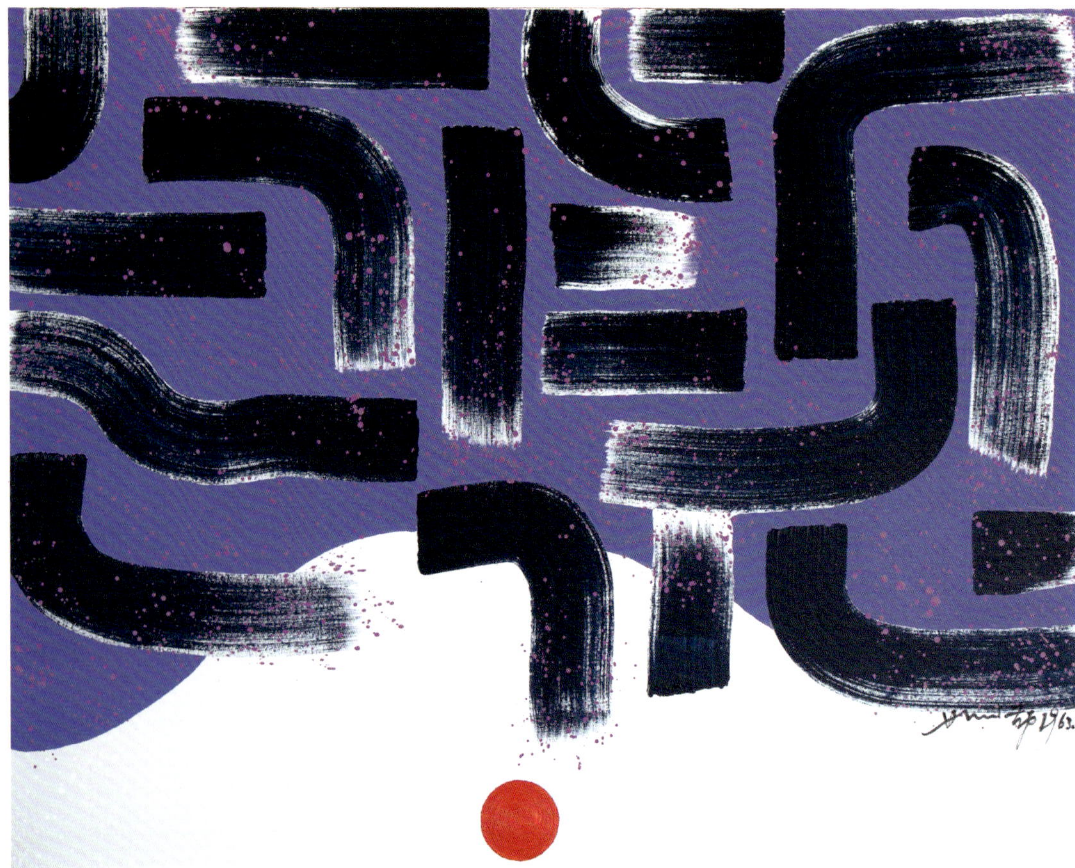

Hsiao Chin
Dancing Light-8, 1963
Acrylic on canvas
110 x 140cm

Hsiao Chin
Three Produces All Things
1963
Acrylic and ink on canvas
230 x 354cm

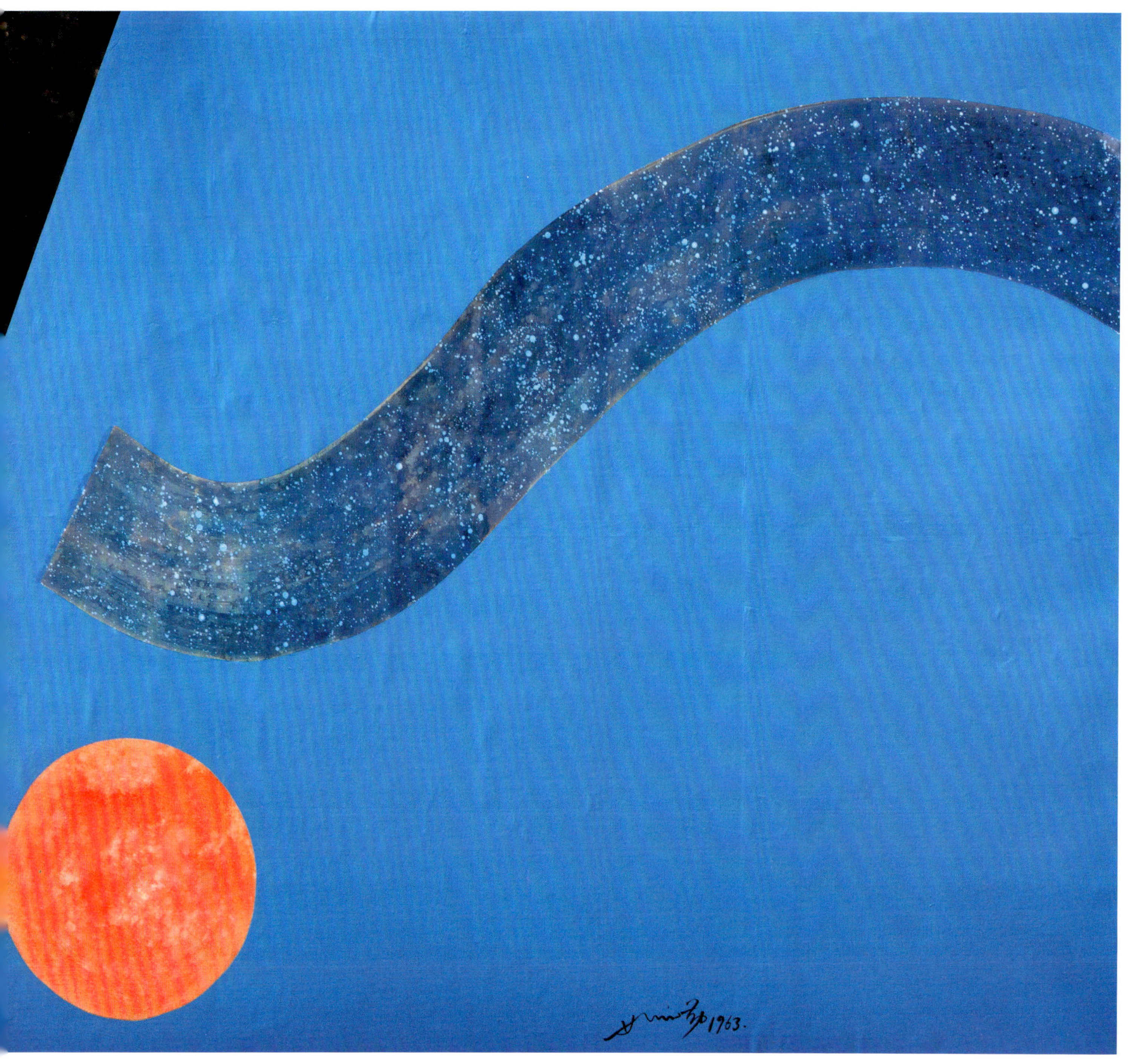

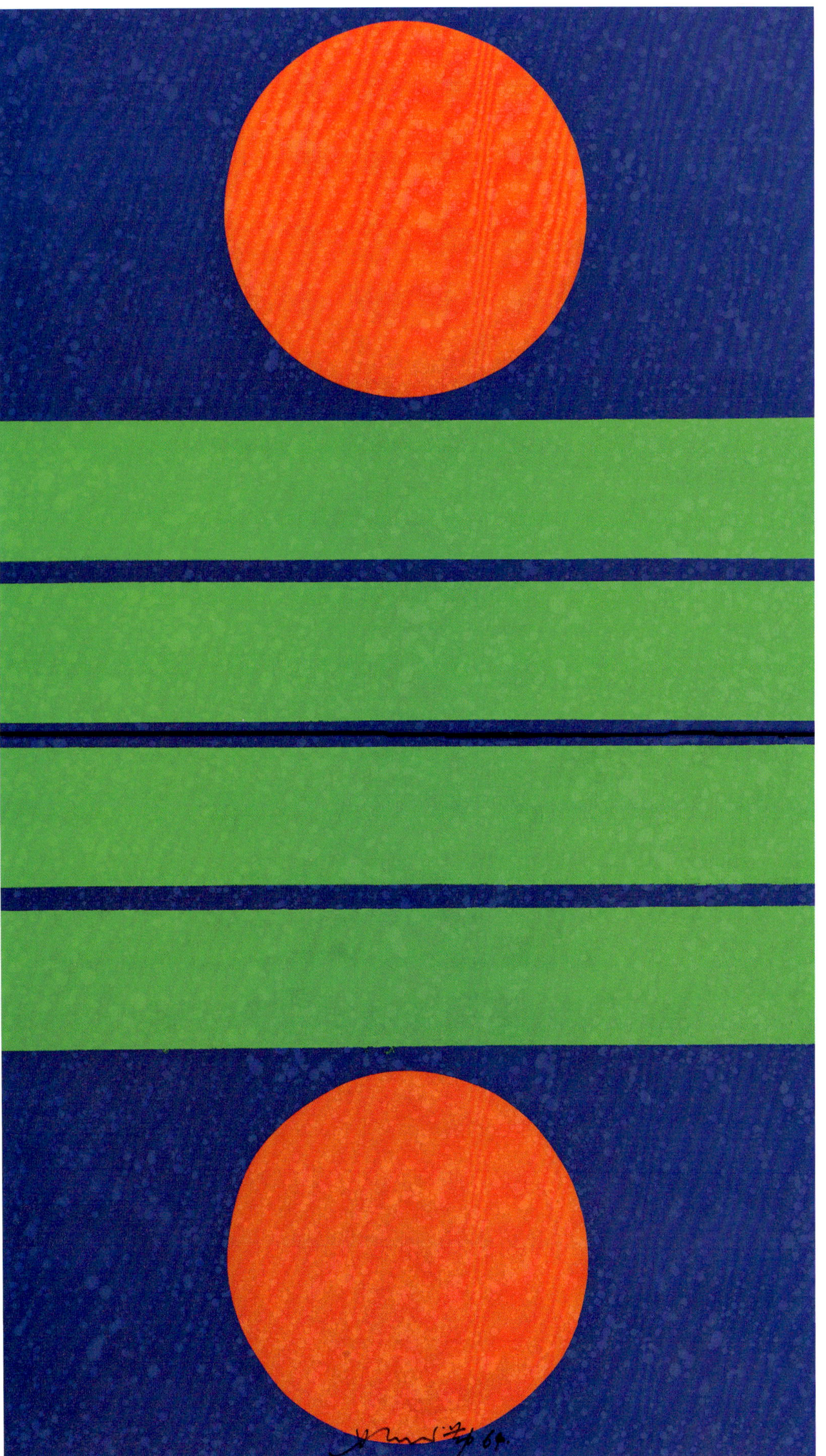

Hsiao Chin
Two Elements, 1964
Acrylic on canvas
120 x 70cm

(*opposite*) Hsiao Chin
Through, 1964
Acrylic and ink on canvas
116 x 91cm

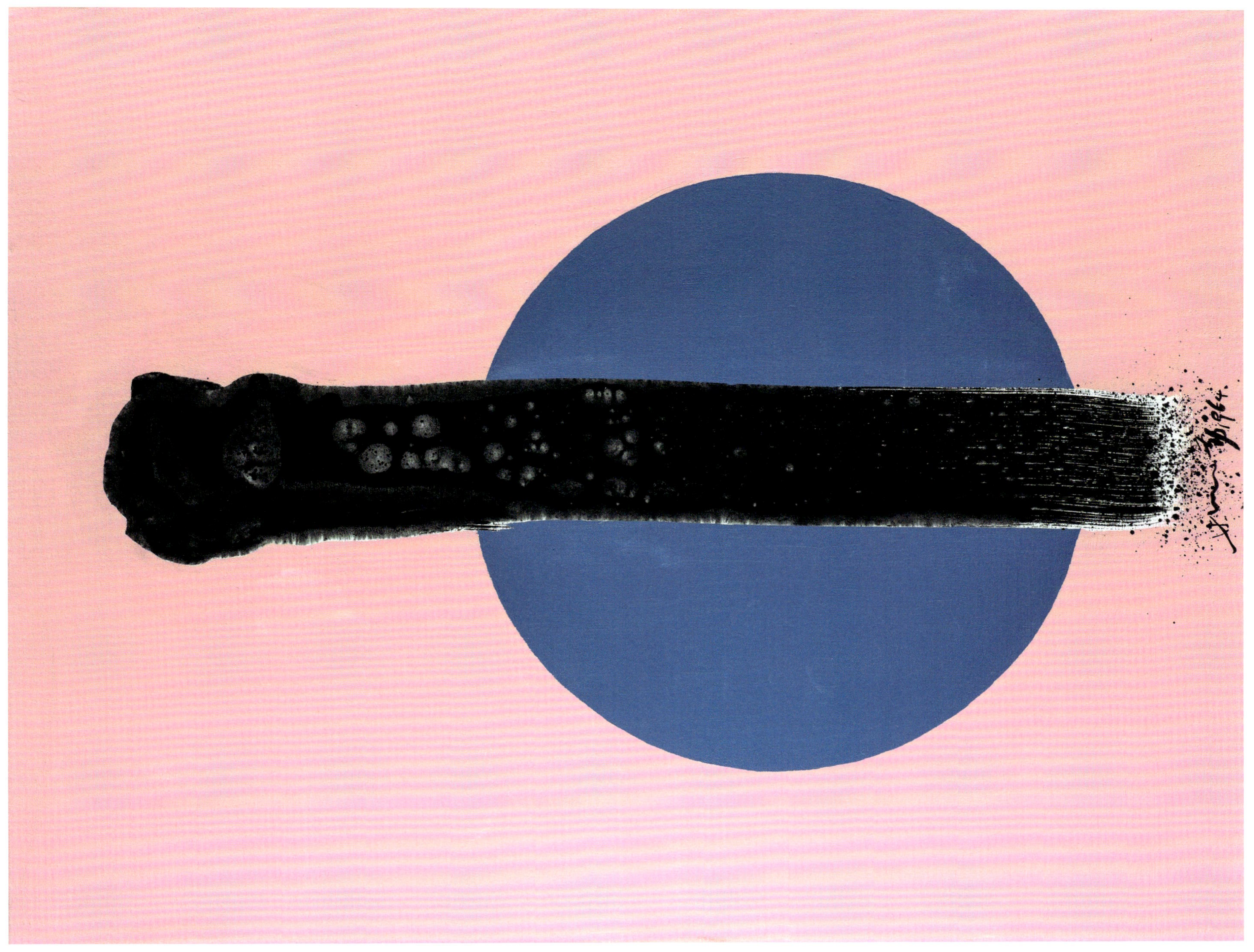

Hsiao Chin
Light Energy, 1964
Acrylic and ink on canvas
70 x 85cm

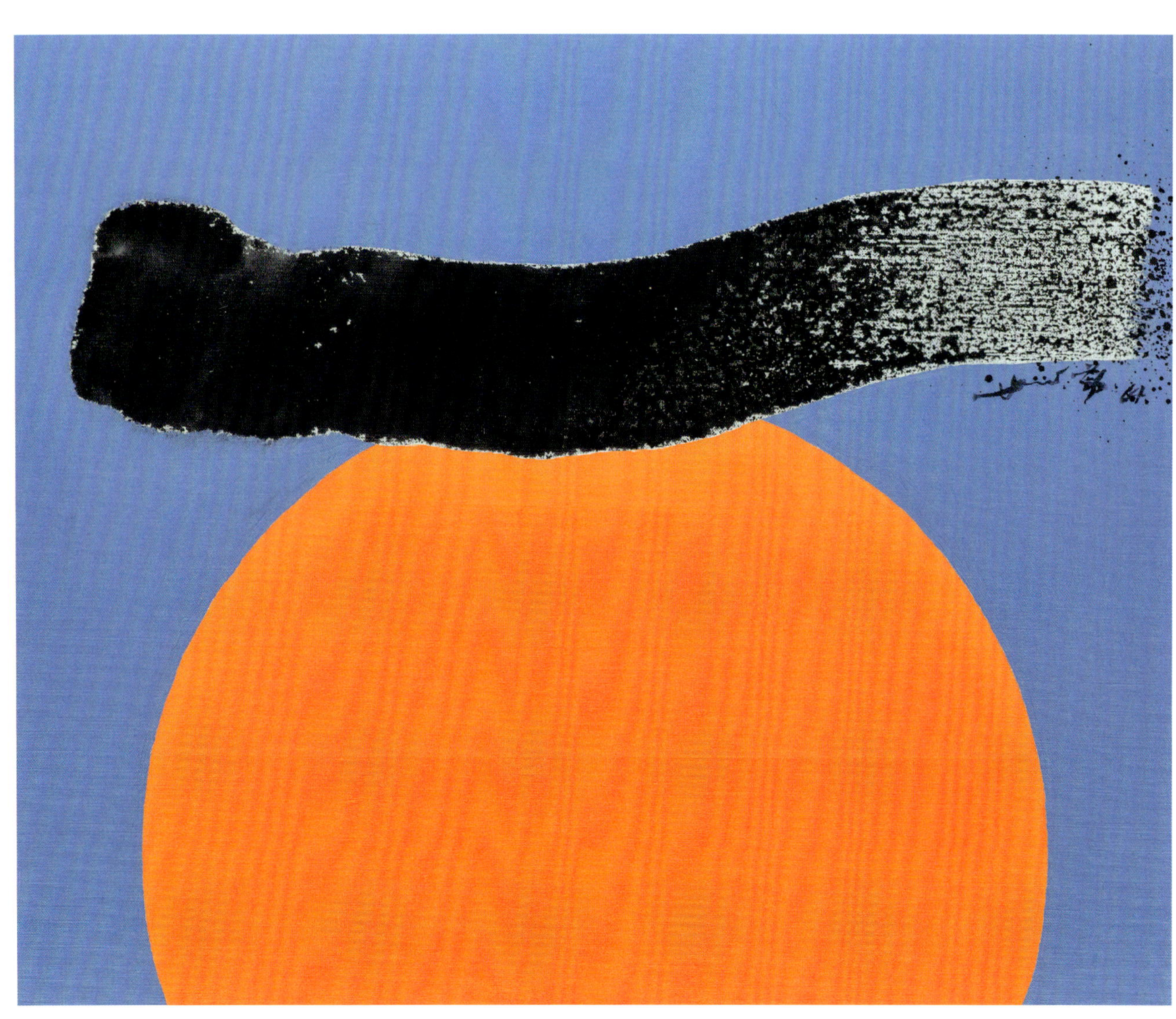

Hsiao Chin
Unlimited Energy, 1964
Acrylic on canvas
101 x 135cm

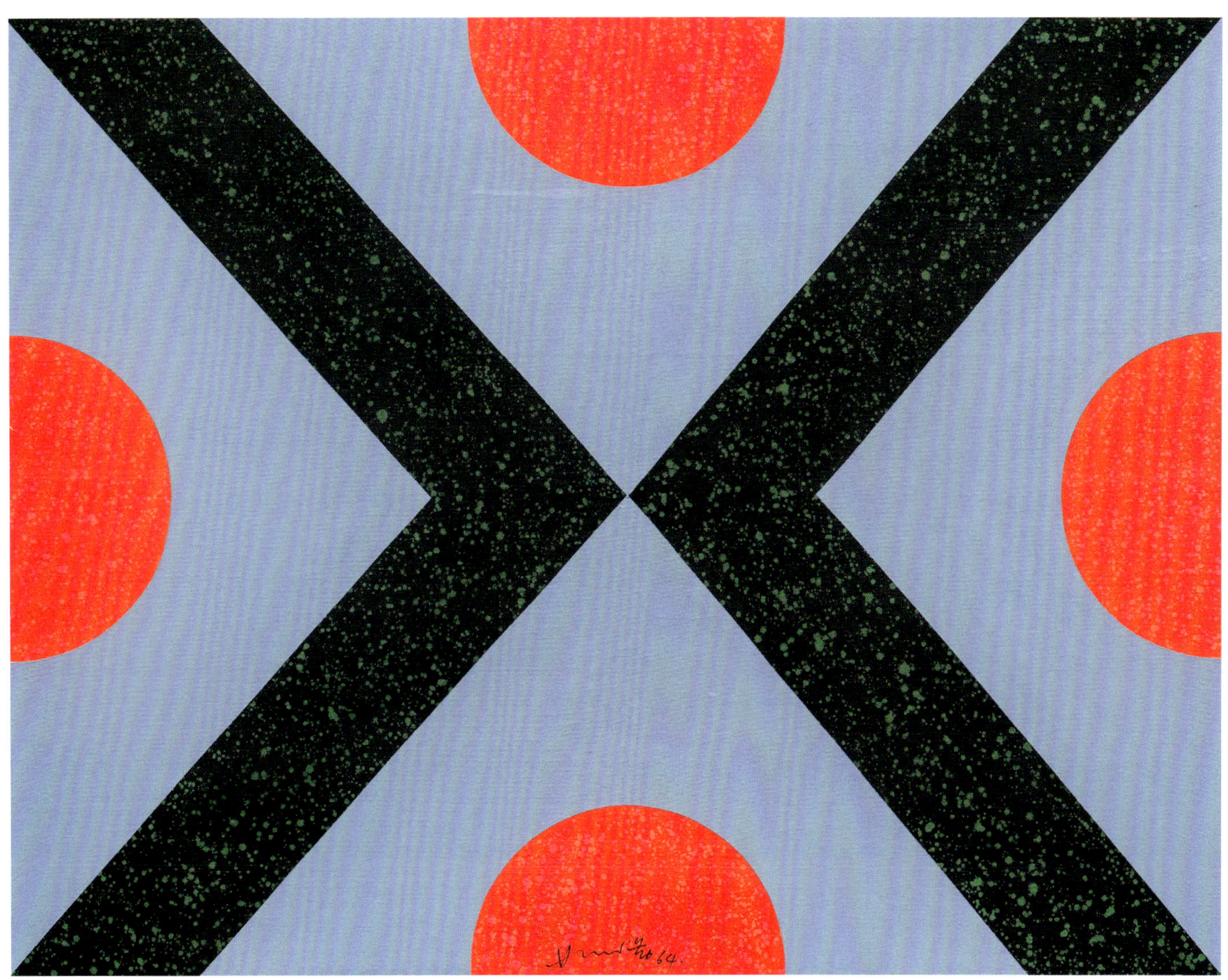

Hsiao Chin
Positive Energy, 1964
Acrylic on canvas
70 x 90cm

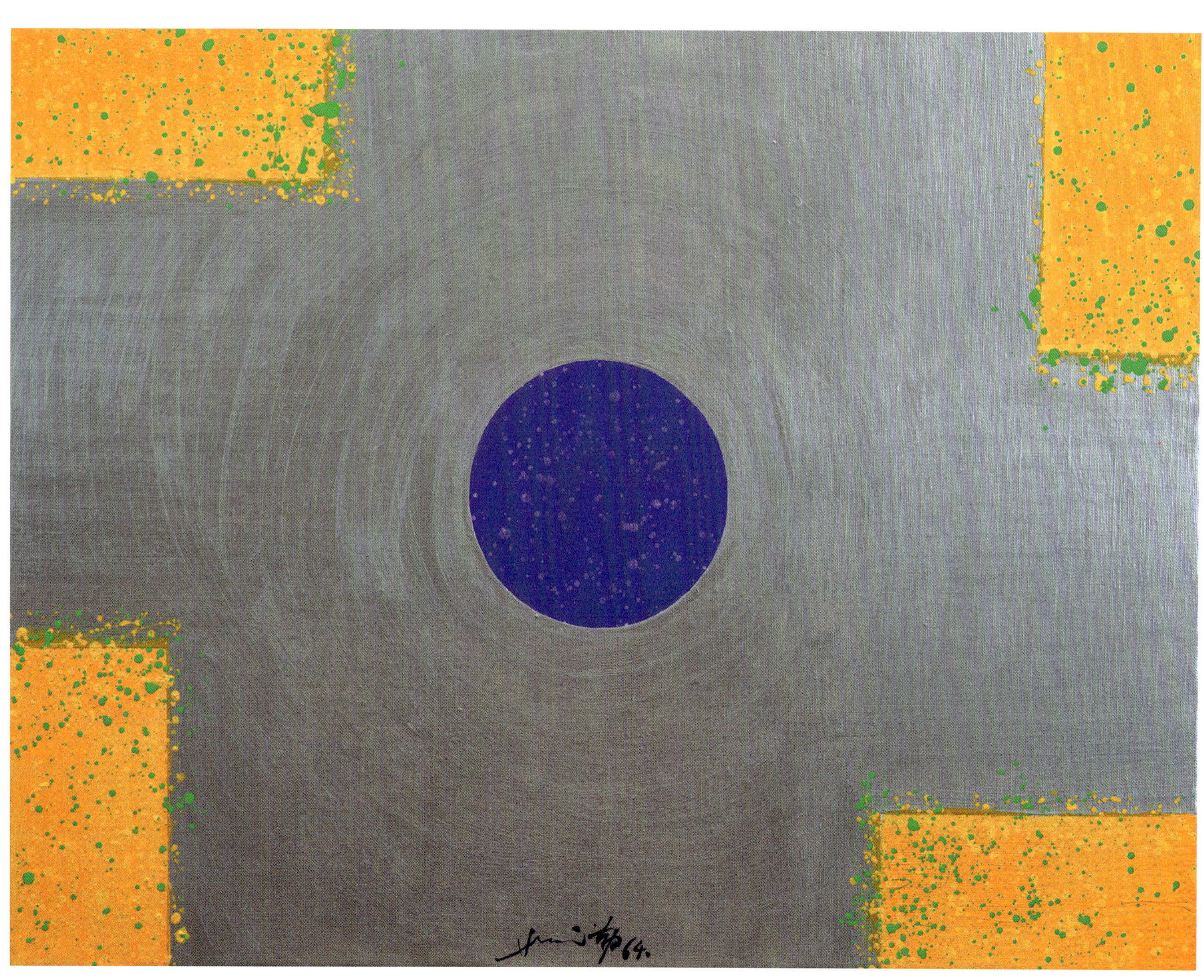

Hsiao Chin
Purple Sun (Il sole viola)
1964
Acrylic on canvas
80 x 100cm

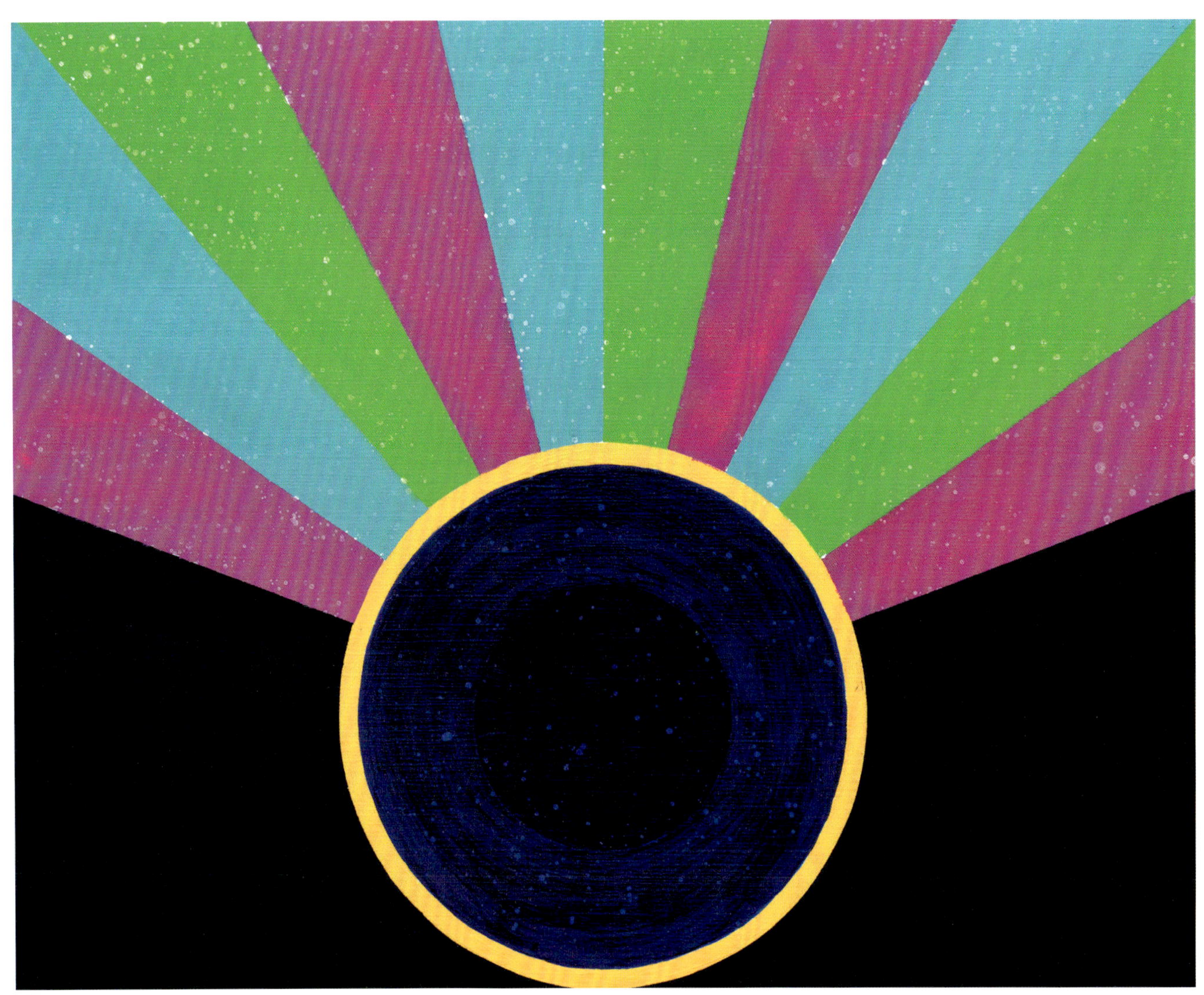

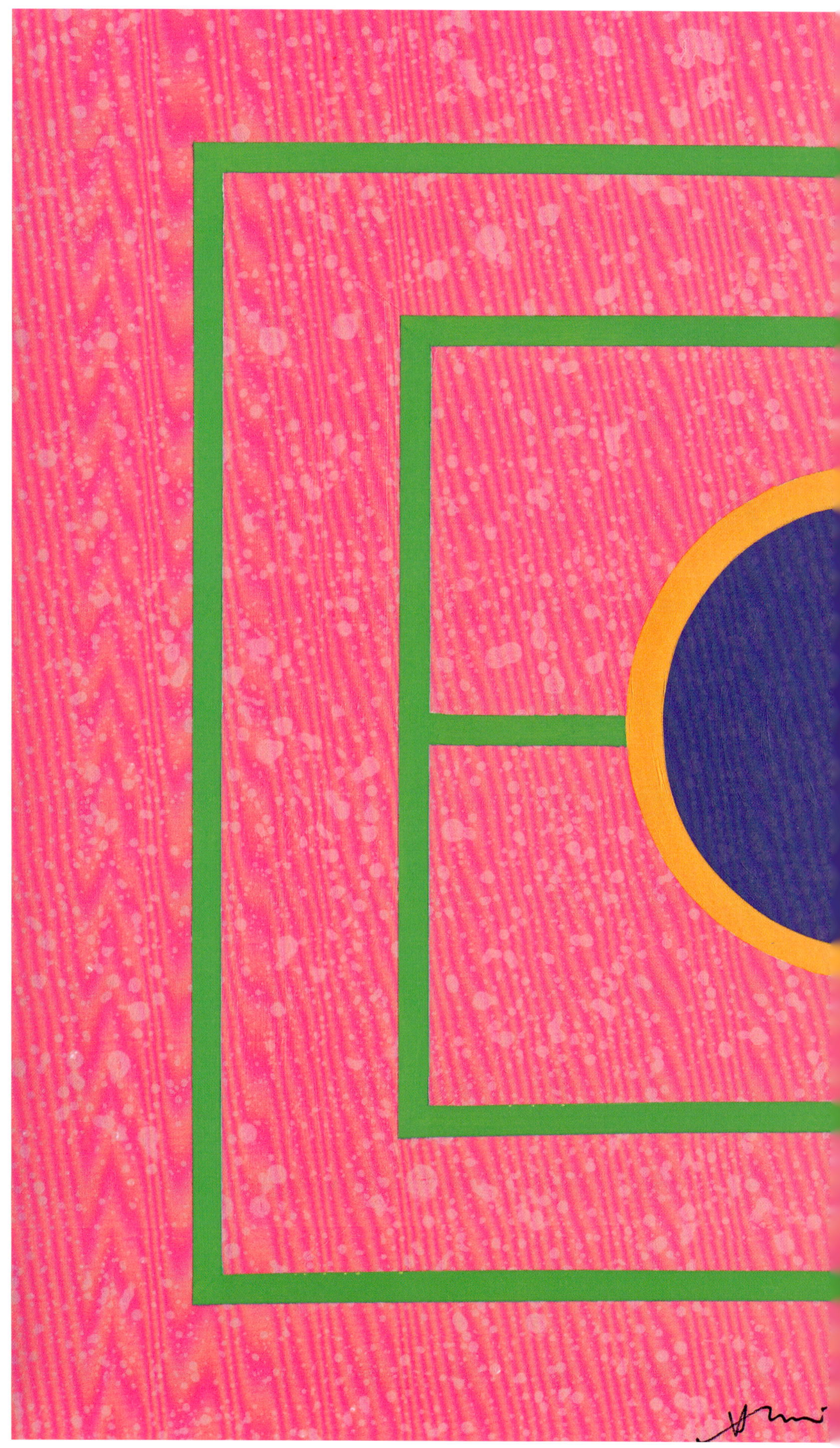

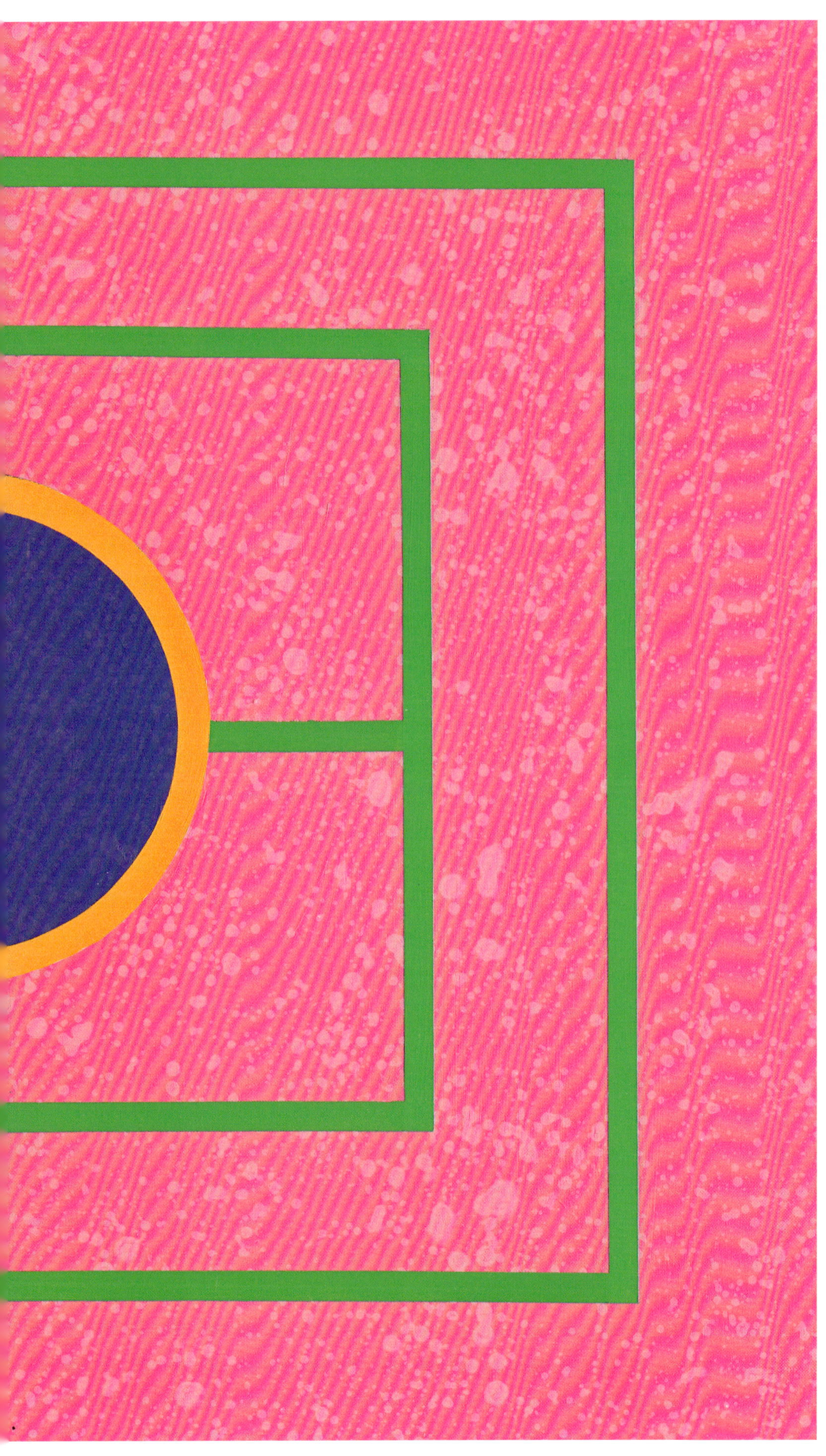

Hsiao Chin
Latent, 1964
Acrylic on canvas
90 x 110cm

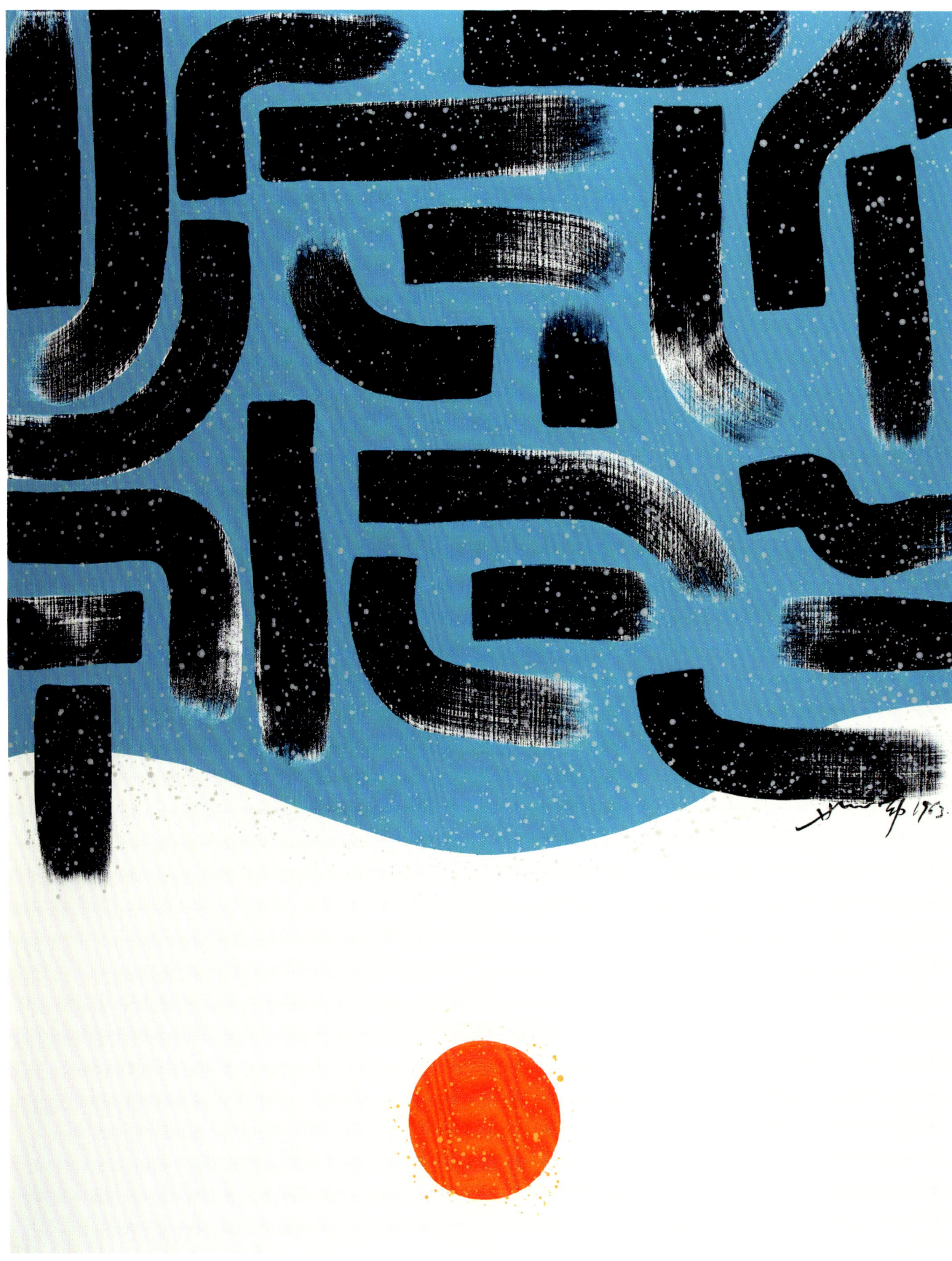

Hsiao Chin
Dancing Light-15, 1963
Acrylic on canvas
140 x 110cm

Hsiao Chin
Dancing Light-17, 1964
Acrylic on canvas
130 x 160cm

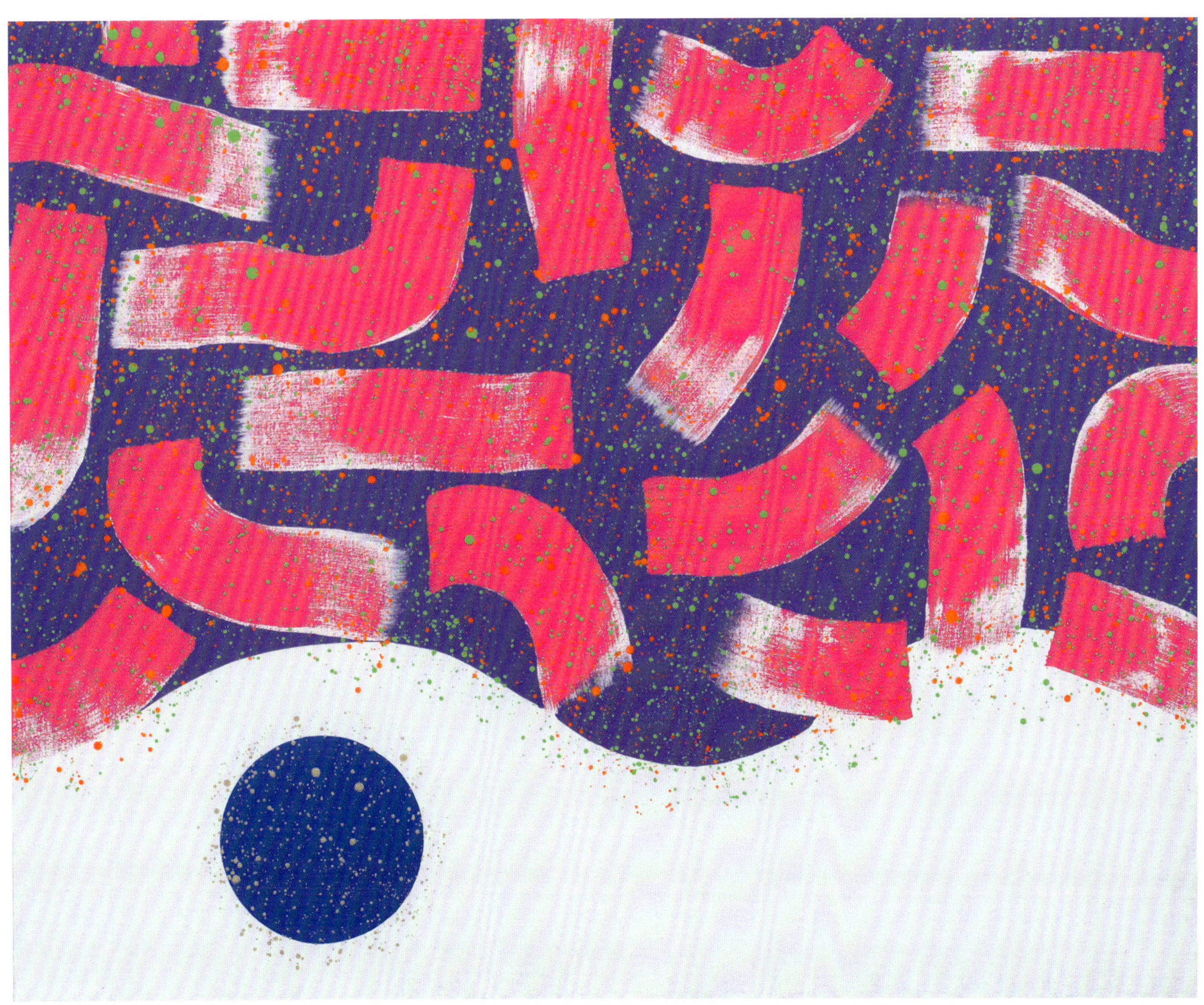

Hsiao Chin
The Sun-7, 1964
Acrylic on canvas
100 x 130cm

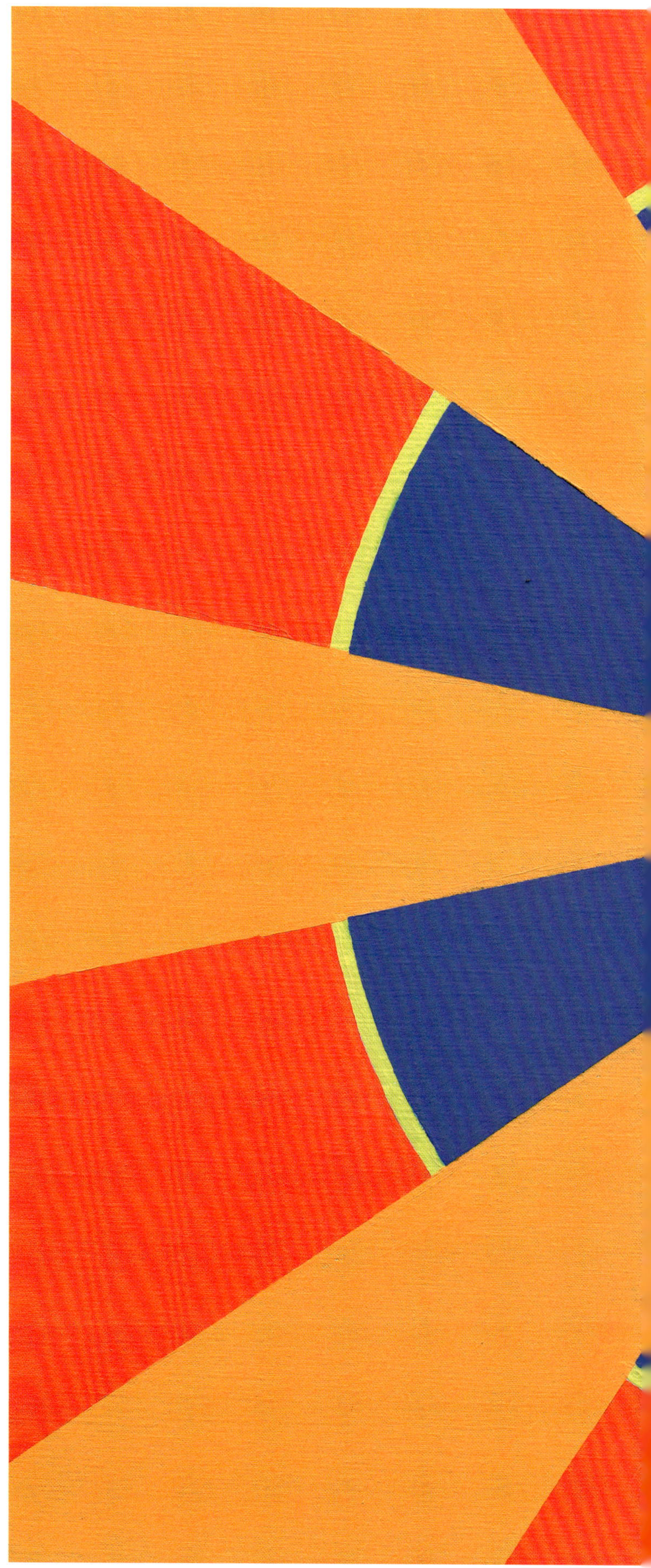

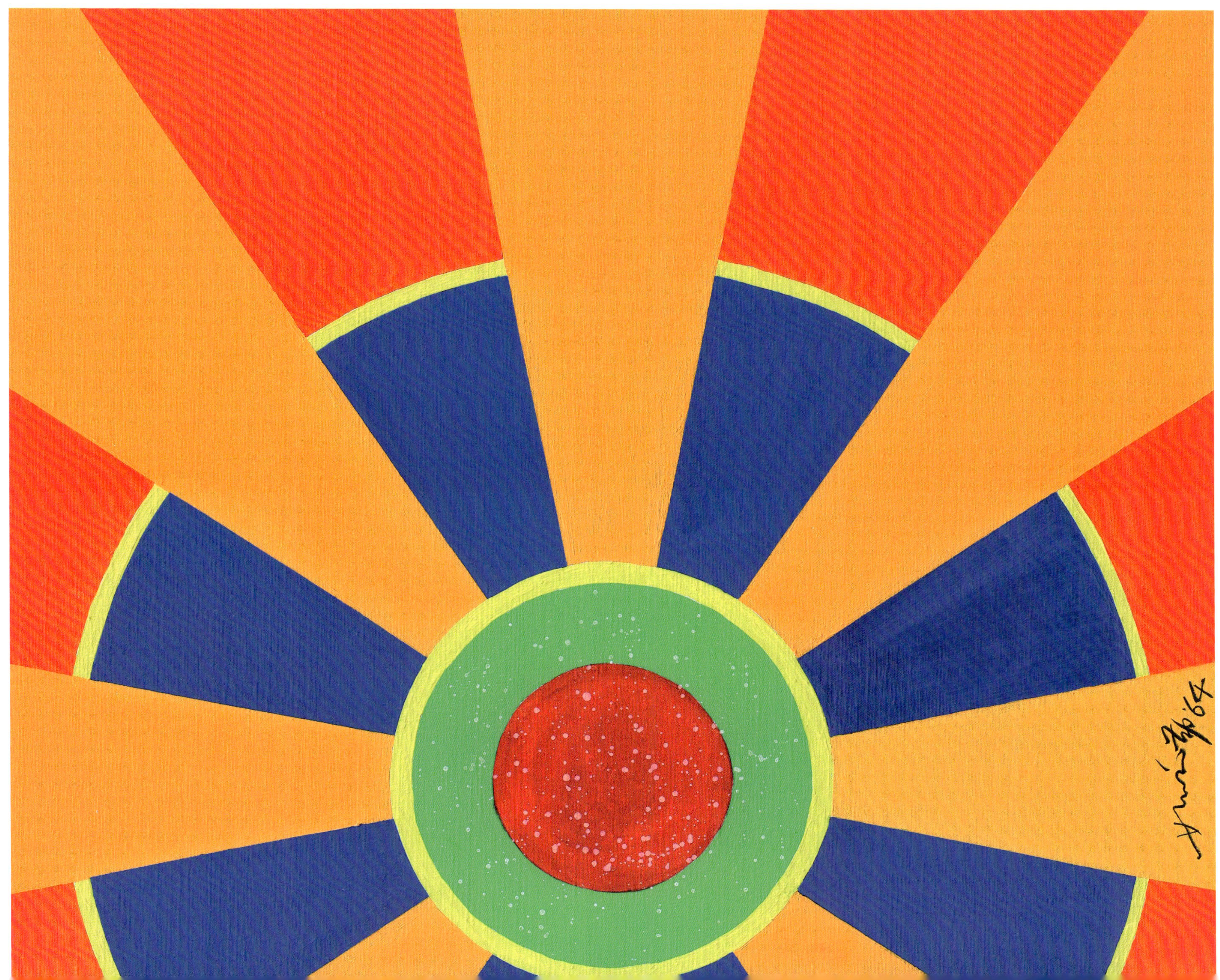

Hsiao Chin
Dancing Light-18, 1964
Acrylic on canvas
110 x 140cm

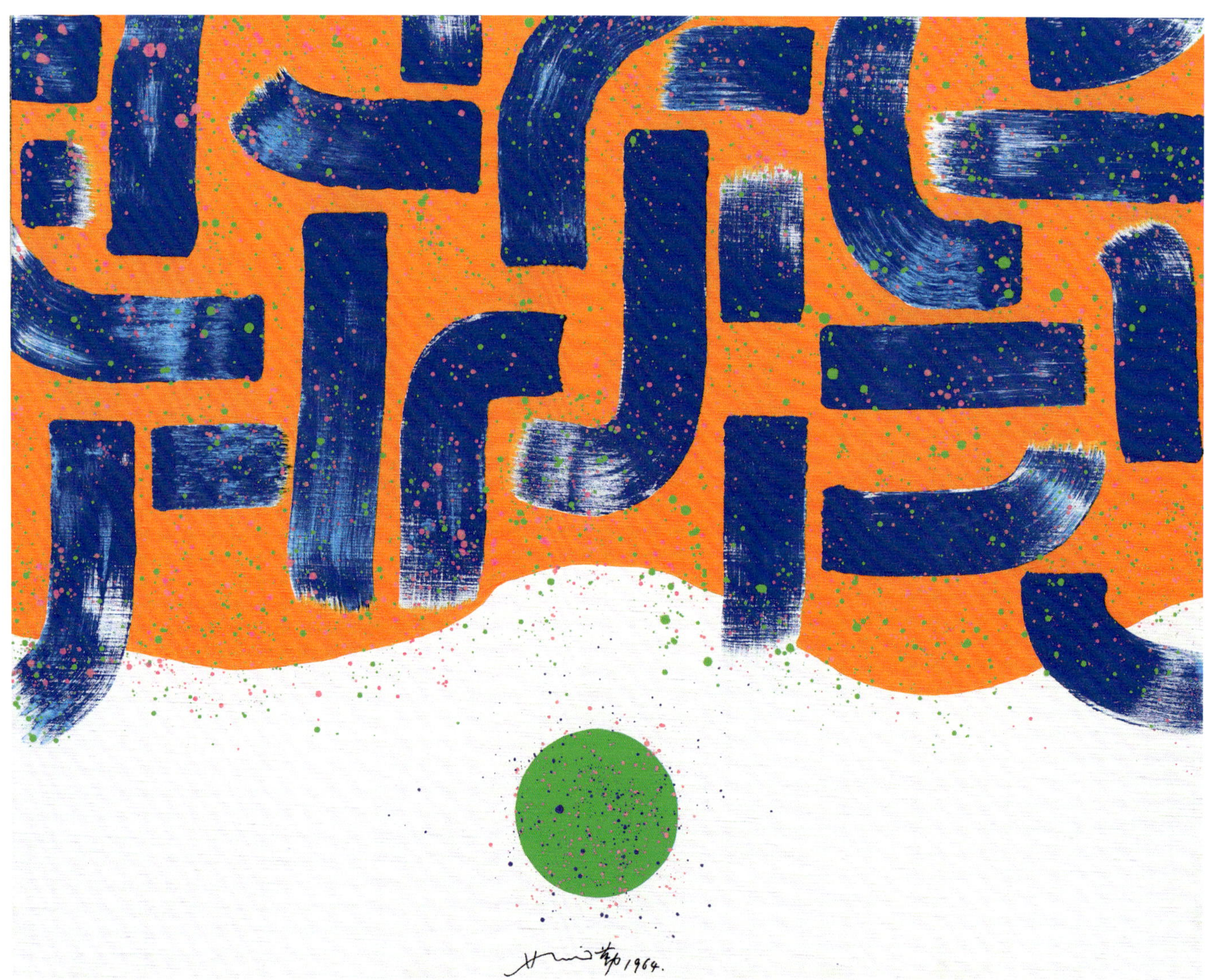

Hsiao Chin
Dancing Light-19, 1964
Acrylic on canvas
110 x 140cm

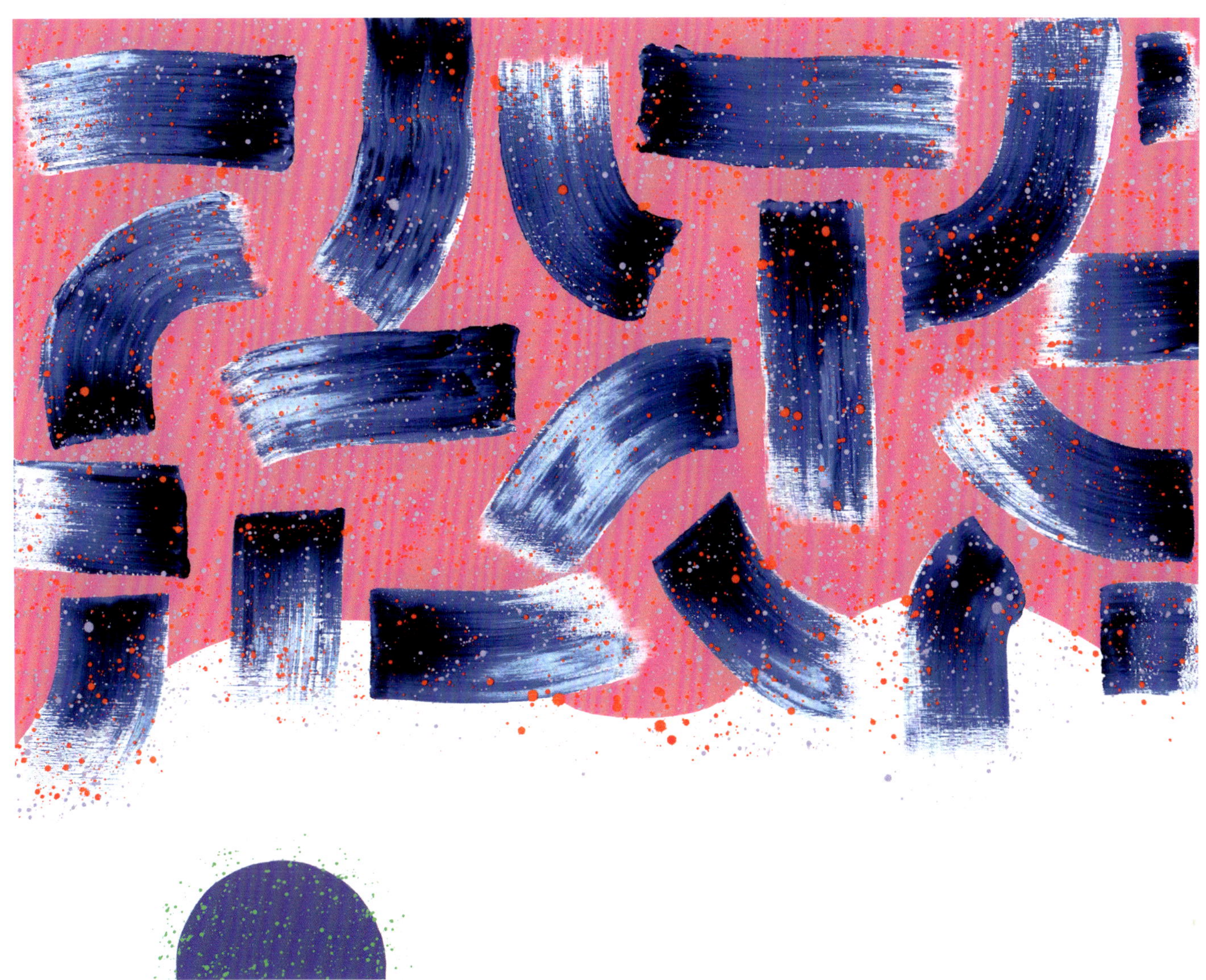

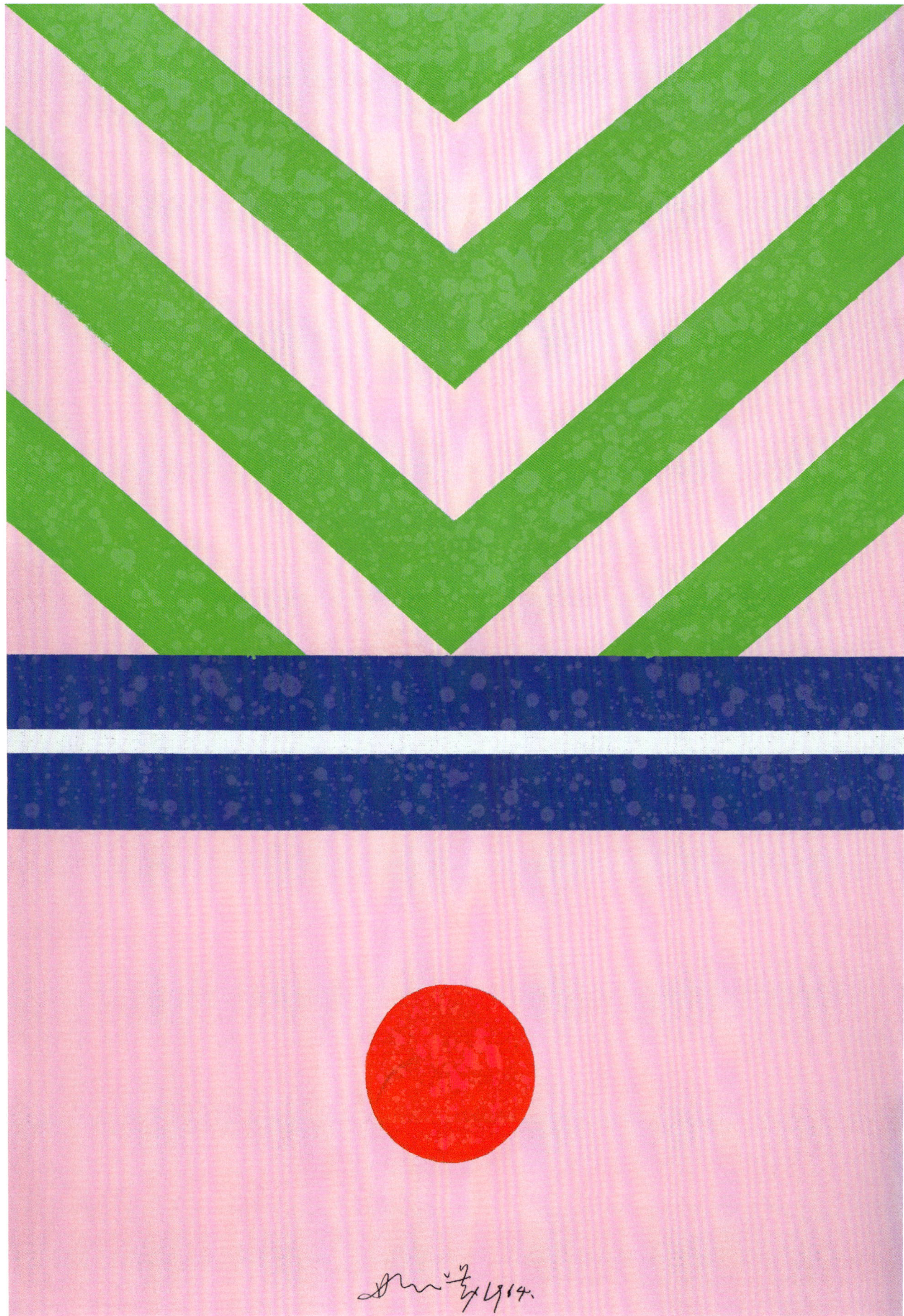

Hsiao Chin
Hope, 1964
Acrylic on canvas
100 x 70cm

Hsiao Chin
Energy Gathering, 1965
Acrylic and ink on canvas
110 x 90cm

Hsiao Chin
La forza della meditazione
1964
Acrylic on canvas
160 x 130cm

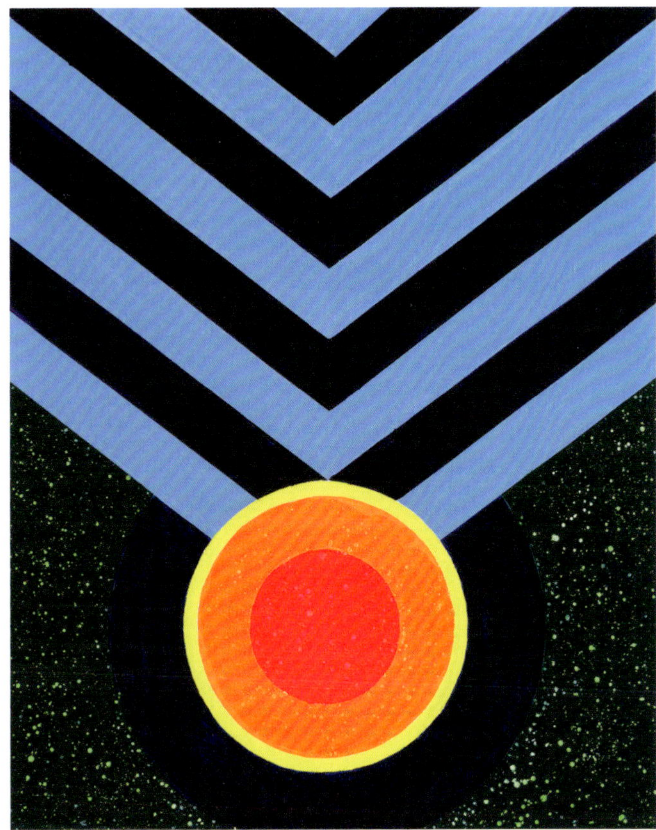

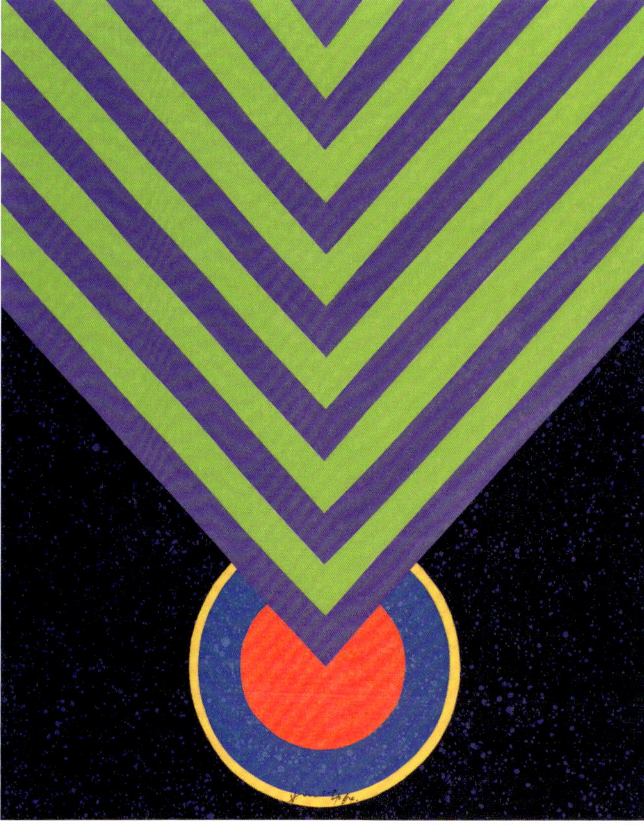

Hsiao Chin
The Vibration of Sun
(La Vibrazione del Sole), 1965
Acrylic on canvas
140 x 290cm

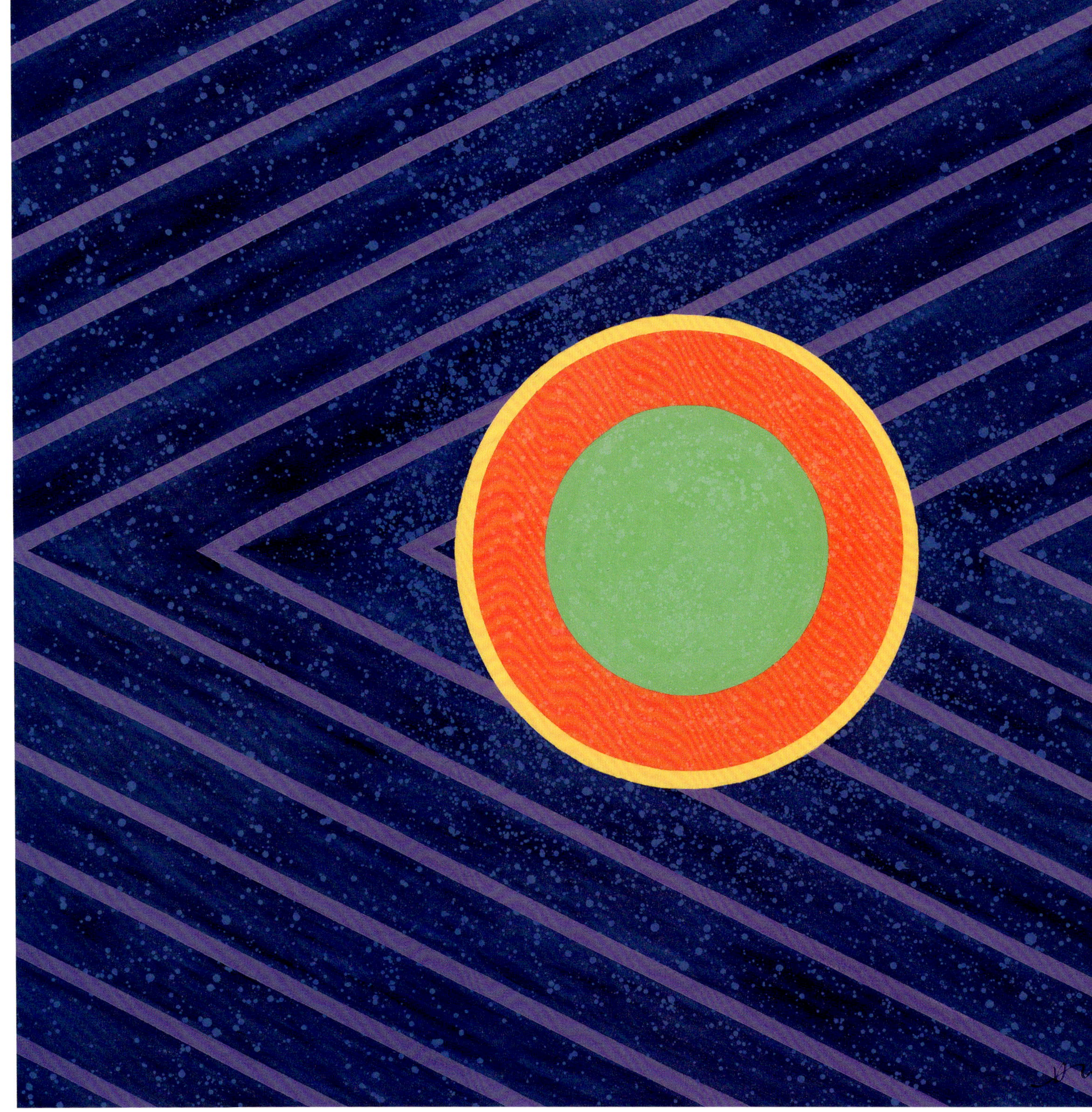

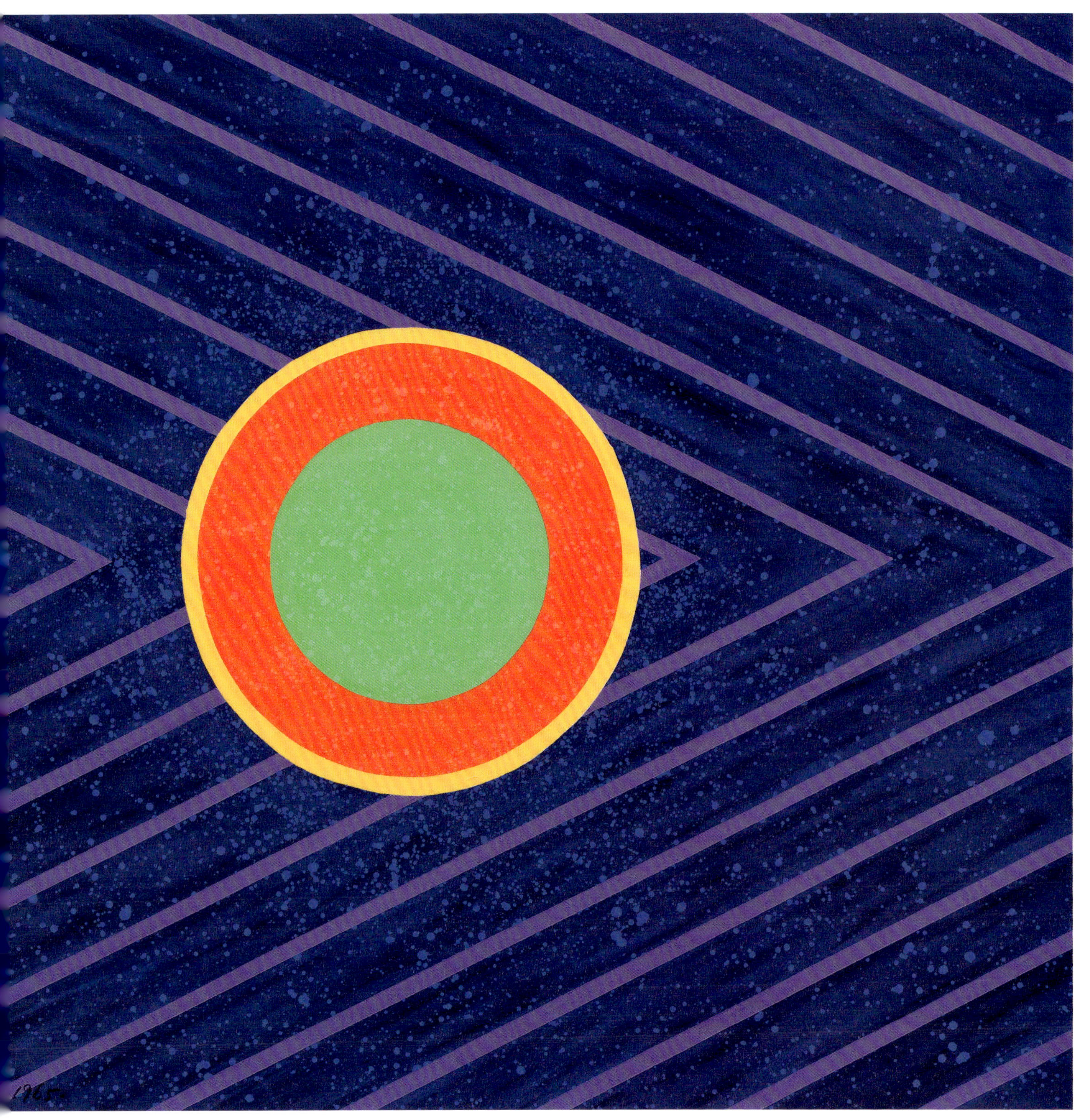

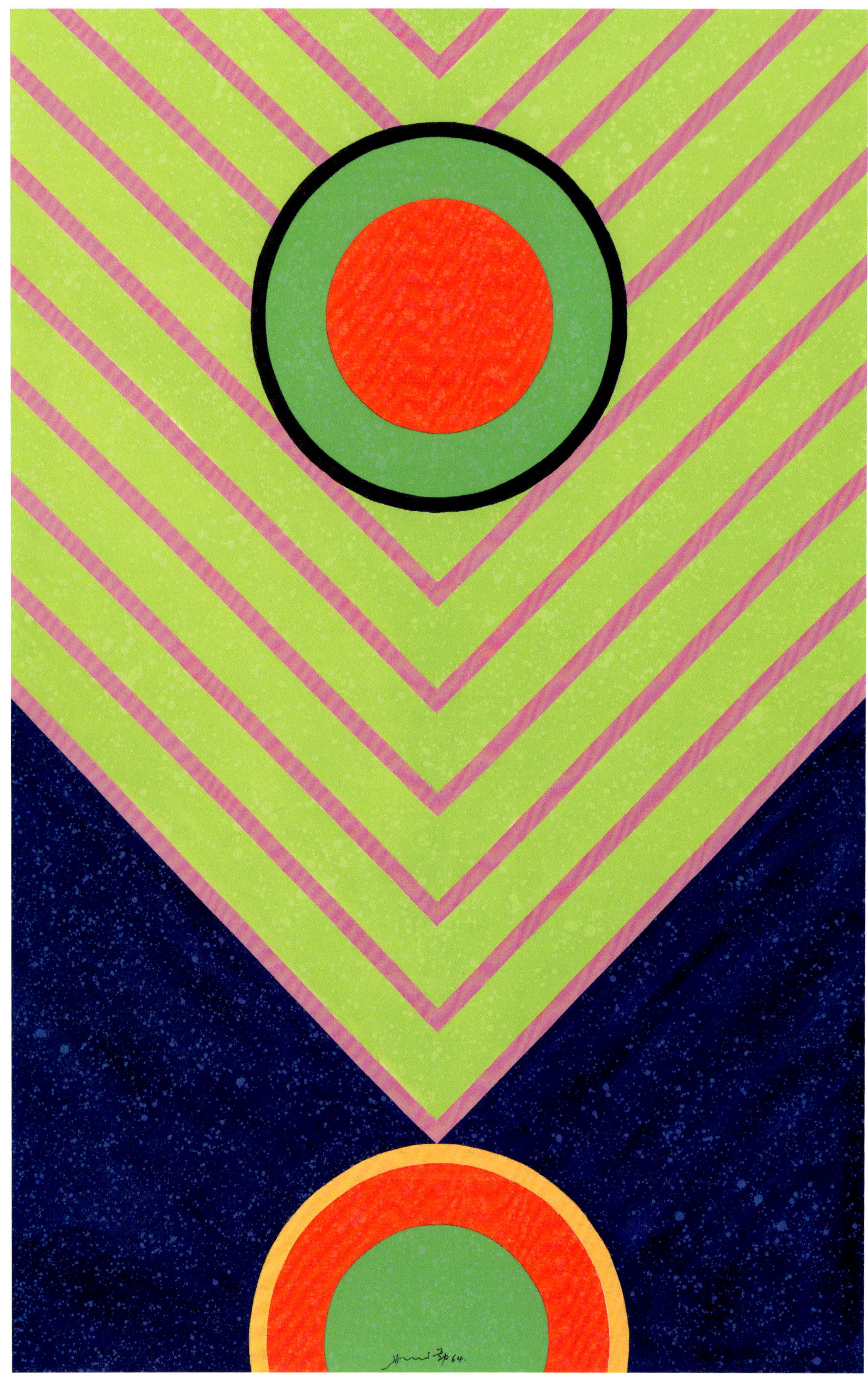

Hsiao Chin
Light of Hope, 1964
Acrylic on canvas
200 x 130cm

Hsiao Chin
Expansion, 1965
Acrylic on canvas
110 x 90cm

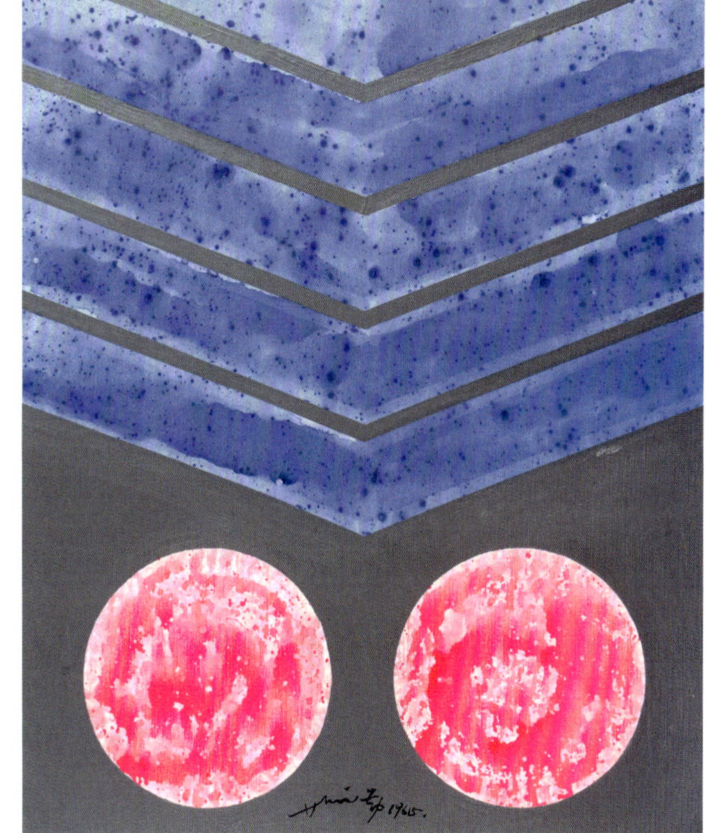

Hsiao Chin
Expansion of Force, 1965
Acrylic on canvas
102 x 133cm

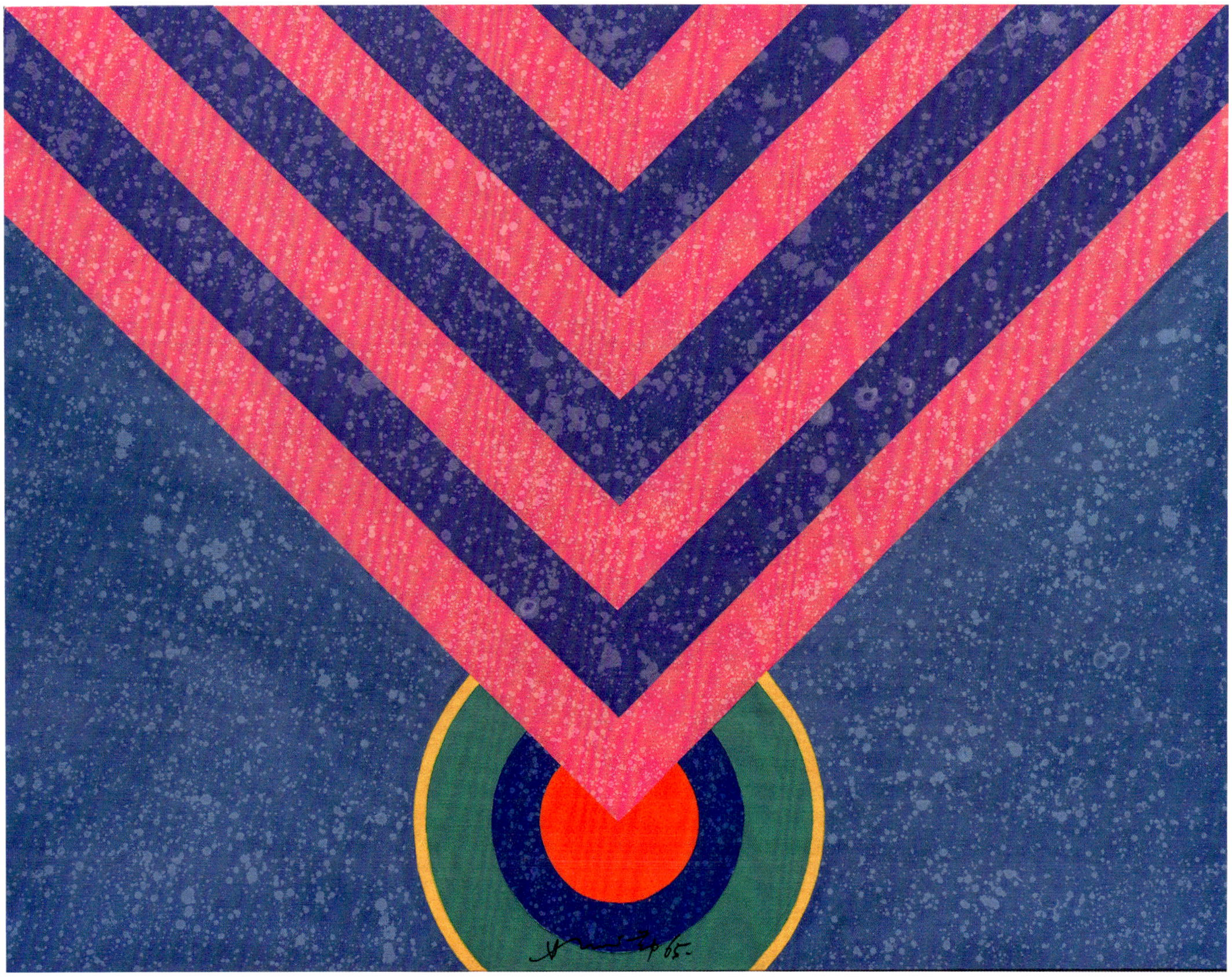

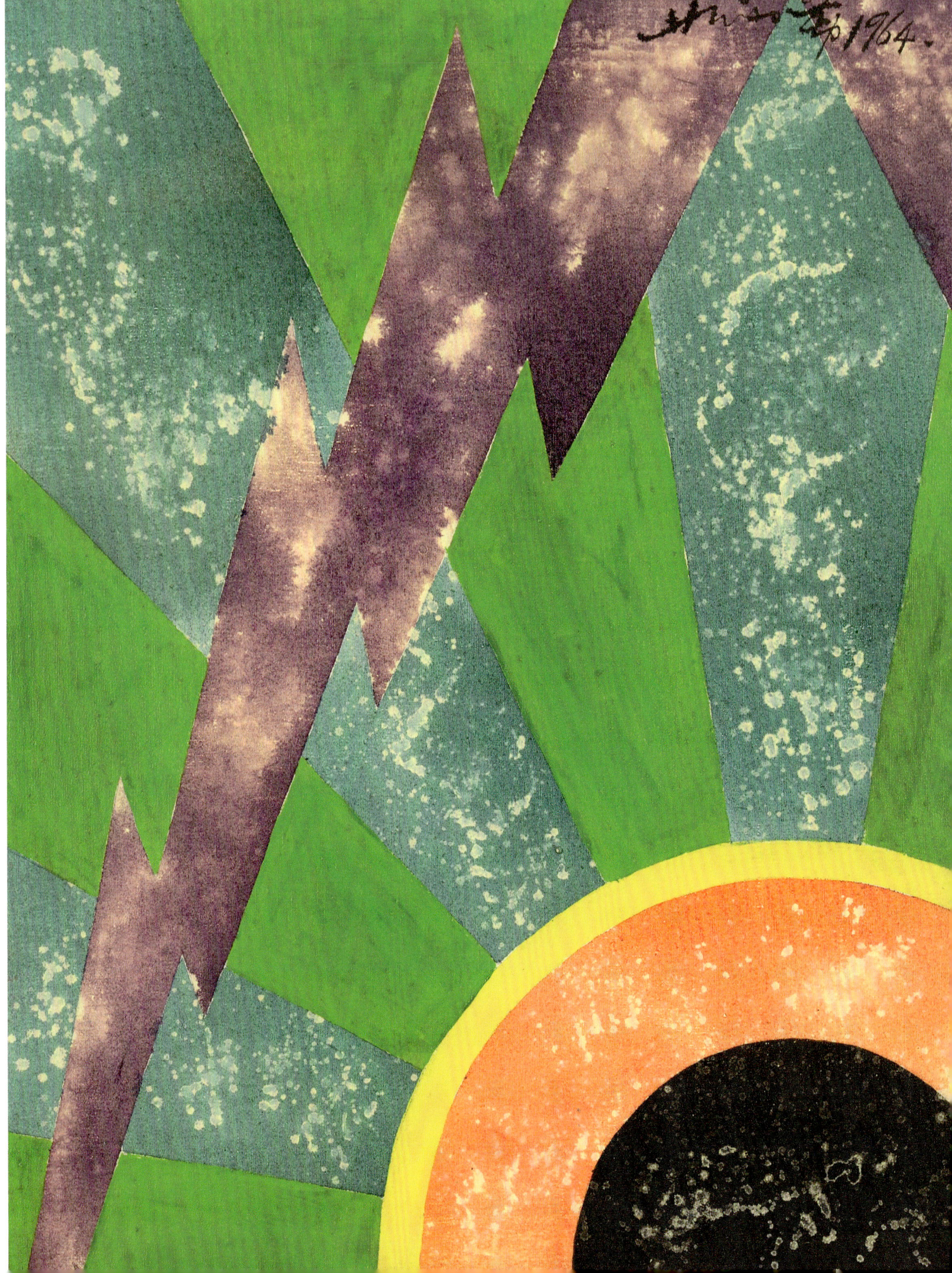

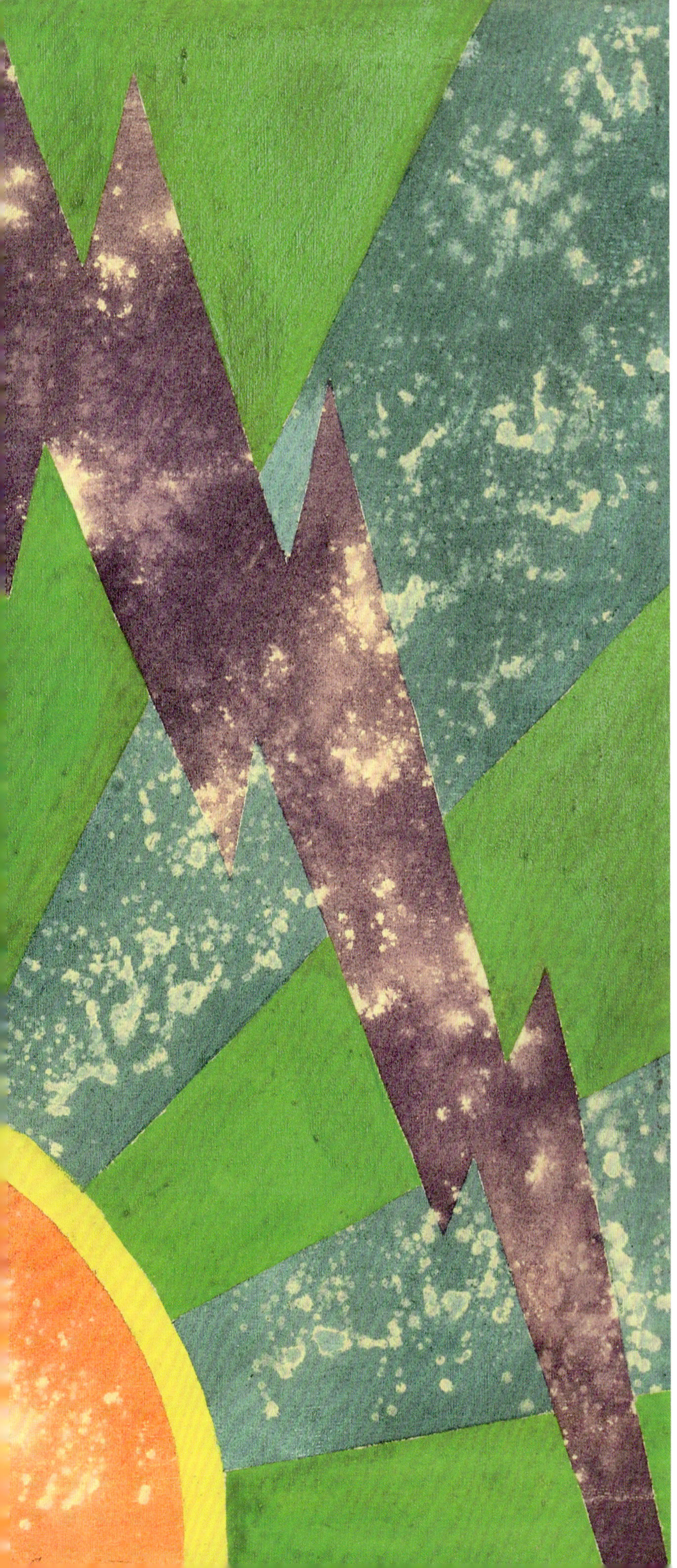

Hsiao Chin
Auuum!!!
1964
Acrylic on canvas
80 x 100cm

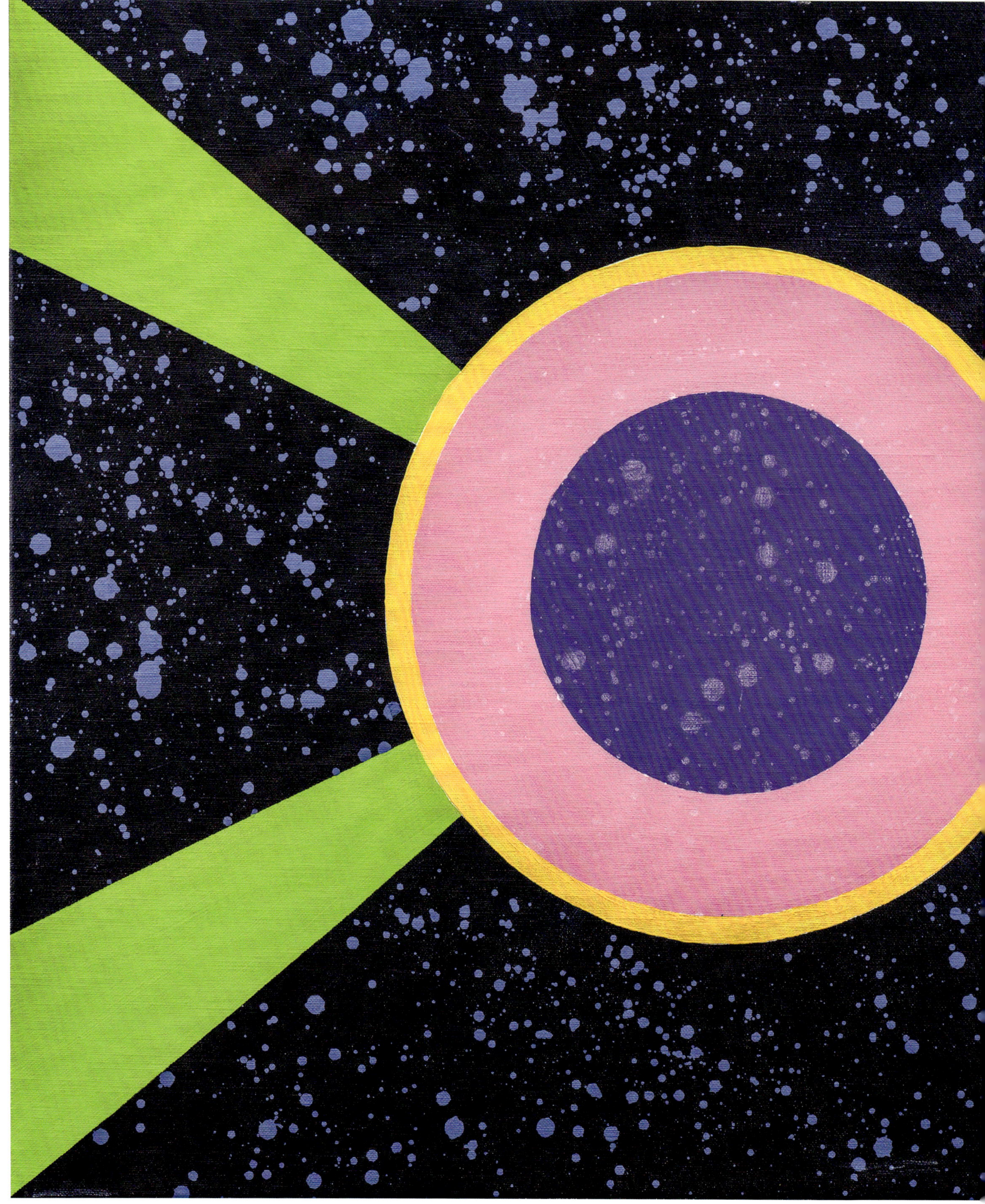

Hsiao Chin
Radiation (La proiezione)
1965
Acrylic on canvas
70 x 85cm

Hsiao Chin
The Sun-9, 1964
Acrylic and ink on canvas
110 x 140cm

Hsiao Chin
Sole con luce viola, 1965
Acrylic on canvas
110 x 140cm

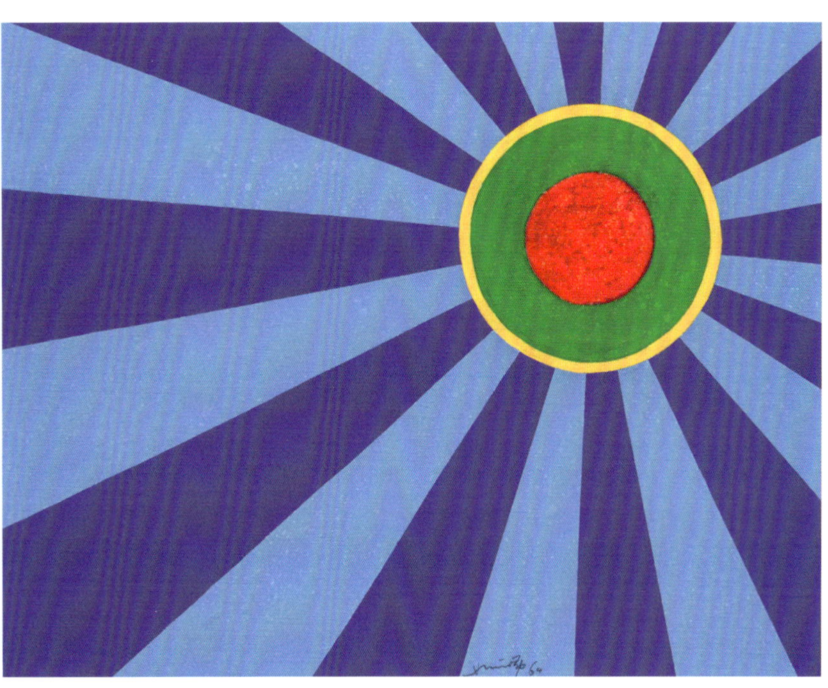

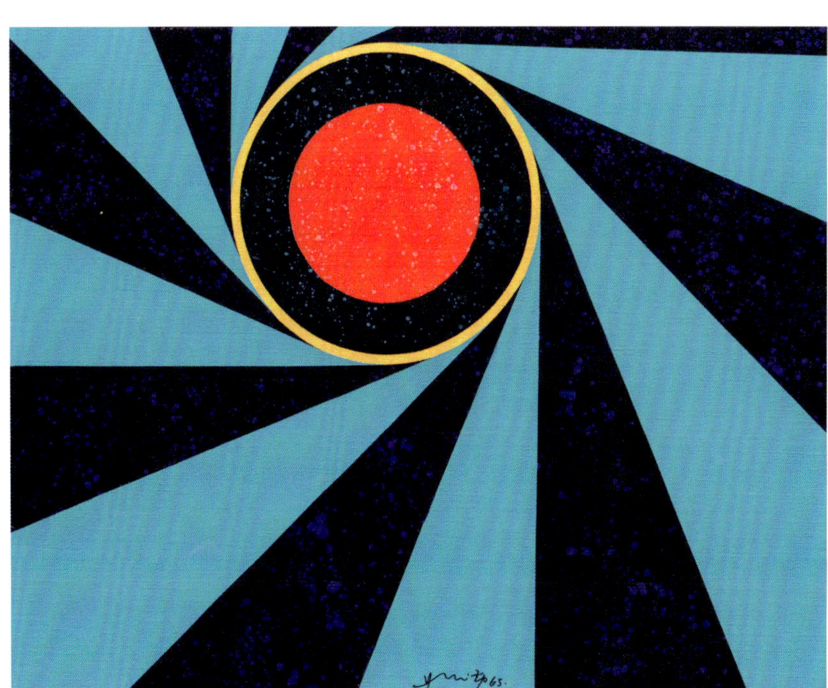

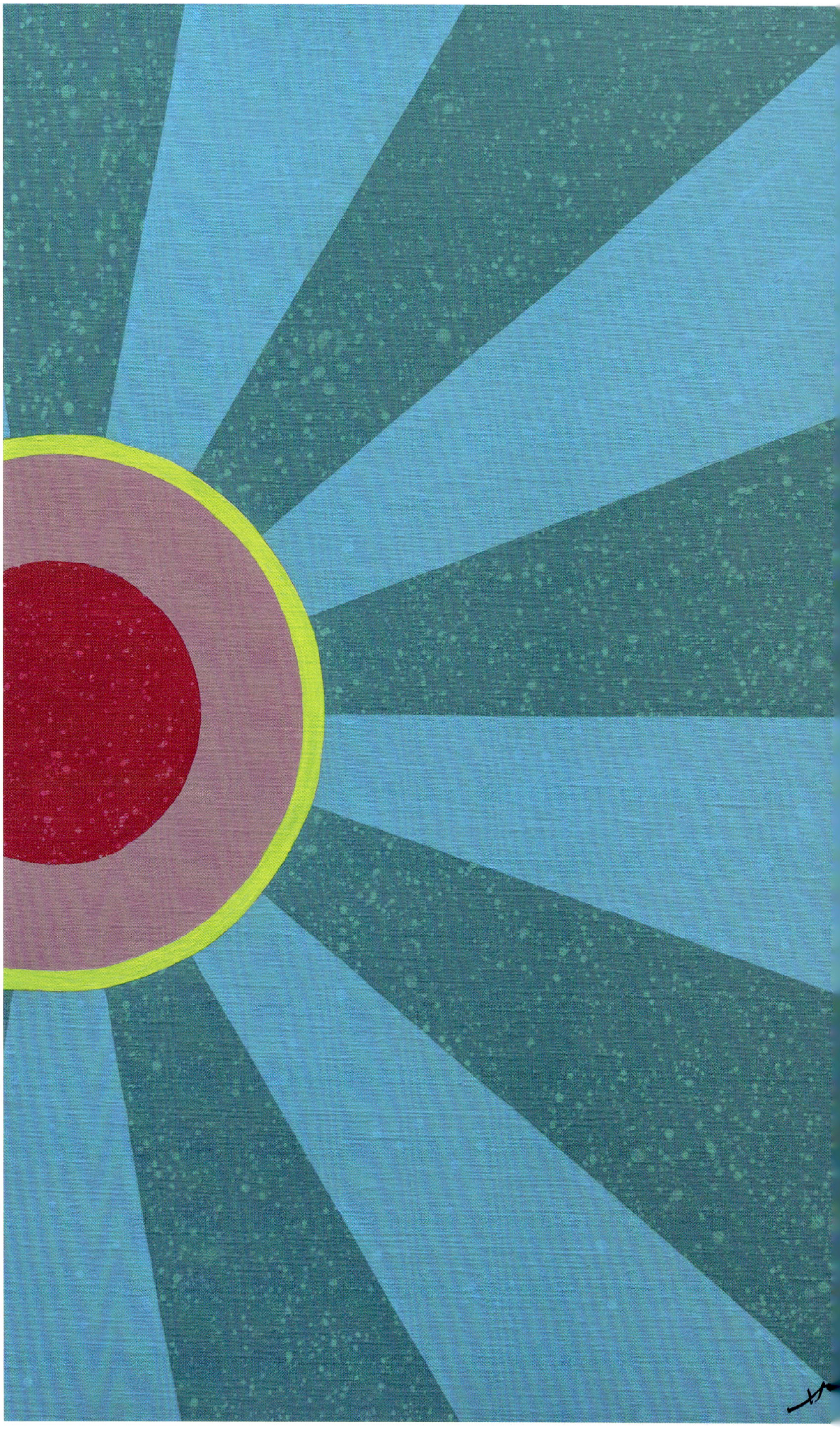

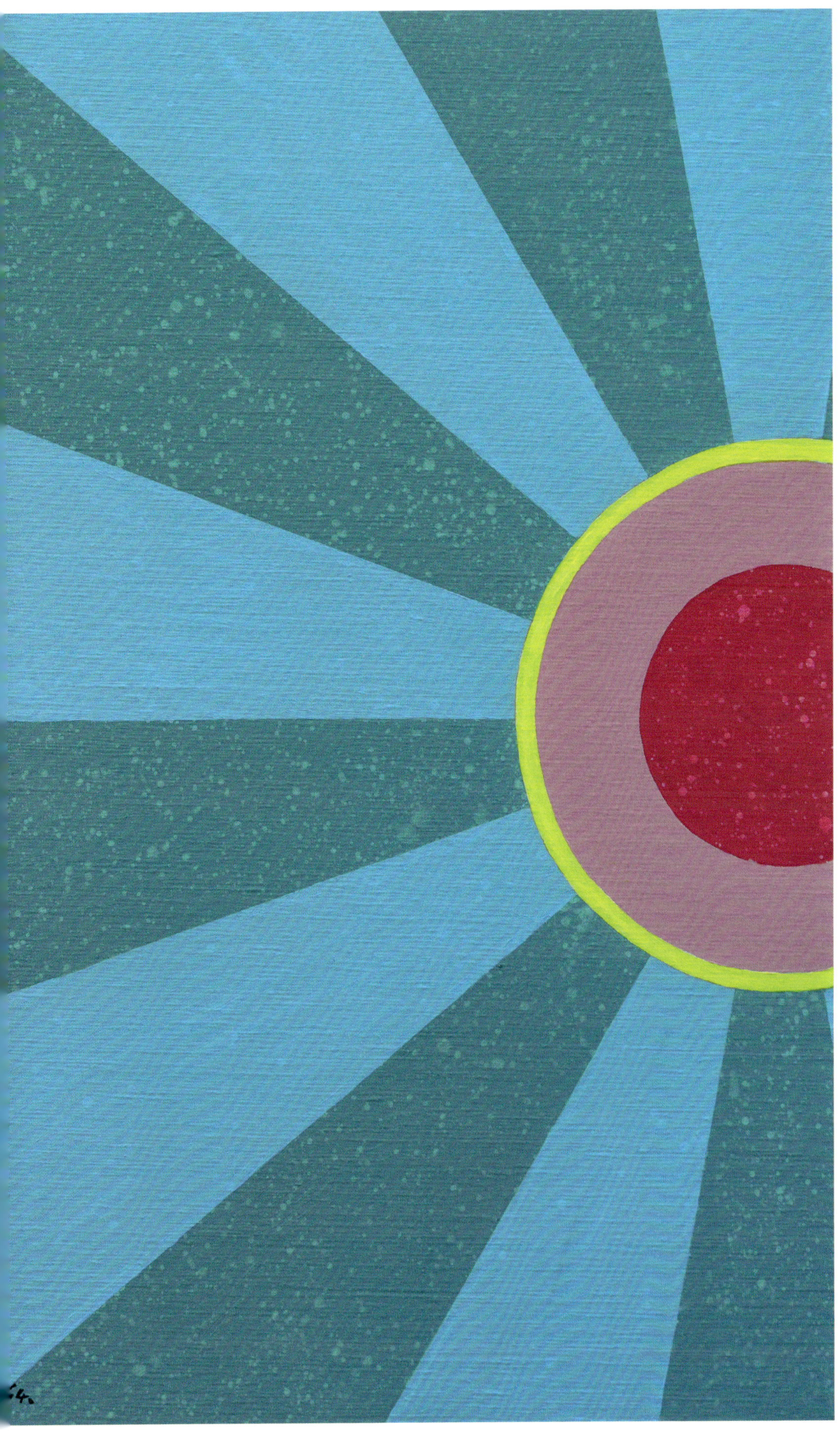

Hsiao Chin
La Luce della Riflessione
1964
Acrylic and ink on canvas
110 x 140cm

Hsiao Chin
The Illusion of Sun-1, 1965
Acrylic on canvas
130 x 160cm

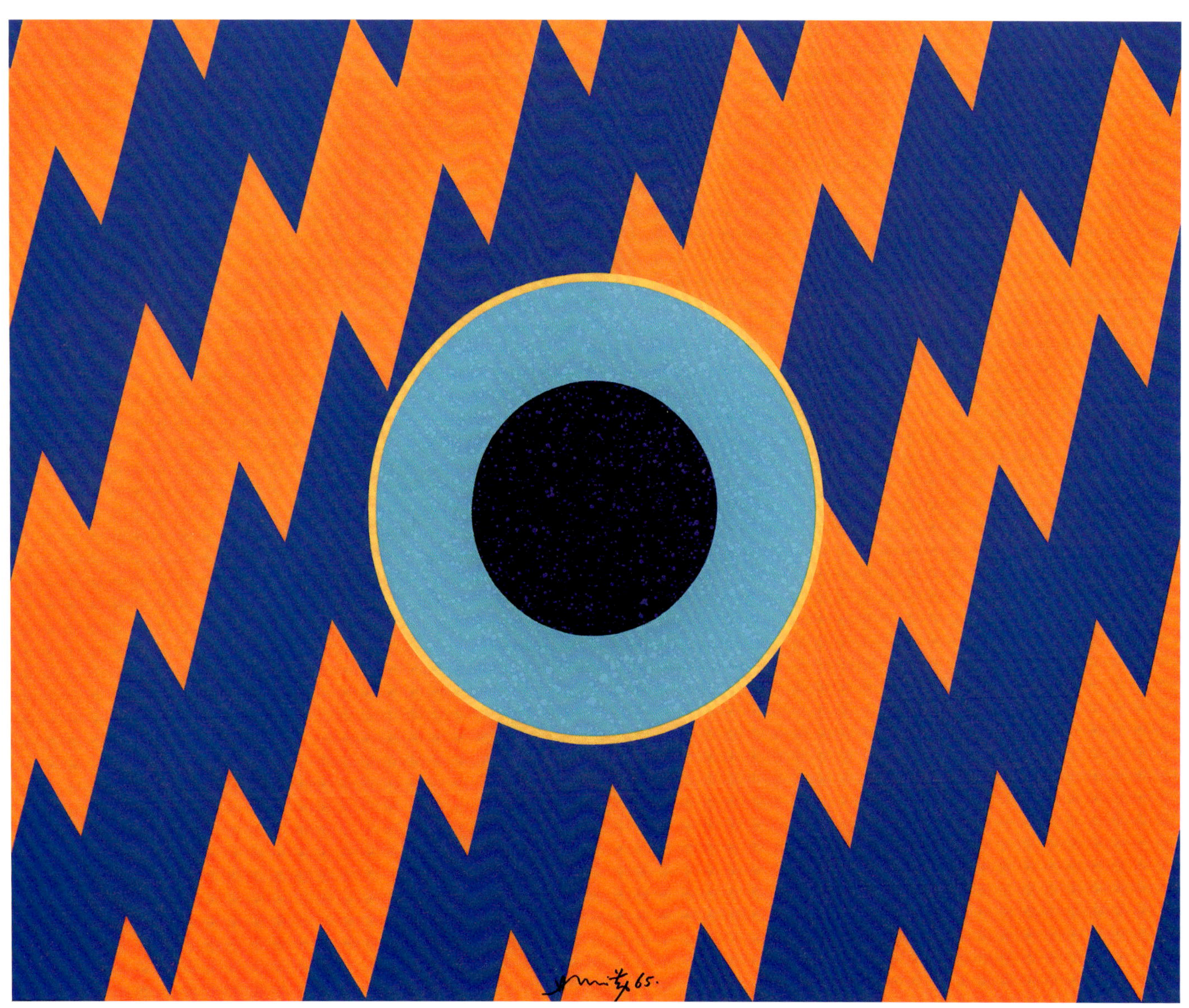

Hsiao Chin
The Illusion of Sun-2, 1965
Acrylic on canvas
130 x 160cm

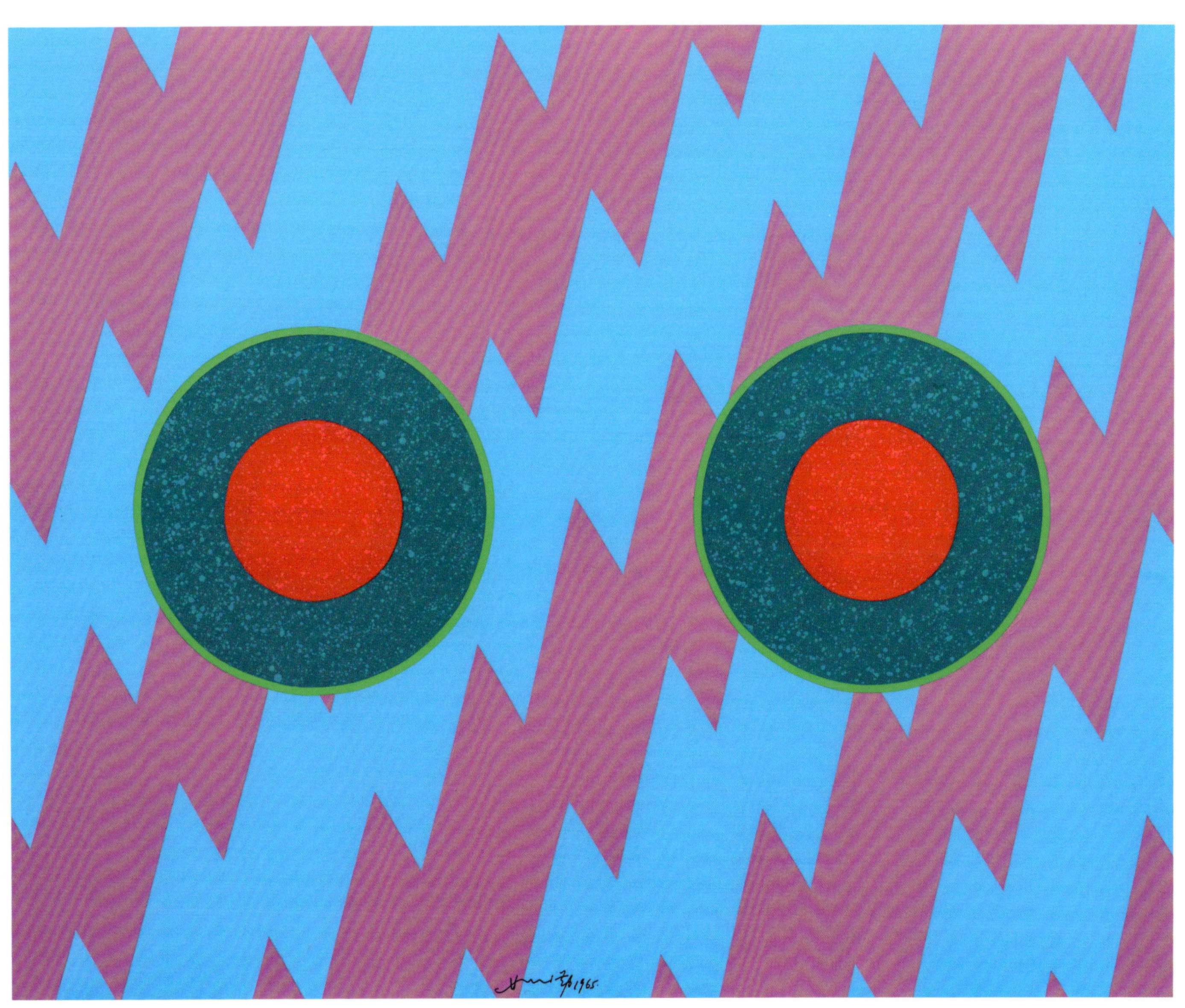

Hsiao Chin
The Universe Projection-3
(La proiezione dell'universo-3)
1965
Acrylic and ink on canvas
100 x 140cm

Hsiao Chin
The Universe Projection-2
(La proiezione dell'universo-2)
1965
Acrylic and ink on canvas
140 x 200cm

Hsiao Chin
The Universe Projection-1
(La proiezione dell'universo-1)
1965
Acrylic and ink on canvas
110 x 140cm

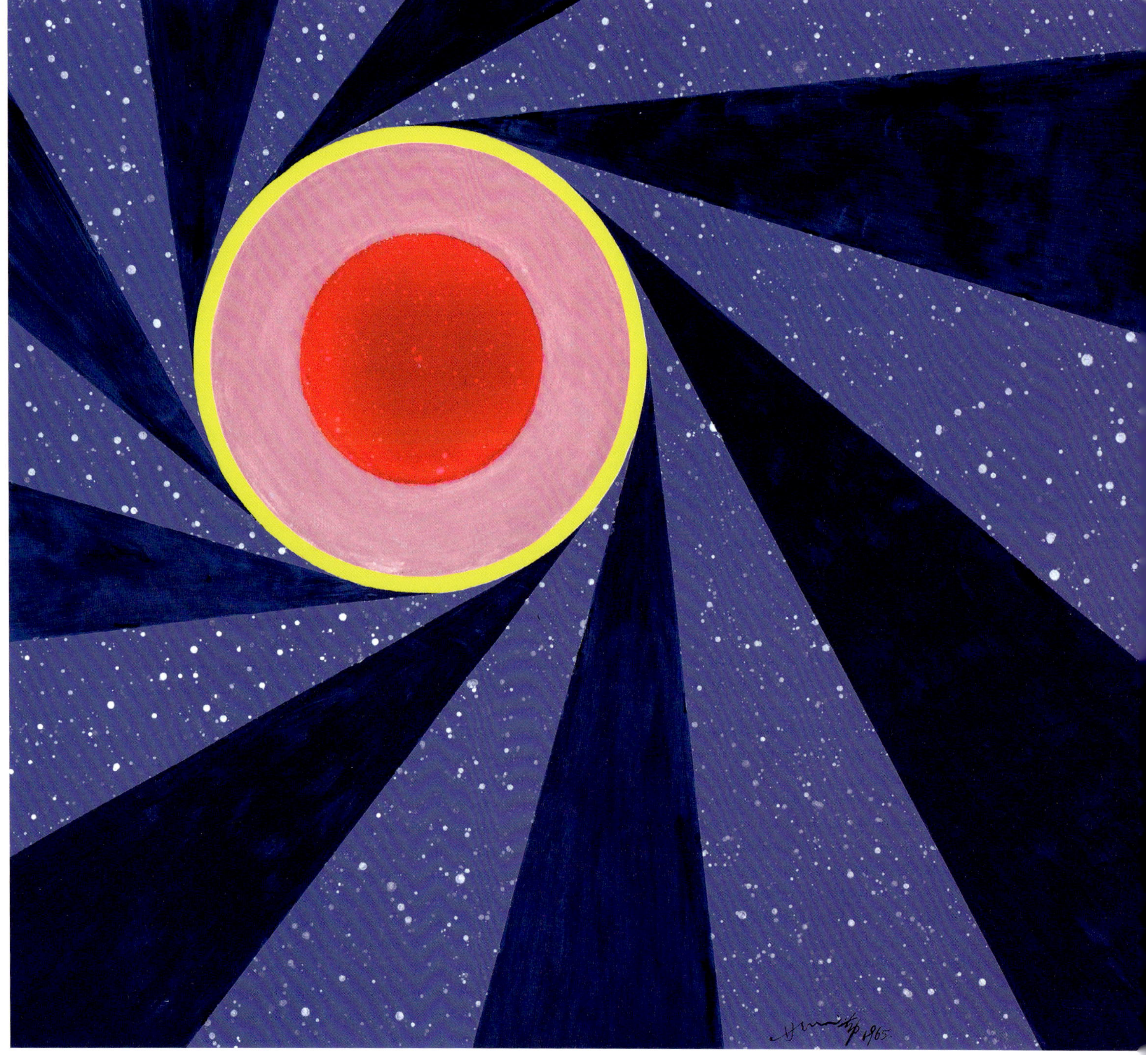

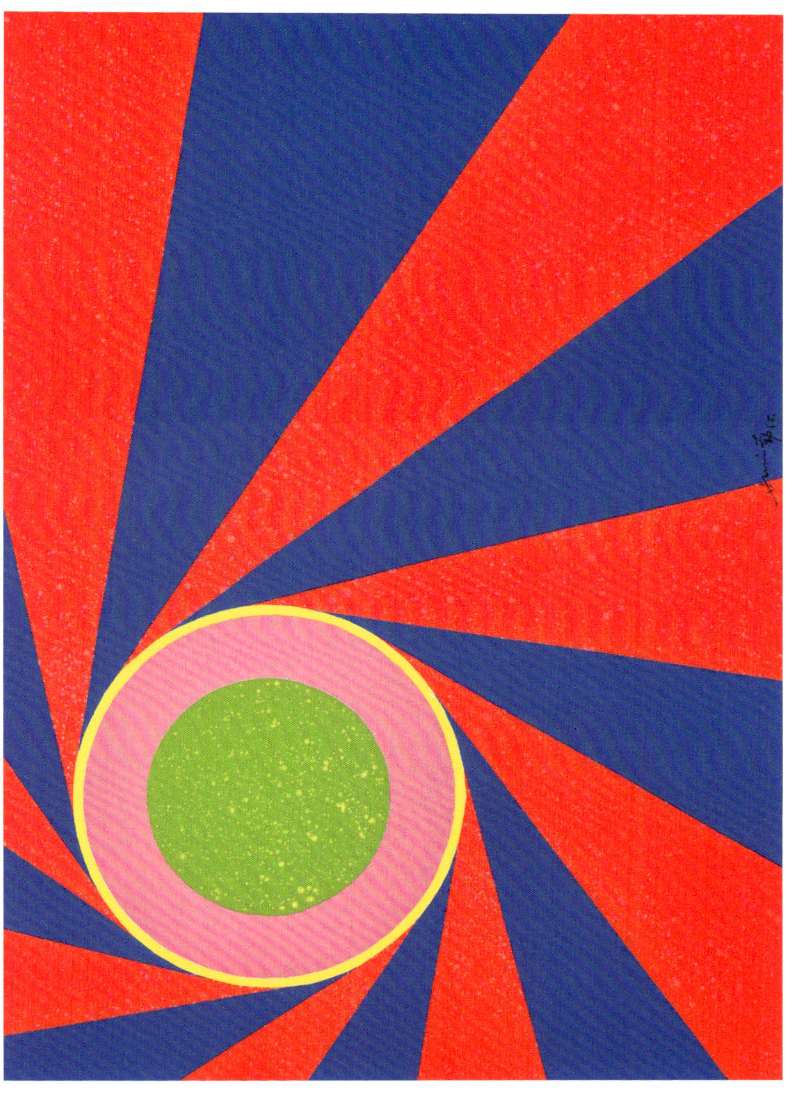

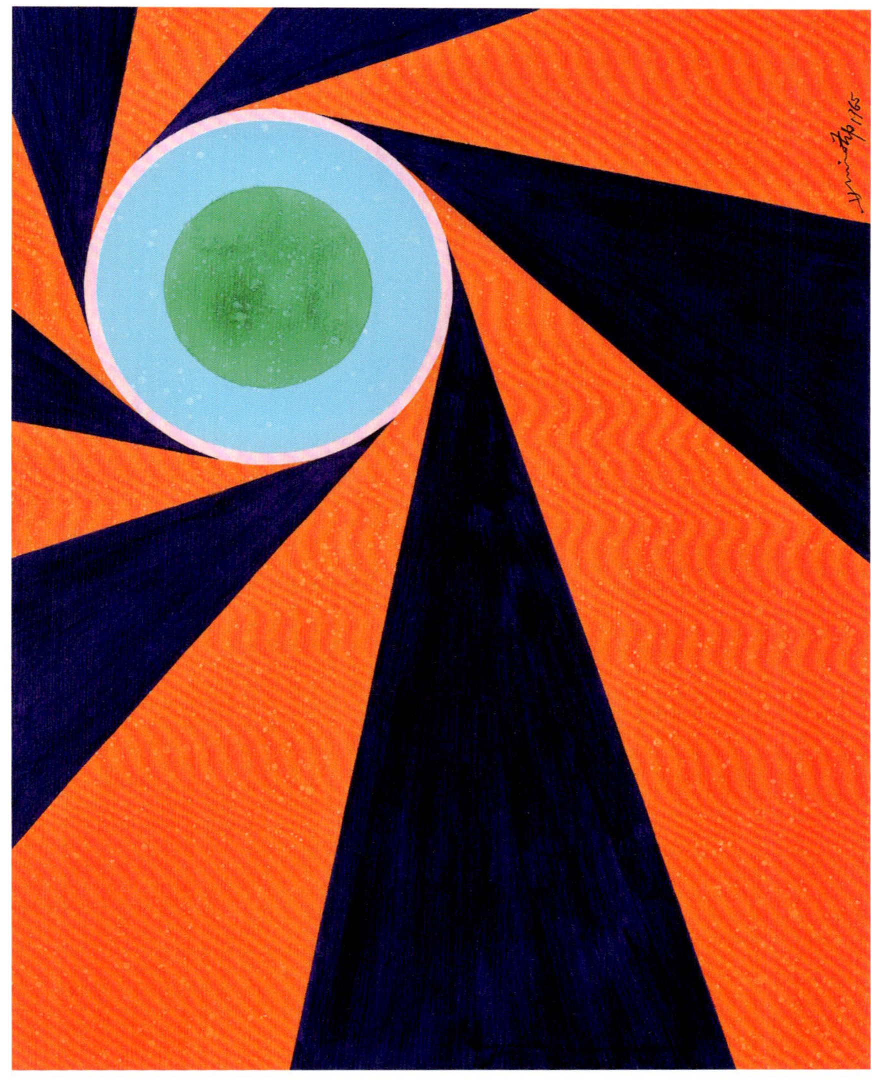

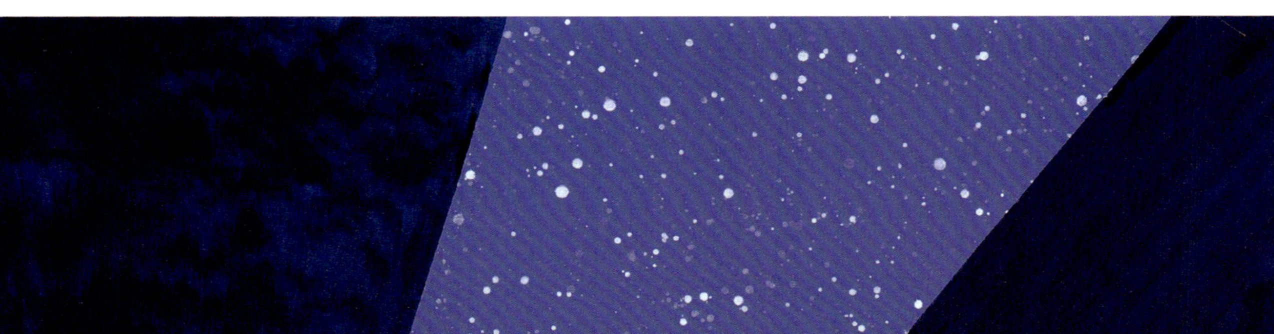

Hsiao Chin
L'illusione del potere
Universo, 1965
Acrylic on canvas
130 x 160cm

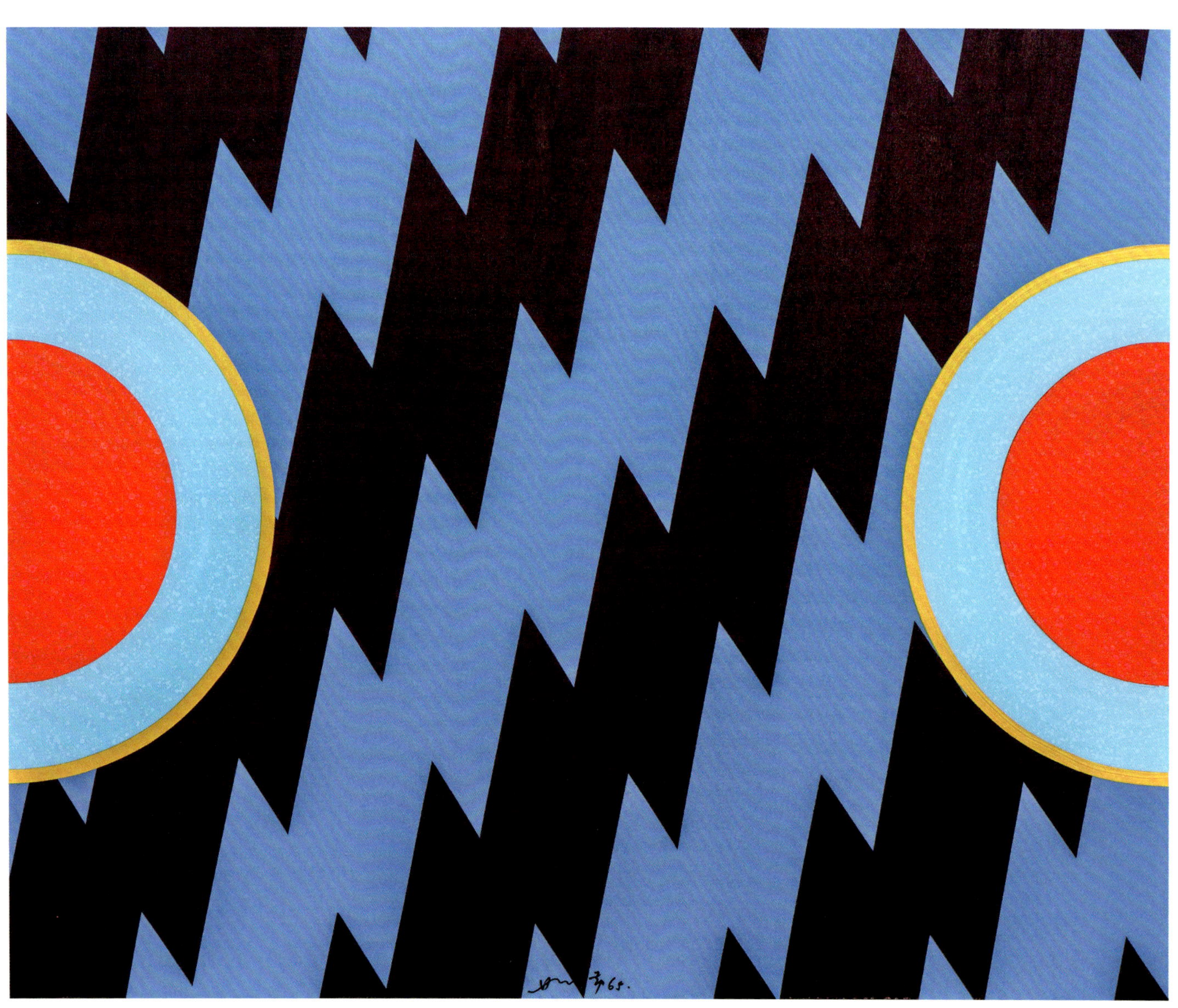

Hsiao Chin
La proiezione del potere
Universo, 1965
Acrylic on canvas
130 x 160cm

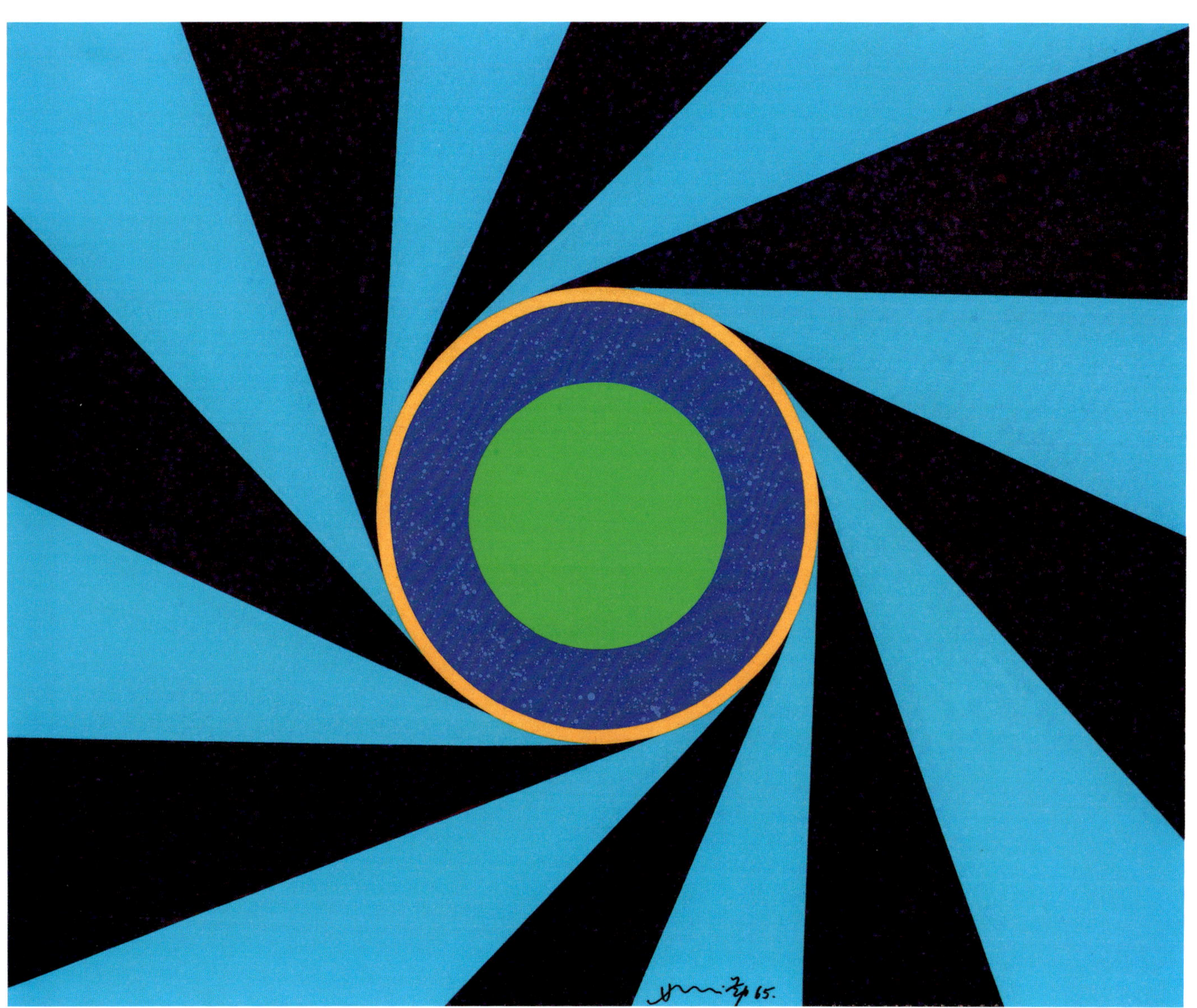

Hsiao Chin
Vibrazione Universale, 1965
Acrylic on canvas
140 x 290cm

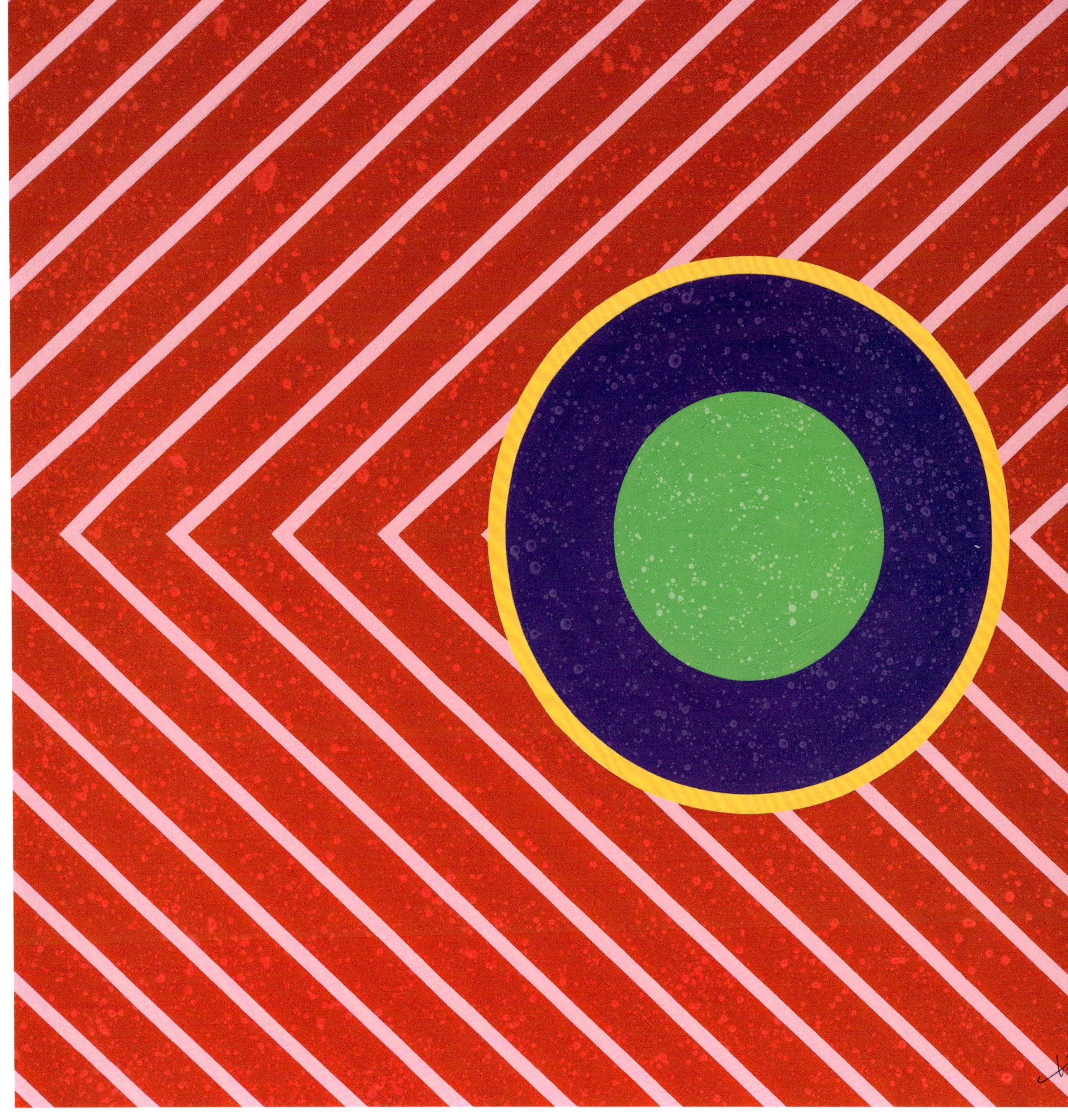

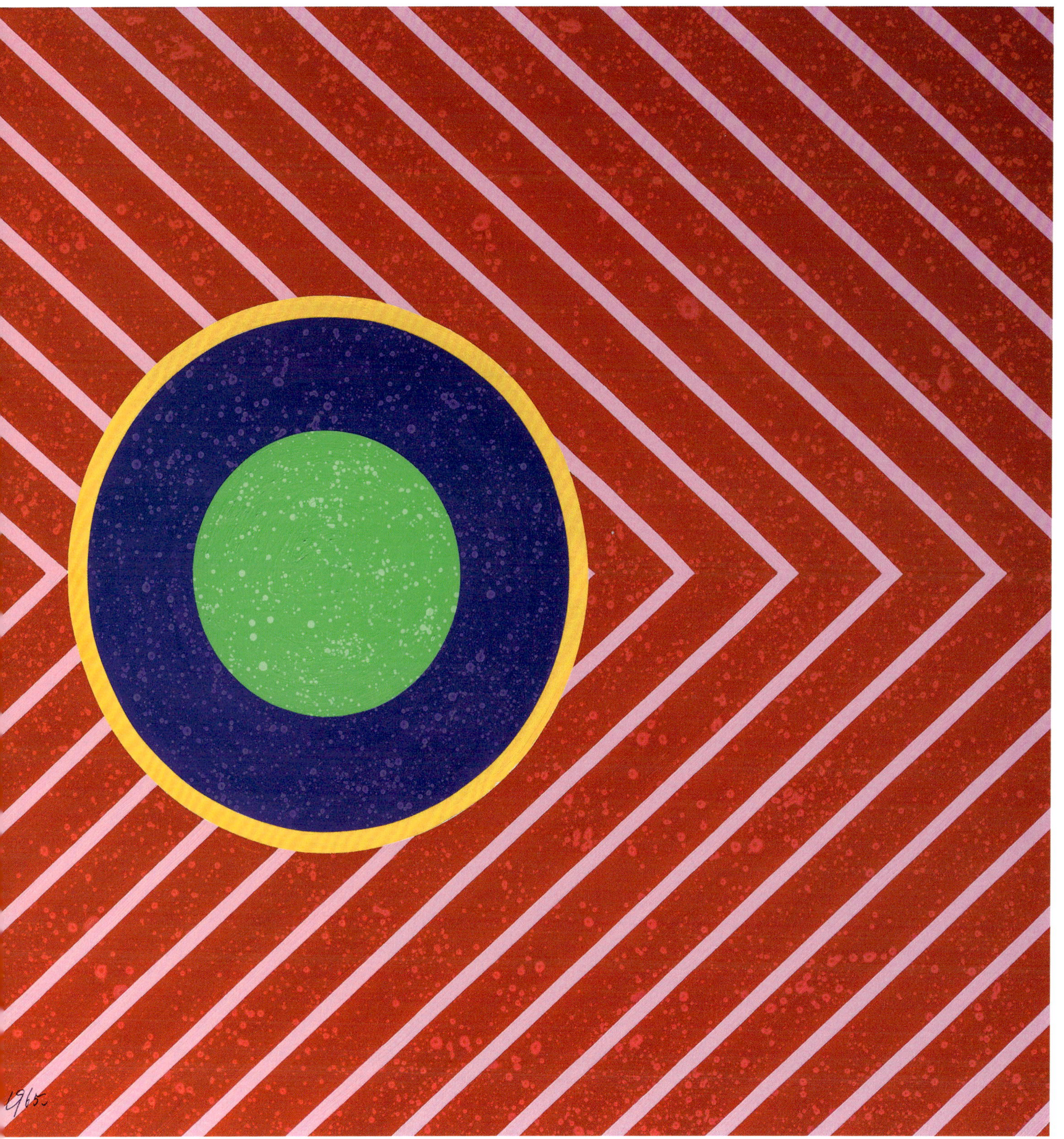

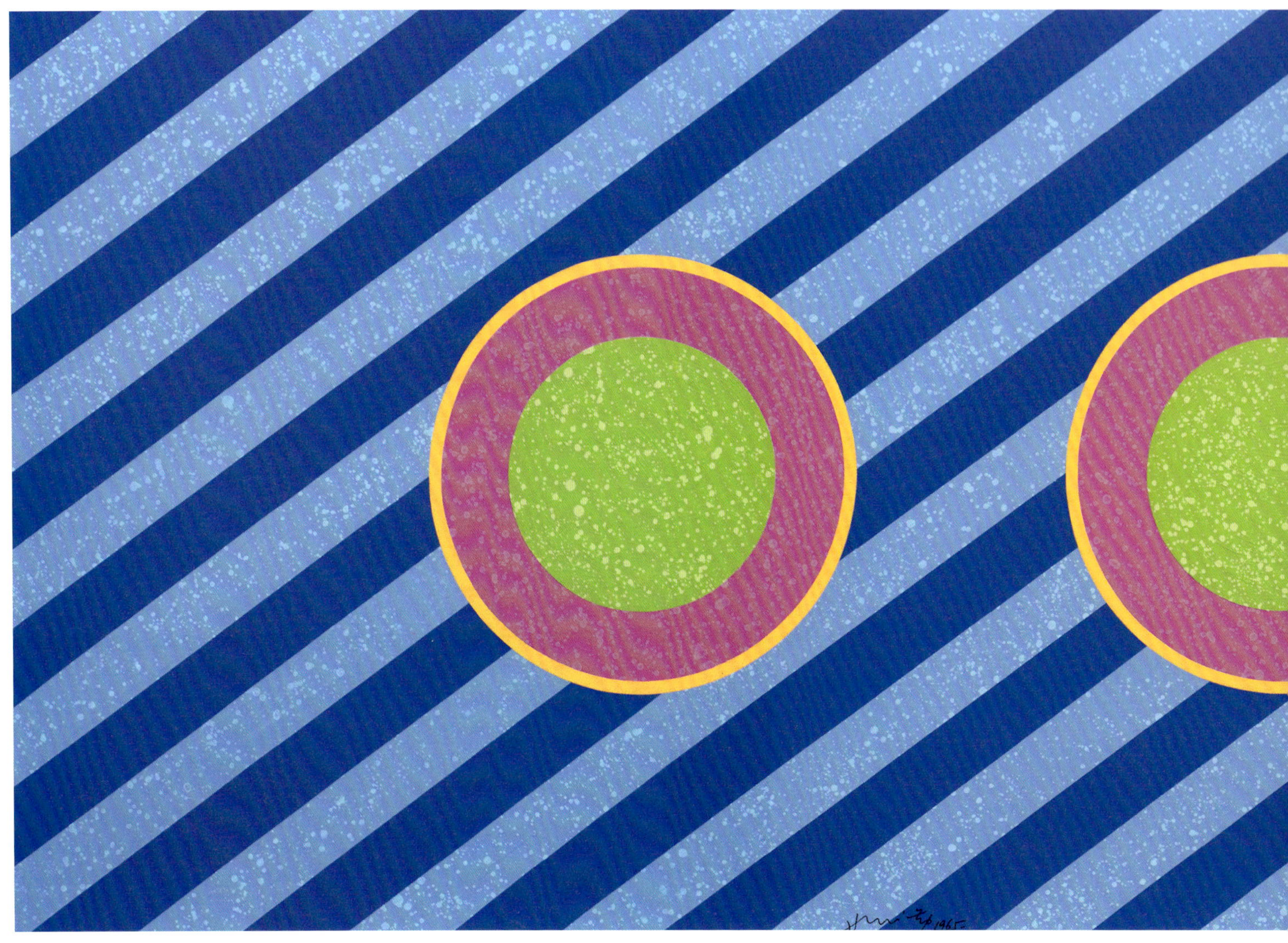

Hsiao Chin
Universal Vibration, 1965
Acrylic on canvas
140 × 290cm

Hsiao Chin
The Universe Projection-5
(La proiezione dell'universo-5)
1966
Acrylic on canvas
130 x 160cm

Hsiao Chin
The Universe Projection-6
(La proiezione dell'universo-6)
1966
Acrylic on canvas
130 x 160cm

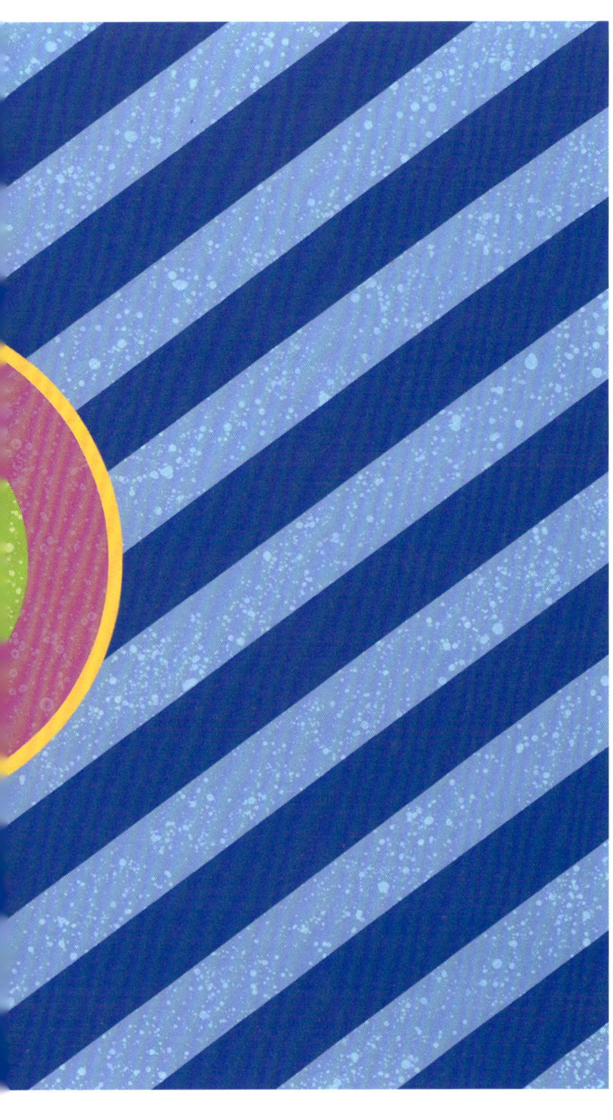

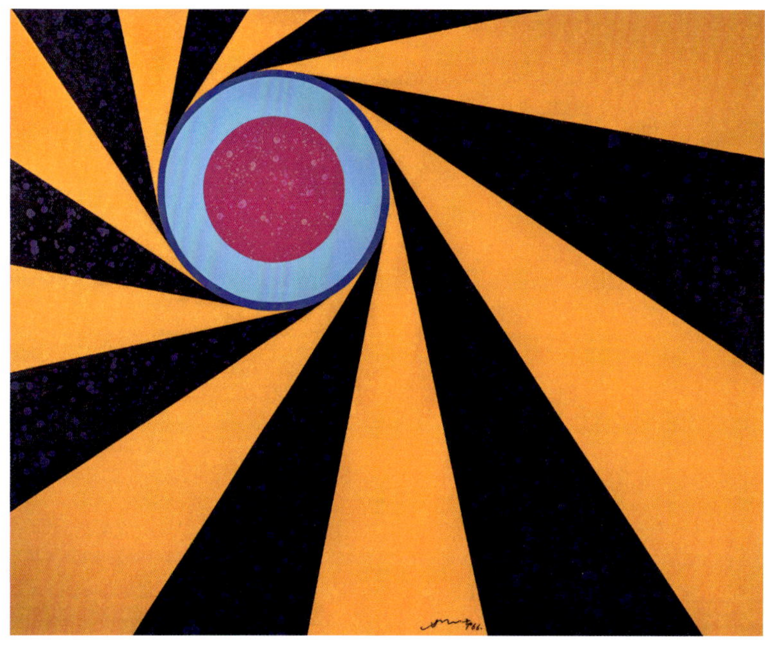

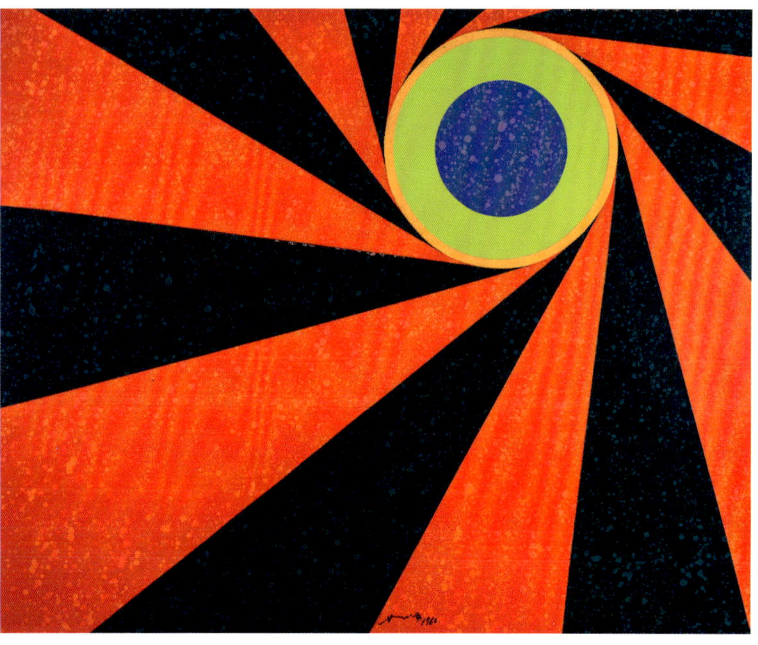

Hsiao Chin
Inner Light, 1966
Acrylic on canvas
102 x 133cm

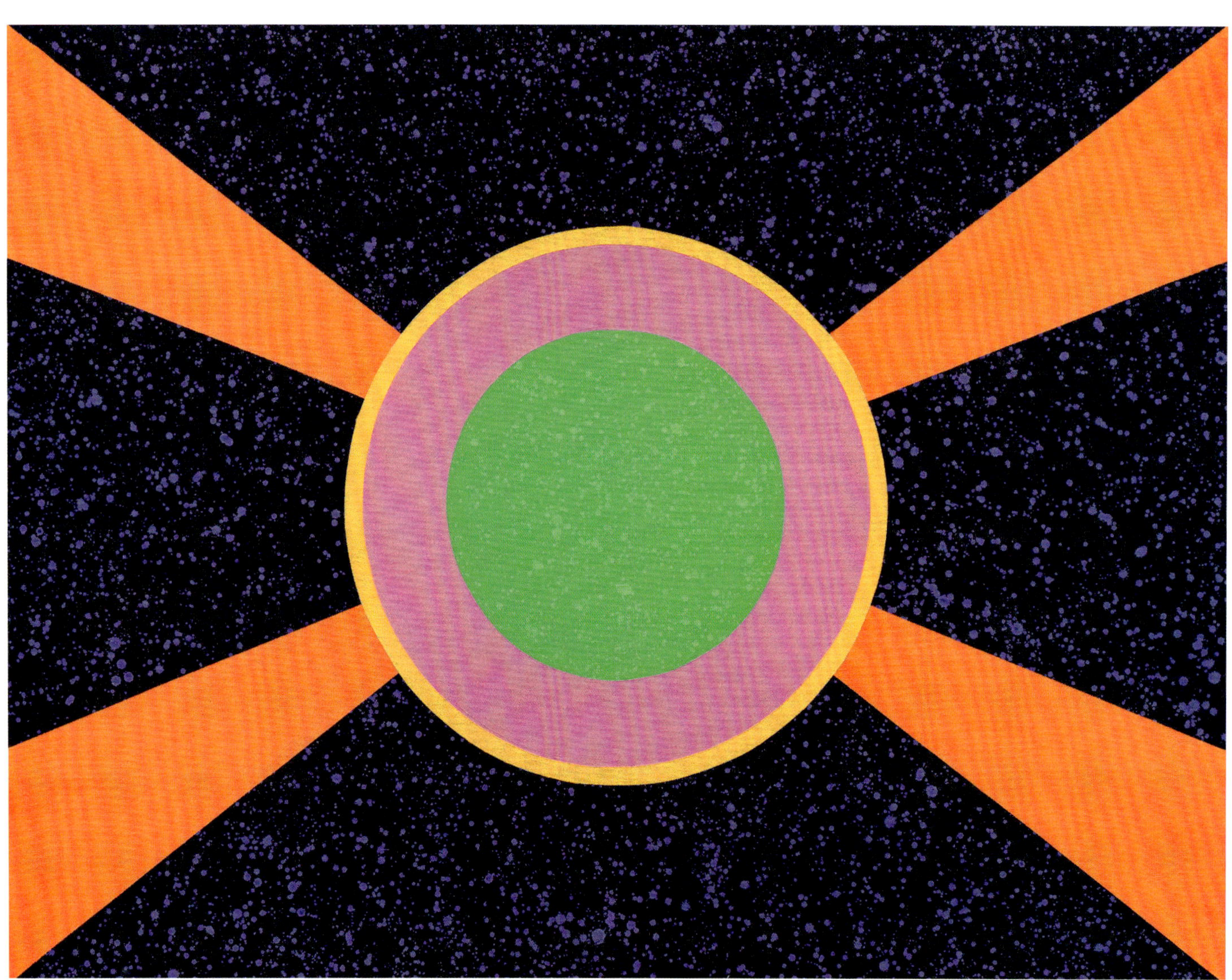

Hsiao Chin
The God from Origin, 1966
Acrylic on canvas
70 x 90cm

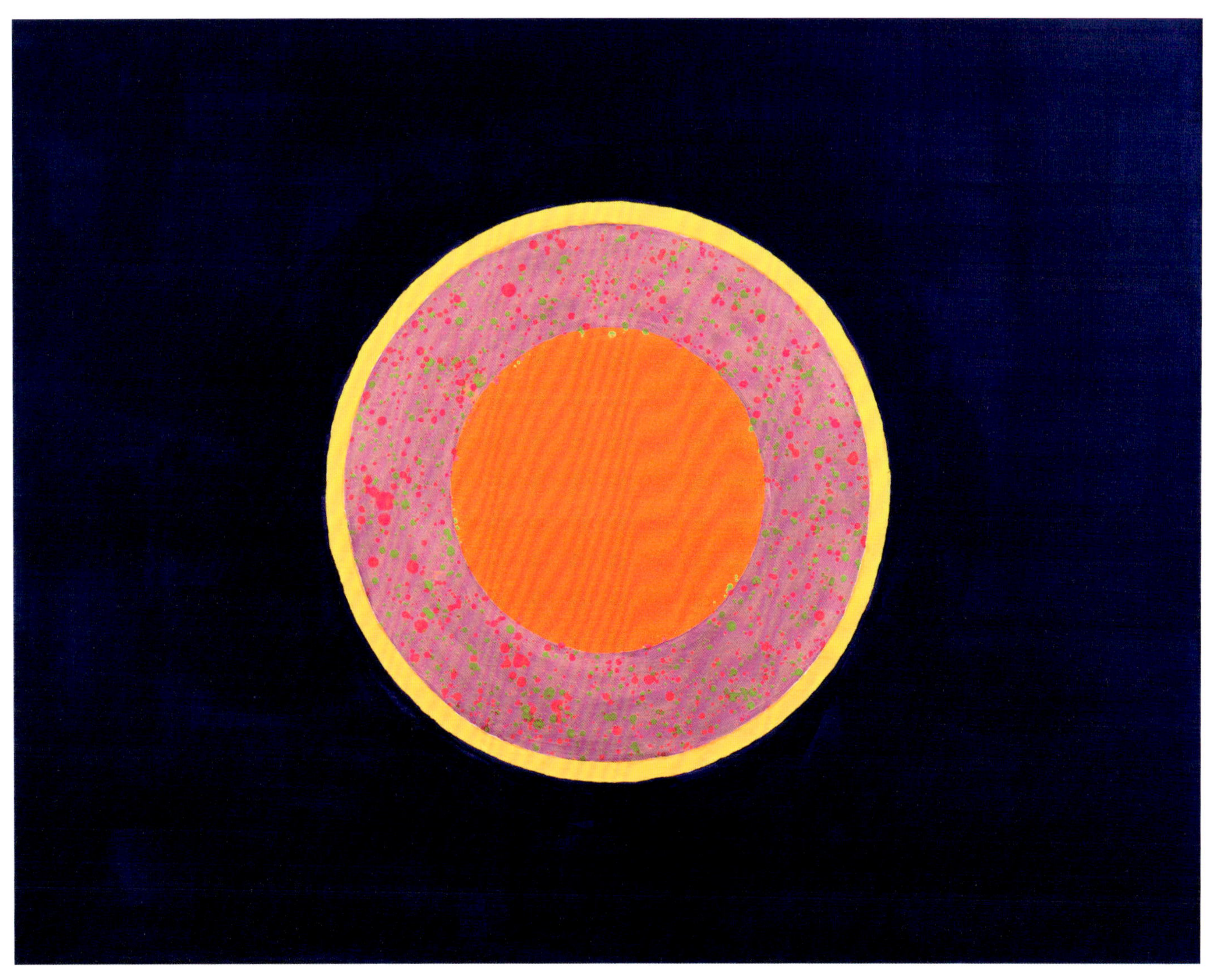

Hsiao Chin
Power of the Light, 1965
Acrylic on canvas
160 × 130cm

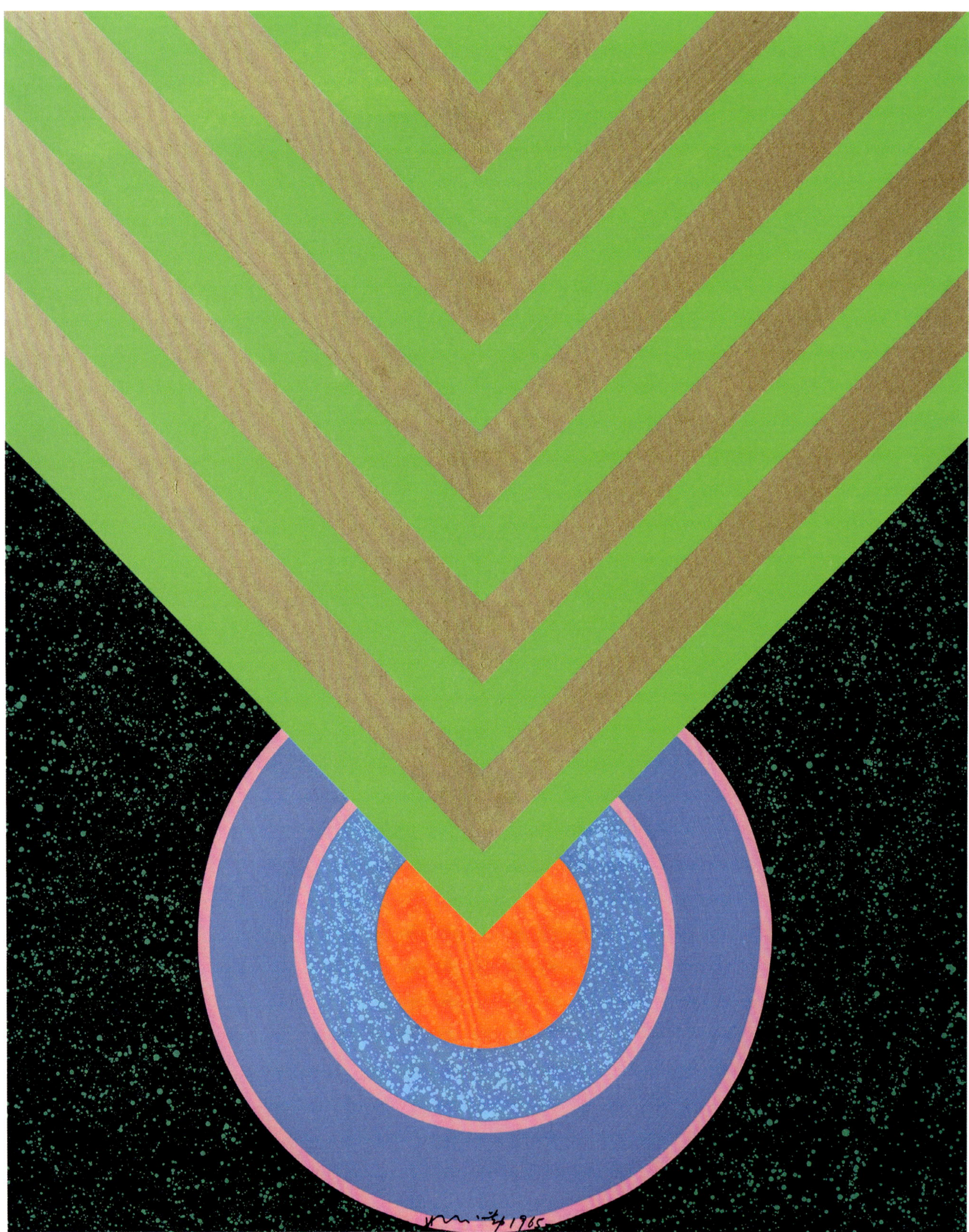

Hsiao Chin,
La Riflessioni di Luce, 1965
Acrylic on canvas
142 x 111cm

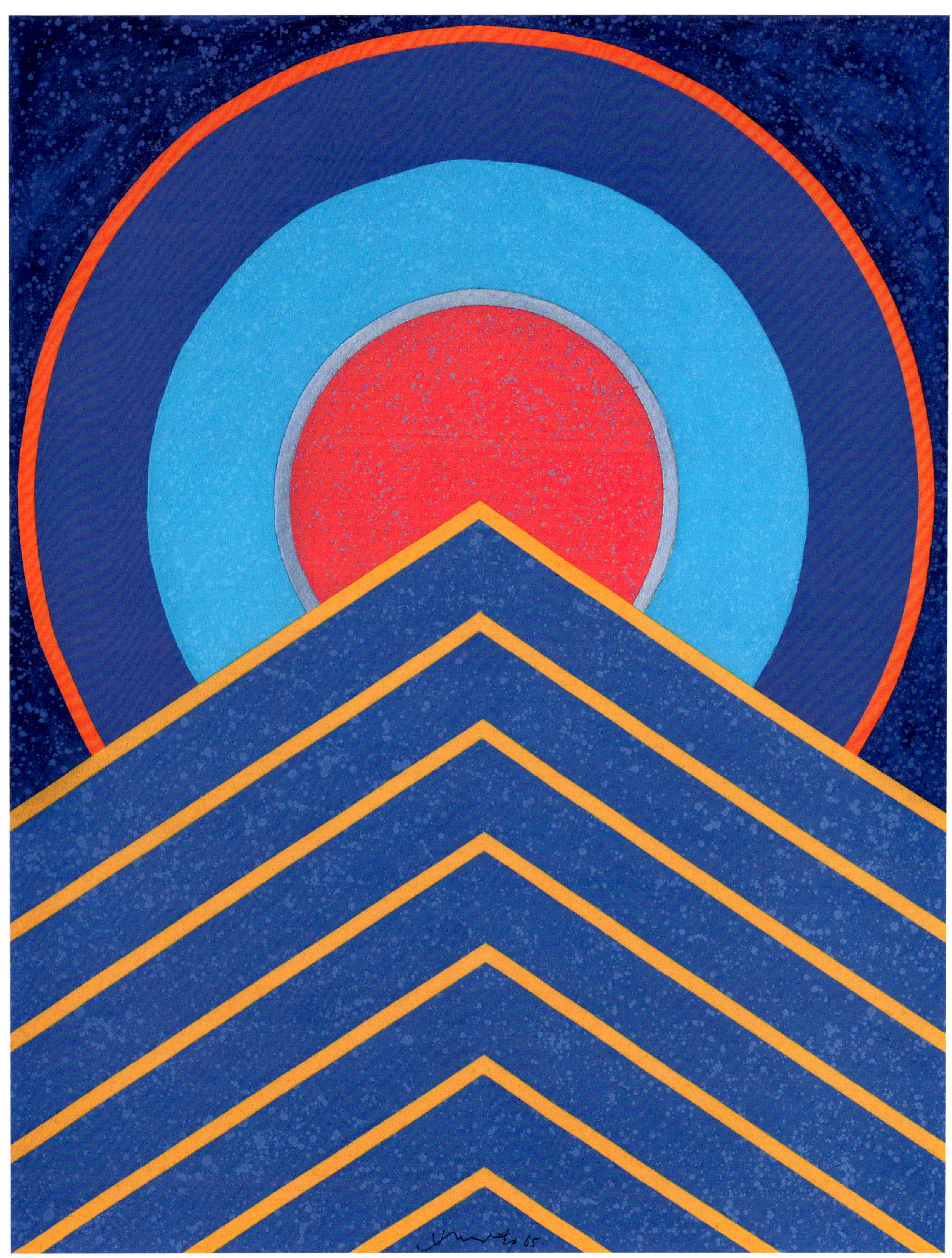

Hsiao Chin
Continuity, 1962
Acrylic and ink on canvas
48.2 x 100cm

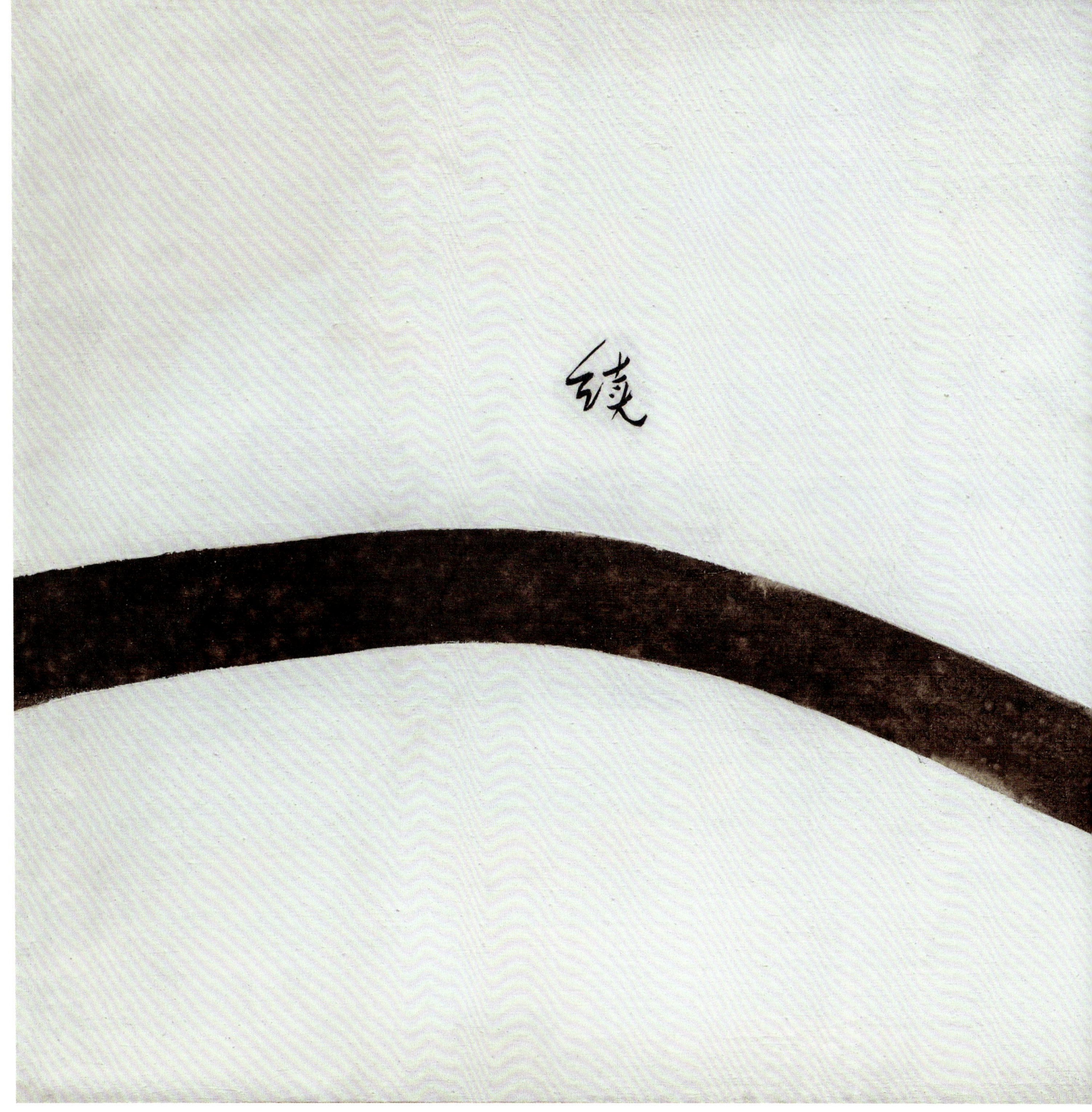

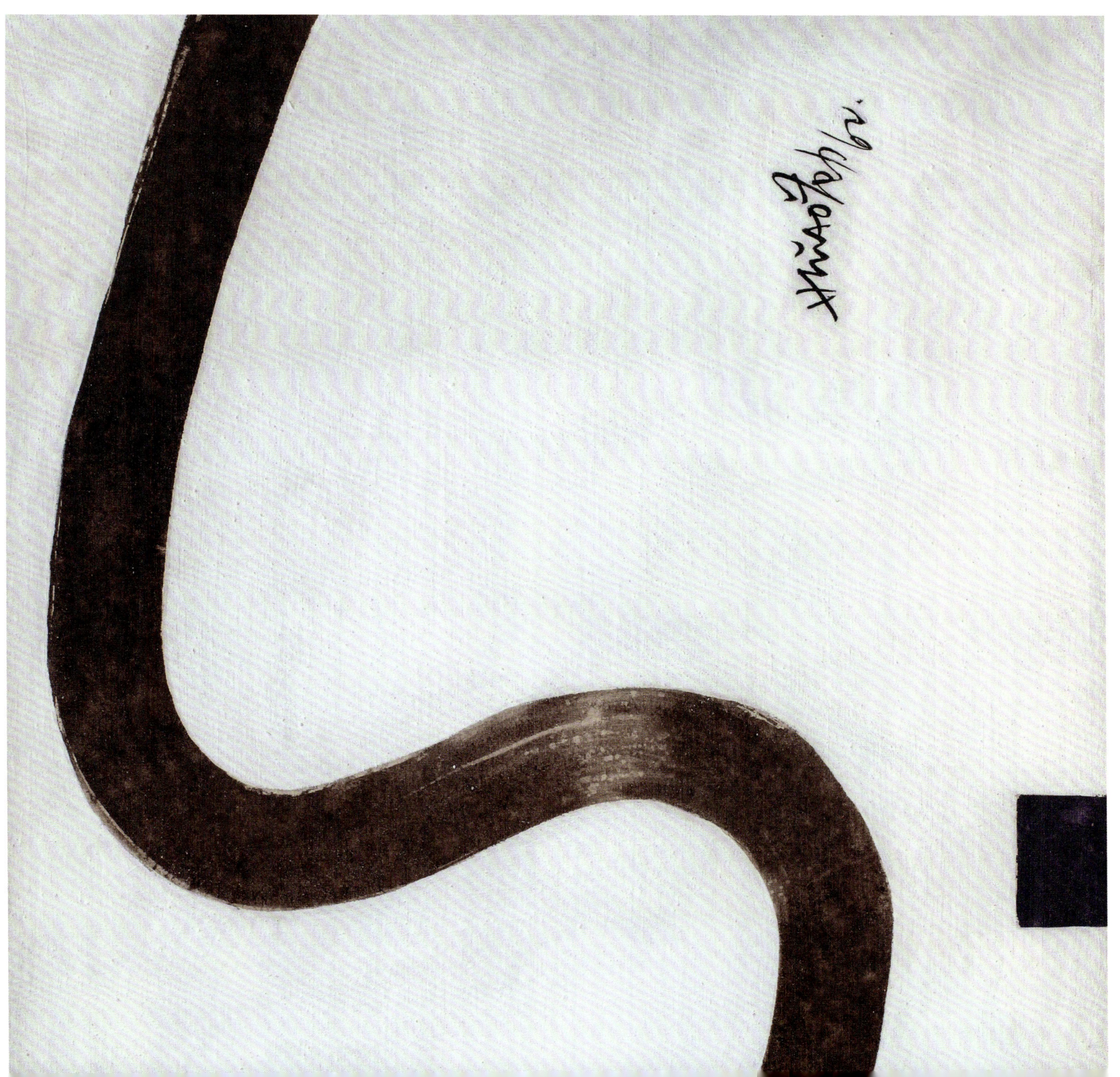

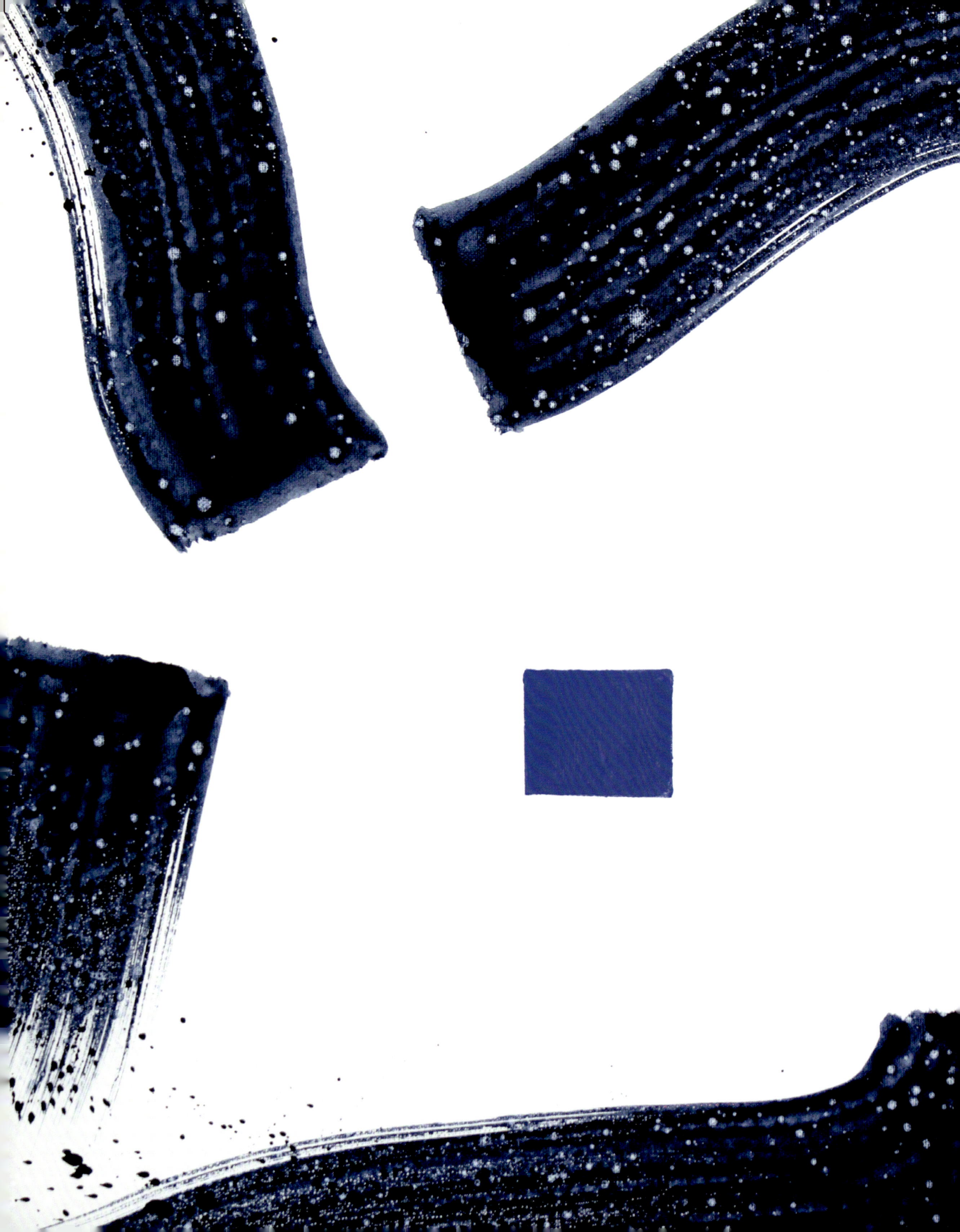

HSIAO CHIN'S **PUNTO**: AN EASTERN TRANSITION IN ABSTRACT ART

Since 1504, when Portuguese adventurers reached China, direct communication between Chinese and Western art has been on a long journey. This history is complicated and controversial, as the Eastern attitude to and trajectory of art are very different from the Western one. Naturalism has different meanings in either field of the cultural sphere. Nevertheless, cultural exchange has enabled artists to be inspired by the diversity and dynamics of communication.

Hsiao Chin and the Punto movement are practitioners in the modern era who contributed significantly to the development of abstract art. The movement has not only revitalised forms and concepts but has also juxtaposed the temporal and the geographical: the traditional and the modern have merged into a new pictorial world; a more profound Zen philosophy fuses the naturalist and the minimalist.

Ton-Fan initiated the Eastern response to Western modernist dissemination in China; while Punto is an Eastern transition into Western art.

Hsiao Chin as an artist started his training with the realisation that the spirit precedes the rules and principles of the form. His art originates through the surge of intuition rather than superficially following the examples of the old masters.

The intuitive origin

Hsiao Chin did not undergo either traditional Chinese ink painting or Western representationalist art training. His mentor, Mr Li Chun-shan (李仲生), encouraged all students to observe the external world with a keen eye for aesthetics. Hsiao Chin did not explore and develop the painterly language by superficially copying iconographies; instead, he drew according to his internal feelings and emotions. Western realist schools that stemmed from the Ancient Greek and were revitalised by the Renaissance have never strongly foreshadowed Hsiao Chin's creativity.

During his formative years Hsiao Chin was inclined to utilise Fauvist bold, vibrant colour and mix the painterly gesture with the themes of Chinese opera. This approach was similar to Chinese avant-garde pioneers such as Lin Fengmian (林風眠, 1900–1991) and Guan Liang (關良, 1900–1986). Despite the similarity in appearance, Hsiao Chin stated that he was not influenced by the two, because his figurative work on Chinese opera themes was encouraged by Li Chun-shan and developed from the mixture of Paul Klee and Matisse as well as ancient Chinese characters carved on metal and stone.[1] It can be explained that in exploring Chinese-ness, Chinese folk art and calligraphy are the apparent subject matter because they are uniquely East Asian. From 1957 to the first Punto, Hsiao tried to minimise forms and colours, inspired by the Daoist discourses, such as 'great art appears to be clumsy' (大巧若拙), 'a wise man seemed to be foolish' (大智若愚), 'great music is simple' (大音希聲), 'a great figure is formless' (大象無形). Those are ideas of relativity and revealed that beneath the complicated and complex façade, the essence is pure. If an artist had a penetrating insight, the principles of art and the painter would be in direct contact. In this case, the artist would be driven by intuition and expose his pure spirit to the audience.

Before Hsiao Chin, a group of Chinese artists of an earlier generation endeavoured to discover the essence of Chinese art, facing the unprecedented influence of Western art. Some insisted on the traditional way, while others fully embraced Western doctrines. Unfortunately,

(*opposite, detail see page 144*) Hsiao Chin, *Movement-2*, 1963

both groups neglected one thing of paramount importance: Chinese national art is not supposed to be bound up with a conservative connotation. Chinese art can be traditional and modern at the same time. The modernisation of Chinese art aims at transcending the traditional and transforming the East into the West: thus making contemporary art universally accessible. Hsiao Chin, to some extent, realised this when living in Spain. Before him, some Chinese pioneers had gradually noticed it while practising their art and feared theoretical arguments.

Lin Fengmian and Guan Liang were educated by traditional ink painting and literature and studied oil painting overseas. They were influential art educators in Chinese history. They both had experience teaching at the Zhejiang Art Academy (now renamed the China Academy of Art). This academy, thanks to its revolutionary educators, was a cradle of Chinese Expressionist and abstract art. Li Chun-shan taught at the academy as a colleague of Lin Fengmian and Guan Liang, before moving to Taiwan. In 1945, Zao Wou-Ki, Lin Fengmian, Wu Dayu, Guan Liang and many other artists from the academy organised the first modernist painting exhibition (現代繪畫聯展) in Chongqing (重慶), the temporary Chinese capital during the war.[2] In the course of this exhibition, the artists shared the vision of juxtaposing Chinese culture with modern art. By modern art, they meant international avant-garde art, from Impressionism to Surrealism. Those artists experimented with abstract art; however, they had not entirely abandoned Expressionist figurative and landscape paintings.

One of Hsiao Chin's teachers in Taiwan was Chu Teh-Chun (朱德群, 1920–2014), who later moved to France, in 1955. It was in France that Chu Teh-Chun began to shift from Expressionist to abstract. Hsiao Chin was under Chu Teh-Chun's instruction learning sketching in 1951. During one month of training, the young artist was amazed by Chu Teh-Chun's vibrant colouring; but he did not appreciate the conservative tutoring.[3]

Wu Guanzhong (吳冠中), Chu Teh-Chun and Zao Wou-Ki formed the triumvirate in the history of Chinese abstract art. They were all educated at the China Academy of Art and studied in France. Wu Guanzhong was not able to embrace abstract art fully. When he went back to mainland China in 1951, his artistic exploration was disrupted by the political changes until the 1980s. Wu Guanzhong's art illustrated the beauty of forms but maintained Chinese gardens and canal villages as his subject-matter. Meanwhile, Chu Teh-Chun and Zao Wou-Ki experimented with abstract art in the second half of the 1950s. Hsiao Chin, as the younger generation, contributed to the abstract trend at almost the same time. Zao Wou-Ki's abstract art was labelled as lyrical abstract; while Chu Teh-Chun excelled in ink brush-strokes.[4] Hsiao Chin respected their contribution and labelled his abstract work as 'Spiritual Abstract', which corresponds with his friend Mark Rothko's statement in 1945:

> The abstract artist has given material existence to many unseen worlds and tempi. But I repudiate his detail of the anecdote just as I repudiate his detail of the material existence of the whole of reality. For art to me is an anecdote of the spirit and the only means of making the concrete purpose of its varied quickness and stillness.[5]

Rothko utilised abstract art to capture and commemorate ever-changing daily life; meanwhile, in a sense, Hsiao Chin made the quickness and stillness of his Spiritual Abstract work by illustrating energy flowing through space on the canvas. Instead of Rothko's creation of colour fields,

Hsiao Chin with Li Chun-shan in Changhua, Taiwan, April 1981

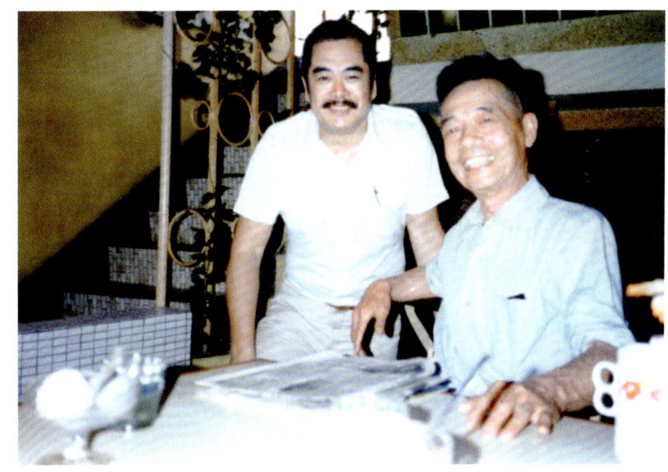

Hsiao Chin created spiritual fields, where the stillness and quickness can be reconciled. Rothko portrayed an immense two-dimensionality and emphasised the sublime beyond the wall; on the contrary, Hsiao Chin paid enormous attention to the space between the strokes, a four-dimensional world co-ordinating with time. Chan Buddhism is sublime in space but more profound in time. The spirituality was not conveyed through the strategy of 'against the grain'; instead it complied naturally with the cosmos, acknowledging the positive and the negative. Hsiao Chin's abstract corresponds with the Heart Sutra, in which Avalokiteshvara (觀自在菩薩) explained:

> This Body itself is Emptiness and Emptiness itself is this Body. This Body is not other than Emptiness and Emptiness is not other than this Body. The same is true of Feelings, Perceptions, Mental Formations, and Consciousness. All phenomena bear the mark of Emptiness; … their true nature is the nature of no Birth no Death, no Being no Non-being, no Defilement no Purity, no Increasing no Decreasing. That is why in Emptiness, Body, Feelings, Perceptions, Mental, Formations and Consciousness are not separate self entities.[6]

The Heart Sutra reveals the way to the unrestrained – heart and body are unified as Emptiness. The crucial difference between Rothko and Hsiao Chin is that Rothko demonstrated the will to live as an artist, Hsiao Chin chose to let go of life for spirituality. Hsiao Chin denounced the author in favour of the reader because the Mantra in the Heart Sutra preaches to the 'realiser' to praise the insight that brings 'us' to the Other Shore, where people all become 'realisers' and can be free of mental suffering.

The origin of Hsiao Chin's art is compassion. To him the spiritual abstract means to be with all beings and his abstract functioned not as a genre but as a medium, through which the audience might find the insight to the Other Shore.

Hsiao Chin, before he went abroad, learned how important it was to create through intuition and was interested in Paul Klee as well as hieroglyphic symbols.[7] It was during Punto that his form started to embrace abstract art. Almost at the same time, Zao Wou-Ki in Paris was thinking of departing from symbolism to abstraction, and he completed his *Black Crowd* in 1954, which was considered by him the first truly abstract painting.[8] Before 1954, Zao spent a significant amount of time exploring the possibility of fusing Chinese calligraphy and Western abstract oil paintings. Meanwhile, Hsiao Chin, a generation younger than Zao, in some way was not particularly interested in the traditional principles of Chinese art. Only until 1957 had his pictorial language been affected by Chinese calligraphy. It was not because he was educated systematically by it; on the contrary, it was because his basic Chinese calligraphy helped create abstract art. Therefore Hsiao Chin's approach to abstract art is different from Zao Wou-Ki's. Zao was brought up by a well-to-do scholarly family and he was educated in an environment in which traditional Chinese ink painting and calligraphy were socially valued and prevalent. Hsiao Chin, even though from a culturally prestigious family, lost both of his parents when he was very young. This may have determined that his way is less bound up with convention. Hsiao Chin had grown up with a strong sense of being an individual, and he had to make most of the decisions by himself, including those about art.

Shifting from figurative to abstract was Hsiao Chin's decisive action. Observing the art world in Europe made him pay considerable attention to the more profound spirituality of Chinese art rather than superficial Chinese symbols.

He later recalled:

> In 1955, before I went abroad, thanks to the inspiration of Paul Klee, I had tried Abstract painting mixed with Chinese calligraphy and epigraphy, but those were only abstract in form. When I arrived in Spain, I saw a lot of things, and I hesitated and thought for quite a while without painting. Later on, I gained new inspiration after meeting those *Informel* artists. There were many artists, particularly in *Art Informel* and American action painting, who had been influenced by the rhythmic beauty of Chinese calligraphy to create new abstract forms. That led me to turn back to the treasures of traditional Chinese art.[9]

The result of this 'turning back' was that Hsiao Chin transformed his work from his previous Fauvist figurative painting to the naturalist abstract.

The term 'naturalist abstract' may seem absurd in the context of Western art history; however, by knowing the evolution of Chinese painting, one would find that Hsiao Chin's composition is a natural evolvement from paintings of Daoist ideology, especially from Chinese landscape.

It can be said that minimalist abstract composition in the West stemmed from Kazimir Malevich and Piet Mondrian, whose utilisation of geometric forms later inspired the Minimalist artists in the 1960s and early 1970s.[10] Although the idea of simplicity for many Western artists is relevant to Japanese Zen (derived from Chinese Chan 禪) philosophy, nevertheless its roots were initially Chinese, as well as its aesthetic practice. Despite the revival of Zen brought by Daisetsu Teitaro Suzuki (鈴木 大拙 貞太郎) to the West, Chan art has at least a millennium of history in the Far East. Unlike the other Buddhist schools originating in India, Chan Buddhism is an exclusively Chinese-born philosophy. Before Chan ideas merged into Chinese art, the concepts of simplicity and naturalism derived from Daoism had already been posited by the scholars who invented theories for landscape painting. In the fifth century CE, the scholar Zong Bing (宗炳) justified the independence of the landscape by acknowledging Confucius' attitude towards the natural. Furthermore, he emphasised Daoist individual freedom by claiming spiritual transcendence through the delight in nature.[11]

Confucius commented on the relationship between nature and wise men:

> The wise find pleasure in water; the virtuous find pleasure in hills. The wise are active; the virtuous are tranquil. The wise are joyful; the virtuous are long-lived.[12]

This non-politically-charged idea is compatible with the appreciation of naturalist simplicity proposed by Laozi, the founder of Daoism:

> The less leads to gaining and the more leads to confusion; therefore, the sage holds in Dao's principle and manifests it to all the world.[13]

The naturalist concept of simplicity was extended by Chan Buddhism later on and exemplified in art practice.[14] Early examples can be found in the Southern Song dynasty (1127–1279), especially in works of art by Liang Kai (梁楷) and Muxi (牧谿). Both Chan masters used black and white colour, as well as simple brush-strokes to represent the external world, for expressing their Chan wisdom.

Hsiao Chin was fascinated with the Chan concept; furthermore, he was inspired by minimalist pictorial language. First, his art shifted in design: with asymmetric composition, he paid great attention to the space between the colour strokes on canvas, as, in Chinese ink painting, blank space (留白) serves to guide the artistic conception (意境). Secondly, the artist changed the palette from oil pigment to watercolour in order to gain a flowing and lighter colour field. Thirdly, his subject matter changed from the figurative to geometric forms; meanwhile, the symbols are recognisable, but not yet conclusively serving as a signifier. The result of this stylistic change demonstrated Hsiao Chin's spiritual transformation. On canvas, he did not deny the influence of Spatialism; meanwhile he believed that Eastern philosophy was the fundamental solution to the artistic conundrum that he confronted by viewing many trends of *Art Informel*. The artist later commented:

> Soon after my arrival, I met Spatialism (*Spazialismo*) founder Lucio Fontana, and his fellow member Robert Crippa. I cannot say I was not inspired in my own creative thinking by this new concept of formal space. Meanwhile, in early 1960 [*sic*], I grew intensely interested in Taoist thinking. This thinking directly influenced my consciousness, which brought me spiritual harmony and balance in the face of the sustained clashes between Eastern and Western culture. My painting changed in turn. I found those symbolic, symmetrical compositions to be too stiff and bland. I also found oil paints to be too thick and insufficiently reserved. Someone once said that 'Western culture and perceptivity are animals, while the East is vegetal.' In many regards, I think this is a very apt metaphor. Taoist thought brought me to a better understanding of this and led me along this path.[15]

With the clarification of cultural, philosophical and aesthetic roots, Hsiao Chin embarked on a lyrical journey in search of the true relation between the internal and the external world – a dichotomy originating from Punto.

Punto opened a gate to a brand-new universe. On canvas and paper, acrylic and ink simplified the form into dots, lines and circles and separated colours into no more than three plus the blank white. It appears that the images signify the sun, the earth and stars; meanwhile, they were decontextualised and transformed into the abstract world. The world was non-formed chaos, just as before an organic being takes shape and is a cell; the development was mysterious and formless. Laozi summarised the mystic point of origin as:

> The way that can be fathomed is not the true way; The Logos that can be expressed in language is not the logos that lasts forever…
> The way produced one; one produced two; two produced three; three produced all things.[16]

Photography liberated artists from imitating the physical appearance of nature, and Cubism endeavoured to interpret appearance with a non-linear-perspective depiction in Western art. Meanwhile, the Western modernist way of image-rendering did not appear alienating to Chinese artists and intellectuals. Hsiao Chin saw the influence of Chinese wisdom in Western art and started to form a distinctive style with a new plasticity and colouring. Abstract elements and multi-point perspective are vernacular in traditional Chinese art. However, abstract painting is a

(*opposite, detail see page 142*) Hsiao Chin, *Gathering the Force-I*

novelty. Hsiao Chin's experiment was groundbreaking and with the contribution of Zao Wou-ki, Chinese abstract art was born.

Traditional Chinese ink paintings may not function as a representation of nature, but they, like Cubism, never tried to break away from the subject matter of the external world entirely. Take Liang Kai's *Portrait of Li Bai* (李白行吟圖) and *Wild Ink Immortal* (潑墨仙人圖), for example: they were categorised as free-hand brushwork (寫意). Liang Kai, as a Chan artist, did not pay great attention to detail in formulating the human figure with anatomical proportions; instead, he portrayed the figure to please the mind. This kind of plasticity was theorised by the first scholarly painter, Gu Kaizhi, in the fourth century, and this 'physical appearance serves the spirit' (以形寫神) doctrine later became the orthodoxy of Eastern Asian art.[17] Hsiao Chin took up this idea with the awareness of avant-garde abstract art in the West: he did not depict images with a sitter or a subject; instead, he followed his intuition and created forms for the distillation of life, and to purify the soul. In many of his paintings during the Punto period, a red dot tends to predominate on the canvas, as if all images or the painterly universe start and orbit around this particular Punto/dot. The viewer might naturally assume that the Punto signifies the sun; however, the meaning extends beyond it. The true principle of the universe is the ineffable, hence Hsiao Chin's artistic translation. Punto does not try to justify the essential property of painting as a medium, and this sets out the difference between Punto and minimalist art. When art historian Rosalind Krauss examined the originality and myth of abstract art, her theoretical formulation was still limited by the Greenbergian mode. She posited that:

> In the early part of this century there began to appear, first in France and then in Russia and in Holland, a structure that has remained emblematic of the modernist ambition within the visual arts ever since. Surfacing in pre-war cubist painting and subsequently becoming ever more stringent and manifest, the grid announces, among other things, modern art's will to silence, its hostility to literature, to the narrative, to discourse.[18]

For Krauss, the grid – a structure – represents the will to defend against the intrusion of speech. This mode referring to violence and war is of the avant-garde, but not of Punto and its Chan roots.

Hsiao Chin in this regard followed the Chinese scholarly doctrine. Ink painting is not a medium or a structure by itself – rather, it is a combination of the three arts: painting, calligraphy and poetry; and the highest value is credited to artistic conception (意境). All forms and literature serve artistic conception in Chinese art. Therefore the conflict between the sense and the mind does not appear as an issue in Chan at all. In this case, the Western avant-garde seems to be bipolar while Eastern art tends to be eclectic (中庸). Hsiao Chin in 1983 explained the relationship between Chan and his creation:

> Zen (Ch'an) has never taught me how to paint a picture. Despite misunderstanding on the part of others, I do not practise Zen (Ch'an) art. As far as I am concerned, Zen (Ch'an) makes me see my own inner mind with a clearer vision, allowing more freedom for me to show the true self in the painting. Most importantly, it lets this pre-existing internal energy be the driving force of the brush-strokes and the colours without any constraints. It also makes me unite with my own inner strength.[19]

Hsiao Chin utilised Chan ideas and the automatic methods from Surrealism and created Punto. The artist felt the energy of image-making with the correspondence of the force of the universe. He simplified the relationship between the individual and the universal and solidified the situation via Punto. Punto moves around from the centre to the edge, reflecting the organic meditation on modern cultural positioning.

The issue of Eastern positioning

Hsiao Chin's eastern positioning did not only suggest the return to his cultural origin, but reflected a revision of a dialectic mode between China and the rest of the world.

During four thousand continuous years of Chinese history, the Chinese intelligentsia had not recognised China as geographically located in the East. Its cultural supremacy had always assumed it to be the centre of the secular world. China's expansion was limited by geography: the Pacific Ocean to the east, the tropical heat to the south, the desert and Tibetan plateau to the west, and the desolation of Siberia to the north. It is only natural for the ancient peoples of China to consider that the most habitual space on earth was taken only by the Chinese, and the margins or edges were left to the rest of the 'barbarians'. The ancient Chinese almost exclusively venerated the Western paradise where Buddhas reside. When the British won the Opium War, Chinese civilisation faced an unprecedented crisis. At the end of the nineteenth century, the ruling class had realised that a total reformation of the power structure had become necessary. Western cultural hegemony peaked in the May Fourth new culture movement (五四新文化運動), and art as part of the high culture sector started to embrace the modern trends of the West.

Traditional values and doctrines at this point were alien to young Chinese people. Many intellectuals endeavoured to catch up with the West. Ton-Fan can be seen as a response to this cultural crisis. Confucius scholars devoted themselves to maintaining social morality and tried to intervene and restore political harmony from chaos. In Ton-Fan, Hsiao Chin focused on the equality of modern art, which could be seen as a Confucian gesture, even though the artist himself believed his artistic realisation stemmed from Daoism rather than Confucianism.[20] Meanwhile, Punto declared a new point of spiritual development in global art, which witnessed a spiritual shift from Daoism to Buddhism.

Hsiao Chin's strategy in translating Eastern philosophy into modern art originated in Daoism, focusing on self-realisation. It can be said that the dots appearing on the canvas signified Hsiao Chin, the image-maker. The positioning of the dot reflects how the artist defined himself in his relationship with his surroundings. It serves the same purpose as action paintings, albeit Hsiao Chin's Punto seeks harmony rather than ostentatiously acting as an agent for emotional catharsis. The power that flows through Hsiao Chin and the canvas dominates the introverted.

Francesca Pola noticed the characteristics of Hsiao Chin's Punto work and put it like this:

> Hsiao Chin's painting is a natural determination of a thought that within itself lives the breathing of the world: it rejects, a priori, offering itself as ideological superstructure, as formal, analytical and visual construction.
>
> One can trace evocations of the Western non-figurative tradition of the twentieth century ranging from Paul Klee to Wassily Kandinsky, Joan Miró to Piet Mondrian, Kazimir Malevich to Mark Rothko, Antoni Tàpies to Lucio

> Fontana, Mark Tobey to Sam Francis – although in the work of Hsiao Chin it's as if this were intentionally filtered through a direct relation with the dimension of the flow of the universe itself and of the flux of life in a vision that is simultaneously dynamic and contemplative.[21]

The first stage of Punto was to filter out some false aspects of specific social and political conditions and to grasp the essence of life. Then the artist utilised and projected the simplicity of human wisdom on to canvas, the procedure of which was experimental. Eventually, through the process of creating, the regulation of beautiful movement was realised. The universality is coded in daily imagery, and it is the artist who captures signs and reproduces the symbols for restoring their meaningfulness.

The 1960s bore witness to a rapid change in the reproduction of mass culture. Images and videos were transmitted to ordinary households within a blink of an eye. Signs were mobilised and directly pushed into the spectrum of the retina. But there is a tendency for signs to be easily manipulated. The minimalists used simplified forms to reject this contamination of signs, while Punto chose to purify the mind without the fanatical obsession of religious conversion.

In a way, Hsiao Chin's depiction functions as a cue for an open-ended interpretation of signs. The artist was not only interested in the macroscopic examination of how the energy of the galaxy moves, but also paid great attention to microscopic scrutiny of biological activities. During the Cold War the two superpowers launched projects exploring outer space, and the competition was fearsome. As a result, from 1960 to 1972, NASA was supported by the government to operate the Apollo program. On 20 July 1969 Neil Armstrong and Buzz Aldrin landed on the Moon. The impact of this human achievement is universal, regardless of its specific political context.

The exploration of space inspired Hsiao Chin to reflect deeply on the universe and civilisation. He was fascinated by mysticism and acknowledged that the significance of the external world as a living organism is greater than that of the ego. When Friedrich Nietzsche declared 'God is dead', he was summarising the consequences of the Age of Enlightenment, renouncing human accountability and condemning the spiritual restrictions imposed by Christianity.[22] Nietzsche, with a sense of moving history on, regarded China as 'a country where large-scale discontent and the capacity for change became extinct centuries ago',[23] which is a negative view, misjudging the Chinese world-view. And this kind of cultural misinterpretation is common.

Western intelligentsia recognised human value from a viewpoint centred on self; however, it was at the cost of neglecting the existence of mystic power, which links to the human mind and body while being beyond the comprehension of the modern mind. The universe exists regardless of the concept of humanity. Buddhism is atheist, as Buddhas are not gods; instead they are 'realisers' who can distinguish the ineffable and eternal from the visible and ephemeral. The more Chan that Hsiao Chin reflected, the more clearly he was able to see the problem of Western art and logic.

Later, Hsiao Chin commented:

> Zen places great emphasis on practice and evidence while ignoring theory. It is also the same as modern art. The theories of others can only serve as references. You must never use them; otherwise, you will be 'speaking the words of others' rather than your own. The most important thing is to find the 'self-nature' within your heart. It

> is true that 'Ten thousand Dharmas do not equal one heart', that 'Dharma is born from the heart', that the 'death of the heart is the death of the Dharma', and that there is 'no one true Dharma'. Huineng said, 'The true nature is the Buddha-nature. There is no Buddha without true nature.'[24]

In Taiwan, Hsiao Chin thought the West could offer a solution to his artistic struggle, while when he dived into the Western world he realised he had to find new methods and experience evolvement via personal and subjective progress. In meditating on Punto he was by himself, but he could find common ground with his fellow Punto artists.

Chinese Abstract Art and Spirituality

The style of Punto progresses from the one-dimensional dot to an infinite variety of shapes, colours and timelines. The artists noticed the lyrical rhythm of the visual, among which Hsiao Chin refined asymmetric symbolism derived from Chinese arts. Abstract art comes naturally to the artists who are educated with Chinese characters. The Chinese language is one of very few analytical languages in the world: the meaning of the sentence is not strongly determined by the conjugations, tenses, or even the sequence of words – on the contrary, the meaning is like the characters, circumstantial and symbolic.

Chinese characters are loosely linked to sounds, and are much closer to the visual. Nevertheless, it would be a mistake to think Chinese characters are concrete pictures. Hieroglyphs in many cases command their users to ascribe the symbolic to the abstract. For example, Air (氣chi) is exemplified by the steam rising from boiling rice, using several strokes to illustrate the variable with a changing form that is fixed from certain principles. Energy (炁chi) is derived from Air but refers to its abstract concept, and the symbol is changed to void (无) plus steam (灬), signifying energy flow.

Chinese calligraphy explores the aesthetic possibilities based on the forms in different scripts: Oracle bone, Bronzeware, Seal, Clerical, Regular, Running, Cursive. The scripts flourished because of a change of media, functions and emotions. Hsiao Chin's Punto images preferred the ancient scripts (Oracle bone script) and the liberal ones (Cursive script), as a way of detaching the lyrical from the verbal.

Even so, some of his spiritual abstraction connotes the Eastern principle of thinking. For example, in Tao (p. 143), the artist depicted one S-shaped stroke horizontally across the canvas and accommodated it with a red square. It can be seen as a simplified version of the bronzeware script (金文) with a red seal, but the whole is disseminated more from the symbol. It neutralised the language of hieroglyphs and put an emphasis on malapropism (hollow strokes 飛白). The spontaneity and the accidental offered a unique form or a special way of making abstract principles physical. The black colour separated the space, and at the same time made the blank space visible and describable.

Similar approaches can be found in *The Beginning of Tao-2* (p. 48), while the artist articulated the ineffable quality of watercolour. Water is praised by Daoism as the most important element in nature, as water exemplifies nature's symbolic power:

> Most benevolent actions resemble water in character.
> Water benefits all things but does not compete with them.
> It puts itself in (low) places which most people do not like.
> As such, it comes close to the nature of Dao.[25]

In Chinese philosophy, Water forms the dichotomy of power, and its infinite energy comes from its fluidity and softness. Hsiao Chin understands the rule of water, and therefore his Punto is like water: organic and soft. This distinguishes him deeply from the masculine quality of American Abstract Expressionism. The spiritual abstraction that Hsiao Chin keeps seeking follows nature, in which, later on, he tried to renounce his ego and to unify with nature. Chinese aesthetic theory suggested 'starting with External Learning from Naturalism and Internal Comprehension' (外師造化 中得心源), and this is a crucial principle in Chinese landscape.[26] In the West, Leonardo da Vinci is probably the first artist who perceived the links between external naturalism and internal comprehension. In this way, he was fascinated by water flow and energy transmission in the human body. Trans-field knowledge stimulated his creativity. No wonder Leonardo was the artist who made a significant contribution to the development of landscape painting in Western art.

From Hsiao Chin's work, his 'learning from nature and supporting the intuition' approach develops into the abstract. The English equivalent could be Imagism (意象). The historic Imagism was a modernist poetry movement in the English world. Ezra Pound played the key role in the movement and his poems are strongly influenced by ancient Chinese poetry. In a sense, Western modernism in ideas first benefited from Chinese Imagism in the field of literature. As for the visual arts, it was only when Hsiao Chin and the other abstract artists from the East such as Zao Wou-ki and Chu Teh-Chun became active in the West that imagist notions made an impact in global visual art.

In Hsiao Chin's work, there are many natural phenomena transcribed into abstraction: water, clouds, the sun, atoms and even photosynthesis. All the concrete phenomena imply energy – the source of creativity. Once again, the relationship between the visible and the abstract can be found in Chan:

> All things contrived are like
> Dream, illusion, bubble, shadow,
> And as dewdrop or lightning,
> They should be regarded as such.[27]

The Diamond Sutra elucidates how Buddhism should deal with all kinds of circumstances in the external world. Dream, illusion, bubble, shadow are symbolic and without substance, being neither absolutely concrete nor abstract. Hsiao Chin's painting, especially the *Dancing Light* series, expresses such a notion – how to find true self from symbols. The artist commented on it thus:

> It is because today's artists engage in 're-creation' as they imitate the work of the creator that their process of 'cultivation' is different from before. They must discover the 'true self'. It is only through the 'true self' that they can approach the 'no-self' state of the creator and be free and unconstrained. But to 'cultivate' to the point of discovering the 'true self' and drive it is just as difficult as the 'enlightenment' of Zen. It can only be attained through strenuous 'gradual cultivation'. We can never gain it from nothing. Otherwise, everything would become empty and meaningless, without content or timelessness.[28]

Wassily Kandinsky had already pointed out in 1911 that the depth of abstract art must reside in 'the internal which conceals the seeds of the future', because there exists a similar inner striving within the whole spiritual/moral atmosphere among human beings. And this similarity of the inner mood of the *Zeitgeist* might be forgotten but can be conveyed to the present through the employment of forms, because the inner logic is inherited.[29] If Kandinsky were to look at the case of China, he would be surprised to find that the dynastic changes seemed to be cyclical – Chinese scholars and historians, as well as artists in writing and creating, often strove for harmony in ancient times. However, many artists in the Qing dynasty neglected abstract or symbolic principles and focused on concrete imitation. Dogmatic learning, which Hsiao Chin disdains, had become an obstacle to volition in motion. Hsiao Chin, in articulating the spirituality of abstract art, endeavoured to recollect empathy flowing from the individual to the collective.

Hsiao Chin's approach to abstract art is eclectic, which is different from the bipolar attitude in the West. Western theorists tended to put the abstract in the co-ordinate against reason, texts, languages, as has been pointed out in the aforementioned statements by Clement Greenberg and Rosalind Krauss. The German art historian Wilhelm Worringer, as early as 1906, even went so far as to say that abstraction and empathy were the two sides of a dichotomy: 'the urge to abstraction finds its beauty in the life-denying inorganic, in the crystalline or, in general terms, in all abstract law and necessity'.[30] The originality of Western abstract art was problematic in distinguishing the 'purity' of the form, medium and concept. Hsiao Chin also laid stress on the matter of 'purity', but he believed in the depths of the soul and spirit, not things that can be sensed on the surface. Western theorists also noticed the vital role that non-Western culture played in stimulating the development of abstract art. For example, Worringer suggested that culturally developed Eastern people manifested the abstract tendency, which remained dominant, whereas from the Ancient Greeks up to the spread of Western civilization, the tendency was gradually to move to representationalism and to favour empathy. In addition, Alfred H. Barr Jr., in mapping the trajectory of abstract art, noted Japanese prints, Near-Eastern Art and Negro sculpture [*sic*] as the source of inspiration. Worringer was mistaken in suggesting that Eastern art exhibits the abstract tendency and does not favour empathy, while Barr was not able to explain the ontology of abstract art. The negligence of Imagism has led many Western theorists to fail to grasp the essence of Eastern abstraction.

Apart from decorative motifs, Chinese art has never been abstract – not even cursive calligraphy – if abstract art means the creation of figures without imitating or portraying existing images in the external world. Hsiao Chin's image-making is not explicitly derived from social lives or landscapes. In this sense, he can be labelled as an abstract artist in the modern sense. Kandinsky, Malevich, Mondrian, Pollock, Rothko and Zao Wou-ki can be said to have belonged to the same group. Hsiao Chin's art contributed more to the trend, not just because of the spirituality reflected in his works, but also through the reintroduction of music, literature, philosophy: the approach is that of cross-cultural fields returning to the visual, without the cost of losing the essence of painting.

Chinese painting appeared to be an art synthesising the beauty of images, poetry and calligraphy, as was mentioned before; Chinese artists are therefore more interested in the artistic concept than in likeness. In a way, the Post-Modernist notion is not alien to Hsiao Chin. When Guillaume Apollinaire was excited by inventing Calligram, mixing texts and images, he, as an optimistic avant-garde practitioner, would be disappointed to find that this is nothing new for the Chinese, as it has been deeply rooted in their civilisation for more than four millennia.

Hsiao Chin's painting did not invite calligraphy or poetic texts directly on to the canvas, and therefore maintained the integrity of abstract painting. On the other hand, he did not go so far as to silence the lyrical and poetical elements projected by brush-strokes and pigments.

The characteristics of Hsiao Chin's spiritual abstract art embody Phenomenology, as the previous chapter has suggested; in other words, it makes manifest that – in order to identify oneself – one must recognise the internal and the external worlds from the start.[31] The notion of transcendental intersubjectivity is not in the consciousness of many Western abstract artists and theorists. Hsiao Chin, through Punto, tried to reveal the more profound connotation of the abstract form in art.

The Other Shore: Post-Modernism

During the Cold War, many artists and viewers were visually burdened with a social façade and the political situation; it was as if the avant-garde demanded to win the war.[32] But a fundamental question is: why are artists required to fight and assigned to march for a goal with the equipment of art? The idea of the 'avant-garde' was originally a military term, and refers to being at the front line of cultural evolution. It was Claude Henri de Saint-Simon who in 1852 wrote in his book *Opinions Littéraires, philosophiques et industrielles*: 'We, the artists, will be the vanguard of the intellectual revolution. The power of art is, in fact, the most effective and the fastest. We have all sorts of weapons: when we want to propose new ideas, we engrave them in marble or we draw them on a canvas.'[33] Meanwhile, Eastern Asian aesthetics does not have a sense of advancing in this regard.

Chinese cultural expansion in East Asia, in general, is natural and peaceful. The ideological hegemony is achieved through friendly communication, even though the China-centric world view is inevitable. The foundation of the civilisation is not race, but culture. In this sense, everyone can be Chinese, as long as they follow or contribute to the Chinese way. For a long time, thanks to its vast territory and cultural variety, China has itself been a small universe. Its vitality and brilliance are derived from communication. The policy of isolation led only to decadence and, eventually, China had to face the imperialist invasion.

Giorgio Vasari coined the term 'Renaissance' to describe the European cultural revival. The second half of the twentieth century could be marked as the beginning of the Chinese cultural revival, after the Opium War. At present, many researchers can see the development of China through its quantifiable economic growth, regardless of which, Chinese intellectuals are aware that the economy is the base for the super-structure – culture, in which art plays a crucial role. Hsiao Chin contributed to the Eastern transition of Western art and became the pioneer in post-war global art. The meaning of Chinese-ness extended throughout the region. When the art historian Craig Clunas wrote his famous monograph on Chinese art, he used the title 'Art in China' to avoid the problem of 'Chinese Art' or 'Art of China'; nevertheless, the geographic conundrum remains. Hsiao Chin's Punto was not made in China, and cannot be referred to as Chinese art. The universalism of Punto transcended the idea of the signifier being limited to the nation. So the more precise term to describe Hsiao Chin's Punto is global art of abstract form.

The Chan master Huineng (惠能) articulated that human beings might be labelled by being from the North or the South, but the Buddhist heart cannot be labelled as from the East or the West.[34]

Post-Modernist perception in art had become more apparent in the 1960s, whereas, in the field of art history, theorists started to discuss the issue systematically in the 1980s. Minimalism witnessed the last hegemony of abstract art in withstanding the prevalent Neo-Dada, Pop and conceptualism. *L'Art pour L'Art* (Art for Art's Sake) had become invalid. When Roland Barthes postulated the post-structuralist theories by claiming 'the death of the author' in 1967, he did not realise that his contemporary fellow thinker Jean Baudrillard had already sensed that the superfluity of communication exhausted both sides of the exchange: the author and the reader.[35] Hsiao Chin sensed the emergence of the consumerist culture and how the advancement of Pop art enfeebled the spirituality he was seeking for:

> Once the concept of consumerism is fixed in place, the strange wonders of the market, as in 'Ugly art', will grow, because the market needs new, fashionable products to promote. So, unfortunately, the majority of young artists working today merely work on 'how to introduce new, fashionable art forms' and 'how to create opportunities for their own success', and ignore the real question of how to make art. In other words, they are trying to learn how to be the most successful manufacturers of art commodities, rather than being an artist with eternal value. Because the concepts of 'eternity' and 'fashion' are at odds with one another, 'art' cannot be like the clothes worn today that go out of style tomorrow. 'Art' is art, and must stand the test of time.

This is a problem of avant-gardism and the modernist era. The poet Arthur Rimbaud, one of the most modernist and avant-gardiste souls of his time, was disappointed by Occidental (European) societies, and eventually decided to leave the West behind, but he was afraid to fall into the kitschy trap of Orientalist claims to wisdom.[36] What he did was to silence himself: he stopped writing poems. He was once fired with imagination and provoked his audience with 'You must be absolutely modern', but in the end, he abandoned liberal arts. Intriguingly, in his period of abjection and passion, he created one of the most influential poems – *L'Éternité*:

Elle est retrouvée.	It has been found again.
Quoi? – L'Éternité.	What? – Eternity.
C'est la mer allée	It is the sea fled away
Avec le soleil.	With the sun.

Hsiao Chin, in confronting the ambiguous function of the avant-garde, chose a different path: he put faith in art. Just as Rimbaud found the Sun and the Other Shore as the symbol of eternity, Hsiao Chin continued to seek enlightenment in the eternal wisdom of the East.

Accordingly, he brought light as a subject into his paintings. There are two stages. The first is in the *Dancing Light* series: the artist utilised two colour fields to indicate the space: a bright colour fills the upper part, and the bottom level is left blank. The division of the two fields is curved naturally, without the suggestion of an artificial symmetric arrangement. The upper field occupies more space, giving the sense of dripping or dropping, so implying gravity. A dot appears in the blank or voided space, the idea of which is derived from Taiji (太極 the oneness before Yin and Yang). Bold strokes are crawling on the upper level. They are like silkworms on a mulberry leaf, exhibiting productivity, while, as a whole, they form a labyrinth permeated by a mysterious aura. The whole canvas can be seen as an analogy of the Other Shore (彼岸 pāra), where humans are cleansed from the suffering of the secular world, and thus become buddhas.

Cultural transcending

The second stage in arranging light on canvas is the *Light Expansion* series (pp. 96-99 and p.102), where rays of light are hard-edged, and therefore the source of power is oriented and determined. The power of light appeared to be so forceful that Punto began to deconstruct. Such a power reflects the Buddhist term *vájra* (金剛), etymologically referring to a diamond or thunderbolt. In Tibetan Buddhism (Vajrayan, the mystery school 密宗), *vájra* is the symbol of the faith, implying indestructibility. During this time Hsiao Chin expanded his interest in esoteric power and tantric symbolism. The *Light Expansion* series reflects his counter-proposal to Pop art and consumerism. For him, sunlight was transformed into *vájra*, guiding the power of light piercing through the context of the spectacle. Guy Debord in 1967 (paralleling the end of Punto) published his famous theses, one of which runs:

> As a negative movement which seeks the supersession of art in a historical society where history is not yet lived, art in the epoch of its dissolution is simultaneously an art of change and the pure expression of impossible change. The more grandiose its reach, the more its true realisation is beyond it. This art is perforce *avant-garde*, and it *is not*. Its avant-garde is its disappearance.[37]

Guy Debord, like many Western intellectuals (viz. Walter Benjamin), fell into desperation in viewing the situation, specifically the problem of modernism, and eventually took the noble way out (suicide). Apparently, Hsiao Chin, equipped with Eastern wisdom, still held hope and gazed at the Other Shore. He continued to practise art after Punto and developed the Hard Edge series because he believed in life. *Vájra* contains absolute power, and sometimes requires solitude; nevertheless, the paintings inspired by it construct 'a symbolic space of the universe' which is also 'a self-contained world of living things'.[38] Love with light as its symbol is the solution to the problem of avant-gardism.

Hal Foster, in formulating Post-Modernist theory, posits that:

> A resistant post-modernism is concerned with a critical deconstruction of tradition, not an instrumental pastiche of pop- or pseudo-historical forms, with a critique of origins, not a return to them. In short, it seeks to question rather than exploit cultural codes, to explore rather than conceal social and political affiliations.[39]

Hsiao Chin's treatment combining traditional Chinese art with Western avant-garde ideas is, in this regard, Post-Modernist. His critical mind synthesised the cultural legacies from the ancient and modern eras, and in facing real and serious social problems, the artist never tried to give up. Sometimes he can be amazed at finding resonance with ancient arts in a mysterious way, but he never borrows them. One of Picasso's famous quotations runs: 'Good artists borrow, great artists steal'. For Hsiao Chin, good artists do not steal, they create.

Pictures, like texts, are part of the symbols of language as a specific form and system. All paintings are related to plasticity, colour, referencing the external world and expressing internal feelings, and those elements simultaneously exist within and alongside paintings. No matter how times change, those principles will be realised in specific ways; sometimes, the projections will be similar, because the principles are pre-determined.[40] Hsiao Chin, as an artist, learned the DNA of abstract art, and he composed with the DNA but created new lives.

There is one particular moment in Hsiao Chin's memory that can exemplify this. It was in the late 1980s, when he visited the Petal Palace in Tibet. He was astonished by the paintings to the left of the entrance, because ancient wisdom had already planted the seed of the abstract in art.[41] Despite this, Hsiao Chin's abstract art is original, in the sense that it holds historical significance, and its aesthetic profundity lies in cultural transcendence.

---

1 Personal correspondence with Hsiao Chin Foundation, 7 December 2019.

2 Qi Lin, 2016, 'The Voiceless Avant-Garde: The Modern Painting Exhibition during the anti-Japanese War', *Anti-Japanese War Culture Research*, pp. 184–98 [漆麟:《无言的前卫:抗战时期的'现代绘画联展'》,《抗战文化研究》].

3 Personal correspondence with the Hsiao Chin Foundation, 8 December 2019.

4 Min Jie, 2017, *The Three Musketeers who studied in France*, HK: Zhonghe Publishing. [閔捷:《留法三劍客》,香港中和出版社2017年].

5 Mary Acton, 2004, *Learning to Look at Modern Art*, London: Routledge, p. 107; Susie Paulik Babka, 2016, *Through the Dark Field: The Incarnation through an Aesthetics of Vulnerability*, Minnesota: Liturgical Press, p. 265.

6 *Heart Sutra*, 2014, trans by Thich That Hanh, Plumvillage, <https://plumvillage.org/about/thich-nhat-hanh/letters/thich-nhat-hanh-new-heart-sutra-translation/>, [9 December 2019].

7 Hsiao Chin, 1983, '1957, My First Solo Exhibition in Mataro Barcelona', *Artist Magazine*, Vol. 96, p. 76.

8 Melissa Walt, Ankney Weitz and Michelle Yun, 2016, *Zao Wou-Ki: No Limits*, Asia Society Museum, p. 86.

9 Hsiao Chin, '1957, My First Solo Exhibition in Mataro Barcelona', p. 77.

10 Brandon Taylor, 1995, *The Art of Today*, London: The Orion Publishing Group, p. 8.

11 Zong Bing, fifth century, *The Preface of Landscape Paintings*, from Zhang Yanyuan, ninth century, *The History of Ancient Famous Paintings*, ancient texts [宗炳:《畫山水序》, 引自張彥遠:《歷代名畫記》]<https://zh.wikisource.org/zh/歷代名畫記/卷第六>, [25 November 2019].

12 Confucius: *Analects of Confucius*, ancient texts [《論語》]<https://zh.wikisource.org/wiki/論語/雍也第六>, [25 November 2019].

13 Laozi: *Tao Te Ching*, ancient texts [《老子》]<https://zh.wikisource.org/wiki/老子_(帛書校勘版)>, [25 November 2019].

14 It can be said that Daoism is nihilistic and individual while Confucianism is positive regarding the secular world, with a societal and collective goal; meanwhile Buddhism is nihilistic, but wishes to rescue all secular beings.

15 Hsiao Chin, 1983, 'Punto Art Movement', *Artist Magazine*, Vol. 103, pp. 66–69. [蕭勤:《藝術家》, 1983年12月第103期].

16 Laozi: *Tao Te Ching*, ancient texts.

17 Gu Kaizhi, *Praising Famous Paintings of Wei and Jin dynasties*, ancient texts [顧愷之:《魏晉勝流畫贊》,東晉], <https://zh.wikisource.org/zh-hant/魏晉勝流畫贊>, [25 November 2019].

18 Rosalind E. Krauss, 1986, *The Originality of the Avant-Garde and Other Modernist Myths*, Massachusetts: The MIT Press, p. 9.

19 Tsai Chao-yi, 2018, 'Topology of Meaning of Life: Retrospect and Prospect of Hsiao Chin's Art', *Hsiao Chin Coming Home*, China Art Museum Shanghai, p. 36.

20 Personal correspondence with Hsiao Chin, 1 December 2019.

21 Francesco Pola, 1987, 'Hsiao Chin: Life, in Equilibrium', *Un Viaggio Attraverso L'universo*, Milan: Robilant+Voena Gallery, 2015, p. 28.

22 Friedrich Nietzsche, 2004, *Why I am so wise*, trans. R. J. Hollingdale, London: Penguin Books, p. 89.

23 Eric S. Nelson, 2017, *Chinese and Buddhist Philosophy in Early Twentieth-Century German Thought*, London: Bloomsbury, p. 84.

24 Hsiao Chin, 1984, 'A Stylistic Turn: on Hard Edges and the Zen Series', *Artist Magazine*, Vol. 104, pp. 68–70.

25 Laozi: *Tao Te Ching*.

26 Zhang Zao, from Zhang Yanyuan, ninth century, *The History of Ancient Famous Paintings*, ancient texts [唐代 张璪,引自張彥遠:《歷代名畫記》]<https://zh.wikisource.org/wiki/歷代名畫記/卷第十>, [25 November 2019].

27 Diamond Sutra, trans by Yutang Lin, [《金剛經》林語堂 譯本]<http://www.yogichen.org/gurulin/efiles/p1/p1488.html>, [9 December 2019].

28 Hsiao Chin, 1983, 'Analysis and Discussion of Artistic Creation', *Artist Magazine*, pp. 46–48.

29 Wassily Kandinsky, 1912, 'Concerning the Spiritual in Art', Quote from *Art in Theory, 1900–2000: An Anthology of Changing Ideas*, 2003, ed. Charles Harrison & Paul Wood, new edition, Blackwell Publishing, p. 83.

30 Wilhelm Worringer, 1910, 'Abstraction and Empathy', Quote from *Art in Theory, 1900–2000: An Anthology of Changing Ideas*, p. 66.

31 Michael Theunissen, 1986, *The Other: Studies in the Social Ontology of Husserl, Heidegger, Sartre, and Buber*, Massachusetts: The MIT Press, pp. 14–18.

32 Brandon Taylor, *The Art of Today*, pp. 8–15.

33 Donald D. Egbert, 1970, 'The Idea of avant-garde in Art and Politics', *Leonardo*, Vol. 3, No. 1, pp. 75–86.

34 Huineng, Platform Sutra of the Sixth Patriarch, eighth to thirteenth century, ancient text, [惠能: 《六祖壇經》] <https://zh.wikisource.org/zh-hant/六祖壇經/行由品>, [10 December 2019].

35 Jean Baudrillard, 1983, 'The Ecstasy of Communication', *Postmodern Culture*, ed. Hal Foster, London: Pluto Press, pp. 126–33.

36 Edmund White, 2008, *Rimbaud: The Double Life of a Rebel*, London: Atlantic Books, p. 114.

37 Guy Debord, 1983, *Society of The Spectacle*, Detroit: Black & Red.

38 Hsiao Chin, 2018, *Hsiao Chin Coming Home*, China Art Museum Shanghai, p. 107.

39 Hal Foster, 1983, 'Postmodernism: A Preface', *Postmodern Culture*, ed. Hal Foster, p. x.

40 Joshua Gong, 2014, *Iconography and Schemata: A Communicating History in Painting between China and the West, 1514–1885*, Shanghai: Commercial Press. pp. 6–7. [龔之允: 《圖像與範式:早期中西繪畫交流史1514-1885》,上海:商務印書館2014年出版].

41 Personal correspondence with Hsiao Chin, 1 December 2019.

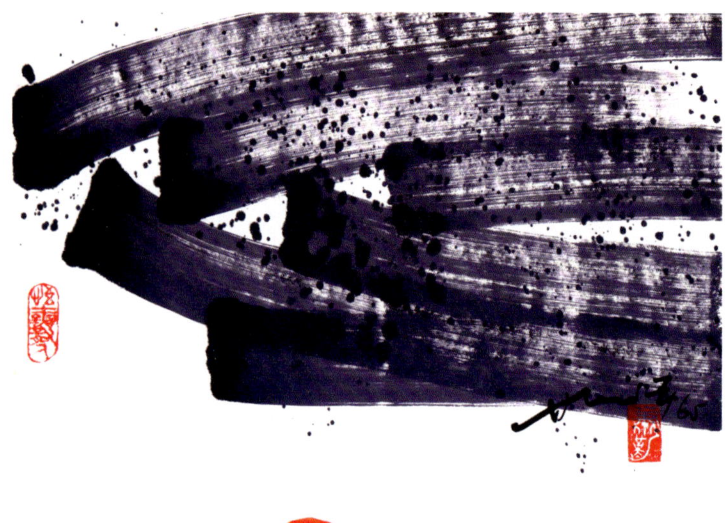

Hsiao Chin
Gathering the Force-1, 1965
Acrylic on paper
45 x 45cm

Hsiao Chin
Tao, 1961
Ink on canvas
60 x 140cm

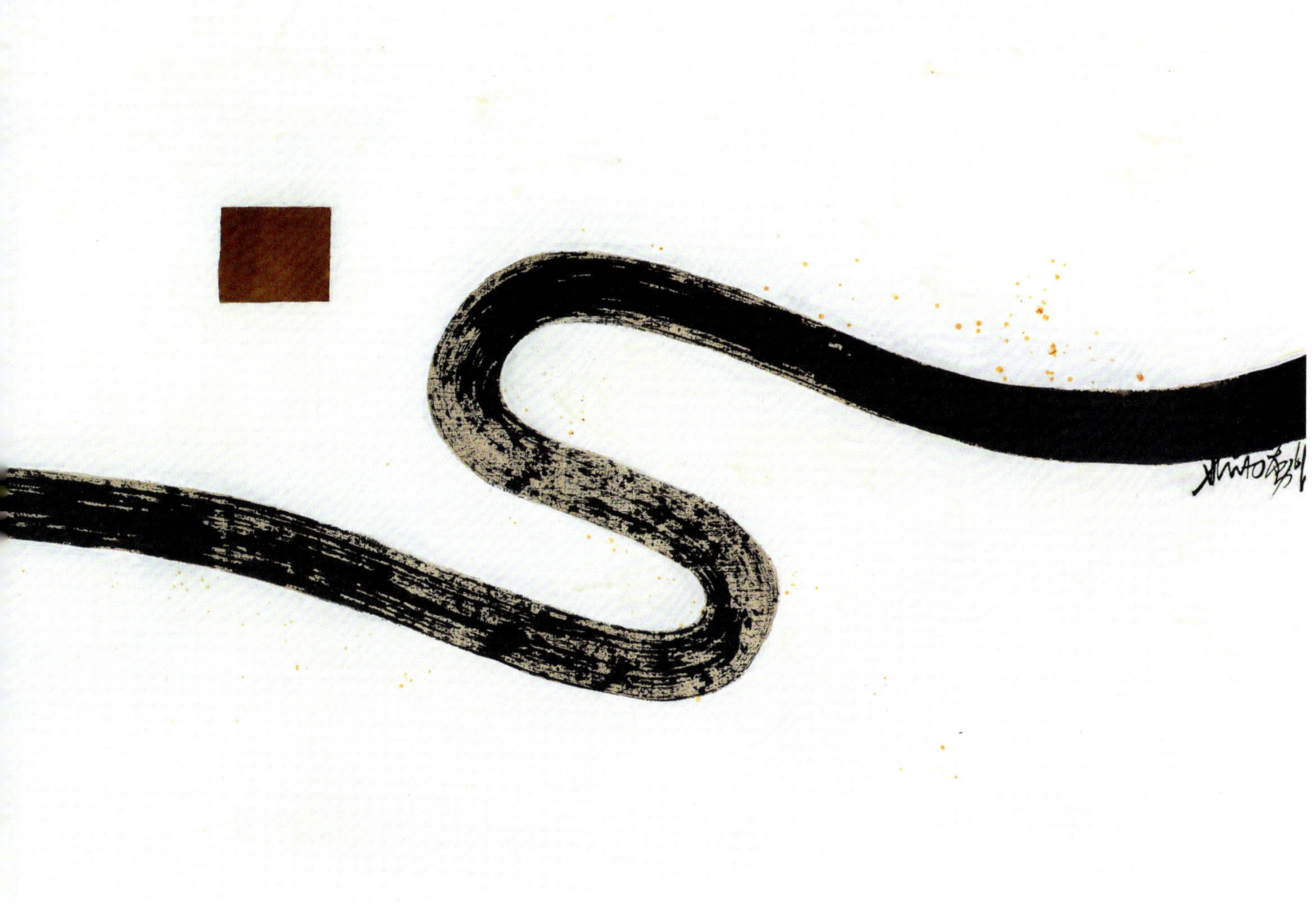

Hsiao Chin
Movement-2, 1963
Acrylic on canvas
60 × 80cm

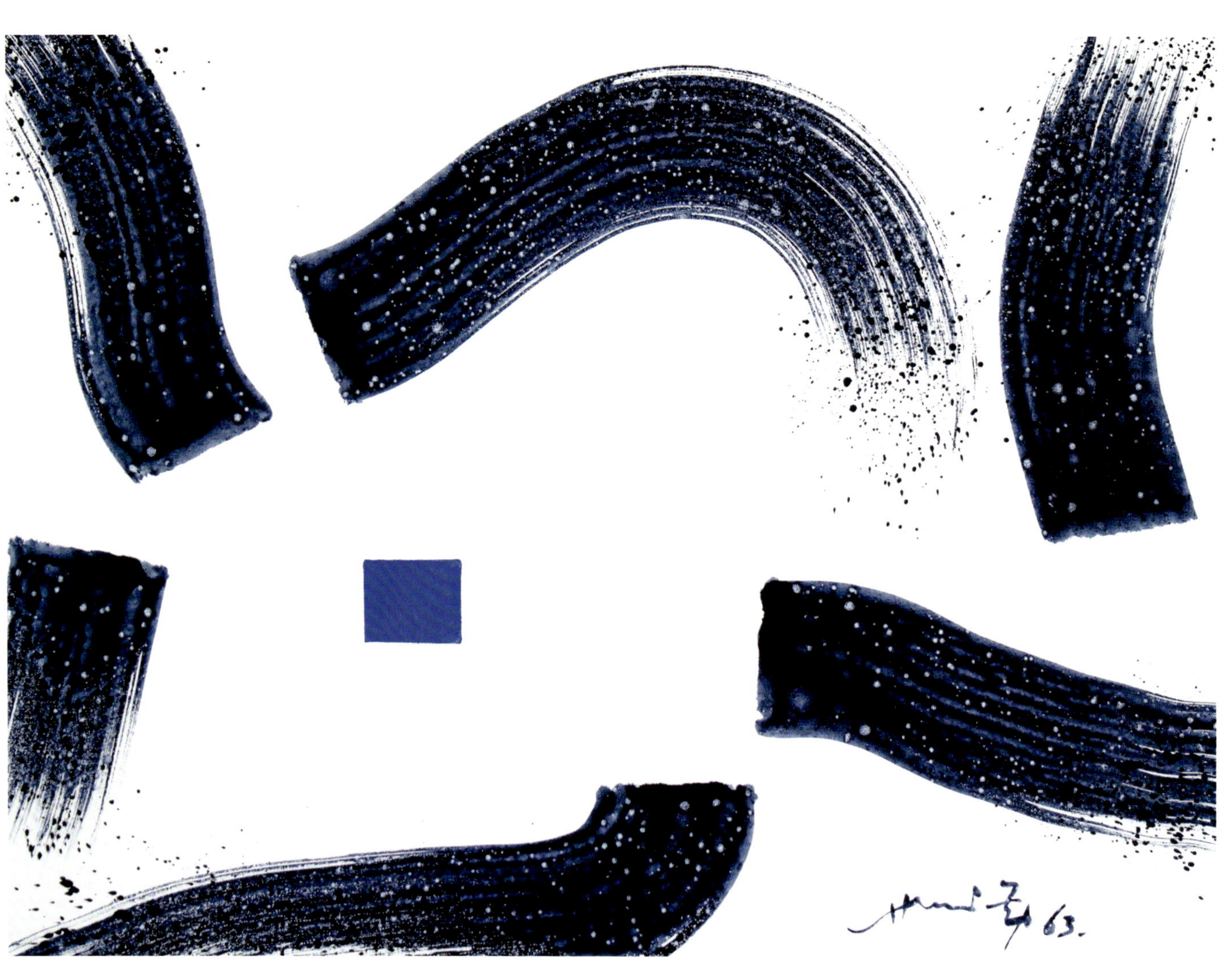

Hsiao Chin
Movement-3, 1963
Acrylic on canvas
60 x 80cm

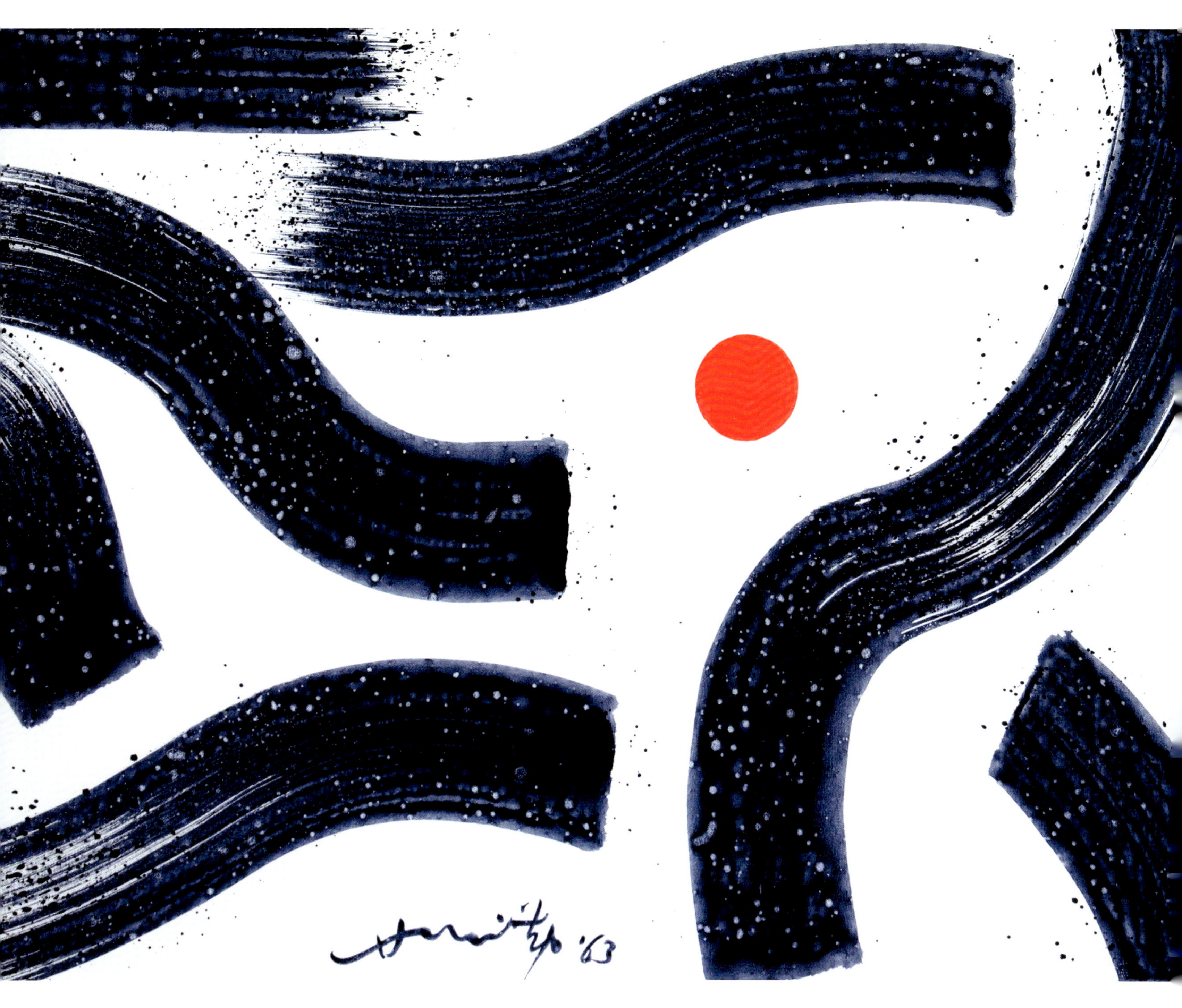

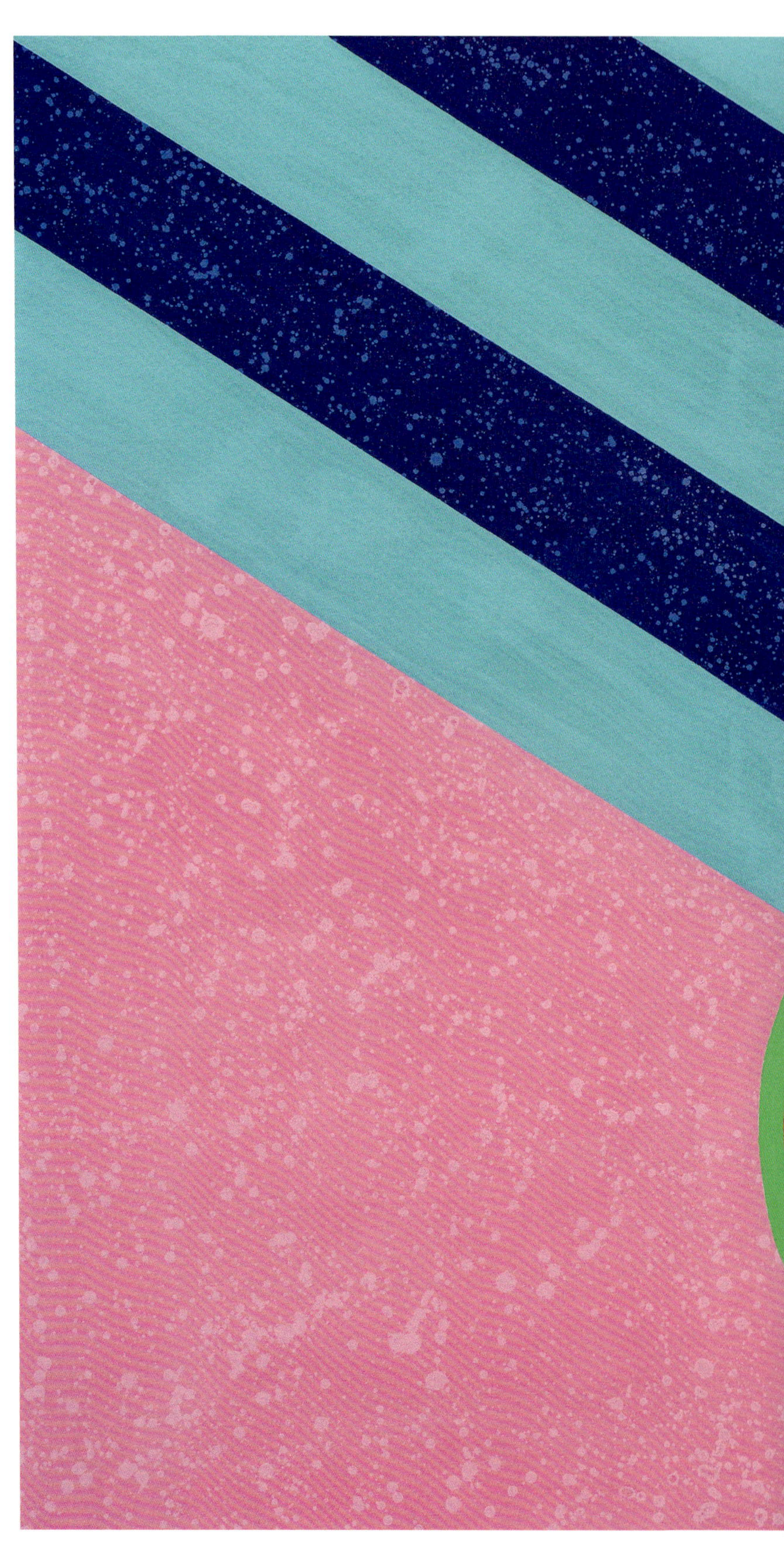

Hsiao Chin
Implication, 1965
Acrylic on canvas
130 x 200cm

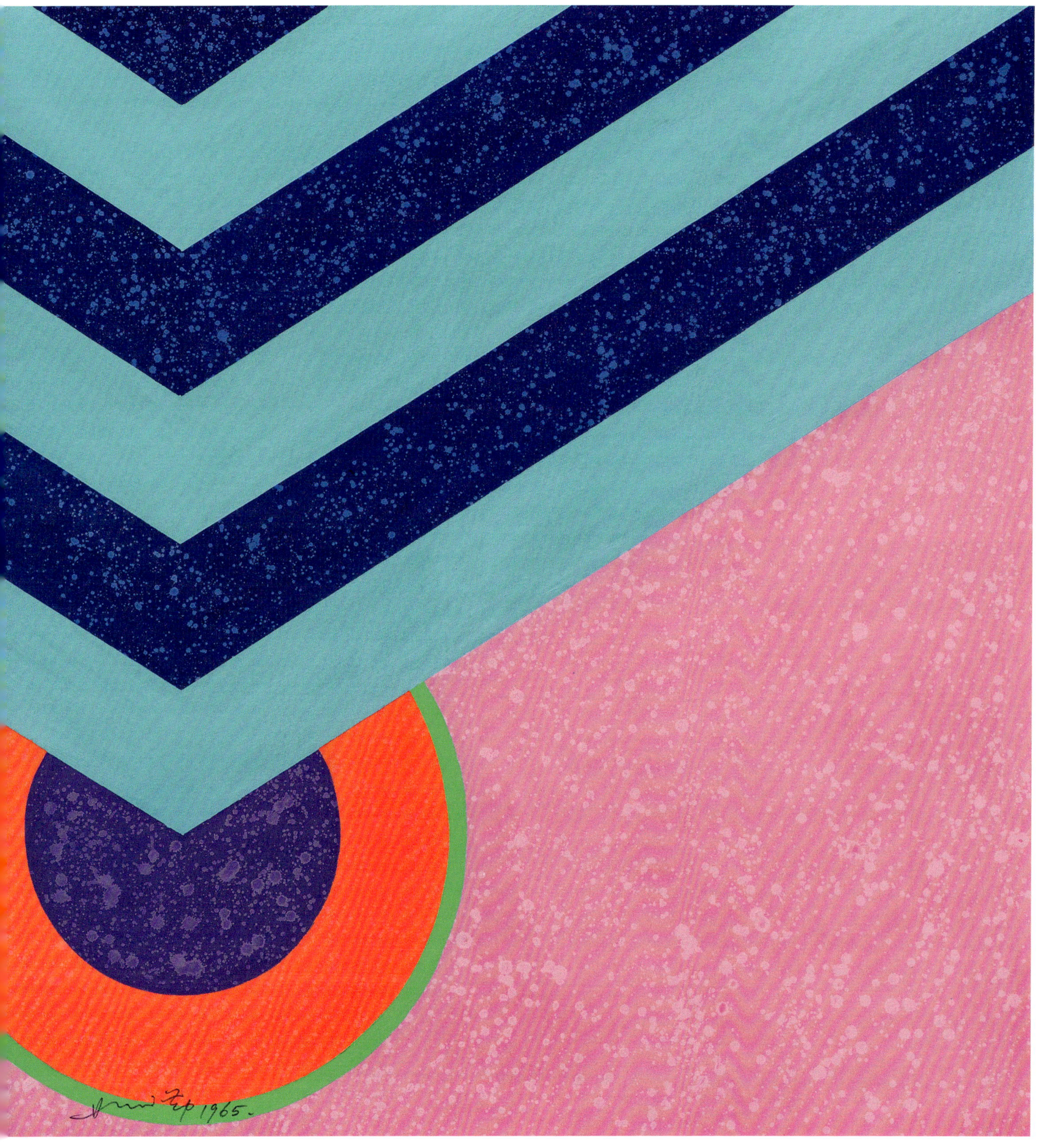

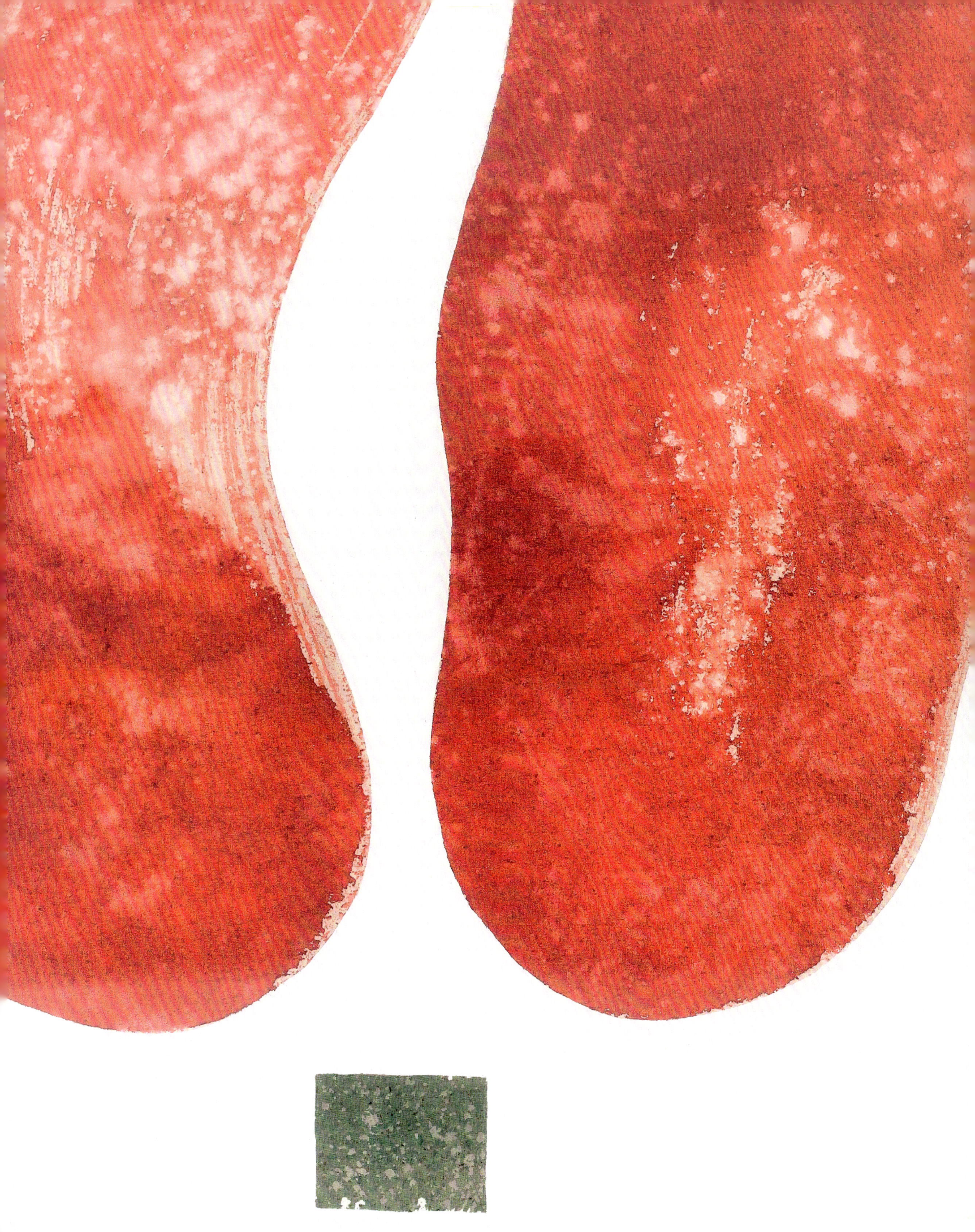

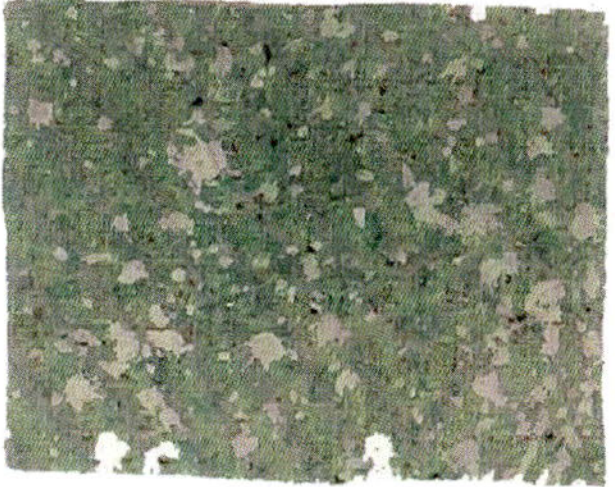

HSIAO CHIN:
A UNIVERSAL JOURNEY

There really is no such thing as Art. There are only artists. Once these were men who took coloured earth and roughed out the forms of a bison on the wall of a cave; today some buy their paints, and design posters for hoardings; they did and do many other things.

– E.H. GOMBRICH[1]

Art is made and recognised by humans, and therefore, like humans, art has a life. Hsiao Chin's Punto is a crucial period in the trajectory of his career. First of all, the artist went abroad, learned foreign languages and adapted Western culture. Secondly, he befriended a group of artists from a different cultural background and formed a global art movement. Furthermore, he was married and had a child; thus the artist also played the roles of husband and father, which were reflected in his paintings. Last but not least, living in Europe led the artist to reconnect with his roots: the value of Eastern culture became apparent, and Asian philosophy has influenced not only Hsiao Chin's way of thinking but also the post-war Western art scene.

The Hsiao family

Hsiao Chin was born into one of the most influential, scholarly and noble families in modern China, especially in the cultural field. Unfortunately, he lost his parents when he was very young.[2] It marked the artist's displaced period in life. He, as the elder brother, had to take care of his younger sister, Hsueh-chen. His two aunts took the siblings into their families separately. Even though the brother and sister were taken care of by their relatives' families, the original small family nevertheless disappeared.

Hsiao Chin's father and mother formed a dichotomy in his philosophical system, and the artist learnt to be independent from an early age. Meanwhile, the civil war in China sent him drifting around the nation, which also determined his character as a wanderer, a man on his own without a family. During his career, Hsiao Chin made various choices under different circumstances; nevertheless, he has always followed his heart. When the artist reviewed the development of his art, he articulated the relation between his life and creativity:

> An artistic creator who really has something to say – a purpose – and a solid motivation to get it across must have his own unique mode of thinking. First, this purpose and motivation tend to be inherently inward. Second, one can readily infer that these traits must be more idealistic than pragmatic. This is quite suitable for me and, in fact, has been precisely the case with my career all along.[3]

Hsiao Chin's father Hsiao Yu-mei (蕭友梅，1884–1940) contributed to the establishment of the Republic of China. He served as the Secretary of General Affairs,

(*opposite, detail see page 165*) Hsiao Chin, *L'incontro*, 1962

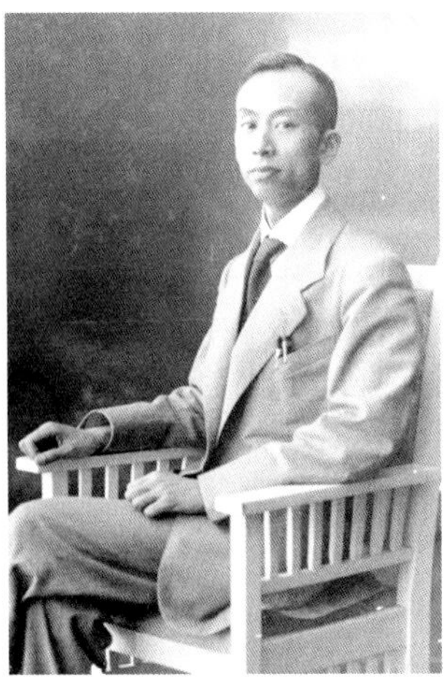

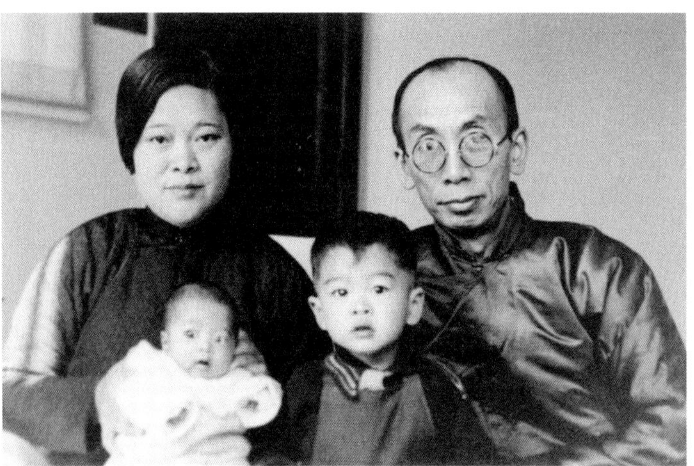

(*far left*) A photo of Hsiao Yu-Mei

(*left*) Family photo of Hsiao Yu-mei couple, Hsiao Chin and his sister Xuezhen in Shanghai home, 1937

Department of the Secretariat at Sun Yat-sen's Provisional Government Presidential Office. Hsiao Yu-mei undertook his formative education in the Macao concession, where new Western culture was prevalent. The family had a close relationship with the Father of the Republic of China, Sun Yat-sen, who at the time was practising medicine in Macao. Hsiao Yu-mei was eighteen years younger than Sun Yat-sen, and they called each other uncle and nephew.[4] In Macao and Canton, he was given both traditional Chinese and Western education. He was particularly interested in the liberal arts, and he studied English and Japanese in addition. After high school, Hsiao Yu-mei went to Japan and was enrolled at the College of Letters of Tokyo's Imperial University. He majored in education. In Japan Hsiao Yu-mei joined the 'Chinese Revolutionary Alliance', and soon afterwards went to Germany, majoring in music. Hsiao Yu-mei was a talented linguist (English, German, Japanese, French, Portuguese, Chinese and Chinese dialects), and Hsiao Chin apparently inherited this ability.

After the establishment of the Republic of China, Hsiao Yu-mei left the office for further degrees in Germany, aiming to realise the ideal of making the nation great by education (教育强國), and obtained a doctorate of Philosophy from Leipzig University. After World War I, he went back to China and helped to found many modern music institutions. He was now commemorated in the mainland as the founder of the Shanghai Conservatory of Music.

Hsiao Chin's mother Chi Chei-chen (戚粹貞) was a pious Christian, and her faith influenced Hsiao Chin in respecting the mysterious.[⊠] Chi Chei-chen's father was a pastor from Jiaxing, a wealthy and cultured city near Shanghai. Hsiao Chin was educated at a Christian school in Shanghai. Because of this background, he did not feel alienated from Western culture, because he accepted his roots on his mother's side.[5]

Hsiao Chin was born in the French Concession in Shanghai in 1935, and his childhood was as a displaced person, especially when his mother passed away. Hsiao Chin moved to Nanjing with his aunt's family (蕭德華) when he was eleven.[6] A few years later, he moved to Taiwan with them. His uncle-in-law Wang Shijie (王世杰, 1891–1981) was one of the most influential educators and justices in the Republican government. Wang Shijie was the first Chancellor of the University of Wuhan (武漢大學) and later served as Minister of Education and Minister of Foreign Affairs as well as the secretary-general of the Office of the President. During the civil war, Wang Shijie acted as a mediator on behalf of the Nationalist party, negotiating terms with the Communist party. Unfortunately, his efforts were in vain. In Taiwan, Wang Shijie devoted himself to traditional Chinese art and became an author and connoisseur.

It can be said that Hsiao Chin's parents, as well as his aunt and uncle-in-law, had a positive impact on his artistic tendencies. His aunt was very strict about his academic choice and was not happy about him taking painting as a career. Due to his unstable childhood, Hsiao Chin became very sensitive, but meanwhile had a strong will to live.[7] He chose to be an artist with unswerving determination. But before he made such a decision, he hesitated for a while, because he was also passionate about music.[8] It is natural to relate music and abstract art – in the cases of Kandinsky and Paul Klee, these abstract artists often explain their compositional ideas as analogous to music. Hsiao Chin's artistic leaning was from his father. As for the visual arts, it was his elder cousin Hsiao Shufang (蕭淑芳, 1911–2005) who opened to him the first impressions of the art of painting.

When Hsiao Chin decided to study art, there were only two higher educational schools offering the course: National Taiwan Normal University and Taipei Provincial Normal College (now National Taipei University of

Education). Hsiao Chin, before becoming enrolled, had just finished a one-year course at an evening high-school; he was therefore not qualified to enter the National University. He had one option: the College; and he knew the goal of the course: to be a primary school art teacher.

Despite the college-level education, the school offered a restricted academic programme, which did not match Hsiao Chin's dream of being a creative artist. He was taught by Chu Teh-Chun (朱德群), but he did not like the severe, strict methods. Chu Teh-Chun at that time followed the path of Cézanne and his style lay between Fauvism and Cubism. Meanwhile, he taught sketching and colouring in a traditional way (Classical Realism). Hsiao Chin hoped he could learn something contemporary. Hsiao Chin's senior, Ho Kan (霍剛), told him that Li Chun-shan was teaching modern art and ideas privately. They went to Li's studio and enjoyed learning from him.

Ton-Fan experience

Li Chun-shan's studio was humble, but the students were delighted and earnest. Hsiao Chin, with his friends, felt the aura of liberty in Li's studio. Eight students there had a similar background. Apart from Hsiao Ming-hsien, they were all from mainland China. Some of them were refugees or professional soldiers. All of them preferred to create artworks worthy of the name of avant-gardism, and Li Chun-shan encouraged their modernist path; they were thinking of establishing an art group. But they did not know that Li Chun-shan was scared about such things, because he had witnessed an artist friend being shot by the Nationalist government on the false charge of conducting espionage with the Communists.[9] It is also possibly why Li Chun-shan did not teach in national universities; instead, he would rather teach as a private tutor. Ouyang Wenyuan (歐陽文苑) was the first student to enter the studio, and as a senior student he started suggesting the founding of an art group. Mr Li did not object openly, but after the session he said Ouyang Wenyuan was too good to be his student, implying that he was banished from his studio.

In summer 1955, another student, Hsia Yan (夏陽), made a proposal suggesting the creation of an art group with a provocative manifesto. This time, Mr Li was intimidated and fell to his knees on hearing the shocking proposal. Next day, he made the excuse of taking a convalescent vacation and closed up his studio.[10]

In 1956, during Chinese New Year's Eve, Hsiao Chin was granted a scholarship to go to Spain. His fellow students held a celebration party, and the gathering encouraged them to activate the dream of creating an art group.

Soon after Hsiao Chin departed, Ouyang Wenyuan and Ho Kan went to the authorities and tried to register an official art group. The authorities refused the proposal, saying that the Chinese Literature and Arts Association (中國文藝協會) had already taken the role of promoting modern art. Because of political restrictions, the group had decided to change its name from 'art group' to 'art exhibition' so that it would be easier to evade censorship. Hsiao Chin in Spain corresponded with his friends in Taiwan and made several suggestions regarding the group's name. Eventually, everyone agreed on Ho Kan's proposal: the Ton-Fan art exhibition.

In Spain, Hsiao Chin made several suggestions for a name, for example, '1957 painting group', 'Andong Painting group' (because Mr Li's studio was located at Andong Road), 'Chinese action painting group'. But eventually the artists agreed to use Ton-Fan, proposed by Ho Kan, for two reasons: first, the Sun rises in the East, signifying vibrancy and vitality, and it reflects that new power of art rising; secondly, all of its members are from the East, and their art emphasises the Eastern spirit and expression.[11]

(*opposite, detail see page 171*) Hsiao Chin, *The Rising Sun*, 1965

Before entering Li Chun-shan's studio Hsiao Chin was tormented by undergoing academic training, because he was not able to follow his own path in creating art. Academic learning confined him to developing modernist pictorial language. Hsiao Chin believed that Van Gogh and Cézanne had already set examples, that it was not necessary for modernist artists to go through the so-called official training. Modern art offers artists the chance to create, derived from their intuition.

Hsiao Chin believes the essence of art is to understand fundamentally how to create, rather than to follow the repetitive and dogmatic practice of a particular training programme. He pointed out:

> Here I would like to emphasise that most teachers and students of fine arts think the academic educational approach is the 'foundation', and that creativity eventually grows on its own from this repetitive teaching method. They believe in 'learning to walk before you run'. This concept is extremely wrong. Art becomes art because of its creative essence. Imitation and plagiarism are not the path for artistic creativity. To put it another way, the academic approach is just like foot-binding of one's thinking; once this foot-binding thought takes shape as a concept, it can never be released. Even if it can be released, such a person could only be a dabbler. How could he ever gallop with his thoughts bound like that?[12]

Hsiao Chin's self-portrait represented the flamboyant feeling inside him. As a young artist, he carried a dream and wished to create, breaking the shackles fixed by academic training. He utilised the method of pointillism to illustrate the uncertainty of shape and the flow of energy through colours. His portrait has the eyes of a rebel, who was ready to create a new world, regardless of tradition.

In Mr Li's studio, Hsiao Chin and his fellow artist friends accepted four points, devoting themselves to creating art:

1. Making art is for the inner needs of the person and a sense of love.
2. There needs to be a sense of accompaniment in terms of artistic practice and it's not enough to rely on internal feelings and love for the work alone. It still depends on individual ability and perseverance. Otherwise, you can only be an amateur, which can beautify life in its own way.
3. Even if you had passion, ability and motivation, you would still need to contemplate artistic interests and perceptual tendencies.
4. Once the artist is determined, it becomes necessary to work to lay the foundation. Using the eyes to carry out sharp observation, and the mind to analyse the object and the ego, then the artist can continue to train himself and the three senses [Eyes, Heart and Mind] to work together and to complete the project of representation.[13]

Hsiao Chin helped to organise exhibitions for Ton-Fan and gained valuable experience. When he started organising Punto, he expanded his communicating circle into a global scale.

Studying in Spain

Because Hsiao Chin was determined to be a modernist artist, he was not satisfied with learning conditions in Taiwan. Not only did the academies not offer relevant courses, but also foreign materials, such as magazines,

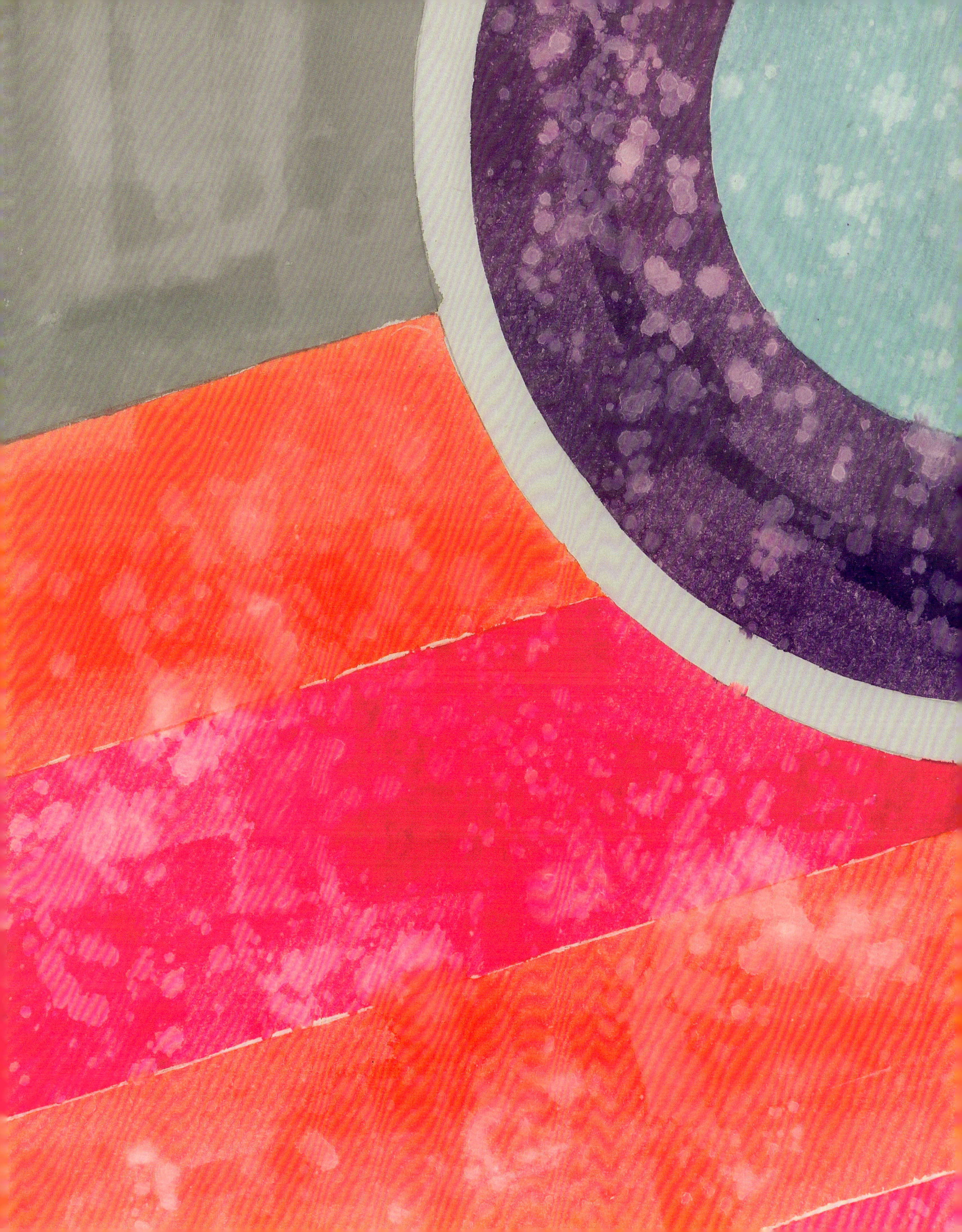

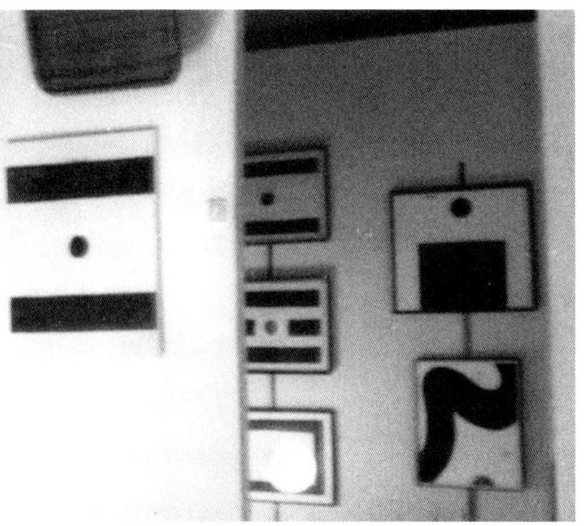

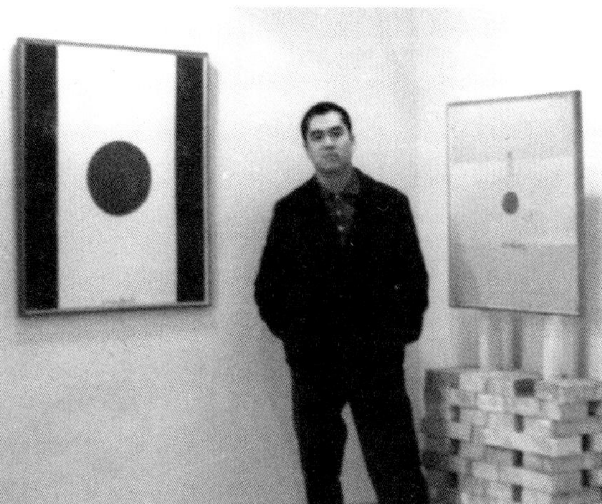

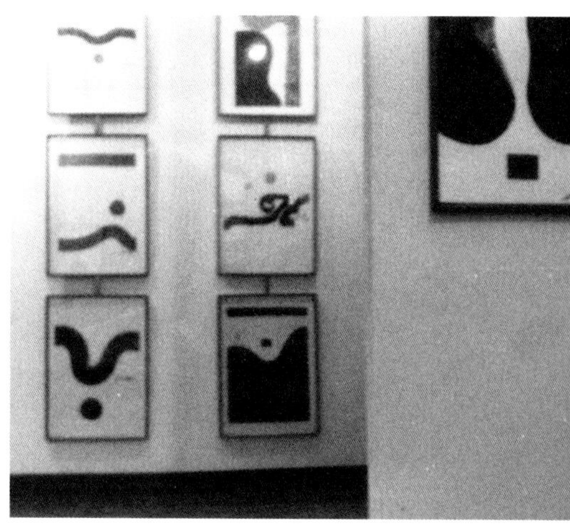

journals and newspapers, were hard to find; most of the time modernist paintings from the West were reproduced in low-quality print. Therefore Hsiao Chin decided to learn at first hand in the West. Once determined, he tried to realise his ambition through actions.

Spain was not an ideal country for people from Taiwan to study in. At that time, the United States was the first choice. The United States had a good relationship with the Nationalist government, although during the Civil War they did not support Chiang Kai-shek (蔣介石, 1887–1975). Hsiao Chin's foster-parents also believed America should be the first choice, but he was too eager to leave. Franco's government, thanks to the common goal of anti-Communism, offered Taiwan fifty scholarships (tuition fees were accepted, excluding the accommodation fees). Hsiao Chin grasped this opportunity and started learning rudimentary Spanish.

It took him more than a month to travel from Taiwan to Madrid. There the students lived in a monastery. Hsiao Chin thought he was familiar with the European environment, considering he was educated in a Christian school and learnt European modernist art. Nevertheless, when he dived into Spanish life, he found himself under tremendously unexpected pressure.

The artist was extremely disappointed by the academic arrangements. He went to visit the Royal Academy of Fine Arts in Madrid, and the teaching was old-fashioned, far from what he was hoping for – inspiration through novelty. He therefore made a tough decision: forfeiting his scholarship and a diploma from an official institution, instead he went to Barcelona to embrace the modern culture of studios, museums, galleries and the market.

This was a decisive moment, and it took great courage for Hsiao Chin to forgo the comfortable living conditions and government funding.

In Barcelona, Hsiao Chin realised there were two significant issues that he needed to deal with: to learn Spanish in order to communicate with the local people; and to earn a living to support his art-making. It took the artist three months to learn enough Spanish to be able to talk to others. He made friends with Spanish people and forced himself to use the language. Sometimes he would spend the entire day listening to the radio and go to the cinema to watch movies in Spanish. To earn a living, he acted as a journalist reporting art news back to Taiwan via the *United Daily News* (聯合報). He made a salary of approximately $30 per month, which barely covered his rent and food. At this time, he was able to give close scrutiny to the Western art world, while redefining himself. He had a wide circle, making friends with local artists.

Some scholars recognised Hsiao Chin's contribution to introducing Western avant-garde art in Taiwan and declared that he enlightened the Taiwanese art circle. Hsia Yan, one of the Ton-Fan artists, even went so far as to say 'after Li Chun-shan, it was Hsiao Chin's era'.[14]

Li Chun-shan believed there are two kinds of people in the world, those who paint well and those who think ahead. Hsiao Chin determined to be one of those who are forward-thinking.[15]

Studying in Spain for Hsiao Chin was a pre-determined accident. With his adventurous character and pious attitude towards modern art, it is not a coincidence that he was willing to give up so-called formal education. He had already been qualified and ready to carve a path in Europe.

In Barcelona, Hsiao Chin not only participated in many group exhibitions but also had the first solo exhibition at the Mataro Fine Arts Museum. According to existing photographs of the show, he had already simplified colours, albeit he remained figurative. At that time, Hsiao Chin began to realise the power of Chinese culture and what Li Chun-

(*left, centre*) Hsiao Chin at the group exhibition at Stadtisches Museum, Leverkusen, West Germany, 1963

(*left and far left*) Hsiao Chin's works at the group exhibition at Stadtisches Museum, Leverkusen, West Germany, 1963

(*right*) Hsiao Chin with friends photographed in his home in Milan, 1963 From left to right: Hsiao Chin, Hsia Yan, scupltor Pizzo Greco, Japanese sculptor Kenjiro Azuma, architect L. Fordes Davanzati

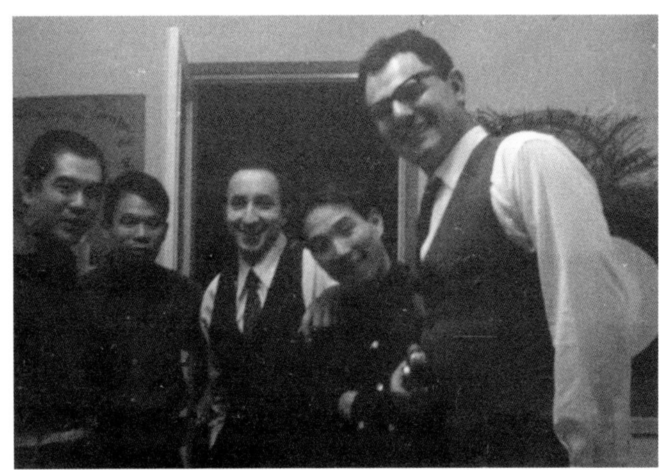

shan had always reiterated: the national stance as a personal aesthetic signature for artists from the non-Western world.

Hsiao Chin was prepared to embrace Western avant-garde art fully, but the more he explored, the more he realised that Eastern wisdom resided in Western modern art. For example, the Impressionists such as Vincent van Gogh took inspiration from the Japanese Ukiyo-e. Mark Tobey (1890–1976) was influenced by Asian calligraphy. Picasso sought pictorial elements from African art. Hsiao Chin discovered that since the 1930s artists such as Mark Tobey, Clyfford Still (1904–1980), Franz Kline (1910–1962), Georges Mathieu (1921–2012), Henri Michaux (1899–1984) and Zao Wou-Ki tried to mix the West and the East to formulate a path to global art.[16] All of this made Hsiao Chin realise it was necessary for him to revisit Chinese culture in order to make an artistic breakthrough.

While Western artists used Eastern elements to complement their personal aesthetic expression, similar methods could not apply to Hsiao Chin, simply because it was impossible for the artist to depict images from a Euro-centric point of view. Hsiao Chin, in revisiting traditional Chinese culture, confronted a dilemma:

> Many have already worked to research, analyse and compare Chinese and Western thought, so I need not say much here. Whether pure Western analysis and logical scientific thought are suitable to give Chinese people a unified view of the universe is certainly a big question.
>
> Excessive analysis and delineation have made Western artistic expression overly radical, and non-theoretical theories, as well as theory for theory's sake, have made it rigid and infertile. In this way, to look back and research China and Eastern thinking about 'nature' should offer a suitable path to redemption. In recent years, the transformation of Western scientific thought has gradually broken down materialism and materialist concepts, reconstructing a philosophical basis in order to balance the material and the spiritual, such that the 'human' and 'nature' can be re-identified as one.
>
> In my opinion, this comparison, reflection, and discovery have determined my life and the trajectory of my art.[17]

In the twentieth century, Western intellectuals had been thinking about how to compensate for the insufficiency of rational thinking, a legacy of the Enlightenment. The result has been to foster a flourishing. First of all, Freudian and Jungian psychology were discovered and discussed as a way to demystify the subconscious; meanwhile, the Dadaists and Surrealists utilised the non-sense and subconscious as a means to portray actuality by exploring the irrational. Moreover, Marcel Duchamp departed from modernism by claiming that since Impressionism art had been made to serve the eye, but he wished to call for the art that serves the mind. Last but not least, the two Great Wars made Western intelligentsia notice the danger of Darwinism and start to revisit humanism as a legacy of the Renaissance. Jean-Paul Sartre and Albert Camus were aware of the absurd condition of Western society and tried different ways to understand human existence.

Hsiao Chin's judgement on the duality of art was very accurate, and he realised that introspection is critical to global art. At first he stopped making art for a while.

When he experienced a block in creating art – in other words, he was not able to find a way to spiritual evolution – he asked friends in Taiwan to send Daoist books. He wished to rediscover the Eastern Wisdom in Daoist ideas:

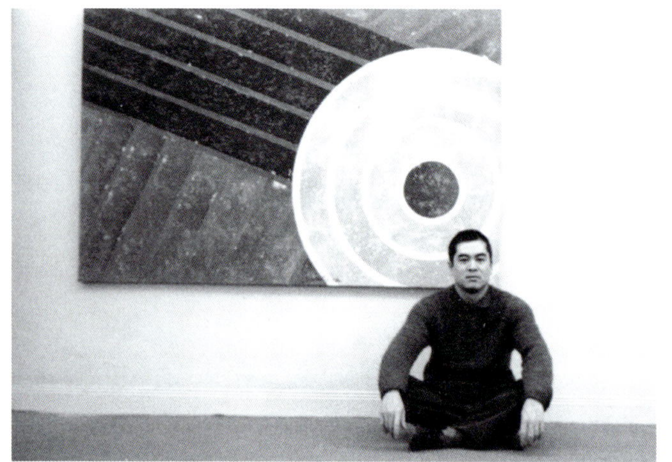

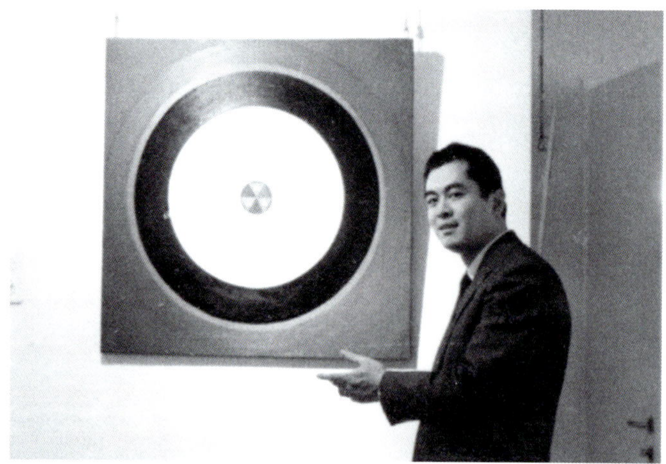

> I rooted my own ideas in Daoism. Though I was living abroad, I had not forgotten the importance of 'spiritual space' that Mr Li Chun-shan had always emphasised. I knew that if my works were lacking in inner experience or failed to persist in creating a unique style, there would be no content of which to speak. Studying the philosophies of Lao-tzu and Chuang-tzu inspired me to develop a new concept of artistic vocabulary.[19]

Hsiao Chin's passion reverted to the origin of thoughts: a dot (punto). The dot implies observance.

The ineffable encounter

In 1959 Hsiao Chin moved from Barcelona to Milan. The city's location in the centre of Western Europe was convenient for the artist to travel around the Continent visiting museums, galleries and artists' studios, and creating exhibitions. It could be said that Hsiao Chin's efforts made Punto exhibitions a reality. Artists entrusted him with their artworks. He personally unframed the paintings and carried them around the Continent, and then did the staging nearly all by himself. At that time, museums and galleries were not as they are nowadays – sponsors and curators were not standard practice. As the key organiser, Hsiao Chin took the roles of curator, shipping and staging company. At first, he was not able to afford a private car, and had to carry twenty to thirty paintings by train.[20]

The experience made of Hsiao Chin a human nexus, bridging the Eastern and Western contemporary art worlds. He also helped promote Chinese art overseas. A few artists a generation older than Hsiao Chin stayed in Europe and America: Pan Yuliang (潘玉良), Sanyu (常玉), Zao Wou-Ki (趙無極), Walasse Ting (丁雄泉), Chu Teh-chun (朱德群), Hsiung Ping-Ming (熊秉明) and I.M. Pei (貝聿銘). Pan Yuliang and Sanyu were celebrated figurative Chinese artists. Zao Wou-Ki and Chu Teh-chun were, like Hsiao Chin, pioneers of Chinese abstract art, although they were a generation older. I.M. Pei was the world's leading Post-Modernist architect, who designed the glass pyramid for the Louvre.

In 1963, thanks to Hsiao Chin's renowned organisational skills, the Städtisches Museum in Leverkusen, Germany, worked with the artist to hold a contemporary Chinese art exhibition (Chinesische Künstler der Gegenwart), featuring works by Zao Wou-Ki, Walasse Ting, Chu Teh-chun, Hsiung Ping-ming and I.M. Pei. This exhibition was one of the most important showcases of Chinese art in history, and it also demonstrated that 'Chinese art' does not mean 'art in China'. Chinese artists, as early as the eighteenth century, had been studying and working overseas. Some of the artists were commemorated in the art history of foreign nations. For example, the Cantonese artist Tan-Che-Qua (Chitqua) was invited by the British king to be an honorary guest in the group portrait of the Royal Academicians by Johann Zoffany.[21] The exhibition at the Städtisches Museum was the first post-war exhibition dedicated to contemporary Chinese art.

Lao-tzu (老子) laid the foundations of Daoism and Chuang-tzu (莊子) expanded the theory, adding romantic elements, using grand allegory and highly imaginative stories to explain the mystic aspects of human life. One of the famous stories in Chuang-tzu gave rise to the question of identifying oneself and the imagined self. Once Chuang-tzu, in a dream, found himself to be a carefree butterfly without realising that he was Chuang-tzu (possibly a personification of secular troubles). When he woke up, he was confused, not sure whether he had turned into a butterfly in the

(*left and far left*) Solo exhibition at the Galerie Internationale d'Art Contemporain in Paris, 1964

(*right*) Sanyu and Hsia Yan visited Hsiao Chin's solo exhibition in Paris, January, 1964

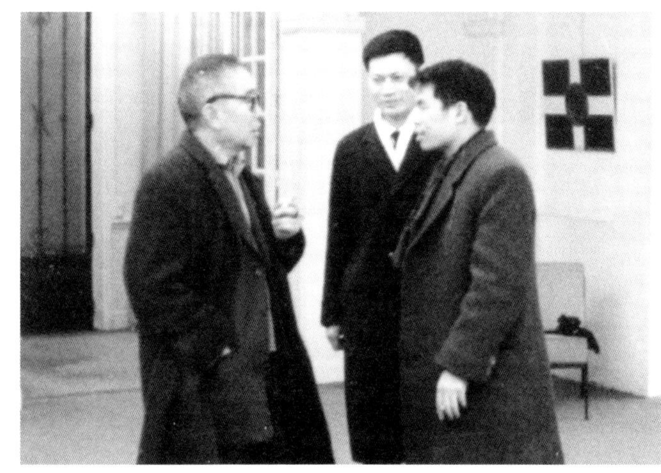

dream, or the butterfly had been transformed into the human Chuang-tzu. The dialectic identity crisis marks the hope of overstepping the boundaries of physical limitation. Dream is the medium of transgression.

Hsiao Chin read the books and was fascinated by their mystic power. He decided to explore oddities and vignettes. At one point, he drove miles in Italy to visit a psychic, who could not read or write but was able to use a typewriter. Hsiao Chin observed how the psychic received revelations from above, and how the energy flowed through the body and conducted the hands to type out some script.[22] The dream world and metaphor inspired an evolution in his thinking. He made a series of paintings as an analogy of some abstract concept: *Crouch* (p. 40), *Dive* (p. 41), *Discover* (p. 42), *Protection for Kindness* (p. 50).

These works illustrated that Hsiao Chin had been meditating on a less aggressive way of living. The superfluid Fauvist flamboyance was reduced to simplicity, and energy concealed its limits so that it could stretch into every corner of the universe.

There is a theme in Hsiao Chin's Punto probing the ineffable encounter: *Follow* (p. 167), *Forward Looking* (p. 58), *L'incontro* (The Encounter, p. 165); and these paintings can be seen as implying his relationship with Pia Pizzo. Pizzo and Hsiao Chin were both signed by the Milan-based gallery Salone Annunciata. Hsiao Chin held his solo exhibition there in spring 1961. At that time the couple had become acquainted, but they did not know each other very well. It was in summer 1961 at the Albissola pottery centre that they began their relationship. In April 1962 the two Punto artists were married. Love was a romantic and mysterious encounter as well as a new experience for Hsiao Chin.

The ineffable encounter, the accidental drawing together, the one generated by the other, and the expansion of space are abstract and abstractly illustrated by Hsiao Chin on canvas. In text, it might be interpreted by Roland Barthes's *A Lover's Discourse*:

> The absence of the other holds my head underwater; gradually I drown, my air supply gives out: it is by this asphyxia that I reconstitute my 'truth' and that I prepare what in love is intractable.
>
> I divine that the true site of originality and strength is neither the other nor myself, but our relationship itself. It is the originality of the relationship which must be conquered. Most of my injuries come from the stereotype: I am obliged to make myself a lover, like everyone else: to be jealous, neglected, frustrated, like everyone else.[23]

The ecstasy of falling in love made one Punto into two fields and may have led to three: a new self within the dialectic masculine–feminine relationship. The intersubjectivity between the self (Hsiao Chin) and the other (Pizzo) seemed to lead to a pure immediacy as a source of inspiration. Husserl distinguished such an immediacy in this way:

> If we look each other in the eye, subject meets subject in an immediate interaction. I speak to him, he speaks to me. I command him, he obeys. These are immediately experiences of Others.[24]

This encounter has an impact on human apprehension, cognition and creativity – a transcendental clue. Hsiao Chin, the abandoned son, has been wandering around the universe, even though he did not lack comradeship with Ton-Fan and Punto artists; nevertheless the artist was

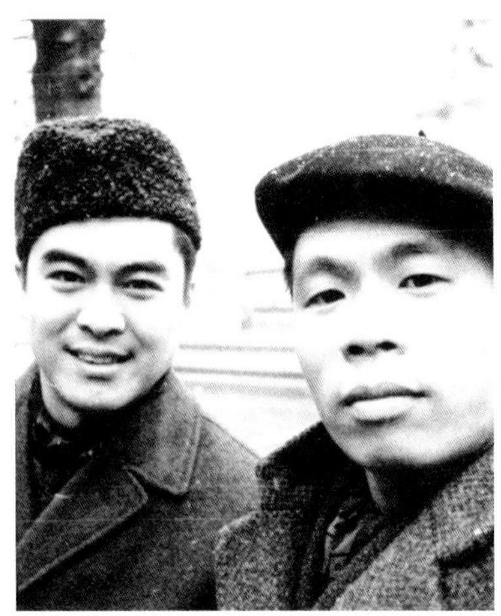

Hsiao Chin and Hsia Yan in Paris, January, 1964

(*right*) Hsiao Chin with Shen Bao-chu, famous artist in Milan, 1973

(*far right*) Photo taken in Ting Yung-yin's place in Hong Kong, October, 1978

without a family. Punto enabled him to have an intimate relationship between the two sexes. Also, the encounter is mysterious, yet a sort of gene code passes from one generation to another. The artist made a particular work derived from the *Encounter* series called *Three Gave Birth to Everything*, seeking analogy from nature:

> On the canvas is a pure, transparent blue; fertile brown soil; a blue, sparkling river; and ample sunlight shining upon everything. Everything is vibrant and full of life, thus allowing all of nature to grow.[25]

Although the artist asserted that he utilised visual language to translate the literary idea of Lao-tsu into the artwork, nonetheless it can be said that he intuitively portrayed the abstract concept, yet the visual opens to another method of interpreting dimension.

Regarding the form, three dimensions formed a hyper-flat space: a red dot represents the origin of all things; a blue line emerges from the left, like the Milky Way, consisting of stars – the high level of energy meets the origin (red dot); finally, a corner of a black square occupies the left corner, implying a space beyond the easel. It might be interpreted thus: that the artist realised his meaning by forming a relationship, knowing the self by recognising the other. The first step of knowing oneself is to acknowledge the importance of the ego, so that one is able to separate the internal and the external worlds. The second step of realising oneself is to relocate oneself in relating to other individuals so that one is able to know and show empathy. Only by equipping himself with empathy can an artist make a work of art as a medium to communicate with the spectator. It is a crucial stage of life, which Jean-Paul Sartre postulated as the Age of Reason.[26] Hsiao Chin emphasised the importance of empathy in creativity:

> Creative artists must first maintain their innate 'vibrant naïve heart', but this by itself is not enough. They must also continuously cultivate this heart's feeling of simple honesty and love of all things. Only in this way can our instinctive 'intuition' and 'perception' become deeper and more sensitive, and only in this way can their works move and resonate with them. These, however, are only the most basic conditions. For a work to become 'art' and stand the test of time without withering, many other factors are necessary.[27]

Predestined Affinity (緣) is a Buddhist concept explaining cause and result. There are infinite predestined affinities generating the various movements and accidents in the universe. *Madhyamika* is the major school of Mahayana (Great Vehicle 大乘), and it believes that the property of predestined affinity is the void. When Hsiao Chin depicted himself in a mandala for meditating on the truth, one thing he had to confront was the nihilistic theory in Buddhism. *Madhyamika* posits that all things have no self-nature but emptiness, and all events have an inevitable cause.

In order to see true nature clearly, Hsiao Chin removed or arbitrarily separated himself from relative connections, and he took more inspiration from Daoism into Buddhism. It can be said that his faith was strengthened. The paintings that resembled the sun acted as mandalas of spiritual energy. The artist wished the spectator to view them with silent contemplation and meditation. The centralised Punto was a gesture through which Hsiao Chin was like a guru master, disseminating his passion, sensitivity and myth. Take *The Sun-7*, *(p. 92)* for instance, the form resembling the sun as well as the wheel of Buddhism (法輪). Although in his art since

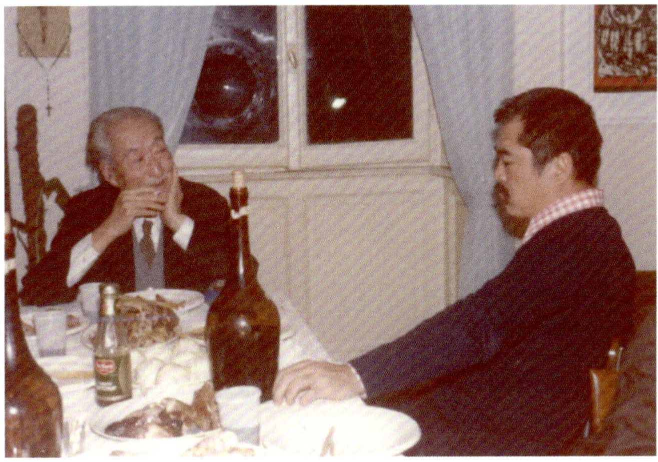

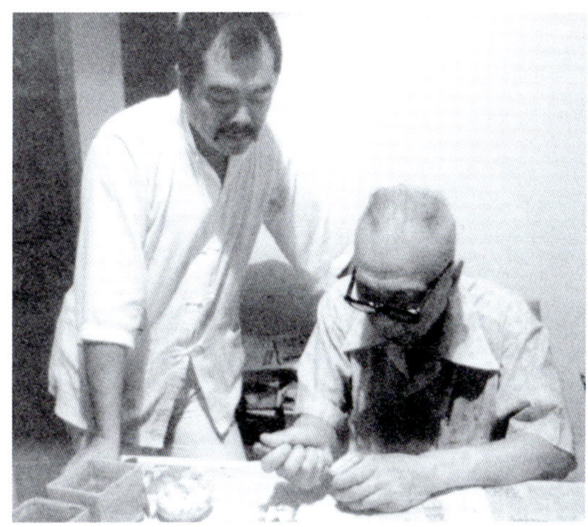

1959 Hsiao Chin had thematically developed a few series of abstract paintings, he alleged that the process was not easy. He admitted the hardship of being a free and creative artist:

> Everyone knows that freedom comes at a great price. It takes great courage and resolve. To be able to 'create freely' in art is also very difficult, whether in terms of achieving 'freedom' in creation itself (how to refine and discover one's 'true nature'), or in terms of maintaining a 'free body' of creation (how to resist the spiritual and material pressures of the outside world). The true artist must have the spirit and courage of the martyr, and the ideals of the Mahayana Buddhist: to use artistic exploration and discovery of one's 'true nature' to give spiritual inspiration to others.[28]

In organising Punto, Hsiao Chin had to overcome a great many issues. Financially, Punto was more of an avant-garde experiment than a commercial operation. Artists who participated in the movement entrusted Hsiao Chin with their spiritual purity. Punto re-centralised human beings as the finite condition of the infinite universe. Artists were supposed to be the spokesperson for humanity.[29] It cannot be denied that commercial success is one aspect in which artists are involved; nevertheless, the essential element is the experience of life and the evolution of the spirit. Hsiao Chin believed that the process and the results of artistic creation are formed by intuition and intellect, and that the process should follow the method of 'gradual enlightenment' (漸悟) with preparation and research; then the action of creating is the result of 'sudden enlightenment' (頓悟).[30] The eureka moment comes with long-term, diligent work, which requires piety and intuition.

The legacy and spiritual significance of Punto

Punto was a success among post-war avant-garde movements. First of all, it was the earliest contemporary abstract art that tried to merge the East and the West, making aesthetic concepts universal and global once again. Moreover, thirteen exhibitions were held in Asia and Europe, and they reshaped the landscape of art history. Artists from different groups participated in and communicated with Punto, all of which developed the meaning of abstract art. Furthermore, the movement had a Post-Modernist spirituality, deconstructing representation to the bitter end, but without compromising creativity.[31] Last but not least, Punto as a movement ended in 1966, when Hsiao Chin moved to London and was not able to organise another group; nevertheless, it has always been the core of the artist's creative thinking. The historic code has already been implanted in global art, and it has been a feature of Hsiao Chin in his long career.

On the other hand, Punto was not seen as influential in commercial terms. No art dealers thought of promoting it as an art group; therefore, the ecology of art was not a complete cycle. Consumer culture, as well as its effect on art, neutralised the edge of experimental art. The art market and its operation have gradually become transcendental. Young, talented artists are not only noticed and supported, but are being evaluated and overpriced. Conceptualist art was invented, in a way, to dematerialise art, yet the capitalists found a way to commercialise the conceptual. Spiritual purity seems to be unable to escape the trap of fame, wealth and power. When Pop artists and Young British Artists lived a life of 'famous for being famous', Punto appeared to be out of fashion.

Another problem of Punto is its theory. Chan was the core aesthetic thinking of the movement. Chan focused

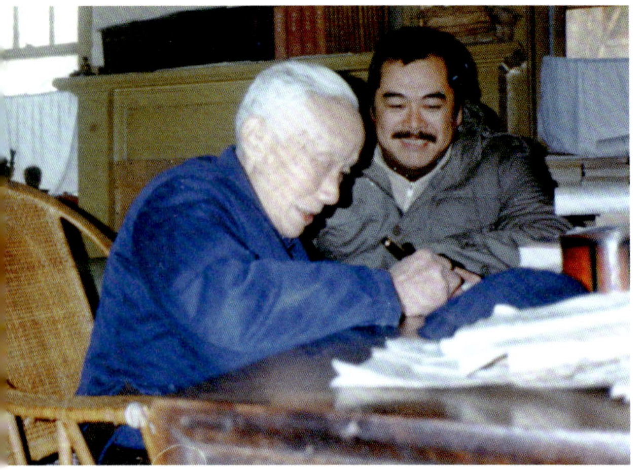
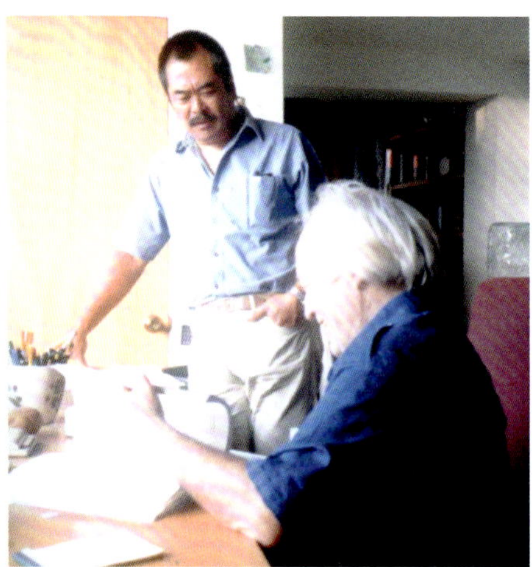
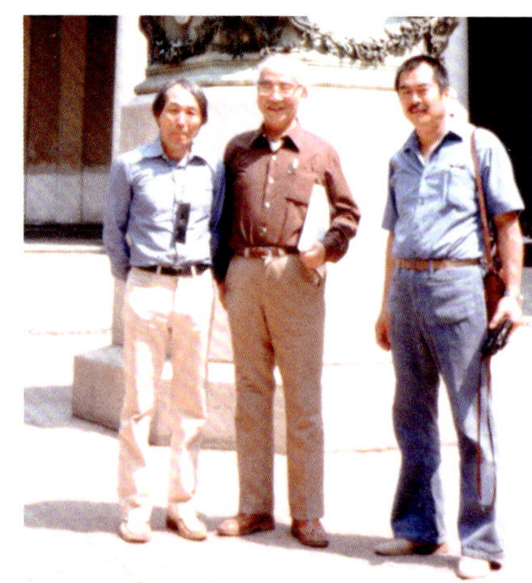

on mediating through practice rather than explaining theoretically – therefore it is hard for theorists to identify and extend its historical significance. Chan decayed in China during the Ming and Qing dynasties precisely because it was difficult for the populace to understand and practise. When it was revived in the 1960s in the West, it was treated as a guide to living, rather than a religious school. Hsiao Chin summarised the problem of Punto:

> The now four-year-old Punto movement had received official affirmation from the art world, and had earned us a place in art history. Internationally, many artists identified with us. The reason it did not make such great waves as many other art movements was that our creative ideas were extremely rigorous and pure. Only a few artists with deep spirituality and determination can carry on the struggle for ideas such as these, and only a small number of people will be able to accept them.[32]

Admittedly, capitalists turned to combining financial ventures with cultural promotion; and sometimes money can contaminate the purity of creation. However, in late consumerist society, money was only a symbol; its significance has long given way to the importance of information. Intellectual capitalists or cultural capitalists in a way co-exist with the traditional bourgeois, if not replacing them. Nationalism (patriotism/populism) is still a significant force in the cultural field of art. The silence of Punto in the late 1960s could be the foundation of its success in the twenty-first century. Ink painting and abstract art in China have already instigated a good creative development. Zao Wou-Ki, Chu Teh-Chun, Wu Guangzhong are recognised academically as great artists of the world and are also recognised by the market. Kumārajāva (鳩摩羅什, 344–413) was forced to marry and fornicate, but this did not become an obstacle on his path to becoming a great Buddhist. Money (capital) is as pure as the human heart, as long as the benign means can justify the benign ends.

After Punto, Hsiao Chin developed Hard Edge and conducted another two global art movements: Surya (1978) and Shakti (1989), all of which inherited the Punto spirit. The art historian Nerio Rosa in his summary said that Punto transcends the limitation of nations, the formality of information, as well as medium and style.[33]

The artist never stopped making art according to the principles of Punto – reflecting its universality and paying homage to the infinite. The transcendental experience of Punto in post-war global art is unique and meaningful, and its significance is beyond the historical, social and aesthetic. It explores the possibility of resolving constant pain caused by greed and violence.

In the twenty-first century, wars are still occurring all over the world. The European Union as a peaceful and respectful model of a universal community might not survive another financial crisis. The complications of feminism, immigration issues and terrorism question the existing model of globalisation. The concept, the validation of democracy in the post-colonial and post-capitalist era have been severely tested. Fake news and digital falsification have started causing contemporary societies to question its validation. China specifically is of paramount significance to the world, especially in the transitional period of global power-shift, and the nation's identity is viewed and conceptualised differently in different regions: mainland China, Hong Kong and Taiwan. Despite the moral problems interwoven with the dilemma of the individual and the collective, the trade war as well as arguments about the internet are pointing to the crucial issue that contemporary society must confront – resources for benefits.

(*far left*) Hsiao Chin in Chu Kuan-qian's home in Beijing, December, 1980

(*centre left*) Hsiao Chin with Sam Francis in Los Angeles, 1982

(*left*) Group photo of Hsiao Chin, Wu Zuoren (middle) and Kenjirō Azuma (left) in Accademia di Belle Arti di Brera, 1983

(*right*) Hsiao Chin with Walasse Ting at the Vigevano Auto Show, May 20, 1990

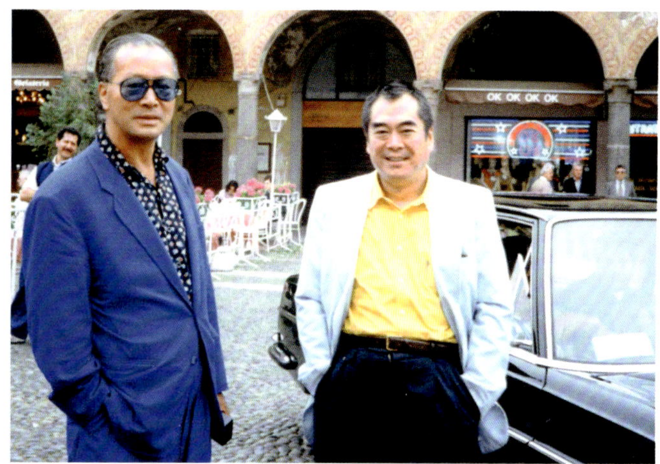

The fundamental source of all crises can be said to be about the distribution of limited resources (the role of politics is to gain power to allocate resources and benefits, whereas economics is the process of generating profits).

In this case, Punto reminds the world that there is a way to counter the problem of all problems: to recognise physical limitations and believe in spiritual infinity. There will be a better way of globalisation, in the course of which human beings can tolerate differences and recognise empathy. The universal value is that of humanity, the existence of which requires great spirituality. If current progress cannot continue, it is suggested that we go back to the beginning and re-examine what went wrong, and find another way. Punto provides such infinity because it revisits the beginning of visual art – a dot.

Hsiao Chin's universal journey has not ended yet: it is certain that Punto will be revived once again.

---

1 E.H. Gombrich, 1996, *The Essential Gombrich*, London: Phaidon, p. 65.
2 His father died when he was five and his mother when he was ten. He had a sister who was separated from him and stayed in mainland China.
3 Hsiao Chin, 2010, 'The universe is my mind', *Infinity of Chi: Homage to the Master: Retrospective of Hsiao Chin*, Kaohsiung: Kaohsiung Museum of Fine Arts, p. 11.
4 Maggie Wu, *Legend of the Rambling King: Side View of Hsiao Chin*, p. 17.
5 *Ibid.*, p. 23.
6 Hsiao Chin, 1983, '1959: My First Two Solo Exhibitions in Italy', *Artist Magazine*, July, Vol. 98, pp. 74–77.
7 Hsiao Chin, 2018, *Hsiao Chin Coming Home*, China Art Museum Shanghai, p. 4.
8 Li Lei, 'Hsiao Chin's Coming Home', *Hsiao Chin Coming Home*, China Art Museum Shanghai, p. 12.
9 Hsiao Chin, 1983, 'Revisiting Key Points of Fine Arts Education', *Artist Magazine*, Mar., Vol. 94, pp. 35–37.
10 Beatrice Peini Gysen-Hsieh, 2002, *The Momentum of the Group Ton-Fan Marked in Shanghai*, Taipei: Taiwan Museum of Art, pp. 7–9.
11 *Ibid.*
12 Hsiao Chin, 1983, '1963 Exhibition at Städtisches Museum, Leverkusen, West Germany', *Artist Magazine*, Jun., Vol. 97, pp. 110–13.
13 Hsiao Chin, 2015, 'Mr. Hsiao Chin Speaks of his Experience as a Student under Mr. Li Chun-shan', *Transmission of the Lamp*, General Association of Chinese Culture.
14 Hsiao Chin, 'Revisiting Key Points of Fine Arts Education', pp. 35–37.
15 Pei-ni Beatrice Hsieh, 2010, 'Preface', *Homage to the Master: Retrospective of Hsiao Chin, Infinity of Chi*, Kaohsiung: Kaohsiung Museum of Fine Arts, p. 6.
16 Hsiao Chin, 2017, 'Hsiao Chin Speaks about Fifth Moon and Ton-Fan Again', *A Historical Dialogue with Art*, Kaohsiung: Punto Press, p. 231.
17 Hsiao Chin, 1983, 'Appreciation and Analysis of Works from the 1950s and the 1960s', *Artist Magazine*, Sept., Vol. 100, pp. 78–80.
18 Hsiao Chin, 1983, '1959: My First Two Solo Exhibitions in Italy', *Artist Magazine*, July, Vol. 98, pp. 74–77.
19 Hsiao Chin, 2017, 'Attitudes Towards Learning', *A Historical Dialogue with Art*, Kaohsiung: Punto Press, p. 65.
20 Hsiao Chin, 1983, '1963 Exhibitions at Städtisches Museum, Leverkusen, West Germany', *Artist Magazine*, June, Vol. 97, pp. 110–13.
21 Joshua Gong, 2014, *Iconography and Schemata: A Communicating History in Painting between China and the West, 1514–1885*, Shanghai: Commercial Press.
22 Personal correspondence between Calvin Hui and Hsiao Chin.
23 Roland Barthes, 2002, *A Lover's Discourse*, London: Vintage Classics.
24 Michael Theunissen, 1984, *The Other: Studies in the Social Ontology of Husserl, Heidegger, Sartre and Buber*, Massachusetts: MIT Press, p. 110.
25 Hsiao Chin, 2017, 'Visual Language and Modelling Language', *A Historical Dialogue with Art*, Kaohsiung: Punto Press, p. 205.
26 Jean-Paul Sartre, 2001, *The Age of Reason*, trans. by Eric Sutton, Penguin Modern Classics, London: Penguin Books.
27 Hsiao Chin, 'Visual Language and Modelling Language', pp. 48–50.
28 Hsiao Chin, 1984, 'A Stylistic Turn: On Hard Edges and the Zen Series', *Artist Magazine*, Jan., Vol. 104, pp. 68–70.
29 Hsiao Chin, 1983, 'Punto Art Movement', *Artist Magazine*, Dec., Vol. 103, p. 66–69.
30 *Ibid.*
31 Aldo Tagliaferri, 'Trip through a Square without Corners', *La via di Hsiao*, La Nuova Foglio, p. 37.
32 Hsiao Chin, 1983, 'Punto Art Movement', p. 66–69.
33 Nerio Rosa, 2005, 'La Poetica di Hsiao Chin tra Oriente e Occidente', *Hsiao Chin*, Città Di Atri: Assessorato alla Cultura.

Hsiao Chin
The Union (L'unione), 1962
Acrylic on canvas
70 x 80cm

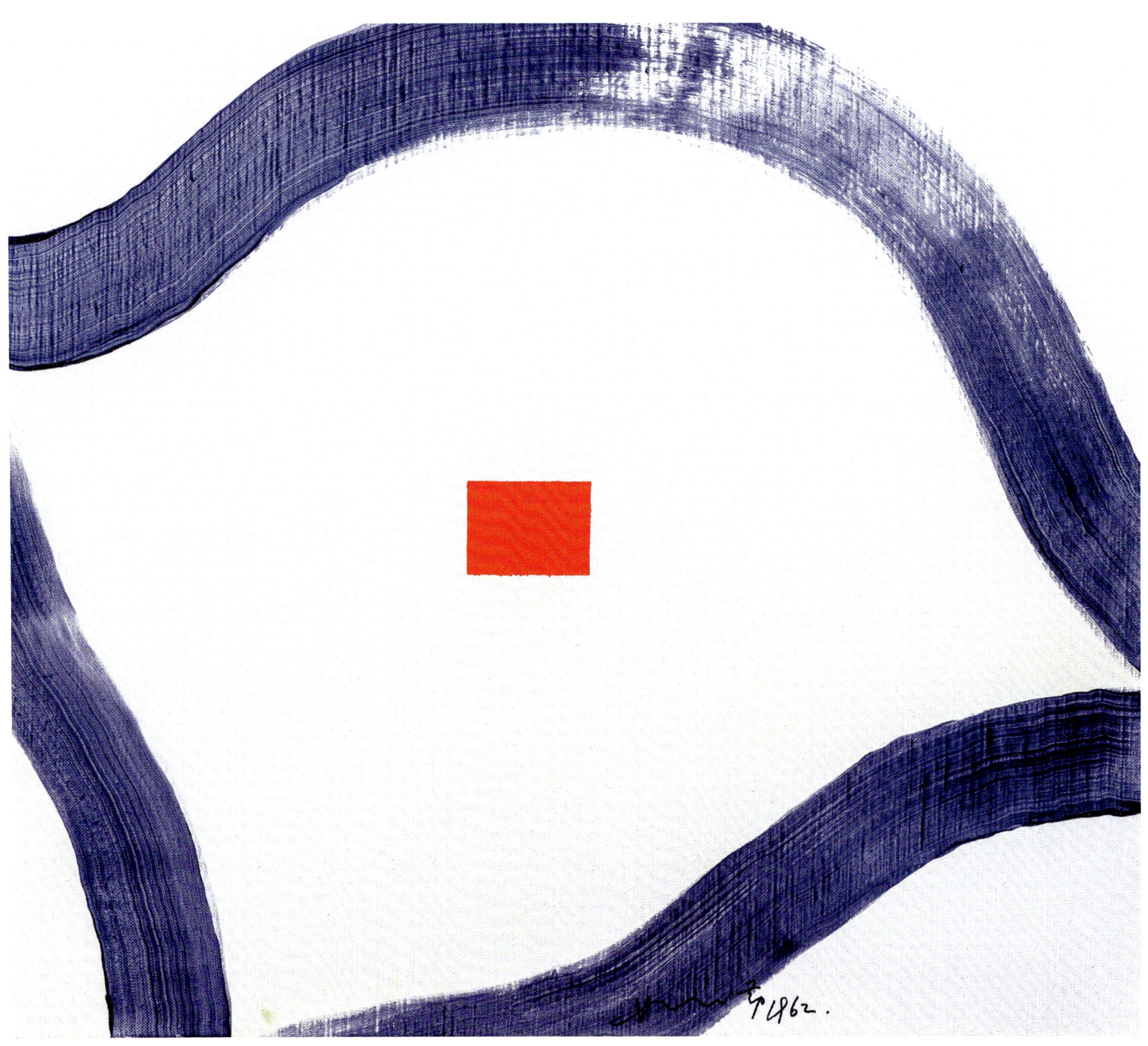

Hsiao Chin
The Vision (La visione), 1962
Acrylic on canvas
60 x 50cm

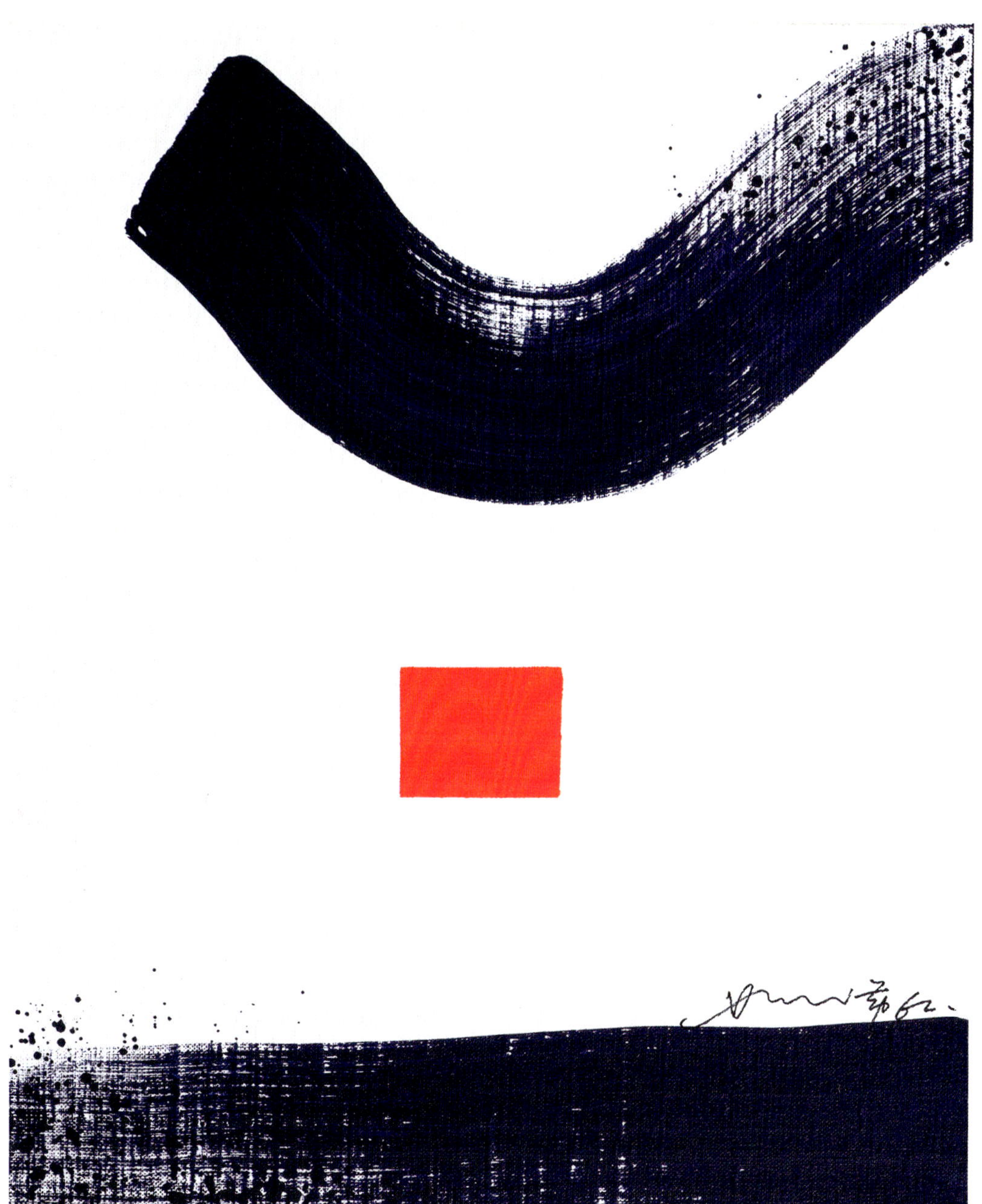

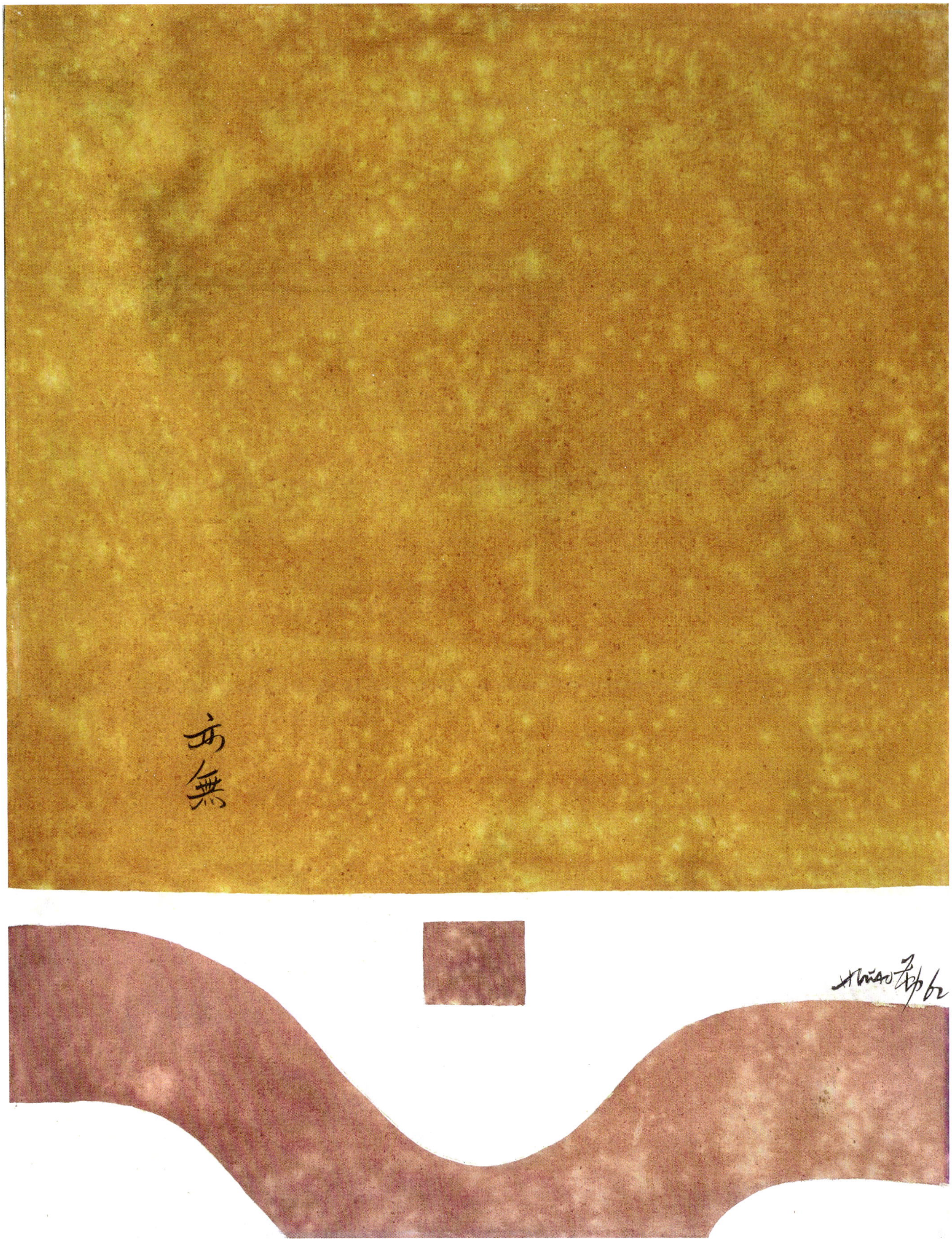

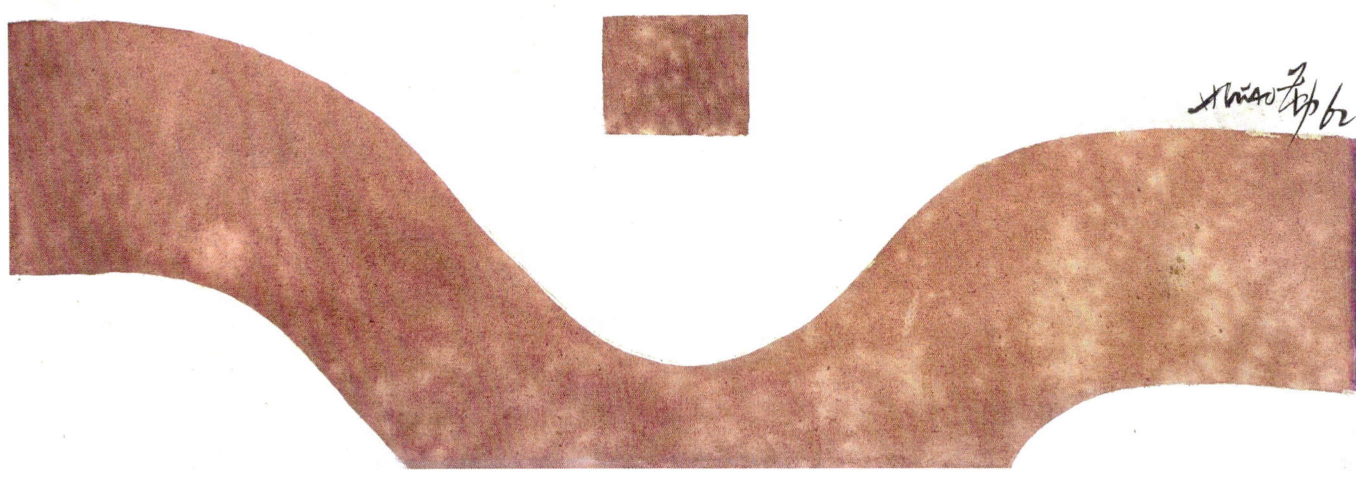

Hsiao Chin
Nothingness, 1962
Ink on canvas
90 x 70cm

Hsiao Chin
L'incontro, 1962
Oil on canvas
70 x 79cm

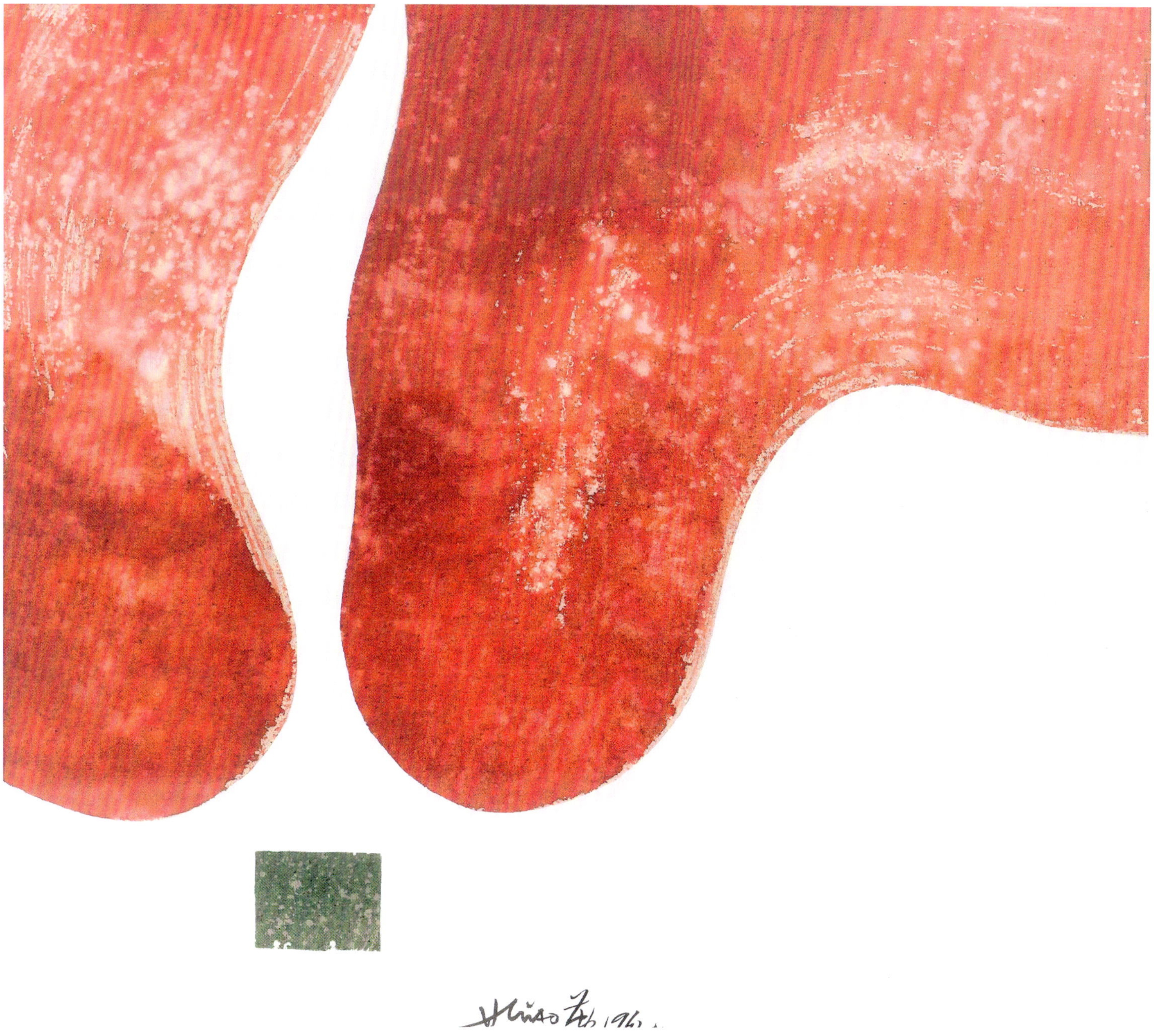

Hsiao Chin
Grand Encounter, 1963
Acrylic on canvas
61 x 36cm

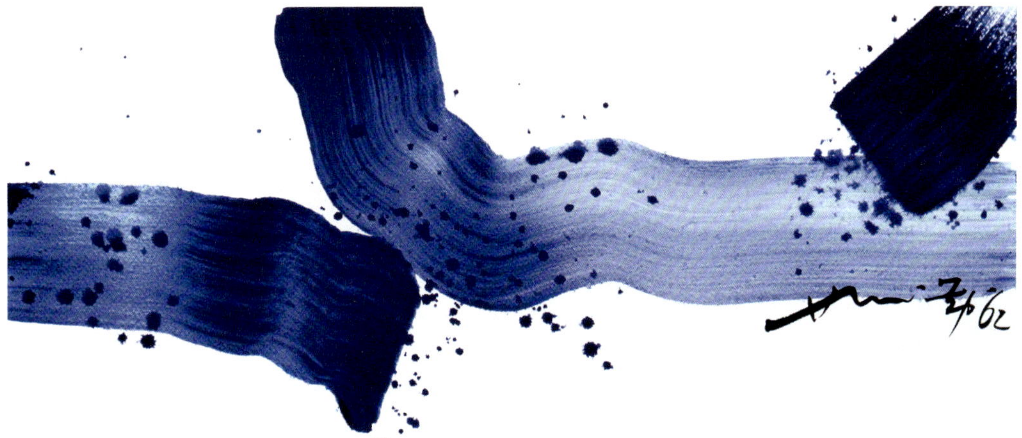

Hsiao Chin
Follow, 1962
Acrylic on paper
39 x 53.5cm

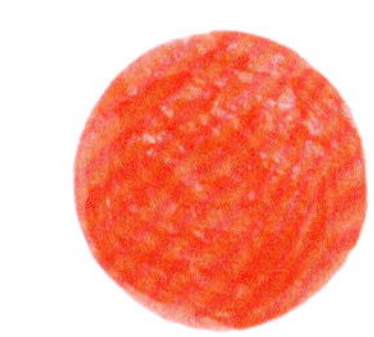

Hsiao Chin
L'attrazione, 1966
Acrylic on paper
38 x 51cm

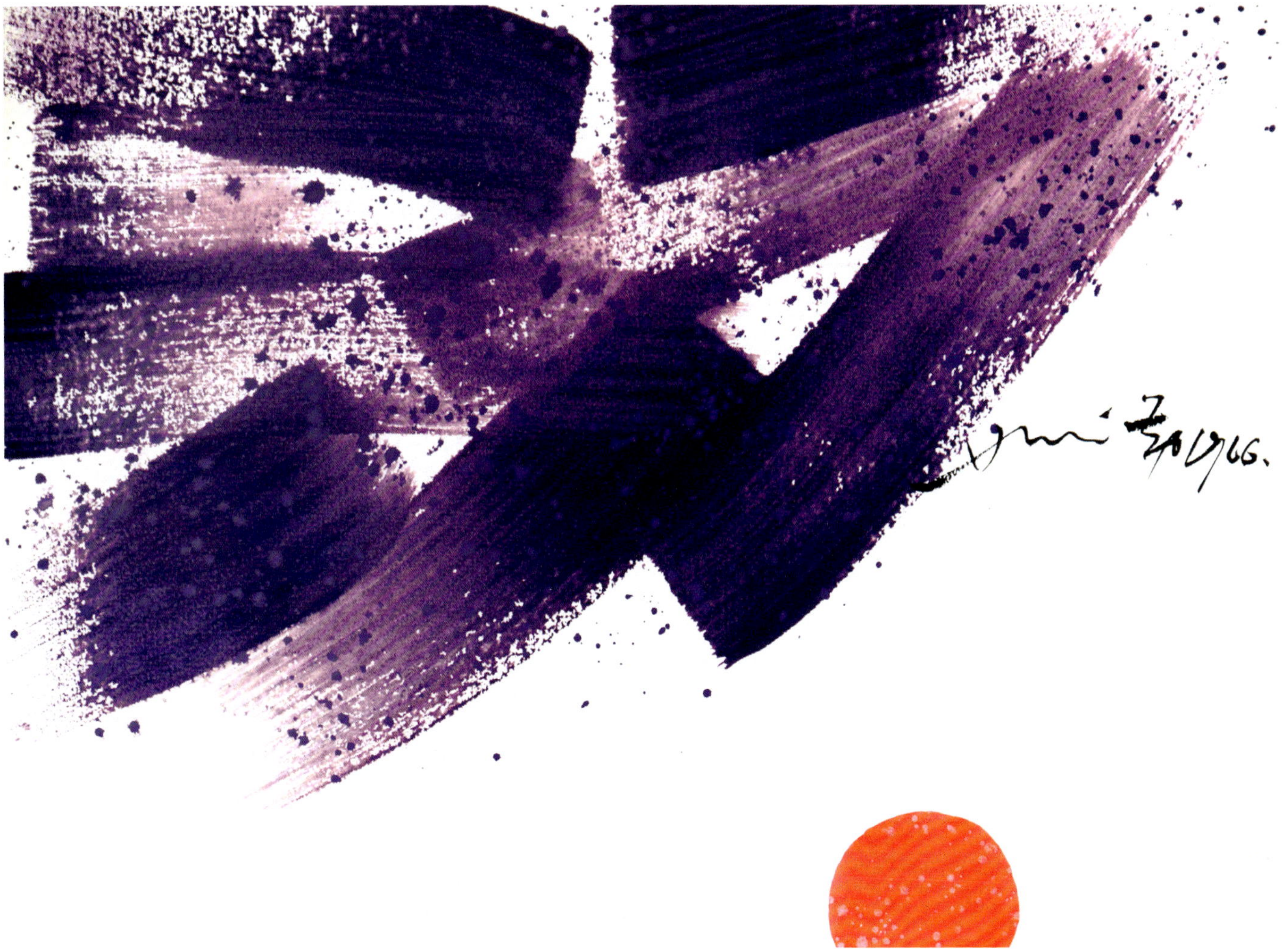

Hsiao Chin
Cause Of Life-1, 1964
Acrylic on canvas
60 x 50cm

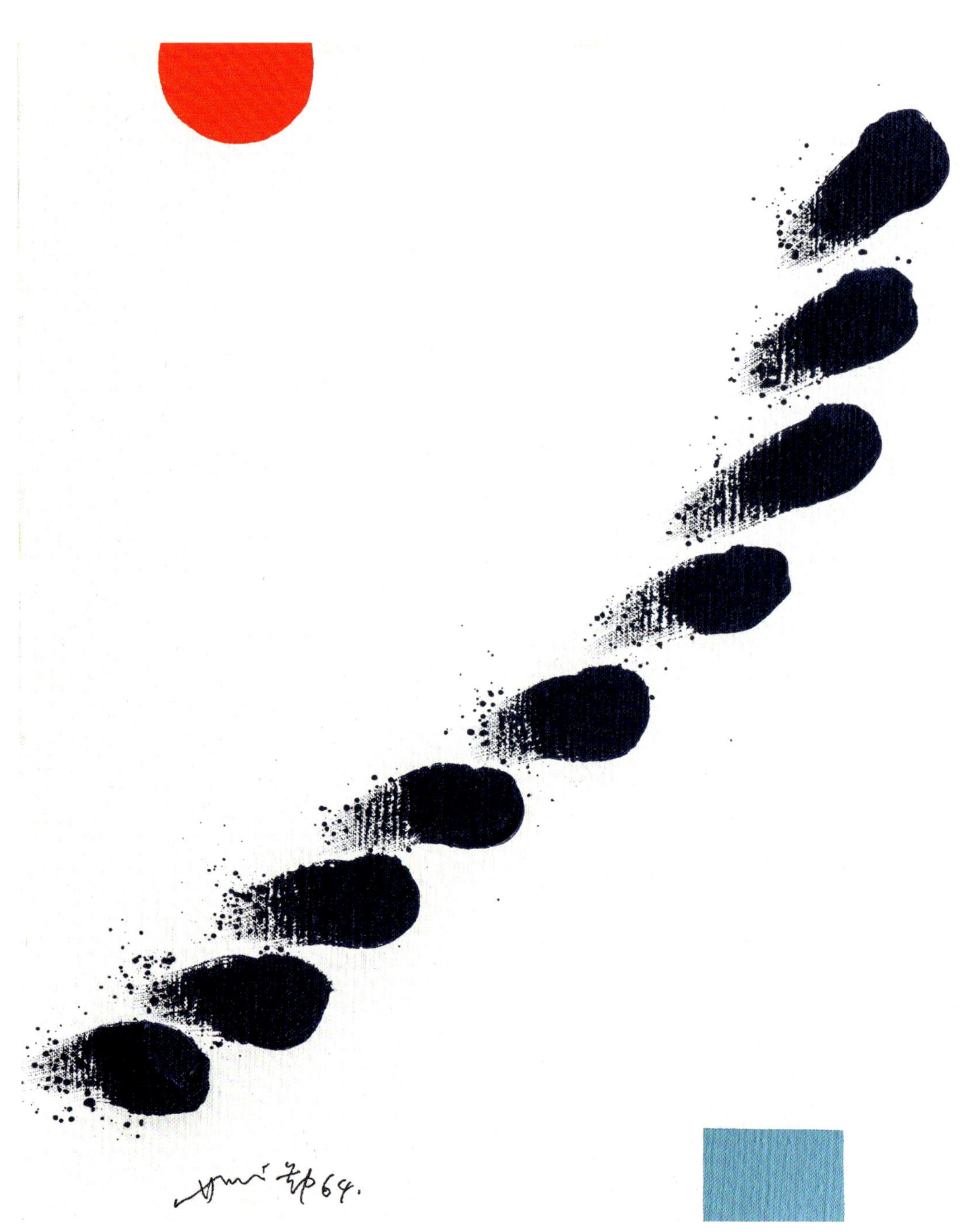

Hsiao Chin
Cause Of Life-2, 1964
Acrylic on canvas
60 x 50cm

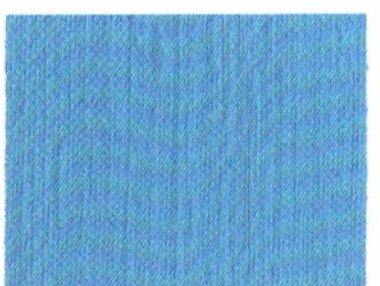

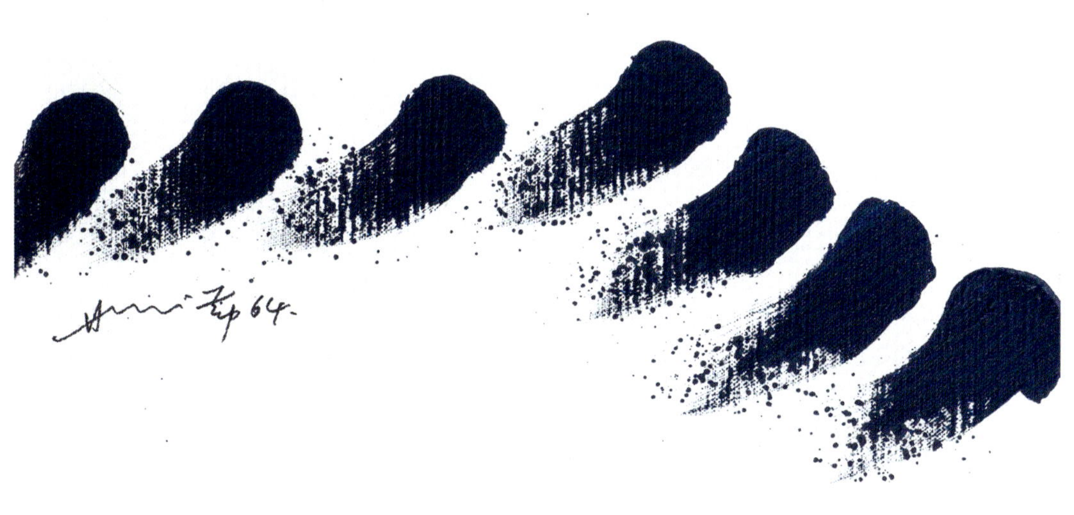

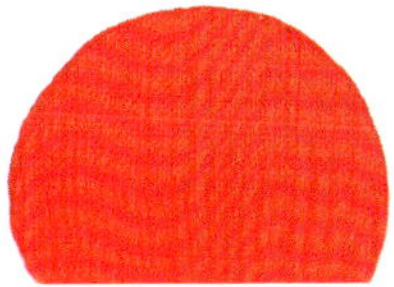

Hsiao Chin
Dancing Light-16, 1963
Acrylic on canvas
90 x 140cm

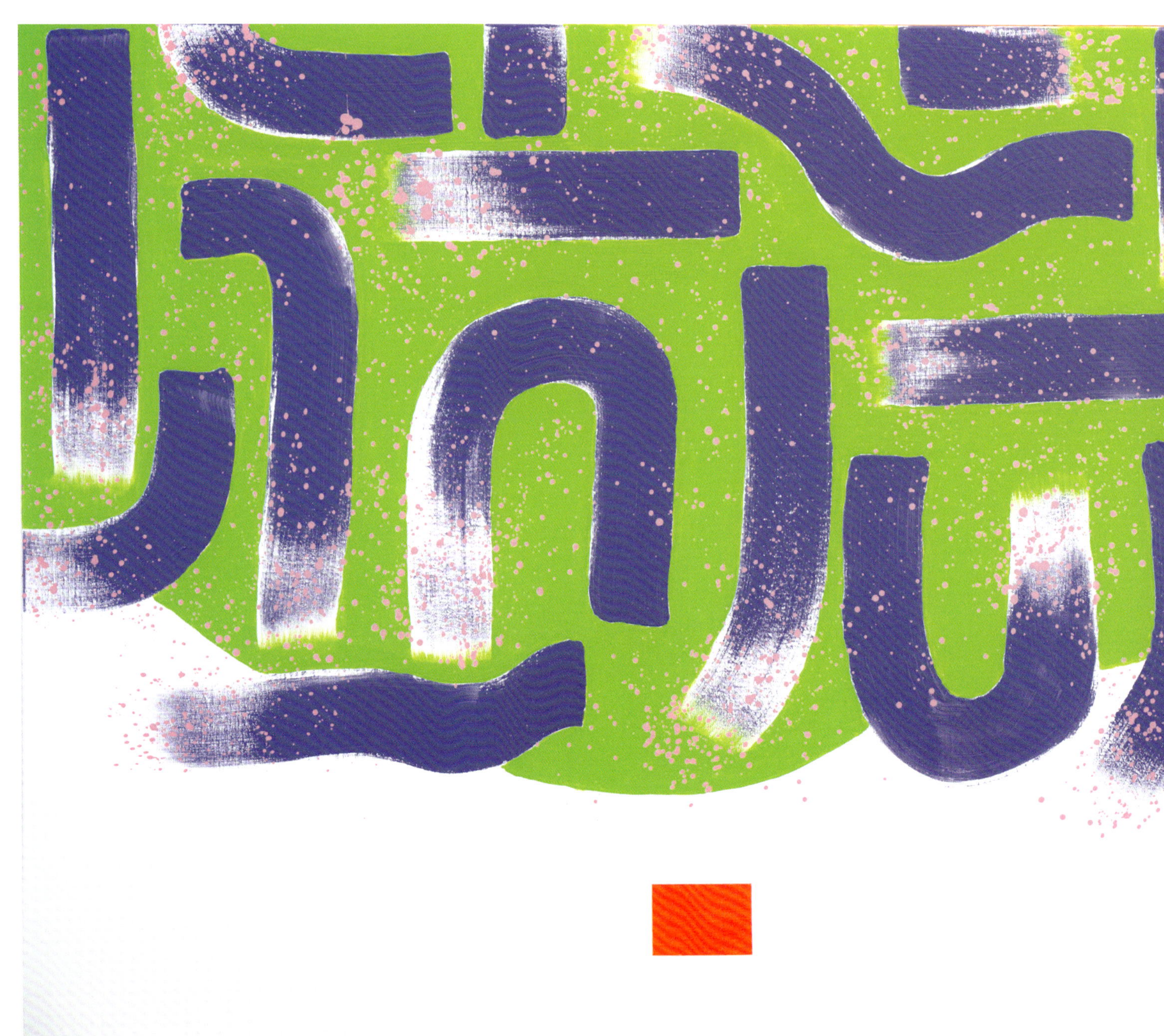

Hsiao Chin
The Rising Sun, 1965
Acrylic on paper
57.5 x 81.5cm

Hsiao Chin
Prevision, 1964
Acrylic on canvas
130 x 160cm

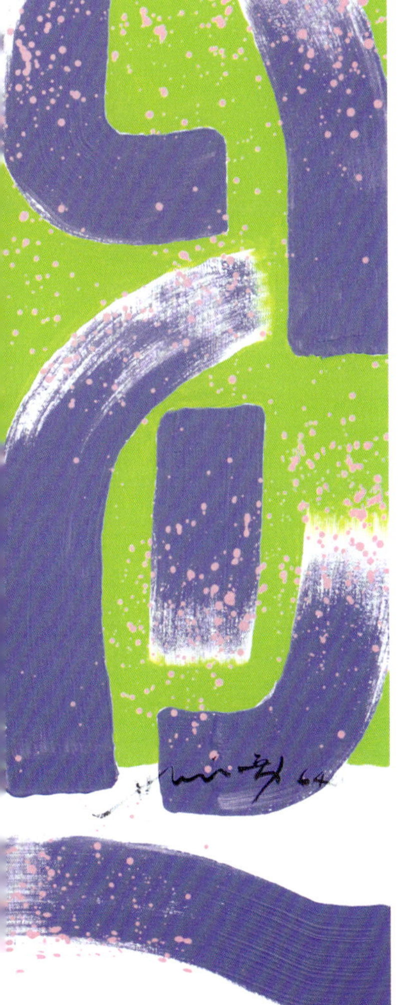

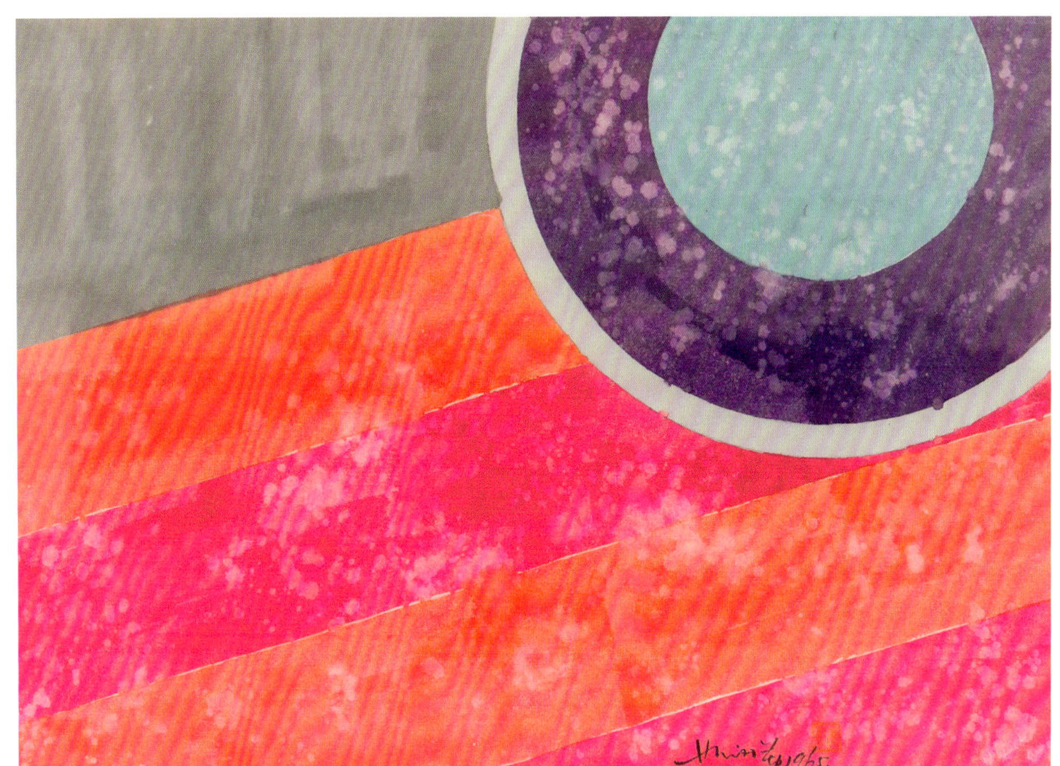

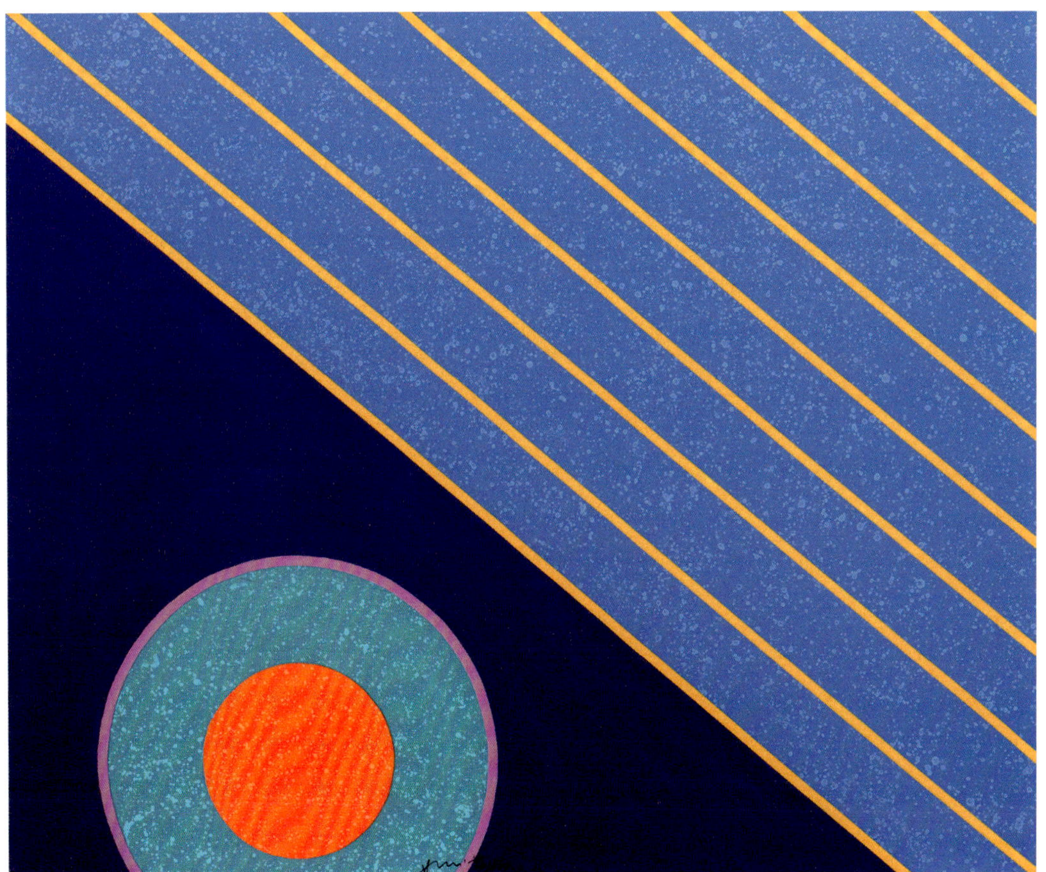

BIBLIOGRAPHY

Acton, M., 2004, *Learning to Look at Modern Art*, London: Routledge.

Babka, S., 2016, *Through the Dark Field: The Incarnation through an Aesthetics of Vulnerability*, Minnesota: Liturgical Press.

Baudrillard, J., 1983, 'The Ecstasy of Communication', *Postmodern Culture*, ed. Hal Foster, London: Pluto Press.

Barthes, R., 2002, *A Lover's Discourse*, London: Vintage Classics.

Bartos, J., 2019, *The Geometry of Beauty*, London: Unicorn Publishing Group.

Cirlot, J., 1958, *Arte contemporaneo: origen universal de sus tendencia*, Barcelona: Edhasa.

Confucius: *Analects of Confucius*, ancient texts [《論語》] <https://zh.wikisource.org/wiki/論語/雍也第六>, [25 November 2019].

Curley, J., 2018, *Global Art and the Cold War*, London: Laurence King Publishing.

Debord, G., 1983, *Society of The Spectacle*, Detroit: Black & Red.

Diamond Sutra, trans by Yutang Lin, [《金剛經》林語堂 譯本] <http://www.yogichen.org/gurulin/efiles/p1/p1488.html>, [9 December 2019].

Egbert, D., 1970, 'The Idea of avant-garde in Art and Politics', *Leonardo*, Vol. 3, No. 1.

Foster, H., Rosalind E. Krauss, Benjamin H. D. Buchloh, Yve-Alain Bois, *Art since 1900*, 2007, ed. Hal Foster London: Thames & Hudson.

Gombrich, E., 1996, *The Essential Gombrich*, London: Phaidon.

Gong, J., 2014, *Iconography and Schemata: A Communicating History in Painting between China and the West, 1514–1885*, Shanghai: Commercial Press. [龔之允:《圖像與範式:早期中西繪畫交流史1514–1885》,上海:商務印書館2014年出版].

Gu Kaizhi, *Praising Famous Paintings of Wei and Jin dynasties*, ancient texts [顧愷之:《魏晉勝流畫贊》,東晉], <https://zh.wikisource.org/zh-hant/魏晉勝流畫贊>, [25 November 2019].

Gysen-Hsieh, B., 2002, *The Momentum of the Group Ton-Fan Marked in Shanghai*, Taipei: Taiwan Museum of Art.

Heart Sutra, 2014, trans by Thich That Hanh, Plumvillage, <https://plumvillage.org/about/thich-nhat-hanh/letters/thich-nhat-hanh-new-heart-sutra-translation/>, [9 December 2019].

Hsieh, P., 2010, 'Preface', *Homage to the Master: Retrospective of Hsiao Chin, Infinity of Chi*, Kaohsiung: Kaohsiung Museum of Fine Arts.

Honour, H., 1973, *Chinoiserie: The Vision of Cathay*, reprinted paperback edition, London: John Murray.

Honour, H. & J. Fleming, 2002, *A World History of Art*, 6th edition, London: Laurence King Publishing.

Huineng, *Platform Sutra of the Sixth Patriarch*, eighth to thirteenth century, ancient text, [惠能:《六祖壇經》] <https://zh.wikisource.org/zh-hant/六祖壇經/行由品>, [10 December 2019].

Hsiao, C-R., 1995, 'The Manifestation of Tao-Hsiao Chin's Continuing Progression of Life', *Hsiao Chin: the odyssey, 1953–1994*, Taipei: Taipei City Museum of Fine Arts. [蕭瓊瑞:《流動的生命——以象成道的蕭勤》,《蕭勤的歷程:1953–1994》,台北市立美術館1995年].

Hsiao, C., 1983, 'Revisiting Key Points of Fine Arts Education', *Artist Magazine*, Mar., Vol. 94.

Hsiao, C., 1983, '1957, My First Solo Exhibition in Mataro Barcelona', *Artist Magazine*, Vol. 96.

Hsiao, C., 1983, '1963 Exhibition at Städtisches Museum, Leverkusen, West Germany', *Artist Magazine*, Jun., Vol. 97.

Hsiao, C., 1983, '1959: My First Two Solo Exhibitions in Italy', *Artist Magazine*, July, Vol. 98

Hsiao, C., 1983, 'Appreciation and Analysis of Works from the 1950s and the 1960s', *Artist Magazine*, Sept., Vol. 100.

Hsiao, C., 1983, 'Analysis and Discussion of Artistic Creation', *Artist Magazine*, Vol. 102.

Hsiao, C., 1983, 'Punto Art Movement', *Artist Magazine*, Vol. 103. [蕭勤:《藝術家》,1983年12月第103期].

Hsiao, C., 1984, 'A Stylistic Turn: on Hard Edges and the Zen Series', *Artist Magazine*, Vol. 104.

Hsiao, C., 2010, 'The universe is my mind', *Infinity of Chi: Homage to the Master: Retrospective of Hsiao Chin*, Kaohsiung: Kaohsiung Museum of Fine Arts.

Hsiao, C., 2015, 'Mr. Hsiao Chin Speaks of his Experience as a Student under Mr. Li Chun-shan', *Transmission of the Lamp*, General Association of Chinese Culture.

Hsiao, C., 2017, *A Historical Dialogue with Art*, Vol. 1, Kaohsiung: Punto Press. [蕭勤:《與藝術的歷史對話》(上), 龐圖出版社2017年].

Hsiao, C., 2017, 'Hsiao Chin Speaks about Fifth Moon and Ton-Fan Again', *A Historical Dialogue with Art*, Kaohsiung: Punto Press.

Hsiao, C., 2018, *Hsiao Chin Coming Home*, China Art Museum Shanghai.

Kandinsky, W., 1912, 'Concerning the Spiritual in Art', Quote from *Art in Theory, 1900–2000: An Anthology of Changing Ideas*, 2003, ed. Charles Harrison & Paul Wood, new edition, Blackwell Publishing.

Kearney, R., 1986, *Modern Movements in European Philosophy*, Manchester: Manchester University Press.

Koenig, J., '*Abstraction chaude* in Paris in the 1950s', *Reconstructing Modernism: Art in New York, Paris and Montreal 1945–1964*, ed. Serge Guilbaut, The MIT Press.

Krauss, R., 1986, *The Originality of the Avant-Garde and Other Modernist Myths*, Massachusetts: The MIT Press.

Laozi: *Tao Te Ching*, ancient texts [《老子》]<https://zh.wikisource.org/wiki/老子_(帛書校勘版)>,[25 November 2019].

Li, L., 'Hsiao Chin's Coming Home', *Hsiao Chin Coming Home*, China Art Museum Shanghai.

Lu, P., 2007, *A History of Art in Twentieth-century China*, Peking University Press. [吕澎:《20世紀中國藝術史》,北京大學出版社2007年].

Lynton, N., 1992, *The Story of Modern Art*, 2nd edition, London: Phaidon.

Mansoor, J., 2016, *Marshall Plan Modernism: Italian Postwar Abstraction and the Beginning of Autonomia*, London: Duke University Press.

Min, J., 2017, *The Three Musketeers who studied in France*, HK: Zhonghe Publishing. [閔捷:《留法三劍客》, 香港中和出版社2017年].

Nelson, E., 2017, *Chinese and Buddhist Philosophy in Early Twentieth-Century German Thought*, London: Bloomsbury.

Nietzsche F., 2004, *Why I am so wise*, trans. R. J. Hollingdale, London: Penguin Books.

Pola, F., 1987, 'Hsiao Chin: Life, in Equilibrium', *Un Viaggio Attraverso L'universo*, Milan: Robilant+Voena Gallery, 2015.

Qi L., 2016, 'The Voiceless Avant-Garde: The Modern Painting Exhibition during the anti-Japanese War', *Anti-Japanese War Culture Research*. [漆麟:《无言的前卫:抗战时期的'现代绘画联展'》,《抗战文化研究》].

Rosa, N., 2005, 'La Poetica di Hsiao Chin tra Oriente e Occidente', *Hsiao Chin*, Città Di Atri: Assessorato alla Cultura.

Rosenberg, H., 1962, 'The Fall of Paris', *Tradition of the New*. Quote from *Art in Theory, 1900-2000: An Anthology of Changing Ideas*, 2003, ed. Charles Harrison & Paul Wood, new edition, Blackwell Publishing.

Sartre, J., 1948, 'The Search for the Absolute', *Alberto Giacometti: Sculptures, Paintings, Drawings*, New York: Pierre Matisse Gallery.

Sartre, J., 2001, *The Age of Reason*, trans. by Eric Sutton, Penguin Modern Classics, London: Penguin Books.

Schapiro, M., 1979, 'The Nature of Abstract Art', *Modern Art, 19th and 20th Centuries: Selected Papers*, reprinted in 2011, New York: George Braziller.

Tagliaferri, A., 1979, 'Trip through a Square without Corners', *La via di Hsiao*, La Nuova Foglio.

Taylor, B., 1995, *The Art of Today*, London: The Orion Publishing Group.

Theunissen, M., 1986, *The Other: Studies in the Social Ontology of Husserl, Heidegger, Sartre, and Buber*, Massachusetts: The MIT Press.

Tsai Chao-yi, 2018, 'Topology of Meaning of Life: Retrospect and Prospect of Hsiao Chin's Art', *Hsiao Chin Coming Home*, China Art Museum Shanghai.

Walt, M., Ankney Weitz and Michelle Yun, 2016, *Zao Wou-Ki: No Limits*, Asia Society Museum.

White, E., 2008, *Rimbaud: The Double Life of a Rebel*, London: Atlantic Books.

Worringer, W., 1910, 'Abstraction and Empathy', Quote from *Art in Theory, 1900–2000: An Anthology of Changing Ideas*.

Wu, M., 2018, *Legend of the Rambling King: Side View of Hsiao Chin*, Kaohsiung City: Punto Press. [吳素琴:《逍遙王外傳:側寫蕭勤》, 龐圖出版社2018年]

Zaffarano, L. & Hsiao Chin, 1987, 'Ten questions asked to Hsiao Chin', in Pola, Francesca edited. *Un Viaggio Attraverso L'universo*. Milan: Robilant+Voena Gallery, 2015.

Zhang Z., from Zhang Yanyuan, ninth century, *The History of Ancient Famous Paintings*, ancient texts [唐代 张璪,引自張彥遠:《歷代名畫記》]<https://zh.wikisource.org/wiki/歷代名畫記/卷第十>, [25 November 2019].

Zong B., fifth century, *The Preface of Landscape Paintings*, from Zhang Yanyuan, ninth century, *The History of Ancient Famous Paintings*, ancient texts [宗炳:《畫山水序》,引自張彥遠:《歷代名畫記》]<https://zh.wikisource.org/zh/歷代名畫記/卷第六>, [25 November 2019].

SOLO EXHIBITIONS		
YEAR	ENGLISH EXHIBITION LIST	CHINESE EXHIBITION LIST
2020	*In my beginning is my end: the art of Hsiao Chin* retrospective exhibition, Mark Rothko Art Centre (Marka Rotko Makslas Centrs), Daugavpils *In my beginning is my end: the art of Hsiao Chin* parallel exhibition, 3812 Gallery, London *Hsiao Chin: The Combination of New Energy* solo exhibition, Hsiao Chin Foundation, Kaohsiung	「在我的開始是我的結束: 蕭勤的藝術」 回顧展, 馬克·羅斯科藝術中心 (Marka Rotko Makslas Centrs), 陶格夫匹爾斯 「在我的開始是我的結束: 蕭勤的藝術」 平行展, 3812 畫廊, 倫敦 「蕭勤 · 新能量之結合」 個展, 蕭勤國際文化藝術基金會, 高雄
2019	*New Energy. Reunification* solo exhibition, Tainan National University of the Arts, Tainan *PUNTO. HSIAO CHIN* solo exhibition, 2019 ART TAIPEI, Taipei World Trade Center, Taipei *Hsiao Chin – Infinite Universe* selling exhibition, Sotheby's S|2 Hong Kong Gallery, Hong Kong *Hsiao Chin: The Colours of Ch'an* parallel exhibition, 3812 Gallery, Hong Kong *Les Couleurs du Zen: Peintures de Hsiao Chin* parallel exhibition, Hsiao Chin Foundation, Kaohsiung *Les Couleurs du Zen: Peintures de Hsiao Chin* solo exhibition, Guimet Museum (Musée national des arts asiatiques-Guimet), Paris	「新能量 · 回歸」 個展, 台灣國立台南藝術大學, 台南 「蕭勤 · 龐圖」 個展, 2019 ART TAIPEI 台北國際藝術博覽會, 台北世界貿易中心, 台北 「蕭勤 — 無限宇宙」 展售會, 香港蘇富比藝術空間, 香港 「禪色: 蕭勤繪畫展」 平行展, 3812 畫廊, 香港 「禪的顏色 — 向蕭勤大師致敬」 平行展, 蕭勤國際文化藝術基金會, 高雄 「禪的顏色 — 向蕭勤大師致敬」 個展, 吉美國立亞洲藝術博物館 (Musée national des arts asiatiques–Guimet), 巴黎
2018	*Hsiao Chin. Spiritual Energy* solo exhibition, Lotus Art Gallery, Kaohsiung *To An Infinite Ascendence* solo exhibition, 3812 Gallery, Hong Kong *Hsiao Chin Coming Home* retrospective exhibition, China Art Museum, Shanghai *ZEN·ART Bright Light – Homage to Ascendence* solo exhibition, Tsz Shan Monastery, Hong Kong	「蕭勤 · 精神能量」 個展, 荷軒新藝空間, 高雄 「向無限昇華 — 蕭勤個展」, 3812 畫廊, 香港 「蕭勤回家藝術大展」, 中華藝術宮, 上海 「禪 · 藝術: 明光 — 向昇華致敬」 個展, 慈山寺, 香港
2017	*Hsiao Chin Art Archival Exhibition: The Origin*, 3812 Gallery, Hong Kong *Hsiao Chin Salon Show: 1960's, An Important Era*, 3812 Gallery, Hong Kong	「源 — 蕭勤藝術文獻資料展」, 3812畫廊, 香港 「重要的六十年代 — 蕭勤作品沙龍展」, 3812畫廊, 香港
2016	*Hsiao Chin Solo Exhibition: Endless Energy*, 3812 Gallery, Hong Kong *Novel Energy: The End is the Beginning*, Tina Keng Gallery, Taipei	「蕭勤 — 無盡能量2016」 個展, 3812 畫廊, 香港 「新能量: 終點亦為起點」, 耿畫廊, 台北
2015	*80 Years of Energy, Hsiao Chin's Retrospect & Prospect*, National Taiwan Museum of Fine Arts, Taichung *60 Years of Abstraction, Harmony and Form*, de Sarthe Gallery, Hong Kong	「八十能量 — 蕭勤回顧 · 展望」, 國立台灣美術館, 台中 「抽象、和諧與形態的六十年歷程」, 德薩畫廊, 香港
2014	*Infinite Energy*, Kuo Mu Sheng Foundation, Taipei *Hsiao Chin Eternal Energy*, Lotus Art Gallery, Kaohsiung	「蕭勤 無限能量」, 郭木生文教基金會, 台北 「蕭勤 永恆能量」, 荷軒新藝空間, 高雄
2013	*Great ALL*, Lin & Lin Gallery, Taipei	「大能量」, 大未來林舍畫廊, 台北
2010	*Infinity of Chi: Retrospective of Hsiao Chin*, Kaohsiung Museum of Fine Arts, Kaohsiung	「大炁之境 — 向大師致敬系列: 蕭勤 75 回顧展」, 高雄市立美術館, 高雄
2009	*Hsiao Chin. In-finite journey 1955–2008*, Bovisa Triennial (Triennale Bovisa), Milan	「無限之旅1955–2008」, 米蘭波維薩三年展 (Triennale Bovisa), 米蘭
2008	*Retrospective Exhibition*, University of Parma (Università di Parma), Parma	「蕭勤回顧展」, 意大利巴爾瑪大學 (Università di Parma), 巴爾瑪
2006	*Glory to the Source, Hsiao Chin 1955–2005*, National Art Museum of China, Beijing	「榮源 — 蕭勤七十回顧展 1955–2005」, 中國美術館, 北京
2005	*Hsiao-Chin 1954–2004 – A Journey Back to the Source*, Guangdong Museum of Art, Guangzhou *Hsiao-Chin 1954–2004 – A Journey Back to the Source*, Zhongshan Museum of Art, Zhongshan *Retrospective Exhibition*, Civic Museum of Villa Colloredo Mels (Museo Civico Villa Colloredo Mels), Recanati *Retrospective Exhibition*, Acquaviva Palace (Palazzo Acquaviva), Atri	「蕭勤 1954–2004 歸源之旅」, 廣東美術館, 廣州 「蕭勤 1954–2004 歸源之旅」, 中山美術館, 中山 「蕭勤歷程展」, 萊卡那迪市立美術館 (Museo Civico Villa Colloredo Mels), 萊卡那迪 「蕭勤歷程展」, 阿德利市阿卦韋伐宮 (Palazzo Acquaviva), 阿德利
2004	*The Journey of Hsiao Chin's Painting 1958–2004*, Shanghai Art Museum (now renamed as China Art Museum), Shanghai	「蕭勤繪畫歷程展 1958–2004」, 上海美術館 (現改稱為中華藝術宮), 上海
2003	*Solo Exhibition*, Leda Fletcher Gallery, Geneva *March to the New World: 2003 Hsiao Chin Touring Exhibition*, Taiwan, presented by National Culture and Arts Foundation, Taiwan	「蕭勤作品展」, 佛萊雀畫廊 (Leda Fletcher Gallery), 日內瓦 「走向新世界——2003蕭勤巡迴展」, 台灣, 由台灣國家文化藝術基金會策劃
2002	*1958–2002: Retrospective Exhibition of Paintings*, Gio Marconi Gallery (Galleria Gió Marconi), Milan *Exhibition of Large-size Paintings*, Mudima Foundation (Fondazione Mudima), Milan *1958–2000: Retrospective Exhibition of Works on Paper*, Lattuada Gallery (Galleria Lattuada), Milan *Ceramic Sculpture Artworks*, Oberdan Space (Spazio Oberdan), Milan	「1958–2002 繪畫作品回顧展」, 馬爾各尼畫廊 (Galleria Gió Marconi), 米蘭 「大幅繪畫近作展」, 姆迪瑪藝術基金會 (Fondazione Mudima), 米蘭 「1958–2000 紙上作品回顧展」, 拉都阿達畫廊 (Galleria Lattuada), 米蘭 「陶塑展」, 米蘭省政府奧拜堂藝術空間 (Spazio Oberdan), 米蘭
1998	*1958–1998: Retrospective Exhibition*, Il Ponte Gallery (Galleria Il Ponte), Florence; Di Meo Gallery (Galerie Di Meo), Paris; Mathildenhohe Darmstadt Institute (Institut Mathildenhöhe Darmstadt), Darmstadt	「1958–1998 回顧展」, 橋畫廊 (Galleria Il Ponte), 佛羅倫斯; 迪. 梅奧畫廊 (Galerie Di Meo), 巴黎; 達姆司特市立美術館 (Institut Mathildenhöhe Darmstadt), 達姆司特
1997	*From Passage through the Great Threshold to Birth of the New World*, Dimensions Art Center, Taipei	「度大限到新世界系列」 展, 帝門藝術中心, 台北
1996	*Journey of Life*, Dimension Endowment of Art Foundation, Taipei	「生之旅程」 展, 帝門藝術基金會, 台北
1995	*Hsiao Chin: the Odyssey, 1953–1994*, Taipei Fine Arts Museum, Taipei	「蕭勤的歷程: 1953–1994」, 台北市立美術館, 台北
1992	*Retrospective Exhibition*, Taiwan Provincial Museum of Art (now renamed as National Taiwan Museum of Fine Arts), Taichung	「蕭勤回顧展」, 台灣省立美術館 (現改稱為國立台灣美術館), 台中
1990	Punto Gallery (Galería Punto), Valencia A. Peola Gallery (Galleria A. Peola), Turin University of Macerata (Università di Macerata), Macerata *HSIAO CHIN 30 Retrospective Exhibition*, National Tsing Hua University, Hsinchu H. Feldmann Gallery (Galerie H. Feldmann), Bern Contemporary Art Gallery, Taichung	點畫廊 (Galería Punto), 瓦倫西亞 倍歐拉畫廊 (Galleria A. Peola), 都林 意大利馬皆拉答大學 (Università di Macerata), 馬皆拉答 「蕭勤30年回顧展」, 國立清華大學, 新竹 費特曼畫廊 (Galerie H. Feldmann), 培恩 當代藝術公司, 台中
1989	La Chiocciola Gallery (Galleria La Chiocciola), Padua Lung Men Art Gallery, Taipei Contemporary Art Gallery, Taichung	基喬拉畫廊 (Galleria La Chiocciola), 巴多伐 龍門畫廊, 台北 當代藝術公司, 台中
1988	*30-year Retrospective Exhibition: 1958–1988*, Gio Marconi Gallery (Galleria Gió Marconi), Milan	「1959 至 1988 回顧展」, 馬爾各尼畫廊 (Galleria Gió Marconi), 米蘭
1987	Alisan Fine Arts, Hong Kong	藝倡畫廊, 香港
1986	Nikolaj Contemporary Art Center (Nikolaj Kunsthal), Copenhagen Mercato del Sale Gallery (Galleria Mercato del Sale), Milan AM Niemeyer Gallery (Galería AM Niemeyer), Rio de Janeiro	尼可拉依展覽廳 (Nikolaj Kunsthal), 哥本哈根 鹽市場畫廊 (Galleria Mercato del Sale), 米蘭 尼邁耶畫廊 (Galería AM Niemeyer), 里約熱內盧
1985	University of Messina (Università degli Studi di Messina), Messina *HSIAO CHIN Solo Exhibition – CHI*, The Hong Kong Institute for Promotion of Chinese Culture, Hong Kong Punto Gallery (Galería Punto), Valencia Waterland Museum (Museum Waterland), Purmerend *HSIAO CHIN·WALASSE TING*, Taipei Fine Arts Museum, Taipei	意大利邁西那大學 (Università degli Studi di Messina), 邁西那 「蕭勤個展 — 氣的系列」, 中華文化促進中心, 香港 點畫廊 (Galería Punto), 瓦倫西亞 瓦特蘭美術館 (Museum Waterland), 普邁朗 「蕭勤 · 丁雄泉」, 台北市立美術館, 台北

YEAR	ENGLISH EXHIBITION LIST	CHINESE EXHIBITION LIST
1984	Gio Marconi Gallery (Galleria Gió Marconi), Milan	馬爾各尼畫廊 (Galleria Gió Marconi), 米蘭
1981	Apollo Art Gallery, Taipei Pancheri Gallery (Galleria Pancheri), Rovereto	阿波羅畫廊, 台北 邦蓋利畫廊 (Galleria Pancheri), 羅凡萊多
1980	Ideogram Gallery (Galleria Ideogramma), Turin *HSIAO CHIN Exhibition*, Printmakers Art Gallery, Taipei	文字畫廊 (Galleria Ideogramma), 都林 「蕭勤畫展」, 版畫家畫廊, 台北
1979	Municipal Gallery of Macerata (Pinacoteca Comunale di Macerata), Macerata	馬皆拉答市立美術館 (Pinacoteca Comunale di Macerata), 馬皆拉答
1978	National Museum of History, Taipei Lung Men Art Gallery, Taipei Kandinsky Gallery (Galería Kandinsky), Madrid	國立歷史博物館, 台北 龍門畫廊, 台北 康定斯基畫廊 (Galería Kandinsky), 馬德里
1977	Palace of Tourism (Palazzo del Turismo), Gio Marconi Gallery (Galleria Gió Marconi), and Zarathustra Gallery (Galleria Zarathustra), Milan	旅遊大廈 (Palazzo del Turismo) 、馬爾各尼畫廊 (Galleria Gió Marconi) 、查拉圖司特拉畫廊 (Galleria Zarathustra), 米蘭
1976	Punto Gallery (Galería Punto), Valencia	點畫廊 (Galería Punto), 瓦倫西亞
1975	Municipal Museum of Modern Art (Museo Civico d'Arte Moderna), Modena Palace of Diamond (Palazzo dei Diamanti), Ferrara	莫登那市立美術館 (Museo Civico d'Arte Moderna), 莫登那 鑽石大廈展覽廳 (Palazzo dei Diamanti), 斐拉拉
1974	Beaubourg Gallery (Galerie Beaubourg), Paris	波布畫廊 (Galerie Beaubourg), 巴黎
1973	Schubert Gallery (Galleria Schubert), Milan	修伯特畫廊 (Galleria Schubert), 米蘭
1972	Brechbuhl Gallery (Galerie Brechbuhl), Grenchen	伯萊許布畫廊 (Galerie Brechbuhl), 格藍欣
1971	Gallery of Modern Art (Galleria d'Arte Moderna), Gaeta	莫登那藝術畫廊 (Galleria d'Arte Moderna), 加埃塔
1970	Orez Gallery (Galerie Orez), The Hague Fonke Gallery (Galerie Fonke), Gent Gio Marconi Gallery (Galleria Gió Marconi), Milan Sant'Andrea Gallery (Galleria Sant'Andrea), Milan	歐雷茲畫廊 (Galerie Orez), 海牙 封克畫廊 (Galerie Fonke), 根特 馬爾各尼畫廊 (Galleria Gió Marconi), 米蘭 聖安德雷阿畫廊 (Galleria Sant'Andrea), 米蘭
1969	Gio Marconi Gallery (Galleria Gió Marconi), Milan Senatore Gallery (Galerie Senatore), Stuttgart	馬爾各尼畫廊 (Galleria Gió Marconi), 米蘭 賽那多萊畫廊 (Galerie Senatore), 司都特卡
1968	The Pollock Gallery, Toronto L. Stevens Gallery, Detroit	波洛克畫廊 (The Pollock Gallery), 多倫多 斯狄芬司畫廊 (L. Stevens Gallery), 底特略
1967	Brechbuhl Gallery (Galerie Brechbuhl), Grenchen Wirth Gallery (Galerie Wirth), Berlin Gio Marconi Gallery (Galleria Gió Marconi), Milan Rose Fried Gallery, New York	伯萊許布畫廊 (Galerie Brechbuhl), 格藍欣 維爾茲畫廊 (Galerie Wirth), 柏林 馬爾各尼畫廊 (Galleria Gió Marconi), 米蘭 若斯. 弗理特畫廊 (Rose Fried Gallery), 紐約
1966	Il Canale Gallery (Galleria Il Canale), Venice Falazik Gallery (Galerie Falazik), Bochum	運河畫廊 (Galleria Il Canale), 威尼斯 法拉濟克畫廊 (Galerie Falazik), 波洪
1965	Maribor Museum (Muzej Maribor), Maribor	馬理堡美術館 (Muzej Maribor), 馬理堡
1964	International Gallery of Contemporary Art (Galerie Internationale d'Art Contemporain), Paris Ariete Gallery (Galleria Ariete), Milan	當代藝術畫廊 (Galerie Internationale d'Art Contemporain), 巴黎 山羊畫廊 (Galleria Ariete), 米蘭
1962	S. Luca Gallery (Galleria S. Luca), Rome	聖・路卡畫廊 (Galleria S. Luca), 羅馬
1961	Trastevere Gallery (Galleria Trastevere), Rome S. Matteo Gallery (Galleria S. Matteo), Genoa HILT Gallery (Galerie HILT), Basel Salone Annunciata Gallery (Galleria Salone Annunciata), Milan Dorekens Gallery (Galerie Dorekens), Antwerp	德拉司代凡勒畫廊 (Galleria Trastevere), 羅馬 聖・馬代歐畫廊 (Galleria S. Matteo), 熱拿亞 希爾特畫廊 (Galerie HILT), 巴薩爾 阿農查德沙龍畫廊 (Galleria Salone Annunciata), 米蘭 多雷肯司畫廊 (Galerie Dorekens), 安特威普
1960	Senatore Gallery (Galerie Senatore), Stuttgart	賽那多萊畫廊 (Galerie Senatore), 司都特卡
1959	Numero Gallery (Galleria Numero), Florence Il Cavallino Gallery (Galleria Il Cavallino), Venice	數字畫廊 (Galleria Numero), 佛羅倫斯 小馬畫廊 (Galleria Il Cavallino), 威尼斯
1958	Fernando Fe' Gallery (Galería Fernando Fe'), Madrid	費爾南多. 費畫廊 (Galería Fernando Fe'), 馬德里
1957	Mataro Fine Arts Museum (Museo Municipal de Mataró), Barcelona	馬達洛美術館 (Museo Municipal de Mataró), 巴塞隆納

GROUP EXHIBITIONS		
YEAR	ENGLISH EXHIBITION LIST	CHINESE EXHIBITION LIST
2018	*Pulse / Thread*, Artists Group Exhibition, 2018 ART TAIPEI, Taipei World Trade Center, Taipei *HSIA Yan and His Times*, Eslite Gallery, Taipei	「脈・絡」, 藝術家聯展, 2018 ART TAIPEI台北國際藝術博覽會, 台北世界貿易中心, 台北 「夏陽的時代」, 誠品畫廊, 台北
2017	*From China to Taiwan: The First Avant-Garde Abstract 1955–1985 Exhibition*, Museum of Ixelles (Musée d'Ixelles), Brussels	「從中國到台灣：抽象藝術先鋒 1955–1985」, 伊克塞爾博物館 (Musée d'Ixelles), 布魯塞爾
2016	*3812 Artists Group Exhibition*, Fine Art Asia 2016, HKCEC, Hong Kong *Summer Show 2016 Artists Group Exhibition*, 3812 Gallery, Hong Kong	「3812 藝術家聯展」, 典亞藝博 2016, 香港會議展覽中心, 香港 「夏季展覽 2016藝術家聯展」, 3812 畫廊, 香港
2014	*Abstract/Symbol/Oriental, Exhibition of Taiwan's Masters of Modern Art*, Liang Gallery, Taipei	「『抽象・符碼・東方情』 — 台灣現代藝術巨匠大展」, 尊彩藝術中心, 台北
2012	*Abstract art in Taiwan*, Taipei Fine Arts Museum, Taipei	「『非行之行』台灣抽象藝術」, 台北市立美術館, 台北
2007	*V Premio Internazionale Biennale d'Incisione*, Contemporary and 1900s Art Museum (Museo di Arte Contemporanea e del Novecento), Monsummano Terme	「第五屆國際版畫雙年展」, 當代及 19 世紀美術館 (Museo di Arte Contemporanea e del Novecento), 蒙蘇馬諾泰爾梅
2005	*Identità e diversità*, Contemporary Art Museum, Moscow	「似性及異性」 展, 當代美術館, 莫斯科
2004	*Identità e diversità*, Medici Riccardi Palace (Palazzo Medici Riccardi), Florence	「似性及異性」 展, 麥地綺・理卡爾地宮 (Palazzo Medici Riccardi), 佛羅倫斯
2000	*7th Biennale Architettura*, Taiwan Pavilion, Venice Biennial (La Biennale di Venezia), Venice	「第七屆威尼斯國際建築展」, 台灣館, 威尼斯雙年展 (La Biennale di Venezia), 威尼斯

YEAR	ENGLISH EXHIBITION LIST	CHINESE EXHIBITION LIST
1998	*15th National Art Exhibition of the ROC*, Taipei *98 Shanghai Art Biennial*, Shanghai Art Museum (now renamed as China Art Museum) and Liu Haisu Art Museum, Shanghai *1st International Ink Painting Biennial*, Guan Shanyue Art Museum, Shenzhen	「第十五屆全國美展」, 台北 「上海美術雙年展」, 上海美術館 (現改稱為中華藝術宮) 、劉海粟美術館, 上海 「第一屆深圳國際水墨畫雙年展」, 關山月美術館, 深圳
1997	*Memory of Ton-Fan Group*, Taipei	「東方畫會四十週年聯展」, 台北
1996	*Due secoli di Incisione*, Brera Academy (Accademia di Belle Arti di Brera), Milan	「兩個世紀的版畫」, 意大利米蘭布雷拉美術學院 (Accademia di Belle Arti di Brera), 米蘭
1995	*L'informale – Materia-Gesto-Segno*, Municipal Museum of Modern Art (Civica Galleria d'Arte Moderna di Gallarate), Gallarate *Anni 90-Arte a Milano*, Milan	「非形象之材質、動作及符號」展, 迦拉拉代市立美術館 (Civica Galleria d'Arte Moderna di Gallarate), 迦拉拉代 「90年代米蘭藝展」, 米蘭
1991	*Colore e Segno nella Materia*, Varese *35th Anniversary Joint Exhibition of Ton-Fan & Fifth Moon Groups*, Taipei	「物質中之色彩及符號」展, 伐萊賽 「東方、五月成立三十五週年聯展」, 台北
1990	*Italian Contemporary Arts*, Taiwan Provincial Museum of Art (now renamed as National Taiwan Museum of Fine Arts), Taichung	「意大利當代藝術展」, 台灣省立美術館 (現改稱為國立台灣美術館), 台中
1989–1993, 1990–1995, 1991, 1994	*International Shakti Exhibitions*, Copenhagen, Aarhus, Gallarate and Milan	「國際 Shakti 展」, 哥本哈根、奧魯斯、迦拉拉代、米蘭
1988	*Contemporary Italian Artists*, Art Palace, Moscow	「意大利當代藝術家展」, 莫斯科藝術宮, 莫斯科
1987	*Contemporary Chinese Painting*, Hong Kong City Hall, Hong Kong *30th International Biennial Print Exhibition*, Milan	「中國當代藝術展」, 香港大會堂, 香港 「第三十屆米蘭全國雙年展」, 米蘭
1986	*Itinerari d'arte Contemporanea*, Lisbon and Porto	「當代藝術巡迴展」, 里斯本、奧波爾多
1985, 1987, 1989	*2nd, 3rd, 4th International Biennial Print Exhibition*, Taipei	「第二、三、四屆國際版畫雙年展」, 台北
1985	*XIII Premio Nazionale Città di Gallarate*, Gallarate	「第十三屆迦拉拉代市全國藝術獎展」, 迦拉拉代
1984	*7th Norwegian International Print Biennial*, Fredrikstad	「第七屆挪威國際版畫展」, 弗萊特列司達特
1983	*Italian Art*, Berlin *3rd Biennial of European Graphic Art*, Baden-Baden *Rigori Astratti della Ragione e Fantasia del Concreto*, Ganna	「意大利藝術展」, 柏林 「第三屆歐洲版畫雙年展」, 巴登巴登 「理性嚴謹抽象及具體之幻想」展, 迦那
1982	*Omaggio a P. Matteo Ricci degli artisti cinesi*, Macerata *The Chinese response – Paintings by Leading Overseas Artists*, Hong Kong Museum of Art, Hong Kong	「中國藝術家向利馬竇致敬展」, 馬皆拉答 「中國海外當代名家畫展」, 香港藝術館, 香港
1981	*25th Anniversary Joint Exhibition of Ton-Fan & Fifth Moon Groups*, Taipei	「東方、五月成立二十五週年聯展」, 台北
1980	*Contemporary International Original Prints Exhibition*, Taipei	「當代國際版畫原作展」, 台北
1978–1979	*Exhibition Surya*, Milan and Macerata	「太陽展」, 米蘭、馬皆拉答
1978	*Ancient Heritage, New Directions*, New York *Grafica '78 Internazionale*, Messina	「古傳統、新傾向」展, 紐約 「國際版畫展」, 邁西那
1977	*X Quadriennale Nazionale d'arte*, Rome *Grafici Italiani Contemporanei*, Ljubljana	「第十屆全國四年藝展」, 羅馬 「意大利當代版畫展」, 留比阿那
1975	*Momenti e Tendenze del Costruttivismo*, Milan	「構成主義之時代及傾向展」, 米蘭
1974	*Asia Oggi – Rassegna di Grafica Contemporanea*, Milan	「今日之亞洲: 當代版畫展」, 米蘭
1971	*Italian Painting*, Dublin and Belfast	「意大利繪畫展」, 都柏林及悲爾法斯特
1970	*III Salon International de Galeries Pilotes*, Lausanne and Paris	「第三屆國際主流畫廊沙龍」, 洛桑、巴黎
1969	*IX Festival de arte '69'*, Cali	「第九屆卡里藝術季展」, 卡里
1966	*Musische Geometrie*, Arts Society of Hannover (Kunstverein Hannover), Hannover	「音樂之幾何」展, 漢諾威藝術協會 (Kunstverein Hannover), 漢諾威
1965	*VI Mostra Internazionale di Grafica*, Ljubljana	「第六屆國際版畫展」, 留比阿那
1964	*International Triennial of Colored Graphic Prints*, Grenchen *III° premio Scipione nazionale di pittura*, Macerata	「國際彩色版畫三年展」, 格蘭欣 「第三屆全國西比翁乃繪畫獎展」, 馬皆拉答
1963	*Chinesische Künstler der Gegenwart*, Municipal Museum (Städtisches Museum), Leverkusen *Art Contemporain*, Great Palace (Grand Palais), Paris *The 7th São Paulo Art Biennial*, São Paulo	「中國當代藝展」, 萊凡庫森市立美術館 (Städtisches Museum), 萊凡庫森 「當代藝展」, 巴黎大皇宮 (Grand Palais), 巴黎 「第七屆巴西聖保羅雙年展」, 聖保羅
1961	*The Pittsburgh International Exhibition*, Pittsburgh *Grand Prix de peinture et sculpture*, Monte Carlo	「匹茲堡國際美展」, 匹茲堡 「繪畫與雕塑大獎展」, 蒙地卡羅
1960	*International Malerei 1960-61*, Eisenbach	「1960/61 國際繪畫展」, 艾森巴赫
1957–1959	*The 1st, 2nd and 3rd May Salon*, Barcelona	「第一、二、三屆五月沙龍」, 巴塞隆納
1957	*Jazz Salon*, Barcelona	「爵士沙龍」, 巴塞隆納